SO-BRI-191

American Arms Supermarket

By Michael T. Klare

University of Texas Press, Austin

Copyright © 1984 by the University of Texas Press
All rights reserved
Printed in the United States of America
First Edition, 1984

Requests for permission to reproduce material
from this work should be sent to Permissions,
University of Texas Press, Box 7819, Austin, Texas 78713.

Library of Congress Cataloging in Publication Data

Klare, Michael T., 1942–
    American arms supermarket.
    Bibliography: p.
    Includes index.
    1. Munitions—United States.   2. United States—
Military policy.   3. United States—Foreign relations—
1945– . I. Title.
UF533.K58   1984   355.8'2'0973   84-13053
ISBN 0-292-70369-4
ISBN 0-292-70370-8 (pbk.)

American Arms Supermarket

This book is dedicated with respect and admiration to my parents, Mildred Smith Klare (1917–1976) and Charles Klare.

Contents

Acknowledgments

I first began work on this book in 1975 and have been working on it more or less continuously ever since. During this time, literally hundreds of people have facilitated my work in one way or another. Even with the best of intentions, it would be impossible to acknowledge all of these people individually. Still, I would like to express my gratitude for all of the help and support I have received. Let me begin, therefore, with a heartfelt thank you to everyone who has assisted me in one fashion or another. Please forgive me if, inadvertently, I have neglected to acknowledge you by name.

Next, I wish to acknowledge those people whose support has been most critical in conducting this project: the staff of the Militarism and Disarmament Project of the Institute for Policy Studies (IPS). These people helped in so many ways—with research, advice and criticism, data collection, fact checking, typing and editing, and plain old-fashioned moral support—that I doubt very much that the book could ever have been completed without them. A very special round of thanks is due, therefore, to Cynthia Arnson, Stephen Daggett, David Leech, Delia Miller, Flora Montealegre, Leslie Parks, and Daniel Volman.

At this point I would also like to thank all of the other fine people at IPS whose friendship and cooperation has been so steady through the years. I particularly wish to acknowledge the long-term support of our two Distinguished Fellows, Marcus Raskin and Richard Barnet, our director, Robert Borosage, and my colleagues Eqbal Ahmad, Saul Landau, Isabel Letelier, Nancy Lewis, Peter Weiss, and Alyce Wiley. Many thanks are also due to my colleagues in the Transnational Institute (IPS's European affiliate), particularly Wendy Chapkis, Ben Dankbaar, Fred Halliday, Mary Kaldor, and Basker Vashee.

During the six years I have worked at IPS, our research on arms sales, conventional conflict, and disarmament has been supported by a number of foundations and charitable organizations. Without this support, it simply would not have been possible to conduct ongoing research of this sort. I am especially grateful, therefore, to the Field Foundation, the Rubin Foundation, the Car-Eth Foundation, the CS Fund, and the Veatch Fund for their generous and sustained support of our work.

Before coming to IPS in 1977, I spent a year as a Compton Fellow in World Order Studies at the Center of International Studies at Princeton University. Under the guidance of Richard Falk, the Albert G. Milbank Professor of International Law and Practice, I used this year to expand my research on arms transfers and to compose drafts of several of the chapters of this book. I am especially indebted, therefore, to the Compton family for providing this extraordinary opportunity, and to the staff and Fellows of the Center for their cooperation and cordiality. Special thanks are due to Corinne and Cy Black, Gladys Starkey, Katie Yablon, and the late Jean McDowall.

During the course of my research on the arms trade, I have had occasion to consult investigators at many other research institutions in the United States and abroad. Their help and cooperation has often proved invaluable. Among the individuals and institutions whose assistance has been most useful are Fred Goff of the Data Center, Oakland, California; Elizabeth Farnsworth, Nancy Stein, and the other staff members (past and present) of the North American Congress on Latin America (NACLA), New York; Tom Conrad, Eva Gold, David Goodman, Marilyn McNabb, Eric Prokosch, Diana Roose, and the other fine people of NARMIC (National Action/Research on the Military-Industrial Complex) of the American Friends Service Committee, Philadelphia, Pennsylvania; David Johnson, Steve Goose, and their colleagues at the Center for Defense Information, Washington, D.C.; Bill Goodfellow, Max Holland, and Jim Morrell of the Center for International Policy (CIP), Washington, D.C.; Ted Lockwood and Chris Root of the Washington Office on Africa, Washington, D.C.; Jennifer Davis of the American Committee on Africa, New York; Joe Stork of the Middle East Research and Information Project (MERIP), Washington, D.C.; Bob Shuey and Richard Grimmett of the Congressional Research Service of the Library of Congress; the Washington Office on Latin America, Washington, D.C.; the Center for National Security Studies, Washington, D.C.; the Military Audit Project, Washington, D.C.; Amnesty International, Washington, D.C.; the Stockholm International Peace Research Institute (SIPRI), Stockholm, Sweden; Asbjørn Eide and Marek Thee of the Peace Research Institute of Oslo (PRIO), Oslo, Norway; Helena Tuomi of the Tampere Peace Research Institute (TAPRI), Tampere, Finland; Peter Lock and Herbert Wulf of the Working Group on Armaments and Underdevelopment of the University of Hamburg,

West Germany; Ulrich Albrecht of the Free University of Berlin; John Saxe-Fernandez of the University of Mexico, Mexico City; Milton Leitenberg of the Swedish Institute of International Affairs, Stockholm, Sweden; Jan Oberg of the Department of Peace and Conflict Studies of Lund University, Lund, Sweden; Steve Wright and Dan Smith of the Richardson Institute, London, England; Sandy Merritt and the staff of the Campaign Against the Arms Trade (CAAT), London, England; and Sherman Carroll of Amnesty International in London, England.

A special debt of gratitude is owed to those people who assisted more directly in the preparation of this book. A number of attorneys—notably Charles Both and Philip O'Neil—contributed their time and effort in litigating Freedom of Information Act cases. Several individuals collaborated on articles and research studies that later served as the nucleus for various chapters of this book: Eric Prokosch of NARMIC on arms transfers to South Africa, Nancy Stein of NACLA on sales of police equipment, Cynthia Arnson of IPS on arms sales to repressive regimes, and Max Holland of CIP on Carter's arms restraint policy. Special thanks are also due to those individuals who read all or part of the manuscript to assist me with comments and corrections: Prof. Irene Gendzier of Boston University, Prof. Richard Falk of Princeton University, Sanford Thatcher of Princeton University Press, Rajan Menon of Vanderbilt University, Joseph Smaldone of the Office of Munitions Control, U.S. Department of State, Max Holland, and Tamara Balter.

On several occasions, I requested and was granted interviews with key officials of the departments of State and Defense. I discovered, somewhat to my surprise, that these officials were quite willing to take time from their busy schedules to answer my questions—some of them provocative—on a wide variety of policy issues. My thanks, then, to the staffpersons in both departments who arranged and/or participated in these often illuminating sessions.

No book project is complete without a publisher, and I have been fortunate to be associated in this endeavor with the University of Texas Press. My special thanks therefore to Scott Lubeck, who brought me to the Press (and served as my editor until his departure in 1983), and to David Catron, Holly Carver, Anne Norman, Kathleen Lewis, and the other wonderful people in Austin who have worked on this manuscript. My gratitude also to the (unknown to me) readers who examined the manuscript and made many excellent suggestions for its improvement.

Finally, I wish to thank those individuals whose friendship and support have sustained me during the long (and sometimes discouraging) years of work on this project: my parents, Charles and Mildred Klare; my brother Karl and sister Jane; my housemates in Berkeley, Charles R. Soulé, Jr., Patricia Morgan, and Shannon Morgan; and all my friends on both coasts and in between. My love to all of you.

MICHAEL T. KLARE
WASHINGTON, D.C.

American Arms Supermarket

CHAPTER 1

The Global Arms Market

A Briefing on the Arms Trade

On March 26, 1979, an exhilarated Jimmy Carter told thousands of guests at a White House celebration of the just-signed Egypt-Israel peace treaty, "We have prayed for peace and we have worked for peace. Now we humbly give thanks to God that we can celebrate the beginnings of peace in the Middle East."[1] Three days later, Secretary of State Cyrus Vance revealed that the "beginnings of peace" carried a formidable price tag: at least $4.5 billion in U.S. military sales and loans, on top of the annual $1.5 billion arms subsidy already promised to those countries. Administration officials defended this largesse on the grounds that U.S. arms transfers are needed to help "enforce the peace," but critics charged that further deliveries of sophisticated arms would probably invite comparable acquisitions by neighboring countries and thus precipitate a fresh round of arms buying in the Middle East. "In the euphoria of success we may be tempted to pay any price," Sen. William Proxmire observed on March 27, "But the payment should not include a new round of the arms race in the Middle East dressed as the dove of peace."[2]

These statements illustrate both the important role played by arms transfers in the implementation of U.S. foreign policy and the intense controversy that such programs often arouse. Since the end of the Vietnam War, military sales have become a major instrument of U.S. foreign policy, eclipsing such traditional instruments as military grants and economic assistance. Arms sales have been used to nourish and sustain America's ties with its overseas allies, to "sweeten" international agreements (such as the Egypt-Israel peace treaty), to woo clients away from the Soviet orbit, and to secure access to overseas bases and energy supplies. "Arms sales are the hard currency of foreign affairs," a senior State Department official observed in 1982. "They replace the security pacts of the 1950s."[3]

Accompanying the increased use of arms transfers as a foreign policy instrument has been a sharp rise in the scale of such transactions. Whereas U.S. military sales rarely exceeded $1 billion per year in the 1950s and 1960s, they averaged $12 billion per year in the late 1970s and reached $21 billion in 1982. All told, the United States sold $97.6 billion worth of arms under the Foreign Military Sales (FMS) program between 1971 and 1980, or approximately eight times the amount for the preceding twenty years.[4]

As arms transfers have grown in scale and importance, they have naturally generated increased attention and debate. "The rather dramatic increase in the volume of the [FMS] program," the General Accounting Office (GAO) noted in a 1976 report, "has sparked considerable controversy over the program's operation and direction."[5] But while it was the volume of U.S. sales that first sparked this controversy, two other factors soon came to dominate the debate over military sales: first, a very large proportion of these arms were going to the underdeveloped nations of the Third World; second, these transactions often involved America's latest and most sophisticated weaponry.

Until 1970, most of the arms supplied through the FMS program were sold to the NATO powers and to such industrialized nations as Australia, Japan, and New Zealand. Since then, however, the bulk of FMS sales have been to Third World countries, with the Middle East alone accounting for three-fifths of the total. And while earlier sales to these countries generally consisted of relatively unsophisticated hardware, since 1970 they have tended to include late-model aircraft, missiles, warships, and armored vehicles. As a result, Sen. Hubert Humphrey observed in 1975, America had become "a kind of arms supermarket into which any customer can walk and pick up whatever he wants."[6]

This perception of America as an "arms supermarket" was a source of particular concern because it occurred at a time when international violence and conflict appeared to be on the rise. The "October War" of 1973 was especially noteworthy in this regard, because it involved the first wide-scale use of modern aircraft and missiles by Third World combatants. As the major suppliers began to reequip Israel and its Arab neighbors with even more sophisticated hardware, many U.S. policymakers warned that conventional arms transfers were fueling a regional arms race that could only end in another round of bloody conflict. Selling arms to these countries may not be "like throwing a lighted match into a gasoline tank," Senator Proxmire affirmed, "but it is like adding more gasoline to a tank that has exploded in flaming destruction over and over in the past few years."[7]

This view, widely shared by U.S. lawmakers at the time, was exacerbated by a sense that the executive branch had allowed the arms transfer program to develop a momentum of its own—reaching a point where sales were being pushed abroad with no real concern for their effect on other U.S. foreign policy objectives. The sales program in Iran, which rose from $133 million in 1970 to $3.9 billion just four years later, was a source of particular anxiety: in 1976, the Senate Foreign Relations Committee released a study charging that "for at least three years U.S. arms sales to Iran were out of control."[8] Spurred by such reports, U.S. legislators adopted a series of measures designed to harness the arms trade and to give Congress a larger voice in major arms transfer decisions. The most important of these, the Arms Export Control Act, was approved on June 30, 1976.[9]

Arms sales also became a major issue in electoral politics. On June 23, 1976, candidate Jimmy Carter raised the arms issue for the first time in a presidential campaign. "I am particularly concerned," he told the Foreign Policy Association in New York, "by our nation's role as the world's leading arms salesman." He had particular scorn for senior officials of the Nixon and Ford administrations, whom he accused of trying "to justify this unsavory business on the cynical ground that by rationing out the means of violence we can somehow control the world's violence." Promising to eliminate such behavior, Carter vowed "to increase the emphasis on peace and to reduce the commerce in arms."[10]

After taking office in 1977, Carter moved quickly to implement this pledge. In January, he ordered the secretary of state, Cyrus Vance, to head up an effort to develop new guidelines for the conduct of U.S. arms sales abroad. Vance completed this effort in April, and, after final review by the National Security Council (NSC), the proposed guidelines were incorporated into a formal Presidential Directive. Then, on May 19, 1977, the new policy was announced in a White House statement. Claiming that "the virtually unrestrained spread of conventional weaponry threatens stability in every region of the world," the president enunciated a new basis for the conduct of military sales: "the United States will henceforth view arms transfers as an *exceptional* foreign policy implement, to be used only in instances where it can be clearly demonstrated that the transfer contributes to our national security interests." In accordance with this principle, Carter imposed a number of specific restraints, including a "ceiling" on total annual sales to a large group of countries, and a ban on the export of sophisticated weaponry to regions where such items are not presently deployed.[11]

Although hailed as a "historical" breakthrough in arms control, the Carter policy soon ran into difficulty as administration officials tried to reconcile its provisions with the exigencies of post-Vietnam diplomacy. To provide for unforeseen contingencies, the policy embodied a number of waivers and exceptions—and before very long

Carter was invoking these on a regular basis to permit sales of so-phisticated weaponry to favored clients in the Middle East. In 1977, for instance, Carter proposed the sale of seven Airborne Warning and Control System (AWACS) aircraft to Iran; in 1978, he announced a $5 billion "jet package" of 200 modern fighters for Egypt, Israel, and Saudi Arabia. These, and other conspicuous sales of high-tech ar-maments, led critics to chastise Carter in the same scathing terms that he had earlier used to condemn the Nixon and Ford administra-tions. During hearings on the 1978 "jet package," for instance, Rep. Clarence D. Long of Maryland charged that the United States had become "the salesman of slaughter."[12]

Dissension over arms sales was not, moreover, confined to the Carter administration. President Reagan, who had criticized Carter's inconsistent decisionmaking during the 1980 campaign, soon found himself in hot water over the arms issue when he announced the sale of five AWACS planes and related equipment to Saudi Arabia in 1981. The AWACS transaction proved to be the most controversial foreign policy decision of Reagan's first year in office, and it was only through a last-minute crusade by the president himself that Con-gress was persuaded not to veto the sale.[13] Reagan's victory in the AWACS sale did not, however, end the controversy over arms transfers. Other proposed sales—of F-16 fighters to Pakistan, South Korea, and Venezuela, of other modern arms to Jordan and Taiwan, and of counterinsurgency gear to El Salvador, Guatemala, and Honduras— have also aroused considerable debate. Given the steady growth in U.S. arms exports, and the frequency of controversial sales, it is likely that arms transfers will remain a major issue throughout the 1980s and beyond.

As this debate unfolds, two broad viewpoints are likely to emerge. While almost all U.S. policymakers agree that some re-straints are needed to prevent risky, excessive, or otherwise coun-terproductive arms transfers, there is wide disagreement as to what constitutes "risky" or "excessive" sales, and what sorts of controls are needed to prevent them. Out of this key difference come the two main approaches to managing U.S. arms exports.

On one side in this debate are those policymakers who believe that uncontrolled military sales tend to provoke local arms races in the Third World, and, consequently, that very tight restrictions are needed to prevent such exports—especially those involving sophis-ticated armaments—from turning these regional contests into real conflagrations. In a characteristic statement of this position, the Democratic Policy Committee warned in 1983, "The quantity and quality of weapons being transferred to developing countries has the potential for creating greater instability and increasing the likelihood that the recipients will respond to political problems with military solutions."[14] Adherents of this viewpoint also caution against sales to Third World countries on the grounds that they consume scarce national resources and thus retard economic development and tend to enhance the repressive capabilities of governments cited for persistent human rights violations.[15]

On the other side of the spectrum are those government and industry officials who believe that military sales can strengthen the self-defense capabilities of friendly nations and thus discourage aggression by hostile powers. "Arms transfers serve as an important adjunct to our own security," Under Secretary of State James L. Buckley affirmed in 1981, "by helping to deter acts of aggression [and] by enhancing the self-defense capabilities of nations with which we share close security ties."[16] Supporters of the military sales program also argue that military sales benefit the U.S. economy by creating jobs, by widening the market for U.S. technology abroad, and by helping to reduce the nation's balance-of-payments deficit.[17]

Naturally, both sides dispute the assertions advanced by their adversaries. The restrainers argue, for instance, that excessive military sales weaken American security by involving the United States in the adventuristic policies of some of our less reliable customers, while their opponents assert that such exports can discourage conflict by correcting regional arms imbalances that might otherwise tempt an aggressor into launching an attack. This side also argues that military exports can spur development abroad by introducing new skills and technologies, while the restrainers suggest that excessive sales damage the U.S. economy by perpetuating the existence of an overblown and waste-producing "military-industrial complex."[18]

Caught in the middle of this sometimes bewildering array of arguments and counterarguments are most U.S. lawmakers and government officials, as well as the vast majority of ordinary citizens. Since this majority will ultimately make the key decisions concerning U.S. arms export policies, it is essential that all major issues be clarified sufficiently for nonexperts to assess the principal options. To facilitate public discussion of this critical topic, this book attempts to analyze and explain recent arms export trends and to chart the likely consequences of existing sales practices.

Among the topics taken up here are the economic and political motives for increased military sales, the evolution of U.S. export policies, and the management of the U.S. military sales program. In addition, special studies are presented on sales of arms-making tech-

nologies to foreign arms producers and on the human rights implications of the trade in police and paramilitary weaponry. These reports
are backed up by in-depth assessments of the performance of U.S.
arms programs in selected Third World areas. Finally, an effort is
made to chart the long-term consequences of the weapons trade and
to establish guidelines for a just and prudent arms export policy.

Before proceeding to all of this, however, it is essential to lay out
the basic parameters of the arms trade. Only by sharing a common
vision of fundamental trends and patterns can we hope to tackle the
more complex policy issues raised in subsequent chapters. Let us
turn, then, to a "briefing" on basic arms export patterns.

A Briefing on the Arms Trade

As I cite a variety of statistics in the course of this survey, it is
useful to begin with a brief note on sources and methodology. While
there are several basic sources of information on the arms trade, no
two references agree entirely on coverage or terminology, and it is
therefore necessary to pick and choose among them to obtain the
data most appropriate for illuminating a particular point. For our purposes, the most useful information can be found in five basic sources:
World Military Expenditures and Arms Transfers, published annually by the U.S. Arms Control and Disarmament Agency (ACDA);
the *SIPRI Yearbook*, published annually by the Stockholm International Peace Research Institute (SIPRI), *The Military Balance*, published annually by the International Institute for Strategic Studies
(IISS) in London, *Foreign Military Sales, Foreign Military Construction Sales, and Military Assistance Facts*, published annually by the
Defense Security Assistance Agency (DSAA) of the U.S. Department
of Defense, and the statistical studies released periodically by the
Congressional Research Service (CRS) of the U.S. Library of Congress. Each of these sources has its particular virtues, and all are
cited throughout the course of this book. It is important to recognize, however, that these references cannot be used interchange-
ably—each uses a different method for computing various trade
patterns—and thus we must be careful to specify what, in fact, is
being reported.[19]

Several distinctions must be made at the outset. First, it is essential to distinguish between arms *orders* (i.e., agreements for the
sale of weapons) and arms *deliveries* (i.e., actual transfers of military
hardware from one country to another), since one may precede the
other by several years. Second, it is essential to identify what is en-
compassed by a particular set of statistics: some of the sources iden-

tified above provide data on military *hardware* only (i.e., weapons, ammunition, and support equipment), while others include military *services* (training, maintenance, technical assistance, construction work, etc.). It is also customary to distinguish between amounts given in *current* dollars (i.e., the actual price recorded at the time of a particular sale), and those in *constant* dollars (i.e., costs measured in dollars of a uniform value, usually the value of one dollar in a specified year). Finally, it is important to remember that U.S. government statistics are usually provided on a *fiscal year* basis (i.e., fiscal year 1981 runs from October 1, 1980, to September 30, 1981) rather than on a *calendar year* basis (January 1 to December 31).

The Global Arms Trade

If there is one factor that all of the basic statistical sources agree upon, it is that there has been a sharp increase in the dollar value of international arms transfers over the past twenty years, with most of the increase representing sales to Third World countries. Looking first at the ACDA figures (given in current dollars) in figure 1, we find that world arms transfers rose from $3–$4 billion per year in the early 1960s to $30–$35 billion per year in the early 1980s, while sales to Third World countries rose from $1–$2 billion to $25–$30 billion.[20] The SIPRI figures, though using a different data base, project a very similar curve: in constant 1975 dollars, transfers of "major weapons" jump from an average of $2 billion per year in the 1960s to $5–$7 billion in the mid-1970s and $9–$12 billion by the end of the decade.[21] Finally, the CRS figures (which include services as well as hardware) show that deliveries to the Third World rose from $6.7 billion in 1973 to $15.7 billion in 1977 and $31.5 billion in 1982 (in current dollars).[22] All of these figures reveal occasional downturns (notably following the worldwide economic recessions of 1974–75 and 1982–84), but on the whole they suggest a strong and sustained upward momentum.

An increase in the dollar value of transfers does not, of course, mean an automatic increase in the quantity of arms supplied. As we shall see, much of the dollar rise in arms sales since 1970 has been absorbed by higher prices and the growing sophistication of the arms supplied, rather than by increased quantities. Even in those categories where there has been no marked increase in the numerical rate of transfers, however, the large boost in dollar values does suggest a substantial boost in the net combat power supplied to recipients, as more advanced and capable systems take the place of older equipment in the pipeline. Of particular significance in this regard are the

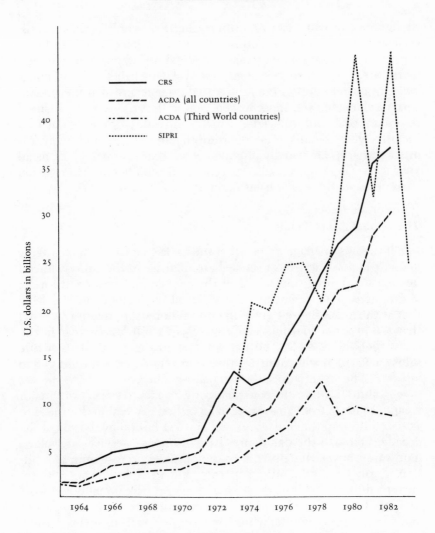

FIGURE 1. *The Global Arms Trade: Dollar value of arms transfers by year as tallied by different organizations*

CRS figures on military orders. As indicated in figure 1, orders have consistently outpaced deliveries over the past decade, indicating a substantial backlog of undelivered equipment that will not show up in the inventories of recipient nations until the mid-1980s. Normally, this backlog consists of the most complex and sophisticated systems on order, since these items usually take longest to produce and assemble. The large inventory of as yet undelivered equipment suggests, therefore, that Third World nations will not receive many of the most advanced weapons they have ordered until the mid- to late 1980s.

The World's Arms Suppliers

Despite the dramatic increase in the volume of world arms transfers, the supply side of the weapons trade continues to be dominated by a relatively small handful of suppliers. According to the CRS, six nations—the two superpowers plus the "big four" European suppliers (France, the United Kingdom, West Germany, and Italy)—accounted for 84 percent of all arms deliveries to the Third World during the 1976–83 period. While other suppliers, including some Third World countries, are likely to capture a larger share of the world market in the years ahead (see chapter 10), these six major suppliers will remain dominant for the remainder of the 1980s: as shown by figure 2, these six nations accounted for 81 percent of new orders received during 1976–83, assuring their continued prominence in the deliveries column for a long time to come.[23]

Of the six major suppliers, the United States has long been the most prominent. According to the CRS, U.S. sales to Third World countries during the 1973–80 period amounted to $66.8 billion, or 34 percent of the world total. The U.S.S.R., in second place, recorded sales of $56.9 billion, or 29 percent of world sales.[24] Some sources, using different methodologies to compute transfer levels, show the Soviet Union in first place. Thus the ACDA, which does not incorporate sales of services and construction in its tallies, showed the U.S.S.R. ahead during this period ($52 billion in deliveries for the Soviet Union, compared to $46.1 billion for the United States). Using still another set of figures, SIPRI puts the United States ahead in sales of major military equipment ($23.6 billion for 1973–80, compared to $20.4 billion for the U.S.S.R.).[25] Although one can debate the relative validity of these different sets of figures, there is no doubt that the United States is a major supplier of arms to the Third World and—if the CRS data on orders prove reliable—will assume a commanding lead in world sales in the mid-1980s.

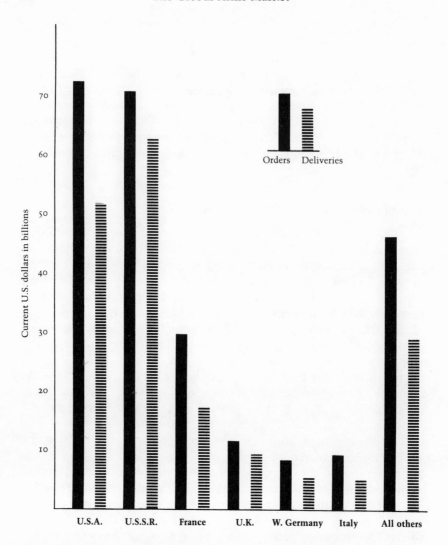

FIGURE 2. *The World's Arms Suppliers: Arms transfers to the Third World, 1976–83*

SOURCE: Congressional Research Service.

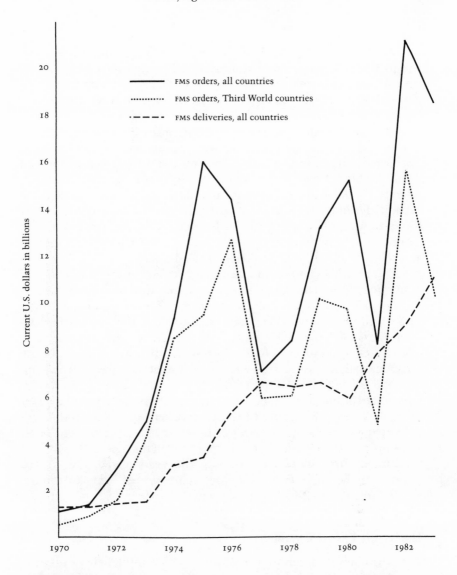

FIGURE 3. *U.S. Arms Exports Trends: Arms transfers through the Foreign Military Sales program, fiscal 1970–83 (includes Foreign Military Construction Sales)*

SOURCE: Defense Security Assistance Agency.

U.S. Arms Exports Trends

Turning now to the United States itself, figure 3 shows the sharp climb in FMS orders that began in the early 1970s and has continued (with occasional slowdowns) ever since. The important role played by Third World countries in sustaining this climb is also demonstrated by figure 3. Three major ascents can be detected: the first, in 1972–76, coincides with the adoption of the Nixon Doctrine and the 1974 OPEC oil price rise; the second, in 1979–80, reflects the Carter administration's efforts to bolster ties with Israel, Egypt, and Saudi Arabia following the fall of the Shah; and the third, in 1982, reflects the Reagan administration's efforts to enhance the defense capabilities of friendly Third World nations. Although FMS sales are likely to level off again in the mid-1980s, as recipient states absorb equipment ordered in the 1981–83 period, total sales should remain at a relatively high level throughout the decade.

Figure 3 also shows the vast gap between FMS orders and FMS deliveries. Although FMS orders have sometimes fluctuated significantly from year to year—dropping from $14.3 billion in fiscal 1976 to $7 billion in 1977, then rising again to $12.9 billion two years later—FMS deliveries have registered an almost continuous ascent, from $1.3 billion in 1971 to $11 billion in 1983. And because of the long "lead times" associated with the manufacture of modern weapons, and the high level of orders in the late 1970s and early 1980s, a large share of the arms ordered by foreign buyers since 1975 have yet to be delivered. According to the Department of Defense, this undelivered balance stood at $62.7 billion in 1983, or 41 percent of all arms ordered by foreign buyers since 1950.[26] This means that even if FMS orders drop off precipitously in the years ahead, the United States will be supplying increasing quantities of arms to foreign buyers for the remainder of the decade.

U.S. Arms Export Channels

Although it is common for analysts to lump all types of arms transfers together when gauging trade patterns, figure 4 shows that the United States exports military hardware through a number of separate channels.[27] These include:

The Military Assistance Program (MAP). Grants of military equipment and services to friendly nations financed by U.S. taxpayers through the Foreign Assistance Act.

The Foreign Military Sales (FMS) Program. Sales of major military equipment and services by the U.S. government to friendly for-

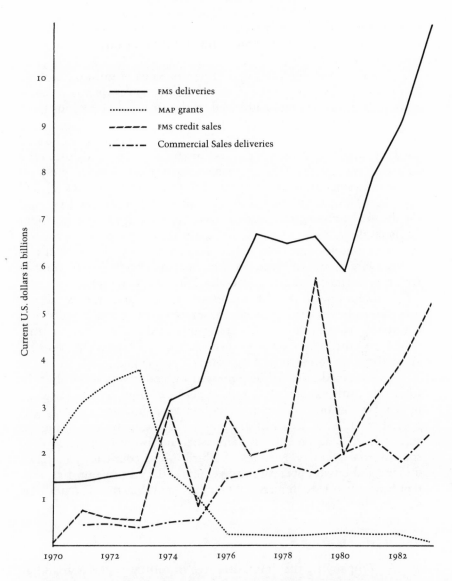

FIGURE 4. *U.S. Arms Export Channels: Military exports through the Foreign Military Sales program, the Military Assistance program, and the Commercial Sales program, fiscal 1970–83*

SOURCE: Defense Security Assistance Agency.

eign governments for cash or credit. It also includes sales of military construction services under the Foreign Military Construction Sales (FMCS) program.*

The Commercial Sales (CS) Program. Sales of military and police hardware by U.S. corporations to foreign governments or companies. Such sales must be licensed by the Office of Munitions Control (OMC) of the U.S. Department of State.

For most of the post–World War II era, the principal channel used for exporting arms was the MAP program, augmented during the Vietnam War by the Military Assistance Service–Funded program (MASF). These grant programs peaked in fiscal 1973 (the final year of the "Vietnamization" effort) at $4.7 billion, then dropped precipitously as Congress grew wary of anything associated with the Indochina conflict. As grant aid declined, military sales soared—reflecting Washington's efforts to reduce its balance-of-payments deficits (caused largely by the OPEC oil price increase) and to shift more of America's defense burden to friendly Third World nations.

Figure 4 also shows the important role played by the FMS credit program in facilitating arms purchases by cash-starved Third World countries. All told, the United States provided $28.7 billion in arms credits to Third World nations between 1950 and 1983, representing approximately 22 percent of the total FMS program.

Commercial sales, while representing a relatively small share of total U.S. arms exports at $2 billion per year (compared to $15–$20 billion for FMS orders), are nevertheless a major channel for the export of small arms, paramilitary gear, police weapons, and other unsophisticated equipment.[28] Because such hardware is often used by the internal security agencies of Third World countries to silence dissent and crush opposition movements, the CS program has a direct bearing on U.S. human rights policy, and thus merits particular scrutiny (see chapter 9).

The Market for U.S. Arms

Accompanying the dramatic surge in military sales abroad has been a significant shift in the direction of this outflow. Whereas prior to 1970 most FMS orders were placed by the industrialized nations (notably Australia, Japan, and the NATO powers), since 1970 the bulk of such orders have come from Third World nations. As indicated by figure 5, the dimensions of that shift have been quite as-

*Unless otherwise noted, it can be assumed that all references to the FMS program incorporate data on FMCS activities.

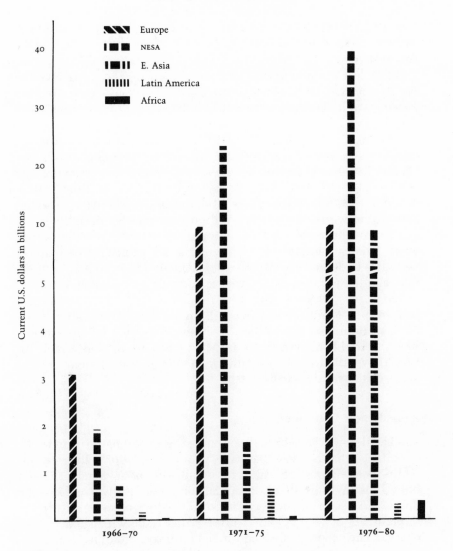

FIGURE 5. *The Market for U.S. Arms: Orders for U.S. arms through the Foreign Military Sales program by region, 1966–80*

NESA = Near East and South Asia, plus Greece and Turkey.
SOURCE: Defense Security Assistance Agency.

tounding: Third World orders jumped from an average of only $250 million per year in the 1960s to as much as $10 billion per year in the mid-1970s. And while the Third World share of U.S. arms exports declined briefly in the late 1970s (following the collapse of the Pahlavi dynasty in Iran), they rose again in the early 1980s and are expected to remain at a relatively high level for the remainder of the decade.

Figure 5 also indicates the dramatic shifts in regional market trends that have occurred over the past twenty years. Since 1972, the Middle East has been the major overseas market for U.S. arms, accounting for well over half of all FMS orders by the end of the decade. All told, the United States sold Middle Eastern countries a total of $80 billion worth of arms and military services between 1972 and 1983, or twenty-nine times the amount sold in the preceding twenty years. The past decade has also witnessed a significant increase in FMS sales to other Third World regions, including Latin America, Africa, and the Far East. Latin American orders rose from $48 million in fiscal 1971 to $696 million in fiscal 1982, while African orders rose from $16 million to $182 million and East Asian orders from $71.2 million to $1,958 million.[29] Although sales to these regions are likely to trail behind those to the Middle East for the foreseeable future, they will probably account for an ever-increasing share of total U.S. sales as the decade proceeds.

Arms Export Commodities

Until now, I have been describing arms export patterns in terms of dollars—that is, the dollar value of annual sales or deliveries. But while these figures are useful for delineating basic trends, they do not tell us anything about the actual commodities involved. It is the unique character of these commodities—their potential utility as implements of warfare—that invests this trade with such significance. "The export of such enormous military potential," Sen. Dick Clark justly observed in 1978, "cannot be controlled in the same way we manage the export of refrigerators or automobiles."[30] Accordingly, we shall next examine the basic data on deliveries of actual hardware. Between 1976 and 1983, according to the CRS, the United States sold Third World nations a total of 5,800 tanks and self-propelled guns; 4,530 artillery pieces; 13,636 armored personnel carriers and armored cars; 122 surface warships and 3 submarines; 1,558 combat aircraft; 422 helicopters; and 8,394 surface-to-air missiles.[31] (For comparable data on sales by the Soviet Union and Europe, see chapter 10.) Clearly, this represents a very substantial transfer of

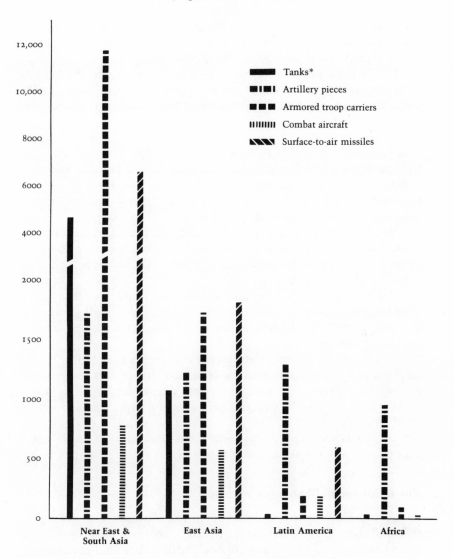

FIGURE 6. *U.S. Arms Export Commodities: Quantities of arms delivered to the Third World by category and region, fiscal 1976–83*

*Includes self-propelled howitzers.
SOURCE: Congressional Research Service.

war-making capabilities to Third World nations. And these figures indicate deliveries only; if we included equipment on order but not yet delivered, the figures would be much higher.

While the United States supplies a very wide range of products within each of these basic weapons categories, certain items are in particular demand abroad. Among those that figure most frequently in U.S. arms export agreements are: [32]

Aircraft. Northrop F-5 series fighters (F-5A Freedom Fighter, F-5B trainer, F-5E Tiger-II, F-5F trainer); General Dynamics F-16 fighter; McDonnell-Douglas F-4 Phantom fighter-bomber and F-15 Eagle fighter; Lockheed C-130 Hercules transport; Rockwell OV-10 Bronco counterinsurgency plane; Bell-Textron UH-1 series utility helicopters and AH-1 helicopter gunship.

Tanks, Guns, and Armored Vehicles. General Dynamics M-60 tank; FMC Corporation M-113 armored personnel carrier; Cadillac-Gage V-150 Commando armored car; GMC-Allison M-109 155-mm. self-propelled howitzer.

Missiles. Raytheon/Ford AIM-9 series Sidewinder air-to-air missile; Hughes TOW anti-tank missile; McDonnell-Douglas Harpoon anti-ship missile and Dragon anti-tank missile; Raytheon Hawk surface-to-air missile.

These are, of course, the "big ticket" items that figure in the largest and costliest transactions—the ones that attract the greatest media and congressional attention. On a day-to-day basis, however, most transfers consist of less impressive hardware: rifles, machine guns, grenades, jeeps, radios, and so forth. Military services (training, maintenance, construction work, etc.) also account for a significant proportion of FMS sales—as much as 40 percent in some cases. [33]

The Diffusion of Sophisticated Arms

Accompanying the increase in the quantities of U.S. arms sold to Third World buyers has been a dramatic increase in the *quality* of arms being offered to these countries. Nations that once received obsolete U.S. hand-me-downs through the MAP program are now buying America's most advanced aircraft, missiles, and warships. As a result, the forces of Egypt, Israel, Saudi Arabia, and other favored U.S. clients are now equipped with many of the same weapons found in America's own arsenals. It is this development, more than anything else, that has spurred congressional and public debate over U.S. arms exports.

This qualitative shift in arms transfers takes two forms: a *horizontal* or geographic increase in the number of countries receiving

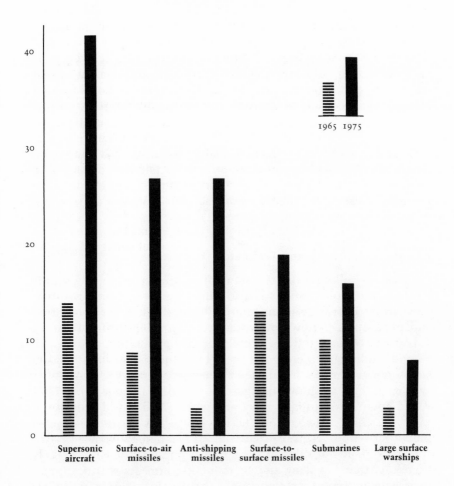

FIGURE 7. *Diffusion of Sophisticated Arms in the Third World: Number of Third World countries possessing selected weapons types, 1965 and 1975*

SOURCE: RAND Corporation.

sophisticated armaments, and a *vertical* or progressive increase in the capacity of arms transferred to any given country over time. Looking first at the horizontal distribution, we find that the number of Third World countries that possess supersonic combat aircraft rose from 14 in 1965 to 42 in 1975. A similar pattern holds for sales of guided missiles and other major equipment (see figure 7). Turning to the vertical dimension, we find that countries that received relatively unsophisticated aircraft like the F-5A in the 1960s are now receiving far more sophisticated aircraft, including F-15s and F-16s.[34] And while President Carter attempted to restrain the transfer of sophisticated arms to Third World countries during his term in office, President Reagan has tended to upgrade the quality of arms sold to many of these nations.

Exports of Arms-Making Technology

Besides selling more and more arms of ever-increasing sophistication, the United States is also exporting the technology to produce arms. Such transactions normally entail the sale of blueprints and production "know-how" via licensing agreements or the involvement of foreign firms in collaborative production schemes via coproduction agreements. For most of the post–World War II era, such arrangements were limited to the NATO powers plus Australia and Japan, but, as shown in figure 8, they now include some Third World countries.[35] In fact, more and more Third World countries—eager to acquire modern production know-how for their domestic industries—now require that such "technology transfers" accompany all major sales of finished weapons systems. It is likely, therefore, that licensing and coproduction projects will occupy an increasingly important role in the international arms trade (see chapter 8).

The stepped-up acquisition of modern arms by Third World nations has also generated an increased demand for another type of nonhardware transfer: the provision of military technical skills and other specialized services. Because many Third World nations lack the trained personnel to operate and maintain all the high-tech equipment they are acquiring from the United States, they increasingly look to U.S. defense contractors to provide such services as part of major arms agreements. Typically, these services are performed by civilian technicians—or "white-collar mercenaries"—hired by U.S. arms firms from the ranks of retired military personnel. According to the Department of Defense, 5,812 civilian

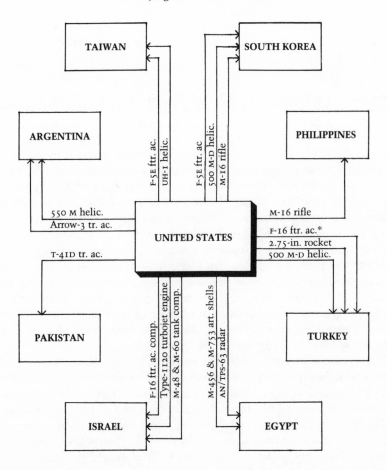

FIGURE 8. *U.S. Exports of Arms-Making Technology to the Third World: Major U.S. arms coproduction and licensing programs, 1982*

*Agreement signed 1984.

ABBREVIATIONS
helic = helicopter
ftr. ac. = fighter aircraft

tr. ac. = trainer aircraft
comp. = components
art. = artillery

SOURCE: U.S. Dept. of Defense, Stockholm International Peace Research Institute.

specialists were engaged in such activities abroad under the FMS program in 1983,[36] and thousands more were involved in related projects.

Exports of Police and Paramilitary Weaponry

Although most of the arms sold to Third World nations by the United States under the FMS and CS programs are intended for use by regular military forces committed to external defense missions, a very significant proportion are sold to police and paramilitary forces engaged in internal security operations. Such transactions typically involve the transfer of small arms (pistols, revolvers, submachine guns), anti-riot equipment (tear gas, chemical Mace, riot sticks, etc.), police and prison hardware (handcuffs, truncheons, leg irons, etc.), paramilitary and counterinsurgency gear (armored cars, jeeps, helicopters, light attack planes, etc.), and related equipment (including computers). Some of these items are provided through the FMS program, but in most cases they are exported through the Commercial Sales program of the Department of State or (in the case of computers and other noncombat items) through normal trade channels administered by the Department of Commerce.

Because transfers of this type usually involve relatively inexpensive and unsophisticated equipment, they rarely come to the attention of Congress or the media. As a result, statistics on such sales are relatively meager. Through use of the Freedom of Information Act, however, I was able to obtain some hard data on these sales. As shown in figure 9, between 1976 and 1979 U.S. firms acquired export licenses from the OMC for the sale to Third World police forces of 126,622 pistols and revolvers, 51,906 rifles and submachine guns, 615,612 tear-gas grenades, 8,870 canisters of chemical Mace, and 55.8 million rounds of small-arms ammunition.[37] Because such equipment can easily be used to suppress dissent by unarmed dissidents or ethnic minorities, and because it is often sold to nations ruled by authoritarian or undemocratic regimes (including embargoed countries like South Africa and Chile), these sales obviously bear directly on U.S. efforts to protect human rights abroad (see chapter 9).

These nine factors represent the empirical backdrop for any comprehensive analysis of U.S. military exports. Essentially, these are the parameters that all policymakers must contend with when attempting to shape or reshape the arms export policies of the United States.[38]

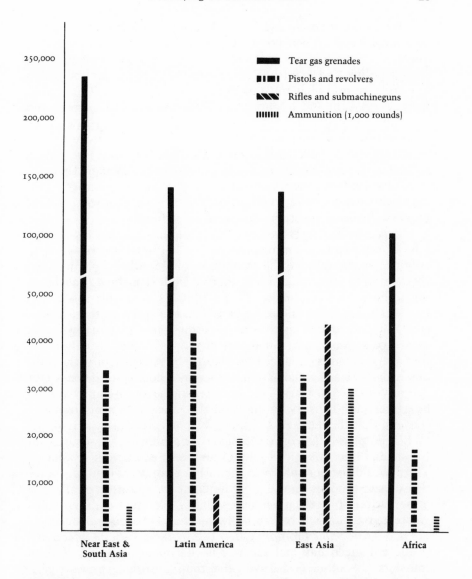

FIGURE 9. *U.S. Sales of Police and Paramilitary Weaponry to the Third World: Quantities of arms delivered to Third World police organizations by category and region, 1976–79*

SOURCE: Office of Munitions Control, U.S. Dept. of State.

While these charts and figures raise many of the issues associated with rising arms exports, they do not address the fundamental questions of policy: questions of war and peace, national security, foreign policy, and so forth. These are the basic issues around which any arms export policy must ultimately be shaped, and the ones that have aroused the most controversy in the press, the Congress, and the public at large. Because we cannot address these issues on the basis of statistics alone, we must examine the actual performance of arms transfers in advancing or retarding basic U.S. objectives. That, indeed, is the task in the remainder of this book. To ensure that this endeavor produces the sort of answers we need to construct a prudent arms export policy, let us conclude this chapter with a summary of the basic questions that must be addressed:

Do Arms Transfers Enhance U.S. National Security? Under U.S. law, all arms transfers must promote U.S. national security by contributing to the self-defense capabilities of U.S. allies, by enhancing their internal security, or by furthering U.N.-sponsored peacekeeping activities abroad. But while U.S. officials invariably assert that this is the case when endorsing particular transactions, there is considerable controversy as to whether arms transfers actually secure these goals in practice. Advocates of proposed sales usually argue that arms transfers enhance U.S. security by strengthening the military capabilities of allied nations—thereby reducing the defense burden of the United States—and by deterring adventurism by would-be aggressors. Those who question the efficacy of arms transfers contend that the recipients of these weapons often use them for parochial purposes that contribute little or nothing to U.S. security interests and that misguided sales of high-tech equipment to volatile Third World regions may provoke rather than deter conflict. Since this debate touches on the most fundamental question of all—the preservation of world peace and stability—it must command our greatest attention when examining the record of arms transfers.

Do Arms Sales Promote Other U.S. Foreign Policy Objectives? While enhanced national security is the major objective of arms transfers, U.S. officials also avow that they contribute to a wide variety of other foreign policy objectives. These "collateral" benefits supposedly include increased influence or leverage over the recipient government, access to military bases and facilities, and close contact with foreign military leaders. Many analysts are skeptical, however, that arms transfers actually deliver on all these promises. These critics argue that any leverage provided by arms transfers is short-lived and unreliable and that the other benefits supposedly provided by arms transfers are obtained only when the receiving nations are predisposed to supply them for reasons of their own. Opponents also argue that arms transfers may actually undermine U.S. foreign policy objectives. In particular, arms transfers have reportedly impeded human rights by contributing to the repressive capabilities of undemocratic regimes and have obstructed economic development by diverting scarce national resources to unproductive activities.

Do Arms Transfers Benefit the U.S. Economy? While economic advancement is not officially recognized as a motive for U.S. arms transfers, government and industry officials have suggested that such exports can aid the U.S. economy at the same time that they promote U.S. security. Specifically, arms transfers can benefit the economy by reducing U.S. balance-of-payments deficits, by maintaining a high level of productivity in the defense industries (and thus preventing cyclical unemployment), and by reducing the amount America must pay for its own military hardware. While these benefits are generally acknowledged by most analysts, there is some dispute as to just how significant they are over the long run. Some critics have argued, moreover, that export sales help sustain an overextended and unproductive arms industry and that America's civilian industries would benefit from a contraction of the over-indulged military sector.

These, then, are the fundamental questions that must be resolved before we can begin to fashion a realistic and prudent arms export policy. To answer them, we must acquire more knowledge on the history, management, and consequences of U.S. arms transfers. As we proceed to these tasks, our perspective will gradually shift: moving from the straightforward transmission of information to the evaluation of competing assessments and options. And while I have, of course, drawn some conclusions of my own, every effort is made to allow the reader—and potential policymaker—to arrive at his or her own conclusions on these vital issues.

CHAPTER 2

Primal Motives

The Political Economy of Arms Sales

"In a perfect world," Assistant Secretary of Defense Paul C. Warnke told the Senate Foreign Relations Committee in 1968, "we wouldn't have to deal with arms sales." In today's imperfect world, however, "we are no more in a position to discontinue our supply of arms to our friends than we are in a position to disarm unilaterally."[1] While this statement suggests that sharply reduced arms exports are the ultimate goal of U.S. policy, the experience of the past fifteen years suggests otherwise. Between 1968 and 1982, U.S. arms exports under the FMS program rose by well over 2,000 percent, from $1 billion to $21 billion. Even under the Carter administration, when "arms restraint" was a formal U.S. policy objective, the Foreign Relations Committee found that "the predisposition in most Executive Branch agencies remains to sell."[2] That "predisposition" outlasted Carter, and subsequently, during the Reagan administration, pushed U.S. military exports to still higher levels.

Many congressional and executive branch studies have concluded that uncontrolled arms transfers can jeopardize world stability. Why, then, does the United States continue to accelerate the outflow of weaponry? To some extent, of course, the arms outflow is driven by the particular economic and bureaucratic interests of specific U.S. corporations and governmental agencies. (See chapter 4 for a discussion of how such vested interests can coalesce around individual arms transactions.) These particular interests can make headway, however, only because there is a persistent, deeply embedded *impulse to sell* at the highest levels of government. As noted by the GAO in a 1979 report to Congress, "From the moment of first interest" by a foreign government, the arms-export process "is geared toward seriously responding to a buyer's perceived needs."[3]

This predisposition or impulse to sell embodies a cluster of political, military, and economic factors that have driven U.S. arms exports to ever-higher levels. Although rarely acknowledged, these motives underlie the formal policy directives that supposedly govern U.S. arms exports. And because the federal government serves as both promoter and controller of U.S. military exports, all previous efforts to constrict the outflow of arms have been frustrated by the prevalence of these factors within the bureaucracy itself. So long as these motives remain unchallenged, it is unlikely that any future efforts in this direction will make any greater headway; it follows, therefore, that the first step in developing an alternative arms export policy is to identify these factors and evaluate their influence.[4]

In undertaking this analysis, however, we immediately encounter one of the most persistent features of the arms trade: the broad gap between official rhetoric and "real-world" motivations. Arms sales, after all, basically involve the exchange of war-making machinery for some form of compensation—and public opinion has rarely looked with favor upon such transactions. There was a time, in fact, when arms suppliers were viewed as "merchants of death" and counted among the lower types of scoundrel. Today, however, arms transfers are considered a legitimate instrument of foreign policy and are normally accorded public approval—so long as it can be demonstrated that they somehow serve the "national interest." This requires, however, that every arms transaction be justified in terms that accord with popular expectations and values. And because economic advantage and political expediency are not normally considered legitimate rationales for such transactions, governments usually advance more idealistic justifications for their arms exports.

Given this requirement, U.S. officials rarely admit to any but the most altruistic motives for approving arms transfers. Typically, such sales are justified on the grounds that they promote U.S. security, regional stability, and world peace. "Arms transfers," Under Secretary Buckley affirmed in 1981, "should be viewed as a positive and increasingly important component of our global security posture and a key element of our foreign policy."[5] An even more striking example of this tendency to characterize arms transfers in "positive" terms is the U.S. Air Force's practice of designating its sales programs with the prefix "peace"; thus the transfer of F-15s to Israel is code-named "Peace Fox"; F-15s to Saudi Arabia, "Peace Sun"; F-4s to Egypt, "Peace Farrow"; F-16s to Israel, "Peace Marble"; and F-15s to Japan, "Peace Eagle."[6]

Although dissimulation of this sort tends to be the rule, U.S. officials occasionally admit to more pragmatic motives for arms sales. "The foreign military sales [program] yields certain indirect military and economic benefits which impact favorably on U.S. security interests and deserve some examination," Deputy Secretary of Defense William P. Clements told the House Foreign Affairs Committee in 1973. "These sales have had a significant favorable impact on our balance-of-payments problem and produce major benefits in

terms of maintaining U.S. defense production lines. . . ."[7] Such "indirect" benefits were also acknowledged in a 1983 essay by Francis J.
West, Jr., assistant secretary of defense for international security affairs. The FMS program, he wrote, "is often the key to the cooperation of strategically important countries in such significant realms
as securing lines of communication and assuring access to critical
raw materials." Furthermore, "Although it is not a pivotal factor in
U.S. arms transfer decisions, . . . defense exports do constitute a
valuable source of income for the United States, contributing to a
more favorable balance of payments and promoting employment in
many sectors of the U.S. economy. . . ."[8]

These and similar statements by other U.S. authorities suggest
that there are a wider range of motives underlying arms transfers than
is normally acknowledged in official statements. Indeed, through
interviews with government officials and a search of government
documents and military trade publications, it becomes obvious that
an assortment of political, military, and economic motives normally
drives the U.S. arms export program. These factors may not arise in
each and every sale of munitions, but they recur often enough to justify their designation as the "primal motives" for U.S. arms exports.

Before proceeding to a discussion of these motives, it is important to note that they represent a set of beliefs or expectations about
the utility of arms transfers in attaining certain foreign policy benefits; we must not assume, however, that they necessarily deliver on
these expectations. As we shall discover, arms transfers are a fickle
and unreliable instrument of policy, often producing the very opposite of their intended result. But because many U.S. policymakers
believe in the long-term efficacy of the arms transfer instrument,
these factors retain their motivational power, and thus it is important that we examine them closely.

Described below are the ten motivations that figure most often
and most decisively in U.S. decisionmaking on arms sales abroad.[9]
Political-military factors are described first, reflecting my belief that
these, rather than economic factors, are most important in motivating U.S. military sales. This does not mean, of course, that political
factors always dominate—in many cases, in fact, economic motives
prevail—but rather that political and economic factors tend to be
most decisive over the long run.[10] Furthermore, within each major
category, individual factors are listed in approximate rank order.
Here again, however, it is important to note that this ranking does
not prevail in each case, but rather reflects my estimation of their
cumulative significance. As we shall see, a somewhat different rank-

ing of motives underlies Soviet and European arms sales (see chapter 10), but here we are talking primarily about U.S. motives.

Political-Military Factors

Support of U.S. Allies. The FMS program, like the Military Assistance Program before it, is intended to enhance U.S. national security by strengthening the military capabilities of allied and friendly governments. "Arms transfers," Under Secretary Buckley explained in 1981, "serve as an important adjunct to our own security . . . by enhancing the self-defense capabilities of nations with which we have close security ties."[11] Such transfers are viewed as a natural concomitant to the NATO Alliance and to our mutual defense agreements with such countries as Australia, Japan, New Zealand, the Philippines, South Korea, and Taiwan.

The precise objective of U.S. support has, of course, changed with time: in the early Cold War period, the emphasis was on buttressing the "forward defense countries" on the periphery of the Soviet Union and China; today, U.S. arms aid is largely intended to enhance the security of friendly Third World nations located in likely war zones such as the Middle East and North Africa. In many cases, U.S. assistance is designed to bolster pro-Western nations that are threatened by hostile neighbors. This is the justification most often cited for U.S. arms transfers to such exposed nations as Israel, Saudi Arabia, South Korea, and Taiwan. In such cases, Buckley noted, U.S. aid can "help our friends and allies provide for their own defense and furnish tangible evidence of our support for their independence and territorial integrity, thus deterring possible aggression."[12]

Military Burden-Sharing. If arms transfers are viewed as a form of assistance to friendly governments, they can also be used to expand the defense burden of friendly nations by encumbering them with some of America's own military responsibilities. U.S. aid is then intended to enhance the self-defense capabilities of allies that might otherwise rely on the United States to provide a direct military presence and to assist in the emergence of "regional gendarmes" that can help protect U.S. interests within their sphere of interests. "Although the United States has become increasingly aware of its inability to police the world alone," a group of analysts from the American Enterprise Institute (AEI) noted in 1982, "it continues to have a major interest in the survival of other nations," and thus arms transfers can further U.S. security interests "by promoting regional security and reducing the potential for direct U.S. involvement."[13]

This motive acquired particular significance after the Vietnam conflict, when, in light of widespread domestic dissatisfaction with prevailing U.S. defense policies, the Nixon administration sought to shift some of America's forward defense role to selected allies in the Third World. Under the Nixon Doctrine, stepped-up U.S. arms aid was extended to such strategically located countries as Indonesia, Iran, and Thailand. And while the collapse of the Pahlavi dynasty in Iran has significantly diminished U.S. confidence in the efficacy of the Nixon Doctrine, military burden-sharing continues to be a major objective of the FMS program. Arms transfers "bolster the military capabilities of our friends and allies," Buckley testified in 1981, thereby "permitting them in some cases to undertake responsibilities which otherwise we ourselves might have to assume."[14]

Political Influence and Leverage. Major arms transfers—particularly those involving high-tech equipment—can provide the supplier with considerable influence over the political behavior of the recipient. "Arms sales may provide political influence," the AEI analysts wrote in 1982, "or they may provide direct leverage over a recipient's behavior in ongoing events."[15] Such influence is believed to stem from the fact that the transfer of advanced munitions creates a bond between the parties involved, implying a commitment on the part of the supplier to the defense of the recipient—and thus a corresponding obligation on the part of the recipient to support the policy objectives of the supplier. This bond is thought to be particularly strong in the case of U.S. relations with such close allies as Israel, Morocco, the Philippines, South Korea, Thailand, and Turkey.

While such ties are assumed to be largely voluntary, they can acquire a coercive character when a recipient becomes dependent on the supplier for continuing deliveries of spare parts, ammunition, and specialized technical services required by most modern munitions. "When you buy an airplane," Lockheed Vice President William D. Perreault once observed, "you also buy a supplier and a supply line; in other words, you also buy a political partner."[16] This dependency can become particularly acute in wartime, when a belligerent may require rush deliveries of critical components, thus investing the supplier with considerable leverage over the recipient's subsequent behavior—and may even, in some cases (the October 1973 Arab-Israeli war is a frequently cited example), enable the supplier to dictate the terms of a cease-fire agreement.[17]

Superpower Competition. Closely related to the motive of influence is the continuing drive of the United States to enhance its global power and authority while diminishing that of the Soviet Union. "Arms sales have become a major component of the American government's approach to the competition with the Soviet Union on a global basis," Andrew Pierre of the Council on Foreign Relations observed in 1982, "perhaps *the* major instrument for action overseas."[18] Arms transfers play an important role in this competition by strengthening America's ties with its existing allies and by helping to induce other nations—including those presently aligned with the U.S.S.R.—to establish fresh ties with the United States. Thus U.S. military assistance to such nations as Jordan, Pakistan, Saudi Arabia, the Sudan, Tunisia, and Zaire is often justified on the grounds that it is needed to help ensure the pro-Western orientation of these countries, while promises of such aid played a key role in Washington's efforts to woo Egypt, North Yemen, and Somalia away from the Soviet orbit.[19]

Superpower competition also stimulates U.S. arms exports in a negative sense, by prompting U.S. officials to approve questionable sales out of fear that the buyer would otherwise turn to the Soviet Union or other suppliers for the desired hardware. "If we refuse to provide the military equipment these nations feel is necessary to their security," Adm. William H. Moorer of the Joint Chiefs of Staff testified in 1973, "the choice they face is to forego the material they consider essential . . . or to acquire it from either Western Europe, the U.S.S.R., or the People's Republic of China." If, however, "we provide the material, our power to persuade is enhanced. . . ."[20] Many experts believe, in fact, that this "negative stimulant" is one of the principal motives for U.S. arms transfers.[21]

Access to Bases. Since the end of World War II, America's worldwide network of military bases and facilities has steadily shrunk as host nations adopted a more independent or hostile stance vis-à-vis the United States. As a result, those bases that remain available to U.S. forces have acquired greater strategic significance; consequently, Washington has generally been prepared to provide host nations with increased military and economic assistance. In some of these cases—notably Greece, the Philippines, Spain, and Turkey—increased arms transfers have been made a *quid pro quo* for continued U.S. occupation of bases on their territory.

Arms sales have also played a key role in U.S. efforts to acquire docking privileges and overflight rights for the Rapid Deployment Force in Africa and the Middle East. As noted by Assistant Secretary West, the FMS program is especially useful "in securing and sustaining the enroute access, overflight privileges, and base rights that are essential to the execution by U.S. forces of a rapid response to crises abroad."[22]

Access to Political and Military Elites. Arms transfers further advance American foreign policy interests by providing U.S. officials with direct and continuing access to high political and military of- ficials of recipient countries. Because arms transactions normally entail long and complex negotiations—often involving the buyer's top military leadership—they offer American leaders a unique op- portunity to establish close working relationships with their foreign counterparts. "The friendships and allegiances that develop as a re- sult of this interaction," the ACDA noted in a 1974 report to Con- gress, "may often yield significant returns to the supplier govern- ment."[23] Such ties are considered particularly important in Third World countries, where military elites often wield considerable po- litical power. Indeed, Washington considers such contacts to be so valuable that U.S. military leaders will often endorse particular sales simply to prevent these political benefits from going to a competitor. As suggested by Secretary of Defense James R. Schlesinger, "The de- gree of influence of the supplier is potentially substantial, and typi- cally, those relationships are long enduring." That is why, he told the House Foreign Affairs Committee in 1974, "When states wish to buy [military] hardware, we prefer that it be American-supplied rather than supplied by some other state that may be hostile or indifferent to . . . the objectives of American foreign policy."[24]

Internal Security. While the U.S. arms export program is pri- marily intended to enhance friendly regimes' defenses against exter- nal attack, it is also designed to strengthen their defenses against in- ternal threats, including insurgent and dissident movements. To a large extent, such transfers reflect the belief—long prevalent in Washington—that pro-Western regimes must be defended against guerrilla or opposition movements that could provide an opening wedge for Soviet (or Chinese, or Cuban) penetration. Accordingly, sales of internal security hardware (police and paramilitary weapons, riot-control equipment, jeeps and helicopters, and so forth) have al- ways figured prominently in the U.S. arms aid effort.

Such transfers played an especially important role in the U.S. arms export program in the 1960s, when defeat of "national libera- tion struggles" was a major U.S. objective and Washington sought to discourage the acquisition of costly high-tech systems by threatened Third World regimes. The fiscal year 1968 arms program for Latin America, Secretary of Defense Robert S. McNamara testified at the time, "will provide no tanks, artillery, fighter aircraft, or combat ships." Instead, "the emphasis is on vehicles and helicopters for in- ternal mobility, [and] communications equipment for better coordi- nation of in-country security efforts. . . ."[25] This perspective was less prevalent in the post-Vietnam era, but has acquired renewed significance under the Reagan administration as the United States has stepped up its support for threatened regimes in Central America (see chapter 5).

Economic Factors

Balance-of-Payments. Ever since the United States first faced the prospect of negative trade balances in the early 1960s, military sales have been viewed as an important tool for improving the nation's international payments accounts. Arms transfers are considered a particularly attractive instrument for this purpose since, unlike most other commodities, their rate of flow is largely controlled by the federal government. This instrument was employed with particular vigor after 1974, when the OPEC nations imposed a fourfold increase in oil prices and America faced a mammoth deficit in its foreign trade accounts. To help reduce the mounting deficit, President Nixon ordered the Pentagon to relax its restrictions on sales of high-tech arms abroad and to invite purchases by the oil-producing nations of the Middle East.[26] As a result of aggressive marketing by U.S. arms firms and large purchases by Iran and Saudi Arabia, the United States sold $49.8 billion worth of munitions to foreign countries in fiscal 1974–77, thereby averting what otherwise would have amounted to a substantial balance-of-payments deficit. "Gains in the U.S. export account offset more than three-fifths of the deterioration in the trade account," the CIA noted in a report on America's 1977 financial condition, "with most of the improvement in service earnings resulting from . . . higher military sales to the OPEC countries" along with increased banking services.[27] And while increased sales of foodstuffs and other nonmilitary products have helped reduce the deficit in recent years, arms transfers remain an important tool for correcting trade imbalances.[28]

Absorbing Surplus Output. Ever since the end of World War II, export sales have been viewed as a critical "safety valve" for ensuring the viability of U.S. military industries. Although U.S. arms firms are primarily committed to the domestic market, they have expanded foreign sales whenever Pentagon procurement fails to consume their total output; without such an outlet, any sustained downturn in Pentagon outlays would cause havoc in the arms industry, eventually resulting in the closure of major plants and assembly lines. This outlet proved particularly critical in 1973, when Vietnam War spending came to a halt and the Pentagon announced cutbacks in many military programs. Rather than reacting to this crisis by closing excess facilities (or converting them to nonmilitary production), many U.S. firms launched aggressive campaigns to sell their surplus products to foreign buyers. These efforts were facilitated by the Department of Defense, which seeks to maintain a "warm production base" for future military emergencies. (By the same token, these efforts were supported by the employees of the affected firms—and their elected representatives—who sought to preserve the jobs involved.) And while domestic military spending has turned upward again, foreign sales are still considered essential to keep some production lines open and to relieve some of the financial burden imposed by persistent inflation in the military industries.[29]

Cost-Sharing. Just as arms transfers are used to shift some of America's global military burden to other nations, they are also used to export some of the economic costs involved in the maintenance of a mammoth military establishment. As military technology has become more complex and sophisticated, the research and development (R&D) and production start-up costs of arms have risen exponentially, forcing the Pentagon to curtail its purchases of many items and forcing the cancellation of some costly programs altogether. However, by shifting some of the R&D and start-up costs to foreign buyers, arms transfers have helped reduce the price that the United States must pay for its own acquisitions of selected systems. According to a 1976 study by the Congressional Budget Office, foreign military sales of $8 billion in fiscal 1976 generated $560 million in savings for the Department of Defense.[30]

Export sales also reduce America's economic burden by increasing the total production run of a particular weapon, thus spreading production costs over a larger number of individual items and reducing the unit cost paid by the Department of Defense for its own supply of that item.[31] Such reductions, however modest, can be of considerable importance when applied to expensive and controversial new projects: Iran's 1974 decision to purchase 80 Grumman F-14 Tomcat fighters, for instance, reportedly saved that project from termination by Congress because of its steadily mounting development costs.[32] As the cost of new weapons continues to rise, therefore, export sales will continue to be seen as an important factor in calculating the overall economic viability of future projects.

The "Clustering" Phenomenon

While other factors may occasionally influence military sales decisions, these ten factors comprise the basic motives which underlie most U.S. arms transfers. Naturally, the relative impact of any particular factor will vary with each transaction and with changes in the political-economic environment, but it is rare to find a major transaction that does not reflect at least several of these motives. Indeed, experience suggests that it is the *clustering* of these motives behind any given transaction that most accounts for its success in winning government approval. Because each participant in the decisionmaking system is likely to advance several factors when promoting a particular transaction (with the Pentagon emphasizing military factors, the State Department political factors, the Treasury economic factors, and so forth), policymakers who advocate restraint are usually faced with a chorus of justifications—each of which appears to harbor legitimacy (see chapter 4).

Because these factors tend to be clustered when introduced in the decisionmaking process, it is almost impossible to determine which individual motives proved decisive in determining the outcome of a particular transaction. It seems reasonable to conclude, however, that the more of them associated with a particular transaction, the greater the likelihood of its success. Certainly this appears to be true when we examine aggregate U.S. sales to a particular country over a given period of time. Looking at Iran in the 1972–74 period, for instance, we find that Washington stepped up its arms deliveries in order to: 1. convert Iran into a "surrogate gendarme" in the Persian Gulf; 2. diminish Soviet influence in the strategic Gulf area; 3. enhance U.S. influence with the Shah of Iran, then viewed as the most stable ruler in the area; 4. reduce U.S. balance-of-payments deficits caused by the fourfold increase in oil prices; 5. offset the recession in the aerospace industry, which was itself partly caused by the OPEC price increase; and 6. help reduce the spiraling costs of new weapons systems sought by the Pentagon.[33] Given this confluence of factors, it is hardly surprising that U.S. sales to Iran increased tenfold, from $325 million per year in the early 1970s to $3 billion per year in the mid-1970s (see chapter 6).

This "clustering" principle can also be applied to aggregate U.S. sales as follows: arms exports will tend to rise when the number of motives at work increases and tend to stabilize or decline when their number decreases.* During the 1960s, military sales were largely motivated by a core group of political-military factors—support for allies, superpower competition, and internal security—that produced few major shifts in the rate of arms outflows. In the early 1970s, however, a host of new political and economic motivations

---

*As we shall discover in chapter 10, this same clustering phenomenon largely explains the shifting levels of Soviet and European arms transfers to the Third World.

emerged—burden-sharing (under the Nixon Doctrine), political influence (in connection with the Mideast peace negotiations), balance-of-payments (following the OPEC oil price increase), absorbing surplus output (to compensate for declining Vietnam War spending), and cost-sharing (as Washington embarked on production of a new generation of high-tech arms)—and weapons sales accordingly rose to record levels.

This constellation of motives did not disappear during the Carter administration, although a new factor, "arms restraint," was added to the decisionmaking process. Carter's emphasis on restraint succeeded in halting the upward trend in U.S. arms exports, but his failure to challenge or eliminate any of the motivational factors described above prevented him from actually reducing the flow of military hardware (see chapter 3).

Having survived Carter's efforts at restraint, this dense cluster of motives received fresh impetus with the advent of the Reagan administration. In his policy directive of July 8, 1981, Reagan explicitly endorsed many of the primal motives underlying U.S. arms exports. "Applied judiciously," he affirmed, arms transfers can strengthen U.S. security by:

- "enhancing the state of preparedness of allies and friends . . . ,"
- "revitalizing our mutual security relationships . . . ,"
- "foster[ing] regional and internal security . . . ,"
- "help[ing] to enhance United States defense production capabilities and efficiency."

Other statements by Reagan and his top foreign policy aides further confirmed the administration's commitment to the basic factors described above, producing a generally positive and permissive attitude toward military sales.[34] If they tended to emphasize political and military factors, it is because the administration's vast military buildup was expected to keep U.S. arms producers fully occupied and thus diminish the overall economic importance of export sales. These economic motives remained in place, however, and helped sustain a major upsurge in U.S. arms exports.

Despite the resurgence of these motivational factors under the Reagan administration, however, there has been a growing tendency for analysts to question the efficacy of arms transfers as a foreign policy instrument. With the collapse of the Pahlavi dynasty in Iran, and the subsequent U.S. failure to halt the Falklands conflict between Argentina and Great Britain (both abundantly equipped with U.S. arms), many observers concluded that arms sales are a relatively ineffective instrument of policy. "We kidded ourselves" in Iran, Sen. Joseph R. Biden, Jr., commented in 1982. "We had close to $30 billion worth of the most sophisticated arms in the world in Iran, [yet] without a shot being fired, the Shah was marched out of the country. [Now] all those weapons are either lying dormant or have become accessible to the Soviet Union."[35] Rep. Tony P. Hall of Ohio, another critic of the administration's arms policies, observed in 1982 that arms transfers are "an extremely seductive but ultimately unpredictable instrument of foreign policy," resulting in "frequent failures."[36] Such comments can only reinforce the cautionary note provided earlier—that the factors described above represent a set of beliefs or expectations about the efficacy of arms transfers, not a record of demonstrated performance. As we proceed in our discussion, therefore, we must always seek to distinguish between the presumed objectives of arms transfers and their actual performance in fulfilling U.S. policy objectives.

Buyer Motives: The "Demand Side" of the Arms Trade

Before concluding this chapter, it is important to recognize that we have until now been looking exclusively at the "supply side" of the arms trade, without considering the corresponding "demand side" of the equation—the factors that motivate purchases by the buyer. Such neglect was permissible because for the time frame we have been discussing—the 1970s and early 1980s—the demand for arms remained relatively strong, and thus the supply side tended to dominate the market environment. Nevertheless, the demand side does affect market conditions, often dramatically. The 1974 OPEC oil price rise, for instance, provided Middle Eastern oil producers with a surplus of petrodollars and thus the capacity to bid for the sophisticated arms once denied to them. On the other hand, the world recession and credit retrenchment in 1982–84 significantly reduced the funding available to Third World nations for the acquisition of costly new munitions—thus constricting the worldwide flow of arms. Because these changing demand factors constitute the backdrop against which U.S. export motives operate, it is useful to identify some of the major import motives at work.

As in the case of suppliers, arms buyers tend to be motivated by a cluster of military, political, and economic concerns. Speaking particularly of Third World buyers, these motives include enhanced defense against external rivals and enemies; enhanced internal defense against dissidents and insurgents; the desire to project an image of national pride and unity by acquiring a mighty arsenal (in imitation of the major powers); the desire to enhance the power and authority of the military establishment; enhanced bargaining positions in negotiations over disputed borders, territories, offshore assets, and so forth; endowing the supplier with a vested interest in the survival of the recipient government; and gaining access to modern technology and industrial processes.[37] While any one of these may predominate in a particular transaction, major Third World arms purchases are normally motivated by several of these factors operating jointly.

Assuming that these buyer motives continue to prevail in the 1980s, and that economic conditions do not worsen significantly, the United States will encounter a steady or increased demand for its military products, and thus the ten primal motives identified above will continue to operate. Already, the permissive policies adopted by the Reagan administration have produced a doubling in FMS agreements, and there is every likelihood that such sales will continue to grow in the years ahead. But while Reagan's advisors clearly believe in the efficacy of arms transfers in obtaining the benefits normally ascribed to them, we must not forget that these represent expectations of success, not guarantees. As we examine the development and implementation of U.S. arms policies in the chapters ahead, we must weigh the actual performance of arms sales in achieving their stated objectives, taking note of failures as well as successes. For only an objective assessment of the arms transfer balance sheet will enable us to compose a sane and realistic weapons export policy.

CHAPTER 3

The Evolution of Doctrine

U.S. Arms Export Policy from Kennedy to Reagan

In chapter 2, we identified the underlying political and economic factors which motivate foreign military sales. In a sense, we examined the subconscious "id" of policymaking—the ever-present desires and expectations which induce U.S. firms and agencies to seek foreign outlets for U.S. arms. Although varying in intensity due to changing political-economic conditions, these "primal motives" are always present, no matter who occupies the White House. In this chapter, we shall consider the conscious side of policymaking, examining how these motives are perceived by U.S. policymakers and transformed by them into formal arms sales doctrine. Specifically, we shall chart the evolution of U.S. export policy from the Kennedy period to the Reagan administration.

The Issue Emerges: Arms Sales Policy from Kennedy to Ford

For most of the post–World War II era, arms sales were generally regarded as a relatively minor adjunct of the Military Assistance Program and thus were rarely subjected to any sort of independent policy review. If a foreign country was already eligible for U.S. grant aid, and could come up with the cash with which to buy its arms, it would normally be shifted from the MAP program to the FMS account without any fundamental change in the arms-supply relationship; any orders placed by that country were processed by the relevant U.S. agencies in the same manner as if they were requests for grant assistance—only the bookkeeping was altered. Because the relatively low level of sales (under $500 million per year in the 1950s and early 1960s) had little impact on the U.S. economy, and because Washington's principal concern was to bolster allied defenses against Communist expansion, the regulation of military sales as such was not considered an important government concern. Insofar as Congress and the White House wrangled over arms transfers, they did so in the context of debate over the level and orientation of the MAP program; once agreement was reached on military aid priorities, FMS policies followed automatically.

The first real distinction between sales and aid was made by the Kennedy administration, which sought to compensate for the growing balance-of-payments problems caused by the deployment of large U.S. forces abroad by inducing the wealthier NATO countries to spend more on U.S. arms. Defense Secretary Robert S. McNamara put particular pressure on West Germany, whose economic recovery had greatly increased the value of the Deutschmark (in relation to the dollar), thus multiplyng the costs of maintaining a large U.S. military presence there. In order to facilitate arms purchases by West Germany and other U.S. allies, McNamara established a military sales agency in the Department of Defense, euphemistically named the Office for International Logistics Negotiations (ILN).[1] Under the leadership of Henry J. Kuss, Jr., the ILN staff converted overseas U.S. military missions into marketing agencies for American arms firms and helped push U.S. military sales over the $1 billion mark for the first time.*

Although McNamara's and Kuss's efforts produced a substantial boost in U.S. sales to the industrialized nations (which together accounted for approximately two-thirds of all FMS orders placed before 1970), there was no significant change in U.S. arms export policy toward the nonindustrialized nations. Most Third World countries were far too impoverished to be buying costly new arms on the international market, and U.S. policy continued to emphasize the arming of friendly regimes through the MAP program. Indeed, as we shall learn in chapter 5, U.S. policymakers actually discouraged purchases of high-tech gear by Third World countries, contending that such spending diverted resources from more critical counterinsurgency and economic development programs. As a result, total FMS sales to all Third World countries for the twenty years ending in 1969 amounted to only $2.8 billion, compared to $9 billion for the developed countries.[2]

As the 1970s began, however, two crucial events occurred which irrevocably altered the political-economic context within which U.S. arms policy is shaped. The first was the U.S. defeat in Vietnam, which produced a fundamental shift in the domestic political environment, and the second was the OPEC oil price rise of 1974, which produced a fundamental change in the world economic environment. In response to the first, President Nixon attempted to shift some of America's global defense responsibilities to "surrogate gendarmes" in the Third World, and in response to the second, he

---

*As a reward for his success in boosting U.S. arms exports, Kuss was named a deputy assistant secretary of defense and awarded the Pentagon's highest medal for nonuniformed personnel.

launched a major drive to increase U.S. exports to the oil-producing countries.

Both of these steps generated enormous upward pressure on U.S. military sales to the Third World. Under the Nixon Doctrine, Washington sought to enhance the military capabilities of selected Third World powers through accelerated arms transfers; because, in light of the Vietnam fiasco, Congress was reluctant to increase spending on the MAP program (which was perceived as a possible precursor to direct U.S. military involvement in overseas conflicts), this inevitably led to increased sales. Similarly, in attempting to improve America's trade balance vis-à-vis the oil-producing states of the Middle East, Washington was forced to sell what the Arabs and Iranians wanted most—namely, sophisticated weaponry. Impelled by these pressures, and the other "primal motives" described in chapter 2, Nixon lifted U.S. restraints on sales of high-tech munitions to Third World countries and encouraged U.S. firms to solicit new orders from the oil-producing nations.[3] When Nixon was replaced by Gerald Ford in 1975, these policies were continued under the leadership of Secretary of State Henry Kissinger.

Nixon's decisions, combined with the sudden affluence of the Persian Gulf nations, resulted in a dramatic rise in U.S. military sales to the Third World. Total orders under the FMS program rose from $1.4 billion in fiscal 1971 to $3 billion in fiscal 1972, $5.3 billion in 1973, $10.4 billion in 1974, and a record $15.8 billion in 1975 (see figure 3). Sales to the Persian Gulf countries posted an even more spectacular rise: from $410 million in 1970 to $11.3 billion in 1976, a five-year increase of 2,500 percent. Despite these sharp increases, and the growing trend toward the sale of high-tech weaponry, no fundamental changes were made in the basic structure of the U.S. arms export program. It was for this reason, more than any other, that U.S. lawmakers concluded that the arms program was "out of control" and in need of serious revision.[4]

The first step toward a revised arms sales policy was taken by the legislative branch, which in 1974 adopted the "Nelson Amendment" (after its sponsor, Sen. Gaylord Nelson of Wisconsin) to the Foreign Assistance Act, giving Congress a limited veto over major FMS transactions. This amendment was subsequently incorporated into the Arms Export Control Act of 1976—the first comprehensive piece of legislation to establish formal policy guidelines for the military sales program,* and the measure which continues (in amended

---

*An earlier measure, the Foreign Military Sales Act of 1968, imposed a variety of procedural requirements and outlawed certain types of credit arrangements, but did not establish an overall policy framework for arms transfers.

form) to govern U.S. exports today. Besides the veto measure, the 1976 act contained restrictions on the "retransfer" of U.S.-supplied arms from one recipient to another and established review procedures for licensing and coproduction programs.[5] (These measures, and other key provisions of the Arms Export Control Act, will be reviewed where appropriate in subsequent chapters.)

Following passage of the Arms Export Control Act, the momentum in reforming U.S. export policies shifted to the executive branch. In 1976, while a candidate, Jimmy Carter raised the issue of arms sales for the first time in a presidential campaign. "I am particularly concerned," he told the Foreign Policy Association in New York, "by our nation's role as the world's leading arms salesman." Arguing that "the United States cannot be both the world's leading champion of peace and the world's leading supplier of the weapons of war," Carter promised that, if elected, he would work, "to increase the emphasis on peace and to reduce the commerce in arms."[6] Following the election, Carter again promised to make arms export control a top priority of his administration. In his first White House interview, on January 24, 1977, he told reporters that the National Security Council had already discussed the problem and had reached a consensus on "the necessity for reducing arms sales" and for placing "very tight restraints on future commitments" to U.S. arms producers and their overseas customers.[7]

To convert this consensus into formal government policy, Carter ordered his secretary of state, Cyrus Vance, to develop a set of recommendations for a new arms export policy. After months of internal debate—in which proposals for a truly massive reduction in military sales were ultimately voted down—Vance presented his recommendations to the White House in April.* After a final review by the National Security Council, the proposed guidelines were adopted on May 13, 1977, with the signing of Presidential Directive No. 13 (PD-13). The new policy was then made public on May 19, with the release of a presidential statement on conventional arms transfers.

---

*One White House insider who followed the internal debate on arms sales told *Aviation Week and Space Technology* in April 1977: "Initially, the guidance was all predicated on finding ways to scale back on arms sales overseas. The thesis was that arms sales are all wrong, but now that has changed, and the guidance for preparing the options is fairly balanced. The people in the White House now realize that there are valid reasons for selling arms."

Carter's "Policy of Arms Restraint"

In the introduction to his May 19 statement, President Carter noted that the new policy was based on two fundamental assumptions: first, that the unrestrained spread of conventional weaponry "threatens stability in every region of the world"; and second, that as the world's leading exporter of arms, the United States bears "special responsibilities" to take the lead in restraining its military sales. On this basis, Carter enunciated a new principle to govern U.S. arms export decisionmaking: rather than view military exports as a normal instrument of U.S. policy, "the United States will henceforth view arms transfers as an *exceptional foreign implement*, to be used *only* in instances where it can be clearly demonstrated that the transfer contributes to our national security interests" (emphasis added).[8]

To implement this "policy of arms restraint," as he called it, Carter imposed several specific controls. These constraints were not, however, to be universal in their application: they did not apply to countries with which the United States had "major defense treaties" (specifically, Australia, Japan, New Zealand, and the NATO countries) and would not be allowed to conflict with America's "historic responsibilities to assure the defense of Israel." They did not, moreover, apply to military services (training, technical assistance, construction work), which account for as much as 40 percent of U.S. military sales. Finally, they could be waived by the president in response to "extraordinary circumstances" or when he determined that "countries friendly to the United States must depend on advanced weaponry to offset qualitative and other disadvantages in order to maintain a regional balance." These exceptions having been established, Carter imposed the following controls:

Ceiling. The total dollar value (in constant 1976 dollars) of U.S. arms transfers to nonexempt countries would not exceed the fiscal 1977 level and would be diminished in subsequent years.

Sophistication. The United States would not be the first supplier to introduce into Third World areas "newly developed, advanced weapons systems which could create a new or significantly higher combat capability."

Modification. The development or "significant modification" of advanced combat systems "solely for export" was prohibited.

Coproduction. The United States would not enter into any new coproduction agreements with the nonexempt nations for the production of U.S. weapons systems.

Promotion. U.S. government personnel assigned to embassies and military missions abroad would no longer be permitted to help representatives of U.S. arms firms to market their products to foreign governments. (This prohibition was subsequently contained in the "leprosy letter" of August 31, 1977, sent to all U.S. embassies and military missions abroad.)

Human Rights. In deciding on proposed arms transfers, the United States would attempt to "promote and advance respect for human rights in recipient countries."

Multilateral Negotiations. Because "actual reductions in the worldwide traffic in arms will require multilateral cooperation," the United States would initiate negotiations with other major suppliers—including the Soviet Union—to develop "possible measures for multilateral action." (Carter subsequently initiated a series of Conventional Arms Transfer [CAT] talks with the Soviet Union, which were held between December 1977 and December 1978.)

When first announced in May 1977, these guidelines were the subject of considerable criticism, both from representatives of the arms industry—who thought they were too restrictive—and from arms control and disarmament experts—who thought they were too weak. The manufacturers and their allies in Congress and the military argued that the guidelines unfairly penalized U.S. companies by permitting firms in other major supplying countries (none of which appeared likely to adopt similar restrictions of their own) to pursue sales that would otherwise have gone to American producers. The arms controllers, on the other hand, argued that the guidelines were of dubious value because of all the waivers and exceptions described above.[9]

Even with the waivers, both camps anticipated major changes in the way the executive branch conducted its arms export operations. "Taken together," Under Secretary of State Lucy W. Benson affirmed in 1979, "these controls and the other requirements of the [Carter] policy represented an ambitious program. They responded to an obvious and long-overdue requirement to lay out a comprehensive and coherent policy for an important foreign policy activity that until then had never had one."[10] As the administration began to process actual arms transactions, however, it behaved more or less as its predecessors had—turning down some of the more dubious orders from abroad, but approving most of the requests submitted by America's principal customers. By October 1977, only a few months after the Carter policy was announced, analysts at the Congressional Research Service of the Library of Congress found that there had been no fundamental shift in U.S. export policy. "Rather than being used as an 'exceptional foreign policy implement,'" the CRS team observed, "arms transfers continue to occur on a rather routine basis." Indeed, such sales "continue to play a very substantial role in support of United States foreign policy and national security objectives."[11]

Despite such criticism, President Carter continued to insist upon the efficacy of his policy, contending that the export ceiling— however imperfect—had produced a slowdown in the level of arms sales. "While high," he observed, the level was "considerably less than it would have been in the absence of new restraints we introduced particularly in sales commitments to the developing countries." Consistent with this outlook, in February 1978, he announced a significant reduction in sales to the nonexempt countries: under this plan, such sales would drop from $9.3 billion in fiscal 1977 to $8.6 billion in fiscal 1978, a reduction of 8 percent in constant FY 1976 dollars.[12]

Unfortunately for Carter's credibility, the increase in sales to the exempt countries exceeded the decrease in sales to the nonexempt countries, and thus the overall level of U.S. exports·continued to rise. (Total FMS orders rose from $8.8 billion in fiscal 1977 to $11.7 billion in 1978.) As these figures became known, Carter's export policy was scathingly described as "doublethink" by critics in both parties. The distinction between exempt and nonexempt sales "sounds as if it were drafted by the ghost of George Orwell," Rep. Stephen J. Solarz of New York observed, "because at the same time total sales are going up, we claim they are going down."[13]

Although such comments became more and more widespread, Carter reaffirmed his commitment to arms restraint and in December 1978 announced yet another reduction in sales to the nonexempt countries, from $8.55 billion in fiscal 1978 to $8.43 billion in fiscal 1979 (a reduction of 8 percent when adjusted for inflation). This time, however, Carter left himself room for a retreat in the future, saying that any further reductions would depend "on the degree of cooperation we receive in the coming year from other nations" in restraining their own exports.[14] Indeed, by this point Carter had already begun to alter his stance on the arms issue, approving several controversial sales to the Middle East and loosening restraints on sales to other regions. In February 1978, he authorized the sale of 200 modern combat aircraft to three Middle Eastern countries (60 F-15s to Saudi Arabia, 50 F-5Es to Egypt, and 15 F-15s and 75 F-16s to Israel) in a move that aroused massive congressional opposition, and in August of that year he gave preliminary approval to the Shah of Iran's request for another $12 billion worth of high-tech weaponry. Finally, in December, he terminated the CAT talks with the U.S.S.R. in response to aggressive Soviet moves in Africa and the Middle East.[15]

Although Carter never formally rescinded the guidelines announced on May 19, 1977, his "arms restraint" policy was effectively abandoned in March 1980 when he barred any further reductions in sales to the nonexempt countries. In conveying this decision to Congress, Secretary of State Vance explained that "in the absence of agreed international restraint, we do not plan to reduce further the ceiling on our own arms transfers."[16] In the remaining months of his administration, Carter announced major new sales to Egypt and Israel and began the series of negotiations with Saudi Arabia that eventually led to the AWACS sale of 1981. While the total level of FMS sales actually dropped during this period (because so many of the orders placed by the Shah of Iran in the late 1970s were canceled by his successors), the pendulum had clearly swung away from a pro-restraint position back in the direction of increased exports.

In attempting to account for this turnaround, most analysts pointed to specific foreign policy constraints—the need to "sweeten" the Camp David accords, the need to tighten U.S. ties with Saudi Arabia following the fall of the Shah, the need to resist Soviet adventurism in Africa and the Middle East, and so forth.[17] Some observers also noted that Carter was a victim of his own overblown promises. "The rhetoric promised a revolution in the United States approach to arms transfers," arms expert Leslie Gelb testified in 1980, whereas Carter in fact "continued a large-scale sales program [and thus] it was inevitable . . . that the Administration would be seen as naive or hypocritical, or both."[18] Similar views were expressed by the Senate Foreign Relations Committee. "From the outset the Carter policy was beset with difficulties," a 1980 committee report noted, "in part because the policy had been oversold" by the administration.[19]

In the final analysis, however, it was not any of these specific factors that led to the demise of the Carter policy, but rather his failure to seriously challenge the cluster of political, military, and economic factors that normally drive arms exports. Such an effort would have compelled Carter to disavow all of the economic and security justifications for arms sales and actively to counter the corporate and institutional forces lined up in support of the export program. As suggested by Rep. Gerry Studds in a 1978 review of the Carter effort, "the forces arrayed against any effort by any President to turn around a policy of such force and long standing as U.S. arms sales policy are awesome. . . ." It is hardly surprising that Carter had difficulty in reducing military sales, Studds observed, because he had run up "against entrenched bureaucracies in the Department of State and Defense, and . . . the powers of industry itself, whose voices are present at all times around us, are very loud and very strong."[20] Unable or unwilling to overpower these forces, Carter was never in a position to make a sharp reduction in U.S. arms exports.

But while the Carter effort was too compromised by its own inconsistencies to achieve substantial results, it did establish a precedent for governmental restraint and test the relative effectiveness of various control measures. "The existence of the ceiling," Gelb testified in 1980, "made a real difference in giving the State Department some real authority, for the first time, in the general management of the sales program."[21] Gelb criticized many of the specific features of the Carter policy, but praised the president for undertaking such a difficult and important effort. A similar perspective was adopted by the staff of the Democratic Policy Committee in a 1983 review of the U.S. arms program. Although condemning the "uneven application" of the export restrictions, the report suggested that "the Carter guidelines represented a serious Executive initiative in attempting to restrain sales and bring them into the mainstream of foreign policy."[22]

The Reagan Reaction

With the election of Ronald Reagan, the pendulum completed its swing back toward a policy of relative permissiveness in the sale of arms. As a candidate, Reagan had expressed his opposition to the Carter restrictions; upon taking office, he ordered the State Department to devise an alternative policy. This task was entrusted to James L. Buckley, the under secretary of state for security assistance and a former Conservative party senator from New York state. Even while this process was underway, however, Reagan approved several major transfers that had been held up by the Carter administration. These transactions—notably the $8.5 billion sale of AWACS patrol planes and other high-tech gear to Saudi Arabia—represented a dramatic introduction to the administration's approach toward arms transfers.

Although many components of this approach were fully visible from the very onset of the new administration, the Reagan policy was not formally unveiled until May 21, 1981, when Under Secretary Buckley addressed an Aerospace Industries Association meeting in Williamsburg, Virginia. Flatly rejecting the notion that military sales are "inherently evil or morally reprehensible," Buckley affirmed that "this Administration believes that arms transfers, judiciously applied, can complement and supplement our own defense efforts and serve as a vital and constructive instrument of our foreign policy." Contending that the Carter restrictions had undermined the defenses of nations whose support was vital to America's own security, he argued that Washington must lift those restraints in order to strengthen the common defense. We must, Buckley declared, substitute "a healthy sense of self-preservation" for the "theology" of the Carter period.[23]

This outlook was subsequently incorporated into a new presidential directive signed by the president on July 8, 1981, and released to the public one day later. This directive formally rescinded PD-13 and established new precepts for the conduct of arms transfers.[24] To a large extent, these guidelines restored the export-oriented policies of the Nixon and Ford administrations, when U.S. arms producers were encouraged to increase their sales to friendly Third World governments. But the Reagan policy represented far more than a return to the *status quo ante*: as we shall discover, it introduced several new features that made it easier for U.S. firms to compete with European and Soviet producers in prime Third World markets, especially in those areas where previous policies had discouraged extensive U.S. penetration. Before describing these measures, however, let us examine the Reagan policy itself. (In doing so, reference will be made both to the Reagan directive of July 8, 1981, and to the Buckley speech in Williamsburg.)

Like the Carter statement of May 1977, the Reagan directive rests on two fundamental propositions: first, that the greatest threat to world stability is the growing military assertiveness of the Soviet Union; second, that the United States cannot defend the free world against this threat by itself, but must "be prepared to help its friends and allies strengthen their [defenses] through the transfer of conventional arms." From this perspective, arms sales are seen not as an independent foreign policy concern, but rather as a vital adjunct to America's own military modernization effort. As Buckley explained on May 21, "We are faced not only with the need to rebuild and modernize our own military forces, but to help other nations in the free world rebuild theirs."

Consistent with this outlook, Buckley enunciated a new governing principle: instead of viewing arms transfers as an "exceptional foreign policy implement," as decreed by Carter, they were to be considered as "a vital and constructive instrument" of American foreign policy. The administration would continue to weigh the merits and hazards of pending transactions on a case-by-case basis, but favorable consideration would normally be given to transfers which would help enhance "the state of preparedness of our friends and allies."

Turning now to the seven specific measures originally introduced by President Carter, the Reagan policy substituted the following:

Ceiling. The ceiling on arms exports to nontreaty countries was abolished. Pending arms transactions were to be judged on their own merits, irrespective of their effect on the total dollar values of such exports.

Sophistication. The United States would take care not to overburden the defense capabilities of less-developed nations, but sales of high-technology arms would be governed more by "their net contribution to enhanced deterrence and defense" than by fears of a local arms race.

Modification. In place of the ban on such activities, this administration would actively "encourage" U.S. firms to "produce equipment which, in terms of cost, complexity, and sophistication, is more appropriate to the needs of non-industrialized nations."

Coproduction. No new guidelines were announced, save that the administration would consider such arrangements on a case-by-case basis, taking into account the economic interests of U.S. suppliers and the need to protect "sensitive technology" against dissemination to hostile parties.

Promotion. The "leprosy letter" of August 1977 was rescinded on April 2, 1981, and Reagan mandated U.S. officials overseas "to provide the same courtesies and assistance" to firms selling arms as to other U.S. companies seeking business abroad.

Human Rights. The United States would no longer withhold essential security support from friendly nations solely because of a poor record on human rights. As Reagan explained shortly after his election, "I don't think that you can turn away from some country because here and there they do not agree with our concept of human rights."[25] This outlook was reflected in the administration's efforts to repeal the embargo on arms transfers to Argentina and Chile and to resume military aid to Guatemala.

Multilateral Negotiations. While the United States would retain "a genuine interest in arms transfer restraint," no major effort would be undertaken by the United States to solicit cooperation from the U.S.S.R. or the other major suppliers.

All of these considerations suggest that, at the very least, the

Reagan policy represented a sharp break with the restrictive approach of the Carter administration and a return to the more permissive approach of the Nixon and Ford administrations.[26] But Reagan went beyond this, introducing several initiatives designed further to enhance the utility of arms sales as an instrument of American foreign policy.[27] These initiatives included:

Liberalized Credits. In order to facilitate arms purchases by credit-starved Third World nations, the administration offered FMS credits to several favored regimes on a special basis—a ten-year grace period followed by twenty-year repayment period (instead of the usual one- to three-year grace period and a nine- to twelve-year repayment span). In fiscal 1982, such terms were offered to Egypt, Greece, Somalia, Sudan, and Turkey.

Special Defense Acquisition Fund. Arguing that previous U.S. efforts to assist allies in times of crisis had been hampered by the time-consuming FMS procurement process, the Reagan administration created a Special Defense Acquisition Fund (SDAF) to stockpile arms in anticipation of future requests. The stockpile, financed by monies received from previous FMS sales, consisted of basic combat gear (tanks, antitank missiles, artillery pieces, etc.) commonly used by Third World forces. Congress established a $300 million limit on the SDAF spending in fiscal 1982 and a $600 million limit for fiscal 1983.

Relaxation of Congressional Oversight. In order to facilitate sales to close allies and reduce congressional involvement in the decisionmaking process, the administration introduced a number of amendments to the Arms Export Control Act. In particular, Congress was asked to exempt Australia, Japan, New Zealand, and the NATO countries from prior notification to Congress of pending FMS transactions and to raise the threshold on notification for other countries from $7 million to $14 million for major defense equipment, and from $25 million to $50 million for other hardware and services. These alterations were needed, Gen. Ernest Graves of the Defense Security Assistance Agency testified in 1981, "to reduce the extensive delays [in the processing of arms transfer requests] that have throttled and raised irritating obstacles to defense cooperation."[28]

Spurred by these initiatives and the adoption of a generally permissive approach toward arms transfers, U.S. sales under the Foreign Military Sales program soared to new heights. Total FMS orders rose from $8.2 billion in fiscal 1981 to $20.9 billion in fiscal 1982—a one-year increase of 155 percent. If transfers approved by the administration but not yet formally accepted by the recipients were added, the FY 1982 total would have been $31.2 billion—more than twice the total for any previous year. Accompanying this jump in the volume of U.S. sales, moreover, was a striking increase in the sophistication of the arms sold to Third World buyers: AWACS patrol planes to Saudi Arabia, F-16 combat jets to Pakistan, South Korea, and Venezuela, AH-1 Cobra helicopter gunships to Jordan, E-2C Hawkeye radar planes to Singapore, and so forth. These sales, coming one after another in rapid succession, led critics to charge that the administration had no real export policy other than a generalized impulse to sell. "The Reagan Administration seems willing to sell more highly sophisticated weapons to a wider variety of countries than any previous administration," Sen. Christopher J. Dodd of Connecticut wrote in 1982, suggesting that Reagan's policy of judging arms transfers on a case-by-case basis "really amounts to no policy at all."[29] Former Assistant Secretary of State Hodding Carter III was even more scathing: the Reagan administration, he wrote, "sells advanced weaponry with promiscuous abandon."[30]

But while increased foreign sales obviously have been an important goal of the Reagan arms policy, the administration has clearly been driven more by political than by economic motives. Indeed, an analysis of administration statements suggest that Reagan has viewed arms transfers as a powerful tool in his drive to restore American influence in the Third World and to diminish Soviet influence. "We intend to employ [arms transfers] as an instrument that can and should be used flexibly and carefully to serve our interest," Buckley testified in 1981. "We believe that with effective U.S. Government control and direction, but without the arbitrary prohibitions and annual ceilings of the past, arms transfers can help to enhance the state of readiness of friends and allies, to demonstrate U.S. determination to respond to threats to our interests . . . [and] to revitalize our alliances and cooperative security relationships and develop new ones. . . ."[31] This view of arms transfers as an active instrument of U.S. policy was reaffirmed in the Pentagon's "Defense Guidance" document for fiscal years 1984–88, which reportedly called for a renewed emphasis on military assistance and training abroad.[32] A similar outlook emerged in a 1982 speech on basic U.S. policy objectives by William Clark, then the president's national security advisor. "An effective security assistance program," Clark declared, "is a critical element in meeting our security objectives abroad." For this reason, "we are planning a priority effort to improve the effectiveness [and] the responsiveness of this vital component of our national security strategy."[33]

Translated into practical terms, this approach tends to result in the approval of transfers that may contribute to the military strength of key U.S. allies, but at the possible expense of other U.S. policy objectives. A salient case in point is the administration's 1981 decision to sell 40 F-16 supersonic fighters to Pakistan as part of a $3 billion arms package. According to the Reagan administration, this sale represented an essential U.S. effort to enhance Pakistan's role as a linchpin of Western security in Southwest Asia. Critics charged, however, that it violated provisions of the Foreign Assistance Act barring security assistance to nations engaged in efforts to develop nuclear arms (as U.S. intelligence suggests is true of Pakistan),* and that it would trigger a new and costly arms race in the Indian subcontinent.[34] A similar debate swirled around Reagan's decision to sell a squadron of F-16 fighters to Venezuela. While administration spokespersons argued that the fighters were needed to bolster Venezuelan defenses against possible Cuban military adventurism, critics disputed the existence of a significant Cuban threat (Cuba's MiG-23 attack planes do not have the range to reach Venezuela) and charged that the sale would precipitate a high-tech arms race in South America.[35] The sale of AWACS radar planes to Saudi Arabia produced an even more vigorous and emotional debate about the role of arms transfers in U.S. foreign policy (see chapter 7).

In all of these cases, administration officials argued that the utility of arms transfers in promoting U.S. security objectives outweighs any damage they may cause to other foreign policy interests. Such an approach is wholly consistent with the Cold War outlook that governed U.S. arms exports in an earlier era, but contrasts sharply with the belief shared by many analysts that arms sales as such represent a direct threat to world stability. When, in the 1950s and 1960s, most Third World countries appeared virtually defenseless against Soviet-inspired aggression, arms transfers seemed to offer a reasonable and expedient response to overseas threats; now that many of these countries are equipped with large arsenals of modern weapons (and, in some cases, nuclear devices), such transfers appear to raise many risks of their own. "The vision of nuclear weapons and F-16 fighters in the hands of [Pakistani president] General Zia," Sen. Mark Hatfield of Oregon declared in 1982, "is as fundamentally frightening a prospect as I can imagine in this age."[36] Similar views

---

*A 1982 report by the Central Intelligence Agency, "Special National Intelligence Estimate 31–81," concluded that Pakistan had been secretly stockpiling fissile material that could be used in making a nuclear device. Under section 669 of the Foreign Assistance Act (known as the "Symington Amendment" after its sponsor, Sen. Stuart Symington), such activities disqualify a nation from receiving U.S. military or economic aid funds.

have been expressed by other policymakers, suggesting that high-tech arms sales will continue to spark debate in the years ahead.

Despite growing criticism of his military sales policies, President Reagan in 1983 appeared fully committed to the continued use of arms transfers as a major foreign policy instrument. In the spring, he asked Congress to step up American military aid to U.S. allies in Central America; in the summer, he promised fresh deliveries of high-tech weaponry to Israel and Saudi Arabia. If this pattern persists, U.S. sales will continue to increase in the years ahead, setting new records for the Foreign Military Sales program and the Commercial Sales program.

But while this effort still claimed the support of a majority in Congress, opposition to the administration's arms policies appeared to be on the rise. A 1983 study by the staff of the Democratic Policy Committee blasted the Reagan policy, claiming that it violated congressional judgment that arms transfers be subordinated to other foreign policy objectives, and called for a return to the restraint-oriented approach of the Carter administration.[37] Opposition to the president's arms program for Central America also became more pronounced in late 1983 and early 1984 (see chapter 5). While it is still too early to predict whether these views will prevail, it is possible that rising sales levels and intensified debate could produce a shift in public opinion, leading to fresh legislative action and/or a new presidential mandate.

Should Reagan be returned to a second term of office in 1984, any new directions in U.S. arms transfer policy would presumably originate in the Congress, where opposition to the president's program is most pronounced; should a Democrat be elected, however, policy innovation could shift back to the White House, as it did in 1976 and 1980. A new presidential initiative could entail restitution of some aspects of the Carter policy and/or the introduction of new control measures. But whichever route is adopted, military sales are likely to remain at fairly high levels unless policymakers are prepared to devise a new policy framework for the management of U.S. arms export programs. So long as the existing cluster of "primal motives" continues to govern U.S. military sales, no meaningful shift in American arms transfer behavior is really possible; only by adopting an entirely new policy outlook—of the sort sketched in chapter 11—can U.S. leaders expect to institute fundamental changes in the day-to-day conduct of arms export activities.

CHAPTER 4

The Implementation of Policy

Arms Export Decisionmaking

On February 14, 1978, President Jimmy Carter notified Congress of his intention to sell 200 modern jet fighters to three Middle Eastern countries—15 F-15s and 75 F-16s for Israel, 60 F-15s for Saudi Arabia, and 50 F-5Es for Egypt—evoking thereby a firestorm of controversy. Critics of the $5 billion "jet package" charged that it would ignite a new arms race in the Middle East and sabotage Carter's efforts to negotiate global restraints on conventional arms transfers. Supporters of Israel also charged that sale of the high-performance F-15 to Saudi Arabia would significantly threaten Israeli security. For these reasons alone, Congress came very close to exercising its veto power under the Arms Export Control Act to block the entire transaction. But while many aspects of the package aroused opposition, what most riled U.S. lawmakers was the fact that the jet sale was presented to Congress only after years of negotiations had produced a *de facto* U.S. commitment to the nations involved—a commitment that Congress could veto only at the risk of damaging U.S. relations with those countries. To many legislators, it appeared that their hands were effectively tied from the start. "We wrote into the law a veto so that we would have some say in matters involving billions of dollars of arms sales," Sen. Frank Church complained, but "when we came around to considering a veto, it was too late. We were told that the exercise of the veto power would create a grievous embarrassment, a serious diplomatic crisis, because everything had been settled between the governments concerned by the time it got to [Congress]."[1]

This incident, so typical of the arms transfer experience, provides an excellent introduction to the next stage of our investigation: a look at how broad export policies are converted into specific sales decisions. In the previous chapter, we learned how basic sales motives are translated into formal government policy; here, we shall discover how these policies are taken up by the key agencies involved and applied to the decisionmaking process. What we will be looking at, in other words, is the "how," "who," and "when" of military sales: how fundamental decisions are made on whether to sell a particular item to a particular country; who makes these decisions; and when in the course of negotiations a given proposal is approved, disapproved, or passed on to higher authorities. Understanding this process is essential because, as Senator Church discovered in 1978, key sales decisions are often largely settled before Congress—let alone the public—is even aware that such a sale is being contemplated. If the public is to play a more informed role in arms export decisionmaking, therefore, it is essential that we become familiar with these key agencies and their operating procedures.

Under law, decisions on arms transfers are the exclusive prerogative of the secretary of state, acting on behalf of the president. In practice, however, most decisions are made by lower officials working in a number of mostly unfamiliar agencies in the departments of State, Defense, and Commerce. These agencies, generally known to insiders by their initials—OMC, SAS, ISA, DSAA—constitute the nerve centers of America's arms export establishment. (These are, respectively, the Office of Munitions Control and Office of Security Assistance and Sales in the Department of State, and the Office of the Assistant Secretary of Defense for International Security Affairs and the Defense Security Assistance Agency in the Pentagon.) Working in close conjunction with representatives of the military services and the munitions companies, these agencies collectively manage an export trade that now exceeds $20 billion per year and is likely to reach much higher levels in the years ahead.

Although a great deal has been written about military sales over the past few years, surprisingly little has been said about the core agencies that actually manage the arms trade. References to these organizations, when they appear at all, usually involve a string of initials and technical terms that are mostly unfamiliar to all but the most informed observers of government operations. All too often, moreover, the activities of these agencies are shrouded in secrecy or otherwise hidden from public inspection. Even when they are discussed in the public literature, very little is said about how they conduct their affairs and under what authority. To learn how they operate, therefore, it is necessary to forsake conventional sources and rely on hearings, specialized government reports, and, most of all, interviews with the key personnel involved. On this basis, we arrive at the following portrait of the arms export establishment.

Before turning to this discussion, however, it is useful to consider the legislative "envelope" within which the arms export establishment operates. U.S. law—specifically the Arms Export Control Act (AECA) of 1976—unequivocably invests the U.S. government with control over foreign military sales. "In furtherance of world peace and the security and foreign policy of the United States," the AECA declares, "the President is authorized to control the import and export of defense articles and defense services and to provide guidance to persons of the United States involved in the export or import of such articles and services."[2] In accordance with this stipulation, the president is instructed to establish a list of military articles and services which fall under such control—the U.S. Munitions List— and to promulgate all necessary rules and regulations governing their sale.[3]

The AECA also identifies two distinct channels for international arms transfers: private sales by U.S. corporations through the Commercial Sales (CS) program, and government-to-government sales by U.S. agencies through the Foreign Military Sales (FMS) program. Commercial Sales, now running at the rate of approximately $2 billion per year, generally involve small arms and combat-support equipment (radios, jeeps, transport planes) which fall at the lower end of the technology spectrum; FMS sales, now running at about $15–$20 billion per year, normally encompass major combat systems as well as technical services performed by U.S. military personnel abroad. Because most of the more controversial arms transactions involve FMS sales, we shall concentrate on such exports when describing the decisionmaking process; CS channels are, however, normally used for exports of police and prison gear, and so we shall pay particular attention to this program when discussing the human rights implications of U.S. military exports (see chapter 9).

Normally, Commercial Sales transactions are initiated by private firms and come to the government's notice only when the company involved applies to the Office of Munitions Control (OMC) for a license to export the items in question. In such cases, the OMC serves essentially as a regulatory agency, either approving or disapproving the license application in accordance with the provisions of the AECA. Under the FMS program, however, the government is empowered to initiate arms transactions on its own and to contract with private companies to produce munitions which it then resells to foreign governments. In such cases, the same government agencies often serve both as arms suppliers and as arms regulators—a paradox which, as we shall see, goes a long way toward explaining why it has proven so difficult to restrain the arms trade.

The Arms Export Establishment

Having briefly considered the legislative envelope within which arms transfers are conducted, we can turn to examination of the arms export establishment itself. At its broadest, this enterprise incorporates all those individuals and organizations in the United States that are involved in the production, sale, and delivery of arms, as well as those government agencies responsible for the management and control of such exports in accordance with U.S. law. In practice, however, these actors fall into three basic categories: private arms suppliers; governmental arms exporters; and governmental arms regulators. Let us look at each category in turn.

Private Arms Suppliers. U.S. arms corporations, of which there are about 1,500, can export their products through two channels: directly to foreign governments and dealers through the CS program and indirectly through the FMS program (in which case the government buys from private industry and then resells to foreign governments). In most cases, the choice is predetermined by law or circumstance: generally, transfers of major military systems originally developed for the U.S. Armed Forces are processed as FMS cases, while transfers of commercially developed weapons and support systems are processed as CS transactions.[4] Furthermore, many Third World buyers prefer to work through U.S. government channels rather than to buy directly from American corporations.

In practice, the FMS/CS distinction tends to divide U.S. arms producers into two categories: the large defense contractors that undertake FMS projects in the course of their ongoing work for the Department of Defense, and the many thousands of smaller firms that may receive some FMS orders but rely mainly on CS channels for their export sales. As shown by table 1, the top fifteen FMS contractors also tend to rank high on the list of the Pentagon's own top contractors. These producers—mostly large industrial firms with a major commitment to military work—regularly garner a substantial portion of FMS awards. In 1980, for instance, the top 25 FMS contractors together received an astounding 78 percent of all contracts awarded through the FMS program. (Also listed prominently are a number of foreign construction firms working on military projects in Saudi Arabia under contract to the U.S. Army Corp of Engineers.) And while the ranking of these companies may vary from year to year, the same big firms—Lockheed, McDonnell-Douglas, Northrop, and General Electric—consistently tend to appear near the top of the list.[5]

In contrast to the FMS program, CS exports tend to be spread among a much wider field of small and medium-sized firms. Total CS revenues have amounted to only $1.5–$2.0 billion in recent years (compared to $15–$20 billion for FMS orders), and this amount is divided up among a much larger number of suppliers. According to the

Table 1. The Top Ten FMS *Contractors, Fiscal 1979–80*
(million current dollars)

1980 Rank	Company	Fiscal year	FMS contracts	% all FMS contracts	DOD contracts
1	General Dynamics	1980	$993.0	12.7	$3,518.0
		1979	518.0	9.7	3,492.1
2	Northrop	1980	$859.4	10.5	$1,227.4
		1979	472.3	8.9	800.3
3	United Technologies	1980	$749.0	9.2	$3,108.9
		1979	249.1	4.7	2,553.6
4	McDonnell-Douglas	1980	$471.3	5.8	$3,246.6
		1979	638.9	12.0	3,229.2
5	Raytheon	1980	$453.5	5.3	$1,745.1
		1979	132.1	2.5	1,249.4
6	Sam Whan Corp.[a]	1980	$266.3	3.3	$ 266.3
		1979	c		c
7	FMC Corp.	1980	$232.9	2.7	$ 834.6
		1979	65.3	1.2	352.1
8	Hanil Development Co. & Al Mabani J.V.[b]	1980	$217.6	2.7	$ 217.6
		1979	c		c
9	Harsco Corp.	1980	$205.4	2.5	$ 280.3
		1979	70.5	1.3	218.6
10	Chrysler Corp.	1980	$197.1	2.4	$ 970.9
		1979	33.9	0.6	808.9

SOURCE: U.S. Department of Defense.
[a] A South Korean company engaged in military construction work in Saudi Arabia under contract to the U.S. Army Corps of Engineers.
[b] A joint venture of South Korean and Saudi firms engaged in military construction work in Saudi Arabia under contract to the U.S. Army Corps of Engineers.
[c] Not among top 25 FMS contractors in 1980.

Office of Munitions Control, some 1,600 U.S. companies and individuals were registered with the State Department in 1983 as exporters of arms. These enterprises included industrial firms which sold "off-the-shelf" support equipment (radios, cameras, automotive parts, etc.) to foreign military buyers as well as producers of small arms and police-type weapons (shotguns, revolvers, tear gas, etc.). Among these companies are some of America's leading gun producers—firms like Colt, Winchester, and Remington—which once dominated the export trade but are now largely overshadowed by the giant aerospace conglomerates.

Governmental Arms Exporters. Under the AECA (and predecessor legislation), the U.S. government is empowered to export arms from existing Pentagon stockpiles or to contract with private firms to produce arms for export through the FMS program. As stated in section 22, "the President may . . . enter into contracts for the procurement of defense articles or defense services for sale . . . to any foreign country or international organization" deemed eligible for such purchases. In such cases—which today represent some 90 percent of all U.S. military exports—the government operates as an international sales agency by buying up the products of domestic manufacturers and then reselling them to foreign buyers. When acting in this capacity, the United States government is, in fact, the world's leading arms exporter, accounting for approximately 34 percent of all military equipment and services sold on the international market.

To do justice to history, Washington did not set out to be the world's leading arms merchant. As we have seen, the FMS program originated as an adjunct of the Military Assistance Program, which was established in the early Cold War period to provide needy allies—many still devastated by World War II—with the wherewithal to defend themselves against potential Communist aggression. Between 1950 and 1973, the United States delivered some $62 billion worth of arms and equipment to friendly governments abroad, with the bulk of this hardware—$48.6 billion worth—furnished through the MAP program. In the aftermath of Vietnam, however, Congress voted to phase out the MAP program and to place most U.S. military exports on a pay-as-you-go basis.[6]

Although the shift from MAP to FMS has required many changes in the government's accounting and billing systems, the basic arrangement has remained the same: after agreeing to provide a particular government with certain items of equipment, Washington either appropriates the items from existing Pentagon stocks or contracts with private industry to produce the specified hardware. The big difference, of course, is that under FMS the recipient ultimately reimburses the U.S. Treasury for the costs incurred, whereas under MAP the tab is picked up by the U.S. taxpayer.* From a managerial

---

*Naturally, not all countries are wealthy enough to pay cash for imported weapons. To ensure that even the poorest Third World governments can buy advanced U.S. arms, the Department of Defense provides credits to foreign buyers through the FMS Credit Program. Since these funds are drawn from the U.S. Treasury, they do constitute a form of taxpayer-provided assistance, although the Treasury is ultimately reimbursed for these outlays. The GAO has found, however, that foreign buyers are not always fully invoiced for all FMS overhead costs, so taxpayers do sometimes subsidize what is meant to be a subsidy-free program.

point of view, however, MAP and FMS have much in common, and an umbrella term—Security Assistance—has been devised by Washington to cover both programs.[7]

Having described the government's export role in general terms, we can turn to a discussion of the particular agencies involved in the management of military sales. Under section 2 of the AECA, the secretary of state is mandated to assume full responsibility for the management of U.S. arms exports. But because FMS orders are normally processed by the U.S. Armed Services in the same manner in which they process their own procurement, the secretary of state has authorized the Department of Defense (DoD) to assume day-to-day management of the FMS program.

Within the Department of Defense, responsibility for management of FMS transactions has been delegated to the Defense Security Assistance Agency (DSAA). Established in 1971 by Secretary of Defense Melvin Laird, the DSAA is authorized to "direct, administer, and supervise the execution of Security Assistance programs." Under supervision of the assistant secretary of defense for international security affairs, the DSAA is empowered to "Conduct international logistics and sales negotiations with foreign countries"; "Serve as the DoD focal point for liaison with U.S. industry with respect to Security Assistance activities"; and "Direct and supervise the organization, functions, and staffing of DoD elements in foreign countries responsible for managing the Security Assistance program."[8] To perform these functions, the DSAA has a staff of about 100 military and civilian specialists headed by a director—usually a two- or three-star general—and a civilian chief of operations. In 1983, the director was Lt. Gen. Philip C. Gast, a former combat pilot who served as chief of the U.S. Military Assistance Advisory Group in Iran and as vice-commander of the Tactical Air Command before moving to DSAA. The chief of operations, Glenn Rudd, has long worked for DSAA as a civilian specialist. Together with their staff, these two men—largely unknown to the U.S. public—supervise the export of far more arms than Basil Zaharoff, the original "merchant of death," ever dreamed possible.

Backing up the DSAA in Washington are Military Assistance Advisory Groups (MAAGs) and military missions in some fifty foreign countries, plus a wide assortment of logistical and supply commands at bases in the United States and abroad. Each of the three military services, moreover, has its own version of DSAA to process FMS transactions.[9] This is because each service normally assumes management responsibility for any item originally developed for its use. All told, some 20,000 U.S. military personnel are believed to work on FMS projects on a full- or part-time basis.[10]

Government Arms Regulators. So far, we have dealt with those agencies which assume the government's role as arms exporter; now we shall look at the agencies which assume the role of arms regulator. By selectively opening or closing the sluice gates of the FMS pipeline, these agencies effectively control the volume, direction, velocity, and composition of U.S. arms exports.

Under law, the locus of this regulatory function is unambiguously centered in the Department of State. As stated by section 2 of the AECA, "the Secretary of State . . . shall be responsible for the continuous supervision and general direction of [military] sales and exports . . . to the end that . . . the foreign policy of the United States is best served thereby." In practice, however, this function is shared among many departments and agencies, including the Defense Department, the Treasury Department, the Central Intelligence Agency, and the National Security Council. Later in this chapter we shall learn how these agencies collaborate in the decisionmaking process, but here we shall simply identify some of the key actors involved.

Within the State Department, primary responsibility for the supervision of arms transfer programs is vested in the Bureau of Politico-Military Affairs (PM). In essence, PM serves as the secretary of state's full-time support staff on all issues relating to military aid, security assistance, and international defense cooperation. Theoretically, the bureau serves as the "point of entry" for all foreign requests for U.S. arms, and normally such requests receive their initial evaluation here before being passed on to other agencies for examination and review. Within PM, Commercial Sales transactions are supervised by the Office of Munitions Control, while MAP and FMS cases are the responsibility of the Office of Security Assistance and Sales. PM, in turn, reports to the under secretary of state for security assistance and the under secretary for political affairs, who jointly share authority for oversight of arms export programs.[11] (Normally the former supervises the noncontroversial cases, while the latter takes responsibility for the more complex cases.)

Within the Department of Defense, arms export decisionmaking is the responsibility of the Office of the Assistant Secretary of Defense for International Security Affairs (OASD/ISA). Often described as "the Pentagon's state department," the ISA staff is responsible for setting Defense Department policy on such issues as security assistance, international defense cooperation, arms control, and foreign policy generally. Like the State Department, it is organized into re-

gional and country desks, and—through the worldwide system of
MAAGs and military missions—maintains delegations in most foreign capitals. Normally, much of the background work on pending
sales negotiations is conducted by the MAAGs and the DSAA before
being passed up to ISA and, in the most sensitive cases, to the secretary of defense.[12] It follows from all this that DSAA and ISA jointly
serve as both arms suppliers and arms regulators, leading to a blur-
ring of identities that tends to favor the former role at the expense of
the latter. As suggested by the GAO in its 1979 study of the decisionmaking process, "From the moment of first interest" by a foreign
government "through the step-by-step process of informal discussions, briefings, surveys, studies, official visits, test-rides, or firing
. . . the process is geared toward seriously responding to a buyer's
perceived needs."[13]

Working closely together, these bodies of the departments of
State and Defense perform most of the initial decisionmaking on
proposed arms transfers. In some cases, however, other U.S. agencies
enter the picture. The Arms Control and Disarmament Agency is
empowered (under section 42 of the AECA) to review pending arms
transfers and to advise the secretary of state as to any adverse arms
control implications. (This occurred fairly regularly during the Carter administration, but has become less frequent under President
Reagan.) The Treasury Department will occasionally become involved if very large sums of money are involved and arrangements
must be made for the financing of FMS projects. Finally, the Central
Intelligence Agency might become involved if there are questions
regarding the stability or intentions of the purchasing government,
or if other security issues arise.[14]

While most FMS decisions are made at the staff level by PM and
DSAA, or by the secretary (or under secretary) of state in consultation
with the secretary (or under secretary) of defense, some cases provoke so much disagreement that they are referred to the National
Security Council (NSC) for further deliberation. Composed of representatives of the Department of State, the Department of Defense,
and the CIA, plus a staff of analysts headed by the assistant to the
president for national security affairs, the NSC is the nation's highest
advisory body covering foreign and military affairs.

Arms Sales Decisionmaking: Before the Beginning

Having identified the principal actors in the decisionmaking
process, we can turn to a discussion of that process itself. Inevitably,
this discussion must be somewhat selective, since no two trans-

actions are exactly alike, and most controversial orders follow long, convoluted, and sometimes unpredictable paths before reaching a final conclusion. Different types of transfers—weaponry vs. support equipment, complete systems vs. spare parts, FMS vs. Commercial Sales—also follow different trajectories within the decisionmaking system.[15] But it is possible at least to identify the various stages in this process and to describe the basic operational approach which governs U.S. decisionmaking on military sales transactions.

First, a note of caution: the U.S. government regularly processes tens of thousands of separate arms transactions each year, most of which are automatically approved or disapproved in accordance with established policy. It is only the rare case that precipitates a full-scale review—usually because it involves the transfer of high-tech gear to a Third World country, because the purchasing government has been cited for human rights violations, or because it is simply too big to be treated any other way.[16] Rather than getting bogged down in discussion of the routine orders, we shall concentrate here on those orders which—like the 1978 Mideast jet package—raise fundamental questions of foreign policy.

What, then, are the steps followed by a proposed transfer as it works its way through the decisionmaking process? Theoretically, that process starts only after the U.S. government receives an official request from a foreign government for a specified set of equipment. As noted by former DSAA director Gen. Howard M. Fish, the arms export process begins "when a country has decided that it is interested in procuring a particular defense article or service [and] makes an appropriate request through diplomatic channels to the Department of State, or through military channels to the Department of Defense and then to State."[17] In reality, however, the process often begins long before the government is formally notified by a buyer that it seeks a particular system. Historical studies of actual arms negotiations indicate that most major transactions have an elaborate "prehistory" involving informal discussions between U.S. and foreign military officials, as well as promotional activities conducted by U.S. arms firms. In some cases, moreover, these promotional activities have included outright bribery of foreign government leaders.

The use of bribery and other promotional activities to generate military sales abroad is a natural consequence of the distorted nature of the FMS program. As noted earlier, FMS production contracts are awarded to U.S. arms firms after the government has agreed to provide a certain item to a foreign buyer. "Under FMS," former DSAA Chief of Operations Leonard Alne once explained, "the buyer . . . is engaging the U.S. Government to buy an item on his behalf—and to do so with the same care and prudence that [the U.S. government] buys for itself." The problem with this formula is that the interests of the U.S. government do not always coincide completely with those of particular U.S. arms firms: whereas Washington normally can select any one of a number of competing systems to perform a particular mission, each individual firm naturally seeks to obtain that contract for itself rather than see it go to a competitor. As Alne put it, "the U.S. defense firm is trying to make a buck. *It is trying to make a buck for itself*—not for its colleague firms in the business" (emphasis added).[18] In order, then, to ensure that a pending FMS order is ultimately awarded to itself, and not to a competitor making the same or similar products, many U.S. firms engage in a wide range of overseas promotional activities designed to persuade potential customers to ask for its products by "brand name" when approaching the U.S. government to supply a particular system. These activities entail advertising and other marketing techniques used by all major corporations to promote sales of their products abroad, but, in the "boom" days of 1972–75, also included extensive use of bribery and other illicit practices.

The widespread use of bribery first came to light in 1974, when the Watergate prosecutors discovered that several American corporations, including Northrop, had made secret contributions to Richard Nixon's 1972 reelection campaign. In probing these payoffs, the prosecutors also found that Northrop had made other suspicious payments from a secret political slush fund, including payments to foreign government officials. The Watergate disclosures subsequently led to investigations of Northrop and other U.S. corporations by the Securities and Exchange Commission (SEC) and the Subcommittee on Multinational Corporations of the Senate Foreign Relations Committee. Although the companies involved at first balked at opening their books to government investigators, they eventually agreed to cooperate under threat of legal action—with dramatic results. On June 15, 1975, the Senate Subcommittee released documents showing that Northrop had spent at least $30 million on bribes and commissions between 1971 and 1975 to secure foreign orders for its military products.[19]

Nor was Northrop alone in employing such tactics. After completing its probe of that company, the Senate Subcommittee focused its attention on Lockheed, which ultimately admitted to making over $200 million in questionable payments abroad, of which some $38 million went for bribes and kickbacks. Among the alleged recipients of this largesse were top government officials in Indonesia, Italy, Japan, Saudi Arabia, Turkey, and West Germany.[20] Other U.S. companies, including Grumman, Raytheon, and McDonnell-Douglas, also admitted making bribes and payoffs to potential customers. Ultimately, the Department of Defense estimated that as much as $200 million was spent by U.S. firms to solicit arms orders abroad between 1973 and 1975.[21]

Following the Senate subcommittee hearings, various laws and regulations were adopted to curb such practices. Section 39 of the AECA empowers the secretary of state to establish controls on the payments of fees and commissions to foreign agents in connection with military sales and prohibits the government from awarding any FMS funds for such purposes when it is found that a particular sale was secured through "improper influence." (In defining "improper influence," Congress studiously avoided the word "bribery" but rather spoke of "influence, direct or indirect, which induces or attempts to induce considerations or action by any employee or officer of a purchasing foreign government or international organization with respect to such purchase on any basis other than such considerations of merit as are involved in comparable United States procurements.") Regulations were subsequently issued by both the Department of State and Department of Defense requiring arms producers to report any large political contributions or commissions proffered in the course of arms negotiations and establishing penalties for the failure to supply such information. Government officials insist that these measures have successfully checked most abuses, but common sense suggests that such practices may reappear as public scrutiny diminishes.[22]

Even if government action is completely successful in eliminating corporate payoffs, U.S. munitions firms can still employ other means of promoting their products to foreign buyers. Each year, America's major military associations (Association of the United States Army, Air Force Association, Navy League, etc.) hold trade shows in which the major producers display their latest products to potential customers.[23] These trade shows, or "arms bazaars" as they have come to be known (after Anthony Sampson's book *The Arms Bazaar*), resemble other trade exhibitions with their elaborate audiovisual displays and scantily clad hostesses, but in this case there is nothing playful about the products on display. One student journalist who attended the Association of the United States Army's 1978 display in Washington reported:

There were helicopters and tanks with awesome firepower, missile launchers, drone missiles, and even a cruise missile pointing ominously through the milling crowd. In most exhibits, slides and test films of the weapon and its destructive potential played continuously. There were battle helmets, collapsible shelters, chain guns, antiaircraft guns, automatic handguns with shoulder extensions, guns mounted on the walls and guns mounted on the floor. Not one sign in sight said "Do not touch."[24]

Federal regulations prohibit U.S. companies from making actual sales at such events, but there is no way to prevent company personnel from making an informal agreement with prospective buyers over drinks in the nearest cocktail lounge or in the "hospitality suites" maintained by all the major suppliers in adjacent hotels.

American producers also try to drum up business by taking new products on around-the-world demonstration tours and by bringing potential customers to their factories in the United States for on-the-scene inspections of new products. U.S. firms are often aided in this process by the military services and the Department of Defense, which may perceive a vested interest in foreign sales of a particular item. Because substantial foreign orders can reduce the unit cost paid by the services for their own procurement of a given product, they often try to facilitate sales of that item. (As noted in chapter 3, these activities were significantly curtailed by President Carter's "arms restraint" policy, but later given White House approval by the Reagan administration.) Such assistance can include high-level briefings for foreign military personnel, test flights or firings of the item in question, or (in conjunction with the producers) display of the item at the Paris Air Show or other international fetes of that sort.[25]

All of these activities—legal and otherwise—occur before the formal initiation of the FMS decisionmaking process. Because they automatically generate vested interests on the part of U.S. producers and agencies in the ultimate sale of the item involved, and because they often leave a potential buyer with the impression that the United States is prepared to offer it for export, they tend to create a momentum behind a particular sale that is very hard to reverse once the formal decisionmaking process begins. As noted by the GAO:

> The incremental nature of the process also tends to continuously reinforce expectations that requests will be approved. Various verbal and written pronouncements to the effect that such actions do not constitute a U.S. commitment to sell appear to be lost . . . in the momentum that builds with each successive step taken on a major case. *It is the actions*

and judgments which normally precede consideration of the formal request which strongly influence the outcome of the formal decision.[26]

It often happens, therefore, that the final yes-or-no decision on a particular transfer will already have been made by the time a formal request is submitted to the Department of State. This is especially common when the appropriate agencies in the departments of State and Defense reach an early consensus on the preferred outcome. It is only when a given case produces substantial disagreement between State and Defense, or when fundamental policy issues are at stake, that the decisionmaking process will be carried forward to its fullest extent.[27]

Arms Sales Decisionmaking: The Plea-Bargaining Process

Officially, the decisionmaking process begins in earnest when a foreign government decides that it wants to buy a particular item, and, in General Fish's words, "makes an appropriate request through diplomatic channels to the Department of Defense and then to State." Such a request can be delivered by a country's ambassador or military attaché directly to the State Department, or by any high-ranking official to the U.S. ambassador or MAAG chief in that country. Whichever channel is used, all such requests theoretically go first to the Office of Security Assistance and Sales in the State Department's Bureau of Politico-Military Affairs. Then, according to Fish, "the State Department determines, after consultation with the Department of Defense, whether the proposed purchase is consistent with U.S. objectives and policy, and whether it will serve our national interest."[28]

To launch this evaluation process, which normally proceeds on a case-by-case basis, SAS serves as a "traffic manager," dividing up the requests into the relevant categories (FMS vs. Commercial Sales, weapons vs. services, cash vs. credit sales, etc.) and dispatching them to the appropriate governmental agencies for review.

Most transactions, as we have noted, are processed by staff officers in SAS and DSAA with minimal review by higher authorities. Although the State Department theoretically retains ultimate control over all military export transactions, the secretary of state has authorized the Defense Department to assume full responsibility for military sales to the NATO powers (except Greece, Iceland, Portugal, and Turkey) as well as to Australia, Japan, and New Zealand. The Pentagon is also empowered to process all sales of noncombat gear (i.e., radios, jeeps, trucks, uniforms, etc.) and spare parts to a much bigger list of friendly countries, including Indonesia, Israel, Jordan, and the Philippines. In such cases, known as "Category-A" transactions, approval is almost automatic unless the transaction involves very large sums of money or raises some fundamental foreign policy issue. What remains, after these cases have been separated out, are sales of "major defense equipment" to the non-NATO countries plus sales of all items to countries with serious human rights problems or where U.S. sales of any sort raise fundamental foreign policy issues (among which are Argentina, Egypt, Haiti, Pakistan, and Uruguay). Such transactions, known as "Category-B" exports, normally receive a full State Department review no matter how small or large the order.[29] (The discussion which follows deals largely with Category-B transactions.)

Now begins what can be termed the "plea-bargaining process": SAS farms out the purchase request to all interested parties—DSAA, ACDA, the country and regional desks within State and ISA, the Treasury and Commerce departments, the CIA, and the NSC—and asks for their opinion on the proposed sale. If all answers come back either yes or no, the transaction is usually processed accordingly, without further review. When, however, there is a divergence of opinion, the various agencies involved often form rival camps and begin to plead their case to higher authorities. In such cases, the entire decisionmaking apparatus is mobilized and a full-scale review commences.

In lining up support for their respective positions, all parties involved in FMS transactions are expected to share a common vision of the "national interest." In calculating this interest, General Fish explained, the officials involved are expected to consider such factors as "the requirements of the requesting country, the possible use to which the equipment would be put, the threat facing the requesting country, the availability of such items from existing U.S. stocks, and our total force policy."[30] The problem with this approach is that U.S. leaders have never agreed on the weight that should be attached to each factor, nor, indeed, on how to determine how any particular sale will perform on these accounts. Since each transaction is treated separately on a case-by-case basis, the officials involved are forced to evaluate each of these factors anew whenever they are presented with a controversial case. What usually happens, as a result, is that each agency tends to advance the position most consistent with its functional identity within the bureaucratic structure. Thus, ACDA argues for restraint, the Defense Department emphasizes common security objectives, the country desks stress bilateral ties, and so forth. Many participants in the process, the GAO noted in 1979, "tend to take predictable positions on requests." Thus, "embassy and regional bureau officials . . . tend to support a country's request," while the ACDA "is seen by some as objecting to every request it sees."[31]

To illustrate this phenomenon, let us try to reconstruct the arguments that were advanced by the various participants in the 1978 decision to sell the F-15s to Saudi Arabia. This obviously represented a major policy decision, and thus the proposal and supporting arguments would have been circulated to all of the appropriate agencies for review and comment. These agencies would probably have lined up approximately along the following lines:

- The Saudi desk in the State Department would argue that any failure to approve the sale would produce a breach in U.S.-Saudi relations and thus undermine U.S. interests in the Middle East.
- The Israel desk would contend that the F-15s could be used for strikes on Israeli territory and thus the sale was inconsistent with the U.S. commitment to safeguard Israel's security.
- ISA might suggest that the F-15 sale was consistent with U.S. efforts to turn Saudi Arabia into an effective counterweight to radical Arab regimes in the area.
- The ACDA would argue that the introduction of the F-15s into the Arabian Peninsula would trigger a new round in the Mideast arms race and thus jeopardize U.S. security interests.
- The U.S. Air Force, which has operational jurisdiction over the F-15 within Defense, might suggest that the Saudi sale would reduce the aircraft's unit cost and thus provide budgetary savings.
- The CIA might contend that the F-15 incorporates classified technologies which could be compromised if any of the aircraft were lost over unfriendly territory.
- Commerce, and the Economic Bureau within State, would argue that cash sales to Saudi Arabia help compensate for growing U.S. outlays for imported Mideast oil.

These views would be collected by SAS and summarized in a position paper for the secretary of state. At this point, the plea-bargaining process would begin in earnest. Each agency would attempt to mobilize the widest possible support for its position and to acquire allies in other agencies. "Decisions on major requests are made through the process of building a consensus," the GAO found. Such a consensus "is sought within organizational units, within agencies, and between departments."[32] If, as a result of this process, a particular viewpoint comes to prevail throughout the bureaucracy, the remaining opponents of that position then concede the issue—

or, in true plea-bargaining fashion, propose a compromise that retains at least some of its position. Such a compromise could involve supplying a less-advanced version of the system requested by the buyer, supplying a smaller quantity of the item, or delaying sale of the item for a particular length of time. Once a final consensus is reached on the original position or on some sort of a compromise, the secretary of state steps in and gives official blessing to the prevailing view.[33]

On those few occasions when the plea-bargaining process fails to produce a satisfactory solution at the under secretary level, the secretary of state may choose to refer the case to the National Security Council for further review. The NSC is, in a sense, the final court of appeal in FMS cases, and each agency normally sends its most persuasive advocates to plead its case. Council members sift through the arguments presented and attempt to identify the outcome which best meshes competing U.S. interests. Such a determination could be a yes-or-no decision or a range of options allowing varying degrees of compromise between the more extreme positions. The NSC then forwards its recommendations to the president, who, in consultation with the assistant for national security affairs, makes the final decision.[34]

Because the plea-bargaining process permits all sides to obtain a fair hearing for their position, this approach theoretically results in the eventual triumph of the "best" solution—that is, the outcome which best serves the national interest. This assumes, however, that large government bureaucracies will accede to the wiser choice even when their own parochial interests are ill-served thereby. In reality, of course, governments do not always work that way, and what usually happens is that the side which musters the greatest array of bureaucratic "muscle" behind a position (as perceived by the participants involved) usually determines the outcome of the debate. In its 1979 report on arms sales decisionmaking, the GAO cited several cases in which persistence by one set of actors led to a favorable outcome for its position—despite the fact that the proposed sale clearly violated President Carter's "arms restraint" guidelines. In one case cited in the report, the U.S. Embassy in a particular country succeeded in mobilizing extensive support in Washington for the sale of a system sought by the host government despite the fact that the State Department itself was opposed; in other cases, the Defense Department succeeded in overriding State Department objections to sale of sophisticated arms to Third World buyers.[35]

Given the importance of sheer bureaucratic weight in the decisionmaking process, it is hardly surprising that the Defense Department often emerges as the winner in intramural contests with the Department of State and the ACDA. The Defense Department not only commands far greater resources in terms of numbers—that is, both of people and of dollars—but also tends to be united in its views on a particular transaction. The State Department, on the other hand, has a much smaller staff with which to lobby for its position and often finds itself weakened by internal divisions over given sales. (It is not unusual, for instance, for the country desk and regional bureau involved to approve of a proposed sale, while the Human Rights Bureau and the ACDA oppose it.) And because Defense can generate considerable momentum behind a particular sale by bringing foreign buyers to the United States for briefings and test-firings—thereby creating expectations on the part of the buyers that cannot easily be frustrated at a later date—the State Department often finds itself compelled to go along with a sale it might otherwise oppose. As noted by the GAO,

> The Defense Department, by virtue of its orientation, mission, expertise, relationships with foreign military, and delegated responsibilities, remains the most active and involved Government entity in foreign military sales. Defense is involved in detailed force planning; in considerations of pricing, availability, releasability, and absorbability [of military gear]; and training, delivery, payment, and continued support of arms sales. Defense thus has tremendous influence on ultimate arms transfer decisions.[36]

It is not surprising, therefore, that advocates of restraint within the Carter State Department experienced so much frustration in attempting to implement the president's policy. During the Reagan period, moreover, the Defense Department appears to have acquired even greater authority over arms sales decisionmaking.[37]

Arms Sales Decisionmaking: The Final Act

Once the secretary of state (or the president) has given formal approval to a particular transaction, the DSAA prepares a Letter of Offer (DoD Form 1513) specifying the item(s) to be sold, the buyer, the estimated cost, delivery dates, and so forth. Once this form is completed—and only then—Congress enters the decisionmaking process. Under section 36(b) of the Arms Export Control Act, all applicable Letters of Offer for major combat systems worth $14 million or more or for complete arms packages worth $50 million or more must be submitted to Congress for examination and review. (Pending sales to the NATO countries and to Australia, Japan, and New Zealand are exempted from this reporting requirement.) Such proposals are then listed with supporting data in *The Congressional Record* (unless, as is often the case, such data are omitted for security reasons), and thus, for the first and only time, the public is informed of pending arms transfers. (Letters of Offer for combat systems worth less than $14 million, or of other hardware under $50 million, are not reported to Congress or the public until after the transaction has been consummated.)

Once Congress has been formally notified of a pending transaction, the House and Senate have thirty days within which to debate the proposal. If, after thirty days, Congress adopts a concurrent resolution opposing the sale (i.e., a resolution adopted by a majority of both Houses), the transaction is nullified and the State Department must negotiate a new agreement with the purchasing government. (As of early 1984, there had been no case of a successful veto of a proposed arms transfer, although Congress had on occasion used the threat of a veto to force the executive to cancel a sale or to resubmit it in scaled-down form.)[38] If, on the other hand, Congress fails to take up the matter or a resolution of opposition fails to win a majority in both Houses, the sale is considered valid and the Pentagon is authorized to submit the Letter of Offer to the buyer. If the buyer then signs the Letter, signifying acceptance of the terms contained therein, it becomes a Letter of Offer and Acceptance (LOA), and takes on the force of a contract between the two nations.

Because any major congressional endeavor requires an immense effort on the part of the initiating senator or congressperson, most FMS transactions are greeted with little or no legislative branch response. On those relatively few occasions on which Congress does debate a pending sale, the plea-bargaining process commences anew. Officials of various government agencies are called before the appropriate committees (usually the Senate Foreign Relations Committee and the House Foreign Affairs Committee) to present the views of their department. At the same time, other interests are likely to emerge: lawmakers from the district in which the item is produced are apt to stress the economic and employment benefits of foreign sales, while representatives of districts with a particular ethnic concentration are likely to argue one way or the other depending on the preferences of their constituents (representatives of districts with a large Greek-American population are likely to oppose sales to Turkey, while those from districts with a large Jewish constituency are likely to oppose sales to Egypt and Saudi Arabia). In some cases, leaders of trade and civic organizations are invited to testify—thus giving the public its sole opportunity to comment on pending arms sales.[39]

Although U.S. lawmakers have occasionally objected to particular arms sales with considerable vigor—the 1978 Mideast jet package and the 1981 AWACS sale to Saudi Arabia are notable examples—the present decisionmaking process does not allow for extensive congressional involvement. Not only are such transactions submitted to Congress only when the key agencies involved have already aligned behind a particular solution (so that all government witnesses sent to testify on the sales endorse the official position), but also, as we have seen, proposed transfers are only presented to Congress after years of negotiation have produced a *de facto* commitment to the buyer involved—a commitment that Congress can reverse only at some cost to U.S. relations with the country involved. To complicate matters further, Congress is rarely united in its position on foreign policy issues, with many lawmakers predisposed by party loyalty or constitutional interpretation to accept the president's leadership in such matters. As noted by Richard Grimmett of the CRS in a 1982 report on executive-legislative consultation on arms sales,

> The President's ability to use the powers and prestige of his office to define or redefine the terms or emphasis of the public debate on a major arms sale makes it difficult for Congress to overrule his decision. The President can overcome serious criticism of a sales proposal by arguing that the national security and important bilateral relations with a client state may be notably damaged if a specific sale is vetoed. This basic power of the Presidency to influence the outcome of a sale case is further enhanced by the institutional difficulty Congress has in achieving consensus on the proper course to take when confronted with a controversial sale.[40]

Although Congress has adopted various amendments to the AECA requiring executive branch consultation with the legislative on pending sales,* Grimmett found that these measures have not fundamentally diminished the president's control over arms sales decisionmak-

---

*These include a requirement that the executive branch submit an annual report detailing the level of arms transfers expected for the coming fiscal year and a quarterly report on any requests made by foreign governments for "price and availability" data on U.S. military hardware. The Department of Defense has also agreed to an informal procedure whereby Congress is notified twenty days before formal notification of a pending sale is submitted in accordance with the AECA.

ing. "Congress has repeatedly tried to establish or perfect procedures
to insure it an opportunity to consult effectively on possible sales
without embarrassing the client state or undermining the President's ability to conduct foreign policy," he observed. "But the Congress is still confronted with the fact that, in present circumstances,
it risks damaging bilateral relations with a client nation and has to
challenge the President directly if it chooses to veto a sale."[41]

Concluding Observations

Having reconstructed the path followed by proposed arms transfers from beginning to end, we can begin to answer the questions
posed at the beginning of this chapter. How are decisions made on
proposed transfers? Who makes these decisions? When in the process of review are such decisions made? The answers, we have
found, involve an intricate matrix of actors, agencies, and procedures—many of which are not identified in existing legislation.

The U.S. arms export establishment, we have discovered, incorporates both private and governmental arms suppliers as well as an
elaborate governmental regulatory apparatus. Most sales are processed in routine fashion by officials in a number of specialized government agencies—the Defense Security Assistance Agency, the
Office of Munitions Control, and the Office of Security Assistance
and Sales—while controversial cases usually entail a complex plea-
bargaining process involving a much wider range of actors, including
the ACDA, the Treasury Department, the CIA, the NSC, and so forth.
U.S. arms corporations, which are not formally a part of this decisionmaking process, often try to stack the deck in their favor by promoting their products abroad or, in some cases, by bribing foreign
government officials. These efforts, and the institutional interests of
particular government agencies, underlie the formal decisionmaking process. Congressional involvement, moreover, does not commence until most of the basic decisions have already been made and
the executive branch is fully aligned behind a given outcome.

This analysis suggests that the decisionmaking process itself—
that is, its particular mode of operation—is a critical factor in the
implementation of U.S. arms export policy. As we have seen, this
process tends to favor the forces lined up in favor of a sale, rather
than those (if any) committed to restraint. If a degree of balance between pro-sales and pro-restraint forces is to be maintained, therefore, or if new priorities are to govern U.S. arms exports, it is obvious
that the decisionmaking process will have to be altered. Such a
change will obviously require considerable give-and-take between

the executive and legislative branches, as well as bureaucratic reorganization within the executive itself. While the scope of this study does not permit us to speculate on all the modifications that might emerge from such an effort, it would appear, on the basis of this analysis, that some fundamental changes are needed to overcome the momentum that almost invariably builds up behind major export transactions—and thus makes it so hard to reject the proposal at a later point in the process. These include:

Reduced Secrecy. Because most of the plea-bargaining associated with arms export decisionmaking is conducted behind a veil of secrecy, critics of a proposed sale often do not learn of its scale and composition until all of the basic decisions have been made and the bureaucracy has already reached consensus on a particular outcome. If other voices are to be heard while they can still have an impact, therefore, it is obvious that some of this secrecy must be lifted. This could involve giving designated committees of Congress access to interdepartmental memos on proposed sales, requiring the DSAA to disclose all discussions between U.S. and foreign officials regarding potential arms transfers, and submitting proposed sales to Congress before the final terms have been decided upon. Such measures may make some foreign buyers uncomfortable, but would reduce the likelihood of controversial sales not being made public until it is almost too late to do anything about them.

Institutional Realignment. Although U.S. law invests the State Department with ultimate authority over arms transfers, it is apparent that the Defense Department tends to overshadow State in the decisionmaking process. If, therefore, U.S. arms exports are to be governed by considerations of foreign policy as required by statute, the power balance between State and Defense will have to be transposed somehow. This will require, at a minimum, expansion of SAS and OMC, and the hiring of many more skilled analysts with a background in the relevant technical fields. It may also require legislative action to define more clearly the responsibilities of State and Defense in the arms transfer process.

Congressional Initiative. Despite considerable effort to enhance its oversight role in the arms export area, Congress is still hampered by its confinement to the final stage of the decisionmaking process. If Congress is to play a more decisive role, therefore, it must enter the process at an earlier stage. Several recent amendments to the AECA have given U.S. lawmakers access to information on pending sales, but at present there is no staff or agency within the legislative branch to act expediently on these data. Thus, one way for Congress to enhance its decisionmaking role would be to establish a special subcommittee in each House to monitor all arms transfer trans-actions and to advise the parent committees (presumably the Sen-ate Foreign Relations Committee and the House Foreign Affairs Committee) when a pending sale requires full-scale review and debate. Such subcommittees would require a small staff of profes-sional analysts to assist member legislators in evaluation of pro-posed transactions.

These steps would not involve a major overhaul of the arms ex-port establishment, but could, if implemented effectively, restore some balance to the decisionmaking process. Any really fundamen-tal change in the way America conducts its military sales program will, of course, require the adoption of an entirely new policy frame-work (such as the alternative framework presented in chapter 11). It is apparent, however, that if U.S. military sales are to be managed so that "the foreign policy of the United States is best served thereby," a new approach to arms export decisionmaking is absolutely essential.

CHAPTER 5

The Limits of Policy

U.S. Arms Exports to Latin America

In the preceding three chapters, we examined the political-economic factors which motivate arms sales, the evolution of U.S. arms export policy, and the decisionmaking process employed in actual transactions. In this chapter, we shall observe how these policies and procedures are applied to a particular region: Latin America. Latin America is a particularly apt choice for such a study for two reasons: first, it can be viewed as a relatively homogenous area from the policymaking point of view (although U.S. policy does distinguish between the individual Latin American countries, such distinctions are not as great as those perceived among the countries of, say, the Middle East or Asia); and second, U.S. officials have historically applied specific policies with more consistency in Latin America than anywhere else. By studying U.S. arms exports to Latin America, therefore, we can better appreciate the shifts that have occurred in U.S. policy over the years and gauge how effective these policies have been in attaining their professed goals.

Latin America has been viewed as a testing ground for U.S. arms policies since the end of World War II, when the United States first became a major supplier to the region. To some extent, this perception reflects Washington's tendency to view the region as a homogenous, cohesive whole—one that can be subjected to a uniform set of policies—rather than as a collection of individual states which must be dealt with separately. It is also true, however, that successive U.S. administrations have exhibited a special interest in Latin America—both because of its physical proximity to the United States and out of a desire to promote certain forms of political behavior in the region. The particular behavior desired by U.S. policymakers has changed during the years—from an emphasis on development during the Kennedy years to an emphasis on regional security during the Reagan period—but the inclination to govern arms sales in accordance with such concerns has remained relatively constant.

To obtain some idea of the vicissitudes which U.S. arms policy toward Latin America has experienced, and to appreciate the sensitivity of such sales to changing U.S. attitudes, we need only compare the annual figures for U.S. sales to this region to those for the Third World as a whole (see table 2). While Latin American sales closely followed total Third World sales for most of the late 1960s and early 1970s—holding steady during the Johnson administration and then rising sharply under Nixon—there is a marked divergence in the late 1970s, when Latin American sales dropped precipitously under the impact of the Carter policy. Figures for both Latin American and Third World sales rose again under the Reagan administration, but Latin American sales—having dropped the furthest under Carter—showed the steepest rise.

An even more precise indication of the shifts in U.S. policy would be some sort of index of the particular characteristics of the weapons exported to Latin America. Such an index, if one could be devised, would show that certain U.S. administrations have emphasized sales of high-tech hardware (jet fighters, modern warships, etc.) while others have favored low technology (transport planes, jeeps, mortars, etc.), and that some have stressed external defense capabilities (air defense systems, antisubmarine warfare ships), while others have emphasized internal defense and counterinsurgency systems (light attack planes, helicopters, anti-riot gear). While similar shifts in priorities can be detected in U.S. exports to other regions, nowhere can they be found with the consistency encountered in sales to Latin America.

Indeed, looking back over the past thirty years, we can distinguish five distinct phases in U.S. arms policy toward Latin America:

The Mutual Security Act Period (1951–60). During this "classical" period of the Cold War, Latin America was viewed as a subsidiary theater in the global East-West struggle. The emphasis in arms exports was on maritime surveillance gear and conventional front-line weaponry for use in repelling a hypothetical Soviet invasion.

The Counterinsurgency Era (1961–68). Following the Cuban Revolution, U.S. strategists emphasized the internal, guerrilla threat to Latin America rather than the external, maritime threat. Accordingly, Washington stressed the export of counterinsurgency hardware and riot-control equipment, while discouraging the sale of high-tech weaponry.

The Open-Arms Approach (1969–76). Eager to recapture the market for high-tech weapons lost to Europe during the counterinsurgency era, President Nixon promoted the sale of supersonic fighters and other modern arms to Latin America.

The Carter Interregnum (1977–80). Under President Carter's leadership, Washington emphasized restraint in its arms exports to Latin America, specifically discouraging the sale of costly, high-tech

Table 2. U.S. Arms Sales to Latin America and the Third World, Fiscal 1966–82 (million current dollars)

Arms Transfer Agreements under the Foreign Military Sales Program

Year	Sales to Latin American countries	Sales to Third World countries
1966	$ 44.8	$ 389.8
1967	37.0	470.9
1968	31.1	462.5
1969	23.3	439.4
1970	24.2	527.8
1971	48.2	871.6
1972	104.3	1,603.1
1973	104.8	4,082.8
1974	206.3	8,459.5
1975	169.3	9,418.1
1976	84.8	12,576.1
1977	82.6	6,293.3
1978	82.4	6,852.4
1979	30.5	9,333.8
1980	31.9	9,822.6
1981	226.1	5,034.6
1982	700.4	15,954.8

SOURCE: U.S. Department of Defense, *Foreign Military Sales, Foreign Military Construction Sales and Military Assistance Facts,* 1982 edition; includes Foreign Military Construction sales.

items. Also, in line with the U.S. commitment to human rights, Congress imposed a variety of restrictions on arms sales to military-dominated countries.

The Reagan Restoration (1981–). Rejecting the restraints of the Carter era, President Reagan relaxed controls on high-tech sales to Latin America. Furthermore, in response to growing insurgency in Central America, he reemphasized the export of counterinsurgency hardware.

In each of these periods (discussed in greater detail below), U.S. arms policy has been fashioned in response to a wider set of foreign policy goals: containment during the Mutual Security Act period, development during the Kennedy era, human rights under Carter, and so forth. Indeed, these relationships have often been stressed with greater persistency in Latin America than in any other region. As we shall see, however, the degree of "fit" between arms policy and larger, foreign policy considerations has always been abridged to a greater or lesser extent by the particular exigencies of the arms trade. Furthermore, there has been a long-term trend toward diversification in arms acquisition sources on the part of the Latin American governments that has progressively eroded the effectiveness of U.S. policy.

Whatever its actual cause, the apparent decline in U.S. influence in Latin America has commonly been blamed on the mistaken policies of a prior administration. The high proportion of European sales, for instance, is often blamed on the restrictive policies of the Kennedy and Carter administrations. Out of this practice has emerged a series of abiding myths about the Latin American arms market: that U.S. arms limitations are inherently "paternalistic"; that Europe and the U.S.S.R. consistently seek to "exploit" U.S. restraint; that U.S. restraint has driven Latin American countries to develop their own arms industries; and so forth. All of these myths have gained wide circulation in Washington and have, on occasion, prompted a shift in policy. And because many of these myths persist today—and still affect the making of policy—it is important that we analyze them carefully.

In the remainder of this chapter, we shall examine the five major phases in U.S. arms policy toward Latin America and consider why they succeeded or failed in achieving their specified objectives. Then, following a discussion of the inherent limits in U.S. arms policy, we shall explore the myths which have arisen around this issue over the past few years. Finally, we shall sketch out the foundations of a more realistic, appropriate policy. Before turning to these endeavors, however, it is perhaps useful to begin with a brief description of the Latin American arms market itself.

The Dimensions of the Marketplace

By all accounts, Latin America spends less on imported weapons than any other similar region. According to the Arms Control and Disarmament Agency, Latin American countries spent $10.2 billion on imported arms between 1978 and 1982, compared to $27.3 billion by African countries, $56.3 billion by Middle Eastern countries, $16.0 billion by East Asian and Pacific countries, and $29.7 billion by European countries. All told, Latin American sales represented only 8 percent of total Third World arms transfers. These figures reflect both the continued weakness of the Latin American economies and the relatively small share of total GNP—1.6 percent—devoted to military expenditures by Latin American governments.[1]

Although small, the Latin American arms market has been growing steadily over the past decade and appears headed for major expansion in the 1980s. According to the ACDA, total military spending by Latin American countries rose by about 50 percent in the 1970s, from $6.2 billion in 1971 to $9.4 billion in 1980 (in constant 1979 dollars). Spending on imported arms grew at an even faster rate during this period, from $410 million in 1971 to $1.6 billion (in constant 1979 dollars), an increase of 293 percent.[2] Furthermore, many Latin American countries appear poised for major purchases of new weapons systems—Argentina alone is expected to spend $2–$3 billion (mostly to replace weapons lost during the Falklands/Malvinas conflict)—and so arms spending should continue to rise at a significant rate well into the 1980s.

This growing market is shared, to a greater extent than in most other regions, by all three major sources of supply: the United States, the Soviet Union, and Western Europe. Again using ACDA figures, we find that the $6.8 billion in current dollars spent on imported arms by Latin America between 1976 and 1980 was divided among suppliers approximately as follows: United States, $725 million (11 percent); U.S.S.R., $2,000 million (29 percent); France $1,200 million (17 percent); United Kingdom, $775 million (11 percent); West Germany, $450 million (7 percent); Italy, $420 million (6 percent); all others, $1,300 million (19 percent).[3] While these figures must be viewed as approximations—the Soviet entry could vary considerably depending on the dollar/ruble conversion factor used—they do suggest the degree to which Latin American buyers have diversified their sources of supply (see table 3).

In general, arms spending by the Latin American countries has tended to emphasize equipment at the low-to-middle range of the technology spectrum. Because such weaponry tends to be significantly less costly than equipment at the upper end of the spectrum, Latin American spending actually generates a far larger volume of orders than the (relatively) low level of spending would suggest. Thus figures compiled by the Congressional Research Service indicate a fairly brisk trade in such items as armored cars and armored personnel carriers, artillery pieces, frigates and patrol boats, and small cargo planes (see table 4).[4] Indeed, Latin America has become a highly lucrative market for producers of counterinsurgency gear and other low-technology hardware. This explains, to some extent, the popularity in Latin America of French and Italian arms, which tend to be less sophisticated (and thus less costly) than their nearest American counterparts.

Before concluding this brief discussion of the Latin American

Table 3. Arms Transfers to Latin America, 1976–80, by Major Supplier (million current dollars)

Recipient	All suppliers, Total	Soviet Union	United States	France
Latin America, Total	6,800	2,000	725	1,200
Argentina	1,100	—	100	340
Bolivia	150	—	10	—
Brazil	800	—	130	30
Chile	600	—	110	170
Colombia	110	—	30	—
Cuba	1,100	1,100	—	—
Dominican Republic	10	—	5	—
Ecuador	700	—	50	390
El Salvador	30	—	5	30
Guatemala	50	—	10	10
Guyana	10	—	—	—
Haiti	5	—	—	—
Honduras	50	—	10	—
Mexico	70	—	20	10
Nicaragua	30	—	5	—
Panama	40	—	40	—
Paraguay	60	—	5	—
Peru	1,500	900	100	170
Trinidad & Tobago	20	—	—	—
Uruguay	70	—	10	20
Venezuela	360	—	90	20

SOURCE: U.S. Arms Control and Disarmament Agency, *World Military Expenditures and Arms Transfers, 1971–1980* (1983); indicates deliveries of arms, ammunition, and related equipment; excludes services and construction.

NOTE: Totals may not add due to rounding.

arms market, something should be said about differences within the region. Although there are many similarities in the buying habits of the various Latin American countries, there are also some important distinctions. Given the relative disparity in purchasing power between the wealthier and poorer countries of the region, it is not surprising that some—notably Argentina, Brazil, Chile, Ecuador, Peru, and Venezuela—spend a lot more on imported arms than others. Between 1976 and 1980, these six countries together accounted for 74 percent ($5.1 billion) of Latin America's arms imports, while the remaining nineteen countries account for the remaining 24 percent. If

United Kingdom	West Germany	Italy	Switzerland	Others
775	450	420	70	1,305
120	120	100	5	360
—	5	—	20	110
460	20	120	—	30
50	30	—	5	260
5	5	—	—	70
—	—	—	—	—
—	—	—	—	10
70	110	5	20	50
—	—	—	—	5
—	—	—	10	20
10	—	—	—	—
—	—	—	—	—
—	—	—	—	40
20	—	—	10	20
—	—	—	—	30
—	—	—	—	—
—	5	—	—	60
10	70	90	5	110
—	—	—	—	20
—	—	—	—	40
30	80	100	—	30

Cuba—a major recipient of Soviet aid—is added to the other six, the combined share of these nations rises to 91 percent. Table 3, meanwhile, shows that there are also some variations in the sources of supply for these countries: only two countries—Cuba and Peru—have turned to the Soviet Union for their arms acquisitions, while some (Argentina, Chile, and Ecuador) have shown a marked preference for French arms and others for a mixture of American and European arms.[5] Finally, it should be noted that Argentina and Brazil have become major producers of arms themselves and have begun to sell their products—mostly small arms and counterinsurgency gear—to other countries in the region.

Table 4. Deliveries of Major Weapons Systems to Latin America, 1975–82

Weapons Category	United States	U.S.S.R.	"Big 4" W. Europe[a]	Total, U.S., U.S.S.R., Big 4
	Quantities delivered by:			
Tanks & self-propelled guns	48	270	130	448
Artillery pieces	1,274	680	210	2,164
APCs and armored cars[b]	194	190	340	724
Major surface combat ships	13	3	28	44
Minor surface combat ships	7	40	70	117
Submarines	5	3	14	22
Supersonic combat aircraft	28	220	60	308
Subsonic combat aircraft	160	10	30	200
Other aircraft	214	80	170	464
Helicopters	112	100	160	372
Guided missile boats	0	13	3	16
Surface-to-air missiles	0	1,090	610	1,700

SOURCE: Congressional Research Service, *Trends in Conventional Arms Transfers to the Third World by Major Supplier, 1975–82* (1983).
[a] United Kingdom, West Germany, France, Italy.
[b] APCs = armored personnel carriers.

The Evolution of U.S. Policy

Having concluded this brief description of the regional arms market, we can now proceed to an analysis of the major shifts in U.S. arms export policy toward Latin America.

Prior to World War II, Latin America obtained most of its munitions from the major European powers—France, Germany, and Great Britain. These nations also provided military instructors for the hemisphere's armies and navies; as a result, Latin American military doctrine tended to mirror that of Europe, which stressed defense against possible attack by rival powers. Once World War II broke out, however, Europe could no longer spare weapons for marginal allies, and thus the United States became the principal arms supplier to the region. Under the Lend Lease Act of 1941, U.S. arms were made available to the Latin American countries in return for access to military bases and strategic materials. As the war progressed, moreover, U.S. personnel gradually replaced most of the European advisors attached to Latin American military forces.[6]

After the war, the United States continued to dominate the arms market in Latin America. Europe was largely occupied with domestic economic recovery, while the United States had large stocks of surplus military equipment which it was willing to give away or sell at relatively low rates. Wartime cooperation also left a legacy of partnership that was perpetuated through the Rio Treaty of 1947 (or, more properly, the Inter-American Treaty of Reciprocal Assistance), which established a framework for collective military action in response to an attack on any of the signatories. It was not until the outbreak of the Korean War, however, that Washington adopted a fully articulated policy on arms exports to Latin America. This policy, incorporated into the Mutual Security Act of 1951, governed U.S. exports during the first of the five major policy phases of the postwar era.

The Mutual Security Act Period (1951–60)

Adopted at the onset of the Cold War, the Mutual Security Act of 1951 reflected the prevailing strategic vision of the time—one that envisioned a bipolar world in which the United States bore primary responsibility for defense of the non-Communist world against the Soviet bloc. Other countries were encouraged to participate in the collective effort to "contain" Communism, but were expected to do so within a framework of U.S. leadership. Thus, under the act, funds were made available for the modernization of Latin American forces engaged in the common defense effort, with the proviso that the United States be assured access to certain critical raw materials.[7] A country became eligible for these funds upon ratification of a bilateral mutual defense assistance pact with the United States. Such agreements were concluded with Chile, Colombia, Cuba, Ecuador, and Peru in 1952; with Brazil, the Dominican Republic, and Uruguay in 1953; with Honduras and Nicaragua in 1954; with Guatemala and Haiti in 1955; and with Bolivia in 1958.

The wording of these agreements, and all references to them by U.S. officials at the time of ratification, suggest that Latin America was viewed by Washington as a subordinate theater in the global struggle to contain Communism. Latin American forces would be assisted to participate where appropriate in the hemispheric defense effort, but were not assumed to play a significant military role otherwise. "Though it galls some South Americans who believe that power and prestige are measured only by industrialization," Sam Pope Brewer of the *New York Times* observed at the time, "the fact is that South America's value to hemispheric defense lies in geography and raw materials rather than in great armies and the industry to equip them."[8]

While this attitude may indeed have galled Latin American leaders, they were hardly in a position to turn down offers of cut-rate arms and training. As noted by Luigi Einaudi in a 1973 RAND Corporation study, "the United States came to be seen as the predominant supplier of arms and training to Latin America, with World War II and Korean War stocks of materiel a source of inexpensive but reliable arms and equipment." The mutual aid pacts also granted the United States a monopoly on military advisory missions, and thus, according to Einaudi, "symbolized de facto U.S. predominance" of the Latin American arms market.[9]

In line with the premises of the Mutual Security Act, U.S. arms policy at the time emphasized the development of hemispheric defense against external, presumably Soviet, attack. Thus as late as 1959, Assistant Secretary of Defense Charles H. Shuff told a congressional subcommittee that "the most positive threat to hemispheric security is submarine action in the Caribbean Sea and along the coast of Latin America."[10] In accordance with this assessment, the United States supplied Latin America with $500 million worth of arms and equipment between 1951 and 1960, with much of it intended for use in coastal defense and antisubmarine warfare.

The Counterinsurgency Era (1961–68)

With the triumph of the Cuban Revolution in 1959, Washington was forced to reconsider the basis for its arms policy toward Latin America. By waging a successful guerrilla war against Batista's U.S.-equipped army, Fidel Castro demonstrated that strategies emphasizing defense against conventional, external attack did not necessarily contribute to defense against unconventional, internal attack. The Cuban upheaval also occurred at a time when U.S. policymakers were beginning to accord the Third World increased geopolitical significance, reflecting growing U.S. trade with this once-neglected area. Together, these developments stimulated a new interest in guerrilla warfare and in strategies for combating the so-called wars of national liberation in the Third World. Out of this effort emerged the strategy of counterinsurgency, which was to dominate U.S. military thinking throughout the 1960s.[11]

John F. Kennedy, who succeeded Dwight D. Eisenhower as president in 1961, placed special emphasis on the development and implementation of counterinsurgency doctrine. "Subversive insurgency is another type of war, new in its intensity, ancient in its origins," he told West Point cadets in 1962. "It requires in those situations where we must counter it . . . a whole new kind of strategy [and] a wholly different kind of force."[12] In line with this outlook, Kennedy established a Special Group for Counterinsurgency at the sub-Cabinet level and ordered a thorough revision of U.S. arms export programs.[13] As a result, counterinsurgency became the principal objective of U.S. aid to Latin America, while external defense was relegated to a decidedly second place. As noted by Prof. Edwin Lieuwen of the University of New Mexico in a 1969 Senate study, "the basis for military aid to Latin America abruptly shifted from hemispheric defense to internal security, from the protection of coastlines and antisubmarine warfare to defense against Castro-communist guerrilla warfare."[14]

Beginning with the fiscal year 1963 Military Assistance Program, Latin American countries which had signed mutual security pacts with the United States (or related military aid agreements) became eligible for grants or credit-assisted sales of counterinsurgency hardware and training. Two years later, MAP director Gen. Robert J. Wood testified that "the primary purpose of the [MAP program] for Latin America is to counter the threat to the entire area by providing equipment and training which will bolster the internal security capabilities of the recipient countries."[15] This approach was reaffirmed in 1967 when Secretary of Defense Robert S. McNamara told a House committee that the primary objective of the U.S. arms program in Latin America "is to aid, where necessary, in the continued development of indigenous military and paramilitary forces capable of providing, in conjunction with the police and other security forces, the needed domestic security."[16]

As viewed by strategists of the Kennedy and Johnson administrations, counterinsurgency implied more than the transfer of military and paramilitary technology: it also implied a commitment to economic and social development on the part of recipient countries. Because revolution thrives in an environment of underdevelopment and stagnation, they believed, the counterinsurgency effort must include a positive effort to advance development if the impoverished masses were to be won over to the government's side. As explained by Secretary McNamara,

> Security is development, and without development there can be no security. A developing nation that does not, in fact, develop simply cannot remain secure for the simple reason that its own citizenry cannot shed its human nature.
> If security implies anything, it implies a minimal measure

of order and stability. Without internal development of at least a minimal degree, order and stability are impossible . . . because human nature cannot be frustrated indefinitely.[17]

The United States could facilitate development, McNamara argued, by providing economic assistance through the Alliance for Progress, by promoting private investment, and by helping the military and the police to maintain the necessary environment of "order and stability."

In accordance with this approach, Latin American armies were encouraged to promote development by lending their managerial and technical skills to civilian development projects, and by curbing their appetite for costly, high-tech weapons which would absorb funds needed for economic modernization. Such expenditures, in the then prevailing U.S. view, were both wasteful and unnecessary. As argued by Raymond J. Barrett, a Foreign Service officer attached to the Department of the Air Force, the official doctrine held that

the need for expensive arms by Latin American countries does not appear great. They are protected against conventional military threats by the effective Inter-American peace-keeping machinery, by the Rio Treaty security guarantees, and by wide oceans . . .

The principal threat to Latin American nations is internal. It is the danger of Fidel Castro–sponsored subversion. The fundamental response to this threat is quicker and better economic development, but strengthening internal security is also important.[18]

To the dismay of U.S. policymakers, however, many Latin American military leaders did not fully accept Washington's strategic outlook. While the Pentagon was generally successful in mobilizing support for U.S.-sponsored counterguerrilla operations in the countryside (such as the 1967 campaign against Ché Guevara in Bolivia), Washington never succeeded in erasing the traditional view that defense against external attack is the primary mission of Latin American armies. In line with this outlook, Peru decided in 1965 to replace its aging F-86 interceptors with a modern replacement, preferably the Northrop F-5A Freedom Fighter. Though the F-5A was only marginally supersonic, U.S. policymakers saw the Peruvian request "as a prime example of wasteful military expenditures for unnecessarily sophisticated equipment at a time when generous U.S. credits were being extended for economic development" and thus rejected the deal.[19]

Washington's refusal to sell the F-5A to Peru set off a chain of events whose consequences can still be felt today. When rebuffed by Washington, the Peruvians turned to Paris, where an export-conscious government was only all too eager to provide credits for the sale of the Dassault-Breguet Mirage-V fighter. Other Latin American governments, in line with their traditional policy of matching the military acquisitions of their rivals, acquired Mirage fighters of their own.[20] U.S. resistance to these moves—at one point Washington threatened to suspend economic aid to Peru—prompted some countries to adopt a policy of diversifying their sources of arms among several suppliers (in order to avoid becoming overly dependent on any single source) and also prompted Argentina and Brazil to step up efforts to establish arms industries of their own. Washington thus discovered, in the words of Einaudi, that

> the U.S. capability to control Latin American acquisitions was sharply limited by the presence of alternative suppliers from Western Europe, many of whom were riding a crest of European economic recovery and aggressive government support. More interested in fostering economic development than in being the exclusive arms supplier, U.S. policy had simply collided with the aspirations and sensitivities of increasingly independent Latin American governments which had more options available to them than those presented by the United States.[21]

Although the Johnson administration continued to adhere to a developmentalist approach to arms sales, other constituencies in the United States began lobbying for a change in export policy. Aerospace executives launched a campaign for the repeal of all restrictions on military exports to Latin America, and many Pentagon officials—concerned that the hemisphere's "turn toward Europe" would undermine their ties with the area's military leadership—joined the lobbying effort. Thus, when Richard Nixon was elected president in 1968, the stage was set for another shift in U.S. arms policy toward Latin America.

The Open-Arms Approach (1969–76)

Ideologically opposed to restraints on arms sales, Nixon immediately set out to reverse the austere, developmentalist approach of the Kennedy and Johnson administrations. As part of this effort, he asked Nelson Rockefeller—then governor of New York state—to assess U.S. arms policies during a "presidential mission" to Latin

America. Upon returning, Rockefeller proposed a less restrictive stance on arms sales, declaring:

> The United States must face more forthrightly the fact that while the military in the other American nations are alert to the problems of internal security, they do not feel that this is their only role and responsibility. They are conscious of the more traditional role of the military establishment to defend the nation's territory, and they possess understandable professional pride which creates equally understandable desires for modern arms.

If the United States is to maintain cordial relations with the region's military leadership, he argued, it must drop its restrictions on the export of sophisticated armaments and permit sales of "aircraft, ships and other major military equipment."[22]

Although the White House immediately endorsed Rockefeller's recommendations, Congress was not so accommodating. Angered by the Mirage sales to Latin America (which seemed to nullify the intent of U.S. economic aid programs), and concerned by the growing unpopularity of the Vietnam War, U.S. lawmakers imposed several new restrictions on arms exports to Latin America. In 1968, a new Foreign Military Sales Act was adopted which prohibited sales of "sophisticated weapons systems" to underdeveloped countries (except to the "forward defense countries" on the border of China and the U.S.S.R.) and imposed a limit of $100 million on military aid to Latin America (including FMS credits but excluding training), with a presidential waiver of 50 percent of that ceiling. At the same time, an amendment was added to the Foreign Assistance Act requiring that aid be cut to any country which diverted excessive funds to the acquisition of sophisticated military hardware.

To overcome these obstacles to a more flexible export program, administration officials conducted a vigorous campaign for the repeal of statutory restraints on arms transfers, particularly the ban on exports of high-tech weaponry. In presenting the administration's case for a permissive approach to high-tech sales, Assistant Secretary of State Charles A. Meyer told the Senate Subcommittee on Western Hemisphere Affairs that "Latin Americans have become puzzled and even suspicious of our motives. Strong nationalist sentiment has arisen over what is seen as United States efforts to infringe on the sovereign rights of a country to determine its own military requirements." Recognizing that the committee members were particularly concerned with preventing needless Latin American spending on sophisticated weapons, Meyer suggested that the net effect of

U.S. restrictions was "the acquisition of more expensive [European] items, higher maintenance costs, and greater diversion of financial resources from civilian purposes."[23]

In pursuing their case, administration officials also charged that the arms export restrictions undermined U.S. national security interests by weakening the ties between U.S. and Latin American military officials. This argument was given special emphasis after 1973, when the maverick military regime in Peru placed an order for 200 Soviet T-55 tanks—the first major purchase of Soviet arms by any South American country. Because arms transfers are believed to provide for a continuing support relationship between supplier and recipient (through the supply of training, maintenance, services, spare parts, and so forth), the shift to European and Soviet equipment naturally diminished U.S. ties while enhancing the influence of other powers. This concern was addressed to the Congress by Gen. Louis T. Seith of the U.S. Air Force, who testified:

> The inflow of European arms, including French Mirage aircraft and French and Soviet armor, has impacted upon our traditional relationship with Latin American leaders.
>
> This has exacerbated further our already declining relationship, which flowed, in part, from the decrease in the security assistance program and the restrictions on sophisticated weapons systems.
>
> We must act now if we are to avoid, or at least mitigate, serious degradation of our lines of communication with Latin American leaders in furtherance of our strategic interests. . . .[24]

Other administration officials also argued that the U.S. restrictions had severely narrowed U.S. access to the Latin American arms market at a time when Vietnam spending was declining and U.S. producers would need to increase their export sales in order to prevent economic hardship.

Although sympathetic to these arguments, Congress was still disinclined to promote expanded U.S. ties with Third World military regimes and thus resisted any changes in its stance on arms transfers. As is often the case, however, Congress had left the president a loophole—and in 1973 President Nixon decided to forego further pleading and to take matters into his own hands. On June 5, 1973, he invoked section 4 of the Foreign Military Sales Act—which allowed the president to waive congressional restrictions on the transfer of sophisticated items when he determined that such sales were "important to the national security of the United States"—in order to permit sales of the Northrop F-5E supersonic fighter to Argentina,

Brazil, Chile, Colombia, and Venezuela. (Brazil subsequently bought
42 F5-ES, and Chile bought 18.) In justifying the president's action in
a memorandum to Congress, Acting Secretary of State Kenneth
Rush argued:

> The prohibition on offering American fighters has had two
> consequences. The first and crucial one is political. Our ties
> with Latin America are rich and varied. Among them is a his-
> toric bond to maintain the security of the Americas. . . . Latin
> American countries have also looked to the U.S. as the major
> source for the supply of its military equipment. These intan-
> gible matters of trust and confidence are important to our rela-
> tions. . . . To pursue a policy which in its effect dissolves a
> confident military supply relationship built over three decades
> carries serious long-term implications for our mutual defense
> bonds with Latin America.
>
> The second and subordinate consequence is economic.
> The U.S. has lost opportunities for making substantial sales
> not only of fighters themselves but also of related equipment—
> as for instance communications networks.[25]

Nixon subsequently invoked section 4 to permit sales of other
high-tech arms to Latin America (specifically, Sidewinder air-to-air
missiles to arm the F-5ES sold to Brazil), and the U.S. sales tally began to turn sharply upward. Total FMS sales to Latin America rose to
$48 million in fiscal 1971, $104 million in 1972, $105 million in
1973, and a record $206 million in 1974 (see table 2). All told, Latin
American countries ordered $769 million worth of U.S. arms under
the FMS program between 1970 and 1976, or triple the amount for
the preceding seven years.[26]

Nixon's pro-sales approach succeeded in winning back some of
the market ceded to the Europeans during the counterinsurgency
era, but it did not restore the commanding position enjoyed by the
United States in the Mutual Security Act period. By this time, the
trend toward diversification had proceeded too far to be reversible,
and the European producers had become too competitive to be excluded from the market. (According to the ACDA, the major European suppliers—Britain, France, West Germany—retained their one-
third share of the Latin American market throughout the 1970s.)
Even with the presidential waivers on high-tech exports, therefore, U.S. producers faced stiff competition from their European
competitors.

Furthermore, even though it enjoyed some success in winning

new orders for U.S. firms, the Nixon approach also generated fresh discord in Washington. Because the 1970s were characterized by a resurgence of military rule in Latin America—coups occurred in Chile in 1973, in Uruguay in 1973, and in Argentina in 1976—many U.S. policymakers began to worry about the attendant increase in human rights abuses. And because conspicuous arms transfers were seen as conferring implicit U.S. support for the newly militarized Latin American regimes, Congress began to view such sales as a cynical negation of the professed U.S. commitment to international human rights.[27] Accordingly, U.S. lawmakers adopted a number of general restrictions on military exports to countries cited for conspicuous violations of human rights and imposed specific bans on certain types of exports to a number of Latin American countries. Section 406 of the International Security Assistance Act of 1976 banned all forms of military aid or sales to Chile, while section 620B of the Foreign Assistance Act (FAA) of 1961, as amended in 1977, banned all forms of transfers to Argentina, and section 503A of the Foreign Assistance Act of 1978 banned military aid and arms credits to Uruguay. Another provision of the FAA of 1978, section 503B, made Brazil, El Salvador, and Guatemala ineligible for arms credits through the FMS program.[28]

The increase in U.S. arms transfers to Latin America also occurred at a time when U.S. leaders were becoming increasingly concerned about the dangers to world stability posed by unrestrained weapons sales to the Third World. The October War of 1973, the OPEC oil price increase of 1974, and the conspicuous purchases by the Shah of Iran which followed all drew attention to the problem of conventional arms transfers. Sensing that the public would applaud a tough stand on this issue, Jimmy Carter criticized the permissive approach of the Nixon and Ford administrations during the 1976 presidential campaign and pledged "to increase the emphasis on peace and to reduce the commerce in weapons."[29] With Carter's election, therefore, U.S. arms policy toward Latin America underwent yet another transformation.

The Carter Interregnum (1977–80)

Soon after taking office, President Carter directed the State Department and National Security Council to develop recommendations for a new policy on conventional arms transfers. After studying the State/NSC recommendations, he announced a new "policy of arms restraint" in a presidential memorandum of May 19, 1977.

This policy also imposed a series of specific limitations on U.S. military exports (see chapter 3 for a full description), of which several had direct application to Latin America:

- A ceiling on total U.S. arms exports to Latin America and other nonexempt countries.
- A ban on the introduction of newly developed high-tech weapons into regions where such weapons have not already been deployed.
- A ban on the development or modification of weapons expressly for export purposes.

Although the administration soon ran into trouble when attempting to apply these restrictions to strategic areas like the Middle East—where the logic of U.S. diplomacy necessitated a continuing series of high-tech exports to key allies—it was rather more persevering when it came to Latin America. As a result, the total dollar volume of U.S. sales dropped sharply. Whereas FMS orders had averaged $140 million per year in the Nixon period (fiscal 1972–76), they dropped to $83 million in 1977, $82 million in 1978, $31 million in 1979, and $32 million in 1980 (see table 2). To some extent, of course, the decline in Latin American sales was mandated by congressional restrictions on arms exports or credit sales to particular countries. But the administration also blocked the sale of F-5ES to Ecuador and Guatemala in accordance with its ban on the introduction of sophisticated weapons and vetoed sales of some counterinsurgency and riot-control weapons to countries which had been accused of persistent human rights violations.[30]

Latin America also figured prominently in the talks between the United States and the Soviet Union on limiting exports of conventional arms to the Third World. These negotiations, known as the Conventional Arms Transfer (CAT) talks, were convened in response to President Carter's call for multilateral initiatives in controlling the international arms traffic. Exploratory CAT talks were held in December 1977, May 1978, and July 1978, in an atmosphere that was generally described as "businesslike" and "encouraging."[31] Then, in September 1978, Secretary of State Cyrus Vance met with Soviet Foreign Minister Andrei Gromyko in Moscow, and the two diplomats agreed to concentrate on Latin America during the forthcoming CAT talks in Mexico City. As reported by Dan Oberdorfer in the *Washington Post*, the Vance/Gromyko agreement envisioned "a round of concrete negotiations aimed at creating common guidelines on the supply of conventional weapons to Latin America."[32] In the intervening months, however, U.S.-Soviet relations deteriorated significantly as a result of the Iranian crisis and other developments, so when CAT negotiators met in Mexico City they were unable to make any significant headway. (East-West relations continued to worsen in the following year, and thus the CAT talks were never reconvened.)

Despite the president's evident commitment to arms restraint in Latin America, the Carter policy was carried out with less and less determination as the 1970s drew to a close. Major sales of high-tech weaponry were concluded with Ecuador in 1979 (Chaparral surface-to-air missiles and Vulcan antiaircraft guns) and Mexico in 1980 (F-5E fighters). Talks also commenced with Venezuela regarding possible sale of the Northrop F-5G supersonic fighter—a plane specifically designed for export to Third World countries and thus prohibited under the Carter policy. (Nothing came of these negotiations until Ronald Reagan became president, at which time the Venezuelans asked for and were given permission to purchase the more sophisticated F-16.) Similarly, Carter eased his restrictions on arms sales to countries with a poor human rights record when the military-dominated regime in El Salvador came under sustained attack from leftist guerrillas in 1980. In the last year of the Carter administration, combined U.S. military and economic assistance to the Salvadoran junta jumped from $15 million in fiscal 1980 to $55 million in 1981.[33]

To a large extent, these reversions from the original Carter policy reflected the decline in East-West relations as well as increasing doubts over the primacy of human rights considerations at a time of growing insurgency in Central America. Cuba's conspicuous military activities in Africa also aroused considerable concern in Washington, while the success of the Sandinista revolution in Nicaragua prompted fears of "another Cuba" on the mainland of North America. A new administration viewpoint emerged in early 1979, when Adm. Gordon J. Schuller of the Pentagon's International Security Affairs bureau testified before the Subcommittee on Inter-American Affairs of the House Foreign Affairs Committee. "During the past year," he noted, "events have revealed vulnerabilities in the security of the hemisphere. Internal problems in Nicaragua have precipitated internal conflict which threatened to become internationalized. Dangers of insurgency and terrorism are rife in Central America. . . ." In response to these new challenges, Schuller called for the repeal of all remaining congressional restraints on arms exports to Latin America.[34]

At the same time, Washington's growing discontent with unilateral arms restraints was reinforced by the failure of America's European allies—especially France and Great Britain—to curb their own arms exports to Latin America. Combined European deliveries rose from about $100 million per year in the 1960s and early 1970s to $320 million per year during the Carter period (in current dollars), while U.S. deliveries rose only slightly and new U.S. orders actually declined. "Our restraint has not invited emulation by other suppliers," Admiral Schuller complained in his 1979 testimony. "More costly and more sophisticated weapons systems have been introduced into the area by a number of eager suppliers."[35] As in the Kennedy/Johnson period, this "profit-taking" by European suppliers provoked widespread resentment in the U.S. arms industry, which again mobilized a public relations effort to reverse prevailing policy.[36]

The administration's arms restraint policy also ran afoul of neoconservative thinkers who felt that human rights and arms control considerations should be subordinated to traditional national security interests. These analysts—many of whom became associated with Ronald Reagan's campaign organization—charged that Carter's policies had made adversaries of traditional U.S. allies like Argentina and Brazil while giving aid and comfort to leftist guerrillas. One of Carter's most persistent critics, Prof. Jeane Kirkpatrick of Georgetown University, wrote in *Commentary* that administration policies "have not only proved incapable of dealing with the problems of Soviet/Cuban expansion in the area, they have positively contributed to them and to the alienation of major nations, the growth of neutralism, the destabilization of friendly governments, the spread of Cuban influence, and the decline of U.S. power in the region."[37] Kirkpatrick, who was subsequently named U.S. ambassador to the United Nations, argued that the United States should assist the "traditional autocracies" which ruled most Latin American countries, rather than, out of a misplaced concern over human rights, allow them to be replaced by "revolutionary autocracies" like Cuba that would directly threaten U.S. security.[38]

Although Carter continued to emphasize the importance of human rights and arms control, by 1980 he had abandoned many of his earlier policies (e.g., the ban on high-tech sales to Latin America) and, in the view of most experts, would have moved toward a more permissive approach to arms sales had he remained in office. However, such speculation became moot when Reagan was elected and the new administration implemented its own approach to arms exports.

The Reagan Restoration (1981–)

As a candidate, Reagan had made no secret of his opposition to the Carter administration's arms policies; once elected, he moved quickly to reverse them. His top foreign policy appointees—Alexander Haig as secretary of state, James Buckley as under secretary for security assistance, and Jeane Kirkpatrick as U.N. ambassador—had all spoken out against the Carter policies and were committed to a shift in priorities. Soon after taking office, Reagan ordered Buckley to draft a new arms transfer policy, while Haig and Kirkpatrick were given a free hand to dismantle what remained of the old one.

Contending that human rights had to be subordinated to traditional security concerns, Secretary Haig asked Congress in March 1981 to repeal the ban on arms sales to Argentina. Three months later, he authorized the sale of army vehicles to Guatemala as the first step toward resumption of military aid to that country.[39] Then, in June, White House sources disclosed that the administration had approved the sale of F-16 supersonic fighters to Venezuela, thereby indicating a new U.S. willingness to sell relatively sophisticated military hardware to Latin America.[40] (The F-16 sale, consisting of 18 F-16A fighters and 6 F-16B trainers, was formally announced in October 1981.)

While Haig proceeded with these concrete steps, Under Secretary Buckley worked on a new set of formal principles to govern U.S. arms transfers. On May 21, 1981, he unveiled the administration's thinking in an address before a meeting of the Aerospace Industries Association in Williamsburg, Virginia. Citing the by now familiar argument that human rights considerations must be subordinated to conventional security concerns in a time of growing Cuban/Soviet adventurism in the Third World, Buckley declared that arms transfers can "serve as an important adjunct to our own security by helping deter acts of aggression [and] enhancing the self-defense capabilities of nations with which we share close security ties."[41]

The administration's new policy was formally announced on July 9, 1981, when President Reagan released a presidential directive on arms transfers which superseded the Carter declaration of May 19, 1977. Noting that the international environment had become significantly more dangerous during the Carter period, Reagan suggested that "the United States must, in today's world, not only strengthen its own military capabilities, but be prepared to help its friends and allies to strengthen theirs through the transfer of conventional arms and other forms of security assistance." To facilitate purchases by America's less affluent allies, Reagan promised to encourage the development of unsophisticated arms specifically for export and to provide arms credits at concessionary rates.[42] (See chapter 3 for a full discussion of the Reagan guidelines.)

Reagan's election, and the promulgation of a new arms transfer policy, led to a dramatic rise in U.S. arms exports to Latin America.

Bolstered by a steep rise in FMS credits, U.S. sales to Latin America soared in the first two years of Reagan's tenure, from $31.9 million in 1980 to $226.1 million in 1981 and $700 million in 1982. Similar increases were posted in military aid grants and Commercial Sales of military hardware.[43] The repeal of the Argentina embargo and the relaxation of curbs on high-tech sales are expected to produce further export gains in coming years. U.S. producers were also expected to benefit from Argentina's efforts to restock its arsenals following the 1982 Falklands conflict, once the Reagan administration succeeded in overcoming resentment caused by Washington's "tilt" toward Great Britain during the fighting.[44]

Despite such optimism, most analysts doubt that the United States will regain its predominant position in the Latin American arms market. Most front-line U.S. arms are too sophisticated—and thus too expensive—to compete with comparable European products, and Argentina and Brazil are not likely to be deflected from their plans to develop domestic arms industries. As noted by Brazilian arms expert Roberto Pereira de Andrade in 1981, we are seeing "a re-orientation in [Brazil's] relationship with the U.S." Although Brazil will remain a major customer for U.S. military hardware, he noted, "now we only buy components, spare parts, and the more sophisticated weapons we can't produce."[45] As their new arms industries flourish, moreover, Argentina and Brazil are beginning to compete with the United States and Europe in sales of counterinsurgency hardware and other low-tech items to the other countries in Latin America. (Brazilian arms exports, for instance, are now estimated to exceed $300 million annually.)[46] Thus, while the Reagan policy will undoubtedly improve America's overall competitive position, it will not alter the basic structure of the Latin American arms market.

While it is still too early to assess the long-term impact of the Reagan arms initiatives in Latin America as a whole, there is one area where administration policy has already had a dramatic impact: Central America. Once the least significant outlet for U.S. arms abroad—total FMS sales to the region amounted to only $58 million by 1979, compared to $97.3 billion to the world as a whole—Central America is now a major recipient of U.S. arms aid and military support. Under the administration's plan, total U.S. security assistance to Central America (including MAP grants, FMS credits, and Economic Support Fund loans and grants) rose from $145.9 million in fiscal 1981 to $303 million in 1982 and $476.2 million in 1983.[47] When Congress balked at further increases in early 1984, Reagan introduced a supplemental military aid request of $443.6 million (raising total 1984 security assistance to $784.6 million) and used emergency "drawn down" authority to provide $32 million in arms aid to El Salvador without congressional approval.[48]

In justifying these moves, the Reagan administration argued that it was responding to a Soviet-Cuban effort to spread subversion and insurgency throughout the region. In line with this view, Nicaragua was described as a heavily armed "staging area" for the export of revolution to El Salvador and other Central American nations. "If guerrilla violence succeeds," the president affirmed in March 1983, "El Salvador will join Cuba and Nicaragua as a base for spreading fresh violence to Guatemala, Honduras, even Costa Rica."[49] Seen from this perspective, U.S. military aid represented an essentially defensive reaction, intended to help defend friendly nations against external aggression. "We do not view security assistance as an end in itself," Reagan told a special Joint Session of Congress on April 27, 1983, "but as a shield for democratization, economic development, and diplomacy."[50]

To a large extent, this rhetoric suggests a return to the Cold War outlook that governed U.S. arms policy during the Mutual Security Act period. Indeed, in his April 27 speech to Congress, Reagan quoted approvingly from President Truman's 1947 "Truman Doctrine" address, implying a direct relationship between current U.S. policy and the Cold War stance of the late 1940s and the 1950s. But while this outlook tends to dominate official rhetoric, the Reagan effort in Central America also represents a partial return to the counterinsurgency approach of the Kennedy/Johnson era. For, however it is described in official statements, the war in El Salvador constitutes a classic encounter with revolutionary guerrillas—and thus the U.S. response, by necessity, has involved the delivery of counterinsurgency hardware (small arms, helicopters, light strike aircraft, etc.) along with training in counterguerrilla operations.[51] To underscore the counterinsurgency orientation of the U.S. effort, Special Forces advisors—many with extensive Vietnam experience—have been brought in to assist government forces in El Salvador and to staff a new "Regional Military Training Center" at Trujillo in Honduras.[52]

By mid-1983, the U.S. military buildup in Central America had become one of the most visible—and controversial—foreign policy initiatives of the Reagan period. While the administration enjoyed some support for its policy on Capitol Hill, many U.S. lawmakers, recalling the frustrations and division of the Vietnam era, were vigorously opposed to the Central American buildup. "There is a sense up here that the Administration has overreacted and undercut our friend's efforts to find a peaceful way out," Rep. Michael Barnes of

Maryland observed in August 1983.[53] (As a demonstration of its concern, the House voted on July 28, 1983, to cut off covert U.S. aid to the CIA-backed "contras" (*contrarevolucionarios*) seeking to overthrow the Sandinista regime in Nicaragua.) Many critics also charged that the administration's aid effort would eventually draw the U.S. forces directly into the fighting, resulting in another divisive and futile intervention. "Unless he is stopped by Congress," former senior editor John B. Oakes of the *New York Times* declared, "Ronald Reagan could plunge this country into the most unwanted, unconscionable, unnecessary, and unwinnable war in its history, not excepting Vietnam."[54]

In order to generate support for his position, Reagan appointed former Secretary of State Henry Kissinger to chair a special National Bipartisan Commission on Central America in 1983. In its report, released on January 11, 1984, the commission verified the administration's contention that the conflict in Central America posed a significant threat to the "direct national security interests of the United States" and that forceful counteraction was essential. "The use of Nicaragua as a base for Soviet and Cuban efforts to penetrate the rest of the Central American isthmus . . . gives the conflict there a major strategic dimension" and represents "a challenge to which the United States must respond." To overcome the insurgent threat in the area, the commission proposed a five-year U.S. aid program of $8 billion, with at least one-fourth of this consisting of military assistance for El Salvador.[55] However, the commission could not reach agreement on other key issues—in particular, on whether to continue covert U.S. aid to the anti-Sandinista "contras" based in Honduras—and its heavy emphasis on military assistance provoked widespread criticism on Capitol Hill. "The central thrust of this report," Representative Barnes complained, "is to recommend military solutions for the region and to deny the viability of political ones."[56]

While the administration still enjoyed sufficient support in Congress in early 1984 to implement the essentials of its Central America policy, it is possible that future events could produce a significant shift in political attitudes—thereby leading to an intensification or diminution of the U.S. military effort. Such a "sea change" could also result in a new policy on arms sales in general. As we have seen, U.S. arms policy toward Latin America has tended to undergo periodic revisions, reflecting shifts in overall foreign policy objectives. It is entirely possible, therefore, that the Reagan policy will at some point be supplanted by yet another policy framework.

Whatever the future course of U.S. arms policy, we have already witnessed enough shifts in orientation to draw a number of conclusions about the relative effectiveness of U.S. efforts to control the arms acquisitions of Latin American governments, and thus their general military orientation. Let us turn, then, to a discussion of these propositions.

The Limits of Policy: Myths and Realities of the Arms Trade

Looking back over the five major phases in U.S. arms policy toward Latin America, it appears that there are distinct limits to Washington's ability to influence Latin American military and political behavior through selective fluctuation in the supply of arms. These limits spring from several basic features of the existing Latin American arms market.

First, U.S. influence is inherently constrained in a market characterized by a multiplicity of suppliers, the absence of binding international export controls, and relative autonomy on the part of the buyers. In the immediate aftermath of World War II, when the European powers were still preoccupied with industrial recovery and the United States alone possessed a stockpile of surplus weapons, Washington was able to exercise a fair degree of control over Latin American purchasing; once Europe had recovered, however, the Latin American marketplace became increasingly pluralistic and U.S. hegemony inevitably disappeared. Although most Latin American governments remain indisposed to acquire Soviet arms (Cuba, which remains highly dependent on Soviet economic aid, is the only major exception now that Peru has reverted to a pro-Western orientation), they feel free to purchase European arms when the price is right and the item in question satisfies their outstanding military requirements. This is also true of most other non-Communist countries, of course, but seems especially disquieting to American policymakers given the earlier experience of U.S. dominance. Nevertheless, the trend toward pluralism in the marketplace appears irreversible and is likely to accelerate as Latin American countries become more affluent and self-assured.[57]

Second, if U.S. efforts to control the buying habits of Latin American governments have been frustrated by the existence of alternative suppliers outside the region, they have also been hindered by the multiplicity of actors within the region. Not only do the various Latin American countries differ in their assessment of outstanding military threats and the strategies needed to counter them, but within most of them there are contending political forces which often hold conflicting views on arms acquisition requirements. Thus, while some Central American countries share the current U.S. view that growing activity by Cuban-backed guerrillas justifies stepped-up U.S. military assistance, others, including Mexico, advocate a nonbelligerent stance toward the insurgents. Similarly, while Latin American military leaders (many of whom have been trained in the United States) may respond positively to U.S. offers of particular weapons, they may be overruled by civilian leaders who seek to diversify their sources of supply, or by economic planners who seek less costly alternatives. Indeed, even in those countries dominated by military juntas, internal differences can arise over the appropriate source of imported weapons. The Brazilians, for instance, have frequently turned to European suppliers despite a long history of close military ties with the United States.[58] It is obvious, therefore, that the Latin American arms market must be viewed as a heterogenous and unpredictable system, rather than as a coherent—and therefore controllable—one.

Finally, if we can say that U.S. efforts to dominate the Latin American marketplace are hindered by the multiplicity of actors and motives involved, it is also apparent that U.S. policymakers must contend with a similar diversity in the United States itself. Although the White House may be firmly committed to a particular policy, differences on how to implement it may emerge between the State and Defense departments and even within State itself—the Brazil Desk may advocate a particular sale, for instance, while the Human Rights Bureau will oppose it. Even if the executive branch is relatively unified in its support for a particular policy, Congress and various trade groups are likely to espouse conflicting views. Indeed, Congress has periodically imposed its own restraints on military sales to Latin America, or otherwise frustrated White House efforts to implement a particular approach to arms exports. And because, over the long run, government decisions tend to represent a compromise between the positions of contending power blocs, presidential efforts to impose a particular arms transfer policy have consistently been frustrated by the contradictions and limitations incorporated into the policy itself.

If this survey of successive U.S. strategies allows us to draw these conclusions about the limits of policy, it also permits us to refute some of the myths that have arisen over U.S. arms sales to Latin America. Although these myths are demonstrably erroneous when subjected to rigorous scrutiny, they have acquired considerable credibility through frequent reiteration and thus have become a significant factor in the policymaking process.[59]

Myth #1: U.S. "Paternalism." U.S. efforts to limit Latin American arms spending have often been described as "paternalism" by those critics who advocate an open-arms approach to military sales. In 1973, for instance, Cecil Brownlow charged in *Aviation Week and Space Technology* that Latin America turned to European equipment when "a 'father-knows-best' Congress refused to sell advanced military aircraft," believing that these countries "should spend its money for more worthwhile projects such as raising the standard of living of its lower classes."[60] Similarly, during the height of concern over human rights, David Ronfeldt and Caesar Sereseres of the RAND Corporation complained that "anti-liberal developments in Latin America have tended to arouse moral outrage, commonly paternalistic, in ways that have often taken the form of . . . restrictive and discriminatory U.S. legislation."[61]

But while moral outrage may sometimes influence the shaping of policy, such concern has rarely been the driving force behind particular measures. Thus, the restraints of the Kennedy/Johnson period were motivated primarily by a desire to ensure the success of U.S. counterinsurgency programs, rather than by any wish to eradicate poverty. Furthermore, while many U.S. lawmakers may have been sincerely committed to the advancement of human rights, the restrictions imposed in the post-Vietnam period were at least partially intended to refurbish America's international image and to preclude U.S. involvement in another debilitating guerrilla war. Indeed, as we have seen, a variety of political, economic, and military concerns have traditionally motivated U.S. arms exports, few of which can be termed "paternalistic" in the sense inferred by critics of restraint.

Myth #2: The "Lost" Arms Market. Advocates of unrestricted arms sales often argue that U.S. constraints on the sale of sophisticated hardware have forced Latin American countries to abandon their traditional preference for U.S. hardware and to turn elsewhere—notably to Europe—for their military needs. Thus Cecil Brownlow of *Aviation Week* charged in 1973 that congressional restrictions on the sale of sophisticated aircraft had "provided a driving wedge for France and Great Britain into wider areas of the aerospace market there and generated [a] turn away from American military hardware."[62] Similar charges were made regarding President Carter's "arms restraint" policy of the late 1970s. "While U.S. policy is trying to restrain the total level of arms transfers," Northrop Vice President C. Robert Gates declared in 1979, "other producing nations are rushing in to fill the vacuum created by the U.S."[63]

However, while it is certainly true that U.S. restraints on the sale of advanced military hardware have on occasion prompted some Latin American governments to shop elsewhere, they cannot be said to have deprived U.S. suppliers of access to a market they would otherwise have dominated. Thus, the record shows that even though the United States provided most of the front-line equipment acquired by Latin America in the immediate postwar period, it confined its transfers to surplus World War II and Korean War stocks, while European suppliers—particularly Great Britain—provided most of the new-construction hardware (fighters, bombers, and warships) acquired at this time.[64] Accordingly, when these countries turned again to Europe in the 1960s and 1970s, they were not breaking with established behavior, but rather reverting to an earlier pattern. Indeed, this was acknowledged at the time in a study released by the State Department's Bureau of Intelligence and Research:

> Heavy South American purchases of arms from European sources during 1967–72 seldom reflected a deliberate policy of turning away from U.S. suppliers. . . . European suppliers were providing much of the same mix of principal combatant vessels, fighter aircraft, tanks, and artillery in the 1950's. . . . [Since] the United States had never been a leading supplier of various kinds of new high-performance equipment being sought [it] could not be said to have "lost" an established competitive position.[65]

Moreover, even if the United States had not imposed such restrictions, Latin American countries would, in any case, have eventually turned to European (and later indigenous) suppliers, both to enhance national independence and by reducing their dependence on any single arms supplier and to facilitate acquisition of the particular items most suited to their military requirements and economic capabilities. That this behavior reflects internally generated policies rather than an unanticipated response to external stimuli—that is, the U.S. constraints—is demonstrated by the fact that many Latin American governments continue to shop in the United States for those U.S. products—helicopters, transport aircraft, artillery, and armored personnel carriers—that are particularly suited to their operational environment and are available at competitive prices.

Myth #3: U.S. Restraints Prompt Domestic Arms Production. Just as U.S. restraints theoretically prompted Latin America's "turn toward Europe," they are also held responsible for the efforts of some countries to establish a domestic arms industry. But while U.S. constraints may have been a contributory factor, they are not decisive. In the first place, it should be noted that U.S. constraints have applied mostly to high-performance combat gear (and particularly to supersonic jet aircraft) which no Latin American nation has yet attempted to build. Rather, current arms programs emphasize small arms, military vehicles, light transport planes, and counterinsurgency gear—most of which are freely available from the United States. Furthermore, many of these programs were begun long before the U.S. restraints were first imposed. Argentina, for instance, established its first military aircraft facility—the Fábrica Militar de Aviones (FMA)—as early as 1927 and began work on a jet fighter soon after the end of World War II.[66] Many of the region's rifle and artillery factories have equally long histories.

Recently, some Latin American governments have launched major programs to expand and diversify their domestic arms facilities. In doing so, however, they have been motivated more by nationalistic and economic considerations than by a desire to escape U.S. export restraints. Thus, Brazilian military leaders argued quite forcefully that a domestic arms capability is a prerequisite for national sovereignty and that such industries spur modernization by stimulating the creation of ancillary industries—electronics, metallurgy, machine tools, and so forth. "The time has come to free ourselves from the United States and Europe," Brazilian Air Force Minister Joelmir Campos de Araripe Macedo declared in 1977. "It is a condition of security that each nation manufacture its own armaments."[67] Furthermore, Brazil—like other Third World powers—also seeks to reduce outlays for foreign arms at a time of growing balance-of-payments difficulties (see chapter 8).

This discussion of the myths and realities of military sales to Latin America obviously has significant implications for U.S. arms policy. As we have seen, previous U.S. efforts to influence Latin American political behavior through selective controls on arms sales have not proved especially successful. This should, it would seem, persuade us that the control of political behavior is not a realistic (nor, indeed, an appropriate) goal for U.S. policy toward Latin America. Instead, we should seek an alternative policy framework—one that reflects an appreciation of the limitations to arms transfers as an instrument of political influence and thus stresses other foreign policy objectives.

Toward a Realistic Arms Policy

What, then, should be the objectives of U.S. arms policy toward Latin America, and how can we ensure that such goals can be met?

In answering these questions, it is useful to begin with a prior question: should we establish a separate arms policy for Latin America, or should we deal with these countries in the same manner that we deal with other Third World countries? This question is important, because we have seen that the failure of previous policies can be at least partially attributed to Washington's tendencies to perceive a special U.S. military role in Latin America and to apply particular policies there with greater determination (and thus greater expectations of success) than was the case elsewhere. In reality, most Latin American countries have long since rejected the notion of a "special role" for the United States, and U.S. assumptions regarding the efficacy of arms transfers in promoting various policy objectives should be seen for the illusions they were. Perhaps, if we view Latin America as only another segment of the Third World when it comes to arms exports, we can begin to fashion a sensible and realistic export policy.

As in the case of any other region, the prime objective of U.S. export policy toward Latin America should be the prevention of local arms rivalries that could trigger a regional war. Historically, Latin American countries have been relatively conservative in their arms purchases, seeking weapons primarily for territorial defense or internal security. Recently, however, many of the larger and more affluent countries have acquired advanced ships and planes with a significant offensive capability. Thus, Argentina, Ecuador, Peru, and Venezuela have all purchased six or more modern frigates (most armed with guided missiles of one sort or another); Cuba, Ecuador, Peru, and Uruguay have ordered modern submarines; and all but a handful of Latin American countries have acquired supersonic combat aircraft.[68] These purchases cannot, of course, be equated with the massive arms transfers to the Middle East; but it is true that we can see the beginnings of classical arms rivalries in several areas—Central America, the southern cone (Argentina, Chile, Uruguay), and the northwest (Ecuador, Peru)—along with a growing inclination to use (or threaten to use) force to resolve local disputes. Because any conflicts in such areas could easily spread and threaten vital U.S. interests, it is essential that we seek to dampen these rivalries through diplomatic means and do what we can to discourage further acquisitions of offensive military gear. The latter is not something we can do on our own—most of these weapons are being acquired in Europe or the Soviet Union—but it is obvious that here as in other Third World areas the United States must work with other nations to curb the flow of modern weapons.

There is also the problem of internal security and human rights. Past experience suggests that U.S.-assisted counterinsurgency campaigns often result in the dissolution of civilian governments by security-conscious military juntas, along with a marked increase in human rights violations. And because Washington is so closely identified with the military authorities involved, democratic and progressive forces tend to view the United States as an obstacle to reform. This means, of course, that opposition groups are more likely to turn to radical solutions in their efforts to topple the prevailing regime, and to adopt anti-American policies when (and if) they come to power. Accordingly, the United States should exercise extreme caution when responding to requests for paramilitary and counterinsurgency hardware on the part of Latin American (and other Third World) governments and withhold equipment which could be used for repression of democratic forces.

These considerations provide at least the framework for a rational arms policy toward Latin America. Clearly, this framework requires much more elaboration and refinement—a task we shall undertake in the context of an overall U.S. policy on arms transfers (see chapter 11). But it is still necessary to say something about the effectiveness of such an approach, given all we have learned about the limits of U.S. policy. Obviously, U.S. restraint can' accomplish only so much if other countries can turn to alternate suppliers for their desired hardware. To be truly effective, U.S. restraint must be matched by comparable efforts on the part of other suppliers—including the Soviet Union—as well as by those recipients with a domestic arms-making capability. Any U.S. effort to control the international arms trade must, therefore, incorporate mutual incentives for restraint on the part of all participants in that commerce. Such incentives—whether economic, political, or diplomatic—must form the cornerstone of any meaningful arms transfer policy, toward Latin America as much as toward any other region of the world.

CHAPTER 6

Arms and the Shah

The Rise and Fall of the "Surrogate Strategy"

Between 1970 and 1978, Shah Mohammed Reza Pahlavi of Iran ordered $20 billion worth of arms, ammunition, and related military hardware from the United States in what one U.S. lawmaker called "the most rapid buildup of military power under peacetime conditions of any nation in the history of the world."[1] This extraordinary accumulation of war-making capabilities was intended by the Shah to transform Iran into a major military power, thereby propelling him into the front ranks of world leaders. American policymakers, who cultivated and nourished the Shah's grandiose visions, hoped in turn that U.S. arms would enable Iran to serve as the "guardian" of Western oil supplies in the Persian Gulf area. U.S. arms sales were also expected to perform other amazing feats: to wipe out America's trade imbalance; to underwrite the costs of U.S. weapons development; to assure high employment in the aerospace industry; and to accelerate the "modernization" of Iranian society. Never, in fact, have arms transfers played such a central role in U.S. foreign policy as they did in Iran. But whatever the presumptions of U.S. policymakers, all these arms could not save the Shah once his subjects were determined to abolish the monarchy. On January 16, 1979, Shah Mohammed Reza Pahlavi, the "King of Kings" and "Light of the Aryans," was forced into permanent exile in the West. While many factors undoubtedly contributed to his downfall, surely one of the most critical was the ill-conceived U.S. arms-supply program.

In this chapter, we shall examine the nature and history of that program and show how it corroded and finally destroyed the Pahlavi dynasty—and with it, the U.S. policy of converting Iran into the "gendarme" of the Persian Gulf. Because the U.S.-Iranian arms relationship was so extensive, however, it is worth beginning with a brief overview of its principal features:

Volume. Between 1970 and 1978, Iran was the leading overseas customer for U.S. arms, accounting for $20 billion in FMS orders, or 25 percent of all FMS orders received during this period. However, since many of the arms ordered by the Shah were not scheduled for delivery until the early 1980s, actual deliveries to Iran had only

Table 5. U.S. Arms Sales to Iran, Fiscal 1950–78
(million current dollars)

Arms Transfer Agreements and Deliveries under the Foreign Military Sales Program

Fiscal Year(s)	Agreements	Deliveries
1950–69	$ 741.2	$ 237.8
1970	134.9	127.7
1971	363.9	78.6
1972	472.6	214.8
1973	2,171.4	248.4
1974	4,325.4	648.6
1975	2,447.1	1,006.1
1976	1,794.5	1,927.9
1977	5,713.8	2,433.1
1978	2,586.9	1,792.9
1950–78	20,751.7	8,715.9

SOURCE: U.S. Department of Defense, Foreign Military Sales, Foreign Military Construction Sales and Military Assistance Facts, 1978 edition.

reached $9 billion when the regime fell in January 1979 (see table 5).[2] All remaining orders were subsequently canceled by the Shah's successors.

Sophistication. Although Washington originally discouraged sales of high-tech weapons to Iran, in 1972 President Nixon agreed to sell the Shah America's most advanced and powerful munitions. The Shah subsequently ordered a wide array of sophisticated arms, including the swing-wing F-14 air-superiority fighter, the DD-963 Spruance-class missile destroyer, and the General Dynamics F-16 multirole combat plane.

Technology Transfers. Iran acquired not only vast quantities of U.S. arms, but also the technology to produce them. Under an ambitious billion-dollar scheme involving many U.S. arms firms, the Shah laid the groundwork for establishment of a modern "military-industrial complex" in Iran.

Military Technical Assistance. Because the Shah was importing high-tech arms faster than U.S. instructors could train Iranians to maintain and operate them, Iran was forced to hire tens of thousands of foreign technicians to perform all the necessary backup functions. By 1978, there were an estimated 10,000 American support personnel working on arms-related projects in Iran.

Police and Paramilitary Sales. In addition to all the conventional military gear supplied to Iran, Washington also sold vast quantities of police weapons and paramilitary hardware (teargas, riot sticks, small arms, etc.) to Iranian security agencies. The United States also provided training to these organizations, among them SAVAK, the notorious secret police.

These are only some of the most conspicuous features of the U.S.-Iranian arms relationship. In addition to these relatively overt transactions, there were a number of hidden dimensions to the arms program that played as great or an even greater role in the U.S.-Iranian relationship. These included bribery and corruption, government mismanagement, and political intrigue. As I shall show, these covert activities combined with the unintended and undesired consequences of the overt transactions to undermine the Shah's position. Before describing this process, however, let us turn briefly to a history of the U.S.-Iranian arms relationship.

Origins of the U.S. Arms Program

In 1941, British and Russian troops occupied Iran and deposed the reigning monarch, Reza Shah, who was considered overly friendly to Germany. Reza, the founder of the Pahlavi dynasty, was succeeded by his son, Mohammed Reza Pahlavi (who served as Shah until his downfall in 1979). In 1941, the United States sent a small training mission to assist the new Shah in his efforts to rebuild the Iranian army. Although Washington provided only small amounts of equipment and training during the war years, this mission served as the foundation for an ever-expanding U.S. involvement in Iranian military and political affairs.[3]

Iran figured prominently in one of the earliest incidents of the Cold War, which began when the Soviet Union offered assistance to the breakaway regimes set up by Kurdish and Azerbaijani rebels in Iran's northern border regions. After forceful protests by the United States, Moscow withdrew its support, thus enabling the Shah to reassert Iranian control over the embattled areas. Nevertheless, President Truman saw Iran (along with Greece and Turkey) as a precarious "first line of defense" against Soviet penetration into the Middle East. Thus, under the Truman Doctrine, Washington stepped up aid to the Iranian military and encouraged Tehran to join with other "northern tier" powers in forming an anti-Soviet military alliance.[4]

Although U.S. military aid to Iran was originally predicated on the then-prevalent doctrine of "containment," it also served another objective: to strengthen the Shah's base of support in the military. At a time when central government revenues from oil production—then controlled by the Anglo-Iranian Petroleum Company—were still very small, U.S. military assistance constituted an important source of arms and equipment for the relatively ill-equipped Iranian army. Because the Shah—as supreme commander of the armed forces—assumed control over U.S. aid disbursements, he was able to assemble a core of loyal officers whose advancement was engineered via the assistance program. From the very beginning, therefore, U.S. military aid had a direct and often powerful influence on Iran's internal political fabric.[5]

U.S. involvement in Iranian military affairs first proved decisive in 1953, when the CIA helped organize a coup against Prime Minister Mohammed Mossadeq. Appointed in 1951, at a time when the Iranian parliament (the Majlis) still retained some autonomy from the royal household, Mossadeq earned Washington's ire by nationalizing Iranian oil supplies and pursuing an independent course in foreign policy. The task of deposing Mossadeq was entrusted to Kermit Roosevelt, who secretly entered Iran and assembled a "coup team" composed of police and army officers loyal to the Shah. On August 19, 1953, these pro-Shah elements took to the streets and crushed the civilian forces loyal to Mossadeq, who was forced to resign.[6] Although this incident was described at the time as a popular uprising, the head of the U.S. military aid mission boasted that "the guns they had in their hands, the trucks they rode in, the armored cars that they drove through the streets, the radio communications that permitted their control, were all furnished through the military assistance program."[7]

Following the coup, U.S. ties with the Pahlavi dynasty became even more extensive. Military assistance was substantially increased, and again the Shah used these funds to expand his base among the military. Other institutions—the Majlis, the clergy, political parties, and so forth—were either dissolved or rendered powerless, and any opposition to imperial rule was quickly silenced by the army, the police, or the gendarmerie. And while U.S. officials stressed the danger of Soviet attack in their official pronouncements, they continued to assist the Shah in his efforts to silence internal opposition movements. In 1957, for instance, the CIA was ordered to help establish SAVAK, the infamous secret police.[8] All told, Washington provided $900 million in arms and equipment to Iranian military and police forces in the post-Mossadeq period—a not insignificant amount in those days of low oil revenues.[9]

The Genesis of the Surrogate Strategy

Throughout the Cold War period, Iran was considered an important ally of the United States, but no more important than any of the other garrison states which anchored the U.S. alliance system extending from Greece to Pakistan and thence around Asia to South Korea. The real turning point in the U.S.-Iranian relationship did not come until December 1967, when Prime Minister Harold Wilson announced that Britain would terminate its military presence in the Persian Gulf area by the end of 1971. Although the British presence had become relatively modest by then, Wilson's announcement caused much consternation in Washington, because U.S. strategists had always relied on London to serve as the official guardian of Western interests in the vital Gulf region. With London now out of the picture, and no apparent successor for the "guardian" role, Washington had to devise a Persian Gulf strategy for the first time.

Wilson's announcement was made during the final days of the Johnson administration, so it was left to the new administration of Richard Nixon to undertake the necessary policy-formulation effort. To facilitate this task, Nixon ordered the National Security Council, then headed by Henry Kissinger, to explore the various policy options open to the United States and to recommend a basic policy framework. Although preoccupied with the Vietnam conflict, Kissinger apparently gave this project high priority, and the resulting document—National Security Council Study Memorandum No. 66 (NSSM-66)—was submitted to the White House on July 12, 1969. After reviewing the recommendations contained in NSSM-66, President Nixon issued a National Security Decision Memorandum, NSDM-92, to govern U.S. policy in the region.[10]

Although NSSM-66 and NSDM-92 were given a very high security classification and their contents never made public, one can reconstruct their findings from various public sources. Of particular value in this regard is a 1969 study released by Georgetown University's Central for Strategic and International Studies (CSIS), *The Gulf: Implications of the British Withdrawal*. Based on the analyses of several top specialists on Middle Eastern affairs, the CSIS study closely parallels the administration's thinking at the time. This document, along with statements made by government witnesses before various congressional committees, allows us to deduce the NSC's reasoning with a high degree of accuracy.

First, the NSC would have set forth Washington's basic policy options. While a wide spectrum of permutations and combinations were no doubt considered, America's choices boiled down to three basic alternatives:

Option #1: Stay Out. The United States would continue to provide military aid to pro-Western governments in the Gulf, but would not assume a direct military role in the area.

Option #2: Move In. U.S. forces would be deployed in the Gulf to perform the "gendarme" functions previously performed by the British.

Option #3: Find a Surrogate. Instead of deploying U.S. forces, Washington would recruit some other power to serve as regional gendarme in place of Great Britain.

In attempting to choose between these three alternatives, the NSC would weigh U.S. strategic interests in the area and then calculate the costs of each option. Here again, while the NSC would have considered a wide range of variables, we can reconstruct the main lines of their reasoning.

Although the United States was, at that time, importing only small amounts (less than 3 percent) of its oil supplies from the Gulf, all reliable projections indicated that such imports would have to rise significantly to meet U.S. energy needs in the 1970s and beyond. Furthermore, America's chief allies in Europe and the Far East had already become highly dependent on Middle Eastern oil. Any interruption in these supplies would, therefore, constitute a major threat to Western security. As affirmed by the CSIS panel in 1969, "The strategic interests of the noncommunist world would be in grave jeopardy if freedom of movement in and out of the Gulf were curtailed or denied."[11]

This finding would almost automatically have eliminated Option #1, Stay Out, from consideration. In the conventional wisdom of the time, the British withdrawal would create a "power vacuum" in the area which the Russians would inevitably fill—unless someone else were there to stop them. "It must be assumed," Alvin Cottrell and David Abshire of CSIS wrote in 1969, "that the Soviet Union will fill the power vacuum resulting from the British withdrawal," since Moscow always moves into "areas where the West shows its inability to safeguard its interests."[12] Given the vast scale of Western interests in the Gulf, such a course would have been deemed wholly unacceptable.

The real problem thus became: who would protect Western interests in the Gulf? No doubt many U.S. leaders would have preferred Option #2, Move In, as the surest way of filling the impending power vacuum. But there were several major obstacles to such a choice. To begin with, this was 1969, and the United States was deeply embroiled in an unpopular war in Southeast Asia. Not only would a Persian Gulf presence divert forces needed for the war effort in Vietnam, but it would arouse the ire of a Congress which had already become disenchanted with America's role as global gendarme. An American presence in the Gulf would, moreover, be viewed by the more radical Arab states as evidence of a U.S. "imperialist" design and thus would frustrate Washington's efforts to wrest these countries out of the Soviet orbit. The only prudent course, therefore, would have been to reject Option #2.

In the final analysis, there was only one choice: Find a Surrogate. This option also accorded perfectly with the administration's newly adopted Nixon Doctrine. But that still left a difficult question: who could be relied upon to serve U.S. interests in the area? Some policymakers may have suggested Israel, but that choice probably would have pushed the Arab countries into an anti-U.S. alliance and thus facilitated further Soviet penetration of the region. Other possible choices—France, perhaps, or even India—were too far from the scene and/or lacked the motivation to take on such a role. The only remaining candidates, therefore, were the countries of the Gulf itself. But even the two most prosperous and advanced nations of the region—Saudi Arabia and Iran—lacked the wherewithal to serve as regional gendarmes without considerable U.S. assistance. That meant, inevitably, that Washington would have to serve as the organizer and quartermaster of this delicate maneuver. "What we decided," former Under Secretary of State Joseph J. Sisco later explained, "is that we would try to stimulate and be helpful to the two key countries in this area—namely, Iran and Saudi Arabia—that, to the degree to which we could stimulate cooperation between these two countries, they could become the major elements of stability as the British were getting out."[13]

Thus, a new doctrine—one that can best be called the Surrogate Strategy—was born. The United States would help Iran and Saudi Arabia to assume a regional peacekeeping role, but would keep its own forces out of the area. In one of the few public references to NSSM-66, Deputy Assistant Secretary of Defense James H. Noyes testified in 1973:

> A major conclusion of that study . . . was that the United
> States would not assume the former British role of protector in
> the Gulf area, but that primary responsibility for peace and sta-
> bility should henceforth fall on the states of the region. . . . In
> the spirit of the Nixon Doctrine, we are willing to assist the

Gulf states but we look to them to bear the main responsibility for their own defense and to cooperate among themselves
to insure regional peace and stability. We especially look to the
leading states of the area, Iran and Saudi Arabia, to cooperate
for this purpose.[14]

As suggested by Sisco and Noyes, this policy originally assumed co-
equal roles for Iran and Saudi Arabia. But, as U.S. policymakers began to undertake the difficult job of implementing the new strategy,
it soon became apparent that the two countries were hardly capable
of assuming an equal share of the burden. Saudi Arabia did not even
possess a navy at that time, and its small army of some 30,000 men
(most of whom were committed to internal security functions) was
hardly capable of performing Gulf-wide peacekeeping missions.
Iran, on the other hand, possessed a sizable navy and air force, and
its well-equipped army of 150,000 was considered among the most
powerful in the region. In practice, therefore, the Surrogate Strategy
inevitably became an Iranian strategy.

Aside from these military considerations, the selection of Iran
as America's principal surrogate was essentially predetermined by
the attitudes of the rulers involved. Whereas the Saudi leadership
was largely concerned with dynastic matters and intra-Arab affairs,
the Shah had long affirmed Iran's role as the "guardian" of the Persian Gulf and was not averse to assuming an even grander role. "Not
only do we have national and regional responsibilities," he told
Arnaud de Borchegrave of *Newsweek* in 1973, "but also a *world role*
as guardian and protector of 60 percent of the world's oil reserves
(emphasis added).[15] Even more important, from the American point
of view, he seemed ready to act on this premise when real threats
emerged: in 1973, for instance, he sent Iranian forces into Oman to
help crush a separatist rebellion in Dhofar province.

A U.S.-Iranian alliance also had the advantage that Washington
need only consult one individual—the Shah—when critical decisions had to be made. Whereas a whole swarm of princes (many of
them inaccessible to U.S. influence) were involved in decisionmaking in Saudi Arabia, in Iran all major foreign policy decisions
were made by the Shah himself. In the decade following the Mossadeq
incident, he had systematically eliminated all remaining challengers
to imperial rule and had established near-totalitarian rule over Iranian society. In the view of U.S. analysts, moreover, the Shah's all-
powerful position seemed unshakable for the indefinite future: with
control over Iran's abundant oil wealth, he could buy off the most
ambitious bureaucrats and entrepreneurs, while the constant vigi-

lance of SAVAK ensured that all dissidents would be quickly dealt with. The only institution with the power to question the Shah's survival—the army—was kept in line by lucrative perquisites on the one hand and the oversight of SAVAK on the other. Echoing the views of American policymakers, *U.S. News and World Report* observed in 1973 that "Iranian society is like a pyramid, with the Shah at the apex and the army a privileged caste." [16]

For U.S. policymakers, forced to grapple with the agonies of Vietnam and growing discontent at home, a U.S.-Iranian alliance must have appeared irresistible. But they soon discovered that there was a substantial price tag for this extraordinary partnership: transfer to Iran of a first-class military arsenal. While the Shah was more than willing to serve as the U.S. surrogate in the Persian Gulf, he expected to acquire military capabilities commensurate with his country's new stature. No longer content with the obsolete hand-me-downs supplied through the Military Assistance Program, he began to eye America's latest and most sophisticated military hardware. At the top of his "wish list" was a modern air force, equipped with America's newest fighters: the McDonnell-Douglas F-15 Eagle and the Grumman F-14 Tomcat.

When the Shah first proposed an Iranian purchase of F-14s and/or F-15s in 1971–72, there were some Pentagon officials who opposed the sale. Never before had the United States transferred such an advanced aircraft to a Third World nation, and there were many in Washington who felt that such a move could compromise U.S. security by entrusting American defense secrets into the hands of foreigners who could not be expected to keep them safe indefinitely. Such hesitations must have infuriated the Shah, who, as a result of the U.S.-Iranian partnership, had come to view Iran's role in increasingly grandiose terms. "Western Europe, the U.S. and Japan see the Gulf as an integral part of their security," he reminded his allies at the time, "yet they are not in a position to ensure that security, [and] that's why we're doing it for them." [17] No doubt Washington tried to satisfy his ambitions with offers of less-sophisticated hardware, but the Shah refused to settle for anything less than the very best, and in the end Washington acquiesced rather than jeopardize the success of the Surrogate Strategy. In May 1972, President Nixon and Henry Kissinger flew to Tehran and signed a secret agreement with the Shah whereby Iran was permitted to order "virtually any weapons systems which it wanted." [18]

Within months of the May 1972 Tehran meeting, the Shah ordered 80 F-14s at an estimated cost of $2 billion, along with dozens of other U.S. weapons systems. Iranian spending on U.S. arms soared

from $500 million in 1972 to $2.2 billion in 1973 and a staggering $4.3 billion in 1974. In addition to the F-14s, major Iranian orders included:
- 169 Northrop F-5E and F-5F fighters for $480 million
- 209 McDonnell-Douglas F-4 Phantom fighter-bombers for $1 billion
- 160 General Dynamics F-16 fighters for $3.2 billion
- 202 Bell AH-1J Cobra helicopter gunships for $367 million
- 326 Bell Model-214 troop-carrying helicopters for $496 million
- 25,000 TOW and Dragon antitank missiles for $150 million
- 4 DD-963 Spruance-class missile destroyers for $1.5 billion.

And this represents only the major items; to round out the Shah's "shopping list," one would have to include billions of dollars' worth of more mundane items like transport planes, armored personnel carriers, and artillery pieces. Finally, one would have to add all of the arms and equipment acquired for the police, the gendarmerie, and other internal security forces.[19]

Critics of Iran's extraordinary arms buildup have charged that Washington lost all control over the weapons program after the May 1972 agreement. In a much-publicized 1976 report, *U.S. Military Sales to Iran*, the staff of the Senate Foreign Relations Committee (SFRC) asserted that "for at least three years U.S. arms sales to Iran were out of control." Not only had the 1972 agreement been concluded without any prior review of U.S. arms policies, but the president's decision also "effectively exempted sales to Iran from the normal arms sales decision-making process in the State and Defense Departments."[20] Administration officials consistently argued, however, that the Nixon-Shah agreement was neither ill-conceived nor hastily contrived. "Our [arms] supply policy is not the result of a series of improvisations," Deputy Assistant Secretary of Defense Noyes told the House Foreign Affairs Committee in 1973, but followed directly from the 1969 decision (i.e., NSDM-92) to encourage Iran to assume "primary responsibility for peace and stability" in the Gulf.[21] Indeed, once Washington elected to convert Iran into a surrogate police power, it had no option but to honor the Shah's requests for the weapons he felt he needed to perform the job.

There was another dimension to the Nixon administration's strategic design that could not be openly used in its defense, but that nevertheless constituted an important justification for its Iranian arms program—the cultivation of an Iranian dependency on U.S. technical support. As noted in chapter 2, modern arms require constant servicing, maintenance, and inspection by skilled technicians, and Iran simply lacked the trained personnel to perform these services. Consequently, each new purchase of sophisticated gear by the

Shah created an additional requirement for backup support which could only be provided by U.S. technicians. And since the more sophisticated a weapon is, the greater its need for specialized maintenance and servicing, the Shah's arms purchases created an ever-expanding demand for such services.[22] By 1973, there were an estimated 3,600 U.S. technicians employed on arms-related projects in Iran (800 U.S. military and 2,800 contractor personnel), and the number swelled to an estimated 10,000 by 1978.[23]

These technicians, or "white-collar mercenaries" as they are sometimes called, rapidly became an essential component of the Shah's high-tech war machine. Thus Washington, by threatening to recall these specialists, could exercise a form of "veto power" over Iranian military activities. "There is general agreement among U.S. personnel involved with the Iranian programs," the SFRC reported in 1976, "that it is unlikely that Iran could go to war in the next five to ten years with its current and prospective inventory of sophisticated weapons . . . without U.S. support on a day-to-day basis."[24] Thus, by continuously expanding the Shah's dependency on American technical skills, the U.S. arms program was meant to ensure that the "surrogate" never operated independently of its preordained role as guardian of Western oil interests.

The "Petrodollar" Imperative

If the Nixon administration's original 1972 decision to sell the Shah "anything he wants" was prompted largely by strategic considerations, its continued adherence to the agreement was soon to be assured by another major consideration: the oil-inspired balance-of-payments crisis. Following the fourfold rise in oil prices announced by the OPEC nations in early 1974, America's balance-of-payments accounts rapidly dropped into the red as its payments for imported oil skyrocketed. With the United States heading into recession, Nixon was under intense pressure to recover as many U.S. "petro-dollars" from the oil countries as possible by selling them whatever they could be persuaded to buy. And there is no doubt what the Iranian government—which is to say, the Shah—wanted most: arms, arms, and more arms. Military sales thus became seen as a critical economic as well as military objective. As Deputy Secretary of Defense William P. Clements told Congress at the time, any slowdown in the arms export program "decreases the potential contribution of sales . . . to strengthening both free world security and the U.S. balance-of-payments position."[25]

If the rise in oil prices created new incentives for Washington to sell weapons, it also furnished the Shah with a vast increase in funds with which to buy them. Iranian income from oil exports rose from $6.3 billion in 1973 to $22 billion in 1974, and a large share of public funding—as much as 25 percent—was devoted to the acquisition of arms. While the Shah spoke in reasoned terms about Iran's role as "guardian" of Western oil supplies, there is no doubt that his arms-buying sprees were also motivated by a desire to convert Iran into a regional superpower. In 1971, he seized three strategic islands belonging to the United Arab Emirates at the entrance to the Gulf and in 1973 sent Iranian troops into Oman. He also began to build a navy capable of operating in the Indian Ocean and beyond. In 1974, at ceremonies marking the forty-second anniversary of the founding of the Imperial Iranian Navy, he affirmed, "In building up a modern navy our aim has not been confined to leadership in the Persian Gulf or Iran's territorial waters . . . because in the world today Iran enjoys a position which gives its duties regional dimension."[26] U.S. leaders did nothing to discourage the Shah's megalomania and indeed continued to provide the arms which made such ambitions credible. In 1974, for instance, Washington agreed to sell the Shah four missile-armed Spruance-class destroyers which were to be stationed at Chah Bahar on Iran's southeastern coast, affording direct access to the Arabian Sea and Indian Ocean.[27]

The Shah's appetite for arms was also fed by what can only be called an obsession with weaponry. A licensed pilot who often test-flew the warplanes he intended to buy, the Shah prided himself on his technical knowledge of military systems and made no effort to hide his zeal in buying arms—as demonstrated by this comment in a 1973 interview with Arnaud de Borchegrave:

> We now have 80 *Phantoms* which cost $2.5 million each, and another 100 coming in that will cost $5 million each that will give us a fighter-bomber force of well over 300. We've ordered 700 choppers, including 200 gunships plus 10 large *Chinooks* and 18 ASW [antisubmarine warfare] Sikorskys. . . . We're also buying 800 *Chieftain* tanks from Britain which will cost us another $480 million and meanwhile we're modernizing the 400 M-47 tanks that we have. That will give us a tank force of about 1,700.[28]

Nor did he have to worry about congressional budget-cutters or worried Treasury officials when he went shopping for still more arms. "What the Shah wants, he gets," one American arms salesman observed in 1974. "There are no inter-service rivalries or bureaucratic squabbles, either. He decides what he wants and those under him carry out his orders—or else."[29]

With Washington anxious to recover as many petrodollars as possible, and with the Shah eager to modernize Iranian military forces as quickly as possible, Iran soon became the principal overseas outlet for U.S. arms. At this point, a new factor entered the arms picture: greed. As the SFRC noted in 1976, "The 1972 [Nixon] sales decision coupled with the increase in Iranian revenues following the quadrupling of oil prices created a situation not unlike that of bees swarming around a pot of honey. Defense industries, both U.S. and foreign, rushed to Iran to persuade the Government to procure their products."[30] With such large contracts in the offing, and many companies competing for the same order, it is hardly surprising that some of them took shortcuts in the marketing process. True, a certain amount of corruption had always been present in Iran, but none of this ever approached the multi-million-dollar bribes and "commissions" paid by U.S. arms firms to secure Iranian military contracts. Grumman reportedly paid as much as $28 million in commissions to Iranian government officials while negotiating its $2 billion sale of F-14s, and Northrop shelled out at least $10 million to expedite sales of its F-5E fighter and other military equipment.[31] (Both companies were later forced to compensate the Iranian government for some of these funds when the payments became public knowledge in 1976.) Other U.S. firms, including Rockwell International and McDonnell-Douglas, were also accused of paying bribes to Iranian officials or unnamed "agents" in the course of arms negotiations, and it is safe to assume that Iranian officials pocketed much of the $200 million which U.S. arms companies reportedly paid to foreign sales agents between 1972 and 1975.[32]

Although the military services lacked purely pecuniary motives for generating arms sales, they had their own reasons for promoting particular sales transactions. Since the U.S. government regularly billed Iran for a share of the development costs of any arms sold to the Shah, Iranian orders could result in a significant reduction in the price paid by the services for their own supplies of that item. And since the various services are often forced to compete with one another for limited Pentagon funds, a major sale to Iran could result in the procurement of one service's product at the expense of the other's. For this reason, the services often sent their own representatives to Iran to assist allied defense contractors in marketing their products, and in some instances this resulted, according to the SFRC, "in fierce competition between the U.S. services." In the case of the proposed F-14/F-15 sale, for instance, the U.S. Navy (sponsor of the F-14) and the U.S. Air Force (sponsor of the F-15) both sent teams to Iran in an effort to secure an Iranian purchase. As a consequence, "vociferous and often conflicting advice was being freely offered to the Iranian military establishment and the Shah by a host of U.S. actors, including the U.S. Navy, the U.S. Air Force, and U.S. weapons manufacturers, each of whom had vested interests in selling Iran different weapons systems."[33]

This is not the kind of atmosphere that would promote restraint, and there is no doubt that high Iranian military officials became immensely wealthy as a result of the American arms programs. One knowledgeable U.S. official, writing in *Armed Forces Journal*, observed:

> Senior military officers obtained vast wealth from commissions. . . . The Shah's brother-in-law and then head of the Air Force, Mohammed Khatemi, became involved in highly publicized contingency deals for Air Force purchases which netted him millions. The Vice Minister of War for Armaments, General Hassan Toufanian, acquired equal visibility for similar commission operations. Lower level officials took their cuts, and money began to pour into safe hiding places in the West.[34]

Corruption on this scale could not be concealed forever, and by 1976 it was common knowledge that high government officials—including members of the royal family—were on the take. Although the Shah belatedly tried to disassociate himself from the spreading infection by arresting a few cronies whose extortions could no longer be hidden, his government had become irreparably tarnished, and he began to lose the support of the smaller merchants and businesspeople who suffered from the omnipresent corruption.[35]

The Gathering Storm

By the late 1970s, the U.S.-Iranian arms program was proving counterproductive in other ways. Back in the halcyon days of 1973–74, the Shah had become accustomed to spending Iran's new oil wealth as if the petrodollars would go on accumulating forever; by 1975–76, however, the West was deep into recession—caused largely by the OPEC oil price rise—and sales of Iranian oil began to decline. Not willing to curtail his massive arms programs, and disinclined to listen to the advice of his economists, the Shah went on buying arms as if his wealth was inexhaustible. Thus, while Iran's oil exports dropped by 12½ percent in 1975, the Shah ordered a 26 percent increase in government spending—with much of the increase going for arms and other military-related projects.[36] The results were predictable: inflation, already a problem in newly affluent Iran, soared out of control. By 1977, it was running at the rate of 30 percent a year, far outstripping wage increases for most salaried workers.[37] Civil servants, oil workers, rank-and-file soldiers, and most of the middle class experienced a drop in real wages at the same time that knowledge of high-level corruption was becoming prevalent. Although the Shah briefly cut back on arms spending, his persistence in buying foreign arms at a time of widespread belt-tightening at home provoked considerable resentment.

Such resentment was particularly acute with regard to the Shah's efforts to create a modern military-industrial complex in Iran. By 1976, he had signed contracts with several U.S. and British firms to begin construction of new arms factories in Iran. Thus Westinghouse and Hughes Aircraft had been wedded with the state-owned Iran Electronics Industry to build a missile repair and assembly plant in Shiraz, and Bell Helicopter was commissioned to construct an entire helicopter industry in Isfahan. And this was just the beginning: before he was forced out of the country in 1979, the Shah had announced plans to establish an indigenous aerospace industry and a tank production facility.[38] These projects were described by the Shah as the cutting edge of his efforts to introduce modern industrial technology into Iran, but many Iranian intellectuals and economists viewed them as a diversion from less glamorous but more important civilian development programs. These critics argued that the Shah's military projects were creating a small enclave of capital-intensive, high-technology enterprises in an otherwise underdeveloped economy, at the same time that more broadly based and labor-intensive projects were being allowed to languish because of Iran's budget crunch. Ultimately, this dispute evolved into a wide-ranging debate over the benefits of what the Shah and his supporters called "modernization," which many Iranians viewed as the intrusion of foreign-dominated military ventures that contributed little to economic and social progress in Iran.[39]

At this point, the presence of large numbers of foreign technicians also began to be a serious problem. Weapons ordered in 1973 and 1974 began arriving at an ever-increasing pace in the mid-1970s, placing enormous strains on Iran's technical support infrastructure. "Mountains of munitions are piling up in Iranian docks and fields," columnist Jack Anderson observed in 1975. "Planes, helicopters, and other sophisticated weapons are left in crates for weeks, waiting to be assembled."[40] In response to this quandary, the Shah invoked his by now characteristic solution: he hired still more Americans to help straighten out the logistical mess. U.S. military technicians working on arms-related programs in Iran jumped from 2,750 in 1975 to 8,700 in 1978, an increase of 215 percent.[41] Other Americans (along with British, French, and West German specialists) were recruited to help manage Iran's overstrained transportation, communications, and energy systems. The conspicuous presence of affluent Westerners at a time of declining real income for most Iranians naturally created much bitterness. Moreover, these foreigners—recruited at high salaries and with lucrative expense accounts—began competing with middle-class Iranians for apartments in Tehran's already tight housing market, thus driving up rents and adding to the growing inflation. The resulting friction was further compounded by religious animosity, as the foreigners began introducing Western behavior patterns—public drinking, revealing clothing, sexually explicit movies, and so forth—that offended Iran's conservative Moslem population.[42]

Within the military itself, the Shah's recruitment policies provoked the alienation of junior officers, cadets, and technicians who found themselves under the *de facto* supervision of foreigners. When we recall the SFRC's finding that "it is unlikely that Iran could go to war . . . without U.S. support on a day-to-day basis," we can appreciate the humiliation and resentment that these fiercely nationalistic young officers must have felt when ordered to obey the instructions of American civilians. Indeed, the Shah's arms program began to cause profound divisions in the Iranian military—once viewed as a monolithic prop to the regime.

As the divisions in Iranian society began to surface, some U.S. analysts tried to warn senior policymakers of the risks posed by the continuing arms program. In 1977, Theodore Moran, an economist on the State Department's policy planning staff, wrote an internal memorandum predicting that Iran "will face rising social and economic tensions unless it reorients government spending." Noting that the Shah was devoting 25 percent of public funds to military purchases, Moran wrote that the regime "will have insufficient financial resources to head off mounting political dissatisfaction, including discontent among those groups that have traditionally been the bedrock of support for the monarchy. . . ." To cope with this problem, Moran proposed that Washington persuade the Shah "to slow down and stretch out the building up of his military forces," so as "to give him more time and more resources to build a cohesive, prosperous (and nonrepressive) domestic base for his defense effort."[43] Similar views were expressed by the staff of the Senate Foreign Relations Committee, and by a number of U.S. lawmakers who were aware of conditions inside Iran.[44]

But even if, for some, the handwriting was on the wall, Washington clung to its faith in the durability of the Shah's rule. By the time Jimmy Carter became president, American policy in the Gulf area had become so rooted in the Surrogate Strategy that U.S. leaders could not conceive of any alternative. Given that "the basic premise underlying America's almost unquestioning support for the Shah of Iran was that he was a rock of stability in a highly volatile region of increasing importance to the United States," Andrew Pierre noted in 1982, there was "little inclination in Washington to question the solidity of the Shah's position in his country until quite late in the regime. . . ."[45] Indeed, even when the signs of discontent were impossible to ignore, U.S. leaders were negotiating the sale of still more high-tech arms to the Shah. In November 1977, Carter met with the Shah in Washington and reaffirmed the "special relationship" decreed by Richard Nixon in 1972, whereby the United States agreed to sell Iran whatever U.S. arms the Shah desired.[46] Nine months later, the Shah returned to Washington to work out the terms of yet another major arms purchase, this one estimated to be in the $10–$12 billion range.[47] Before the final details could be settled, however, the Shah was forced back to Tehran to deal with the accelerating domestic crisis.

By early 1978, the long-simmering revolt against the Shah had come out into the open, as students and young workers took to the streets in ever-larger numbers. The demonstrations first broke out in January 1978, when troops opened fire on protesting religious students in the holy city of Qom, and recurred at forty-day intervals in accordance with the traditional Moslem mourning cycle. Thousands of unarmed civilians lost their lives in these confrontations, and many more were wounded or hauled off to Iran's notorious prisons. Gradually more and more segments of Iranian society joined in these protests, until it appeared that the entire population was united in its opposition to the Shah.

As the protests were gaining momentum, American arms sales again became controversial when Iranian troops used their U.S.-supplied weapons against unarmed civilians. Just as the Shah was ordering martial law throughout Iran, the Carter administration announced an emergency delivery of riot sticks, tear gas, helmets, and shields to the Iranian army, thus providing a highly visible sign of U.S. support for the faltering regime.[48] Once Iranian troops were ordered to occupy Iranian cities, moreover, the distinction between arms supplied for conventional defensive purposes and those for internal security rapidly disappeared. As army units patrolled the streets in their American tanks and armored vehicles, the United States became irretrievably identified with the Shah's bloody efforts to retain power. It is hardly surprising, therefore, that the anti-Shah demonstrations eventually took on an anti-American cast as well.

Long before the Shah's final departure on January 16, 1979, it had become painfully obvious that the extraordinary U.S.-Iranian arms relationship would never be restored to its original stature. With oil production approaching zero, and the economy devastated by months of turmoil, there was no money left in the Iranian treasury with which to pay for imported arms. (Most of the millions acquired by Iranian officials through shady arms transactions had, of course, long been sequestered in numbered bank accounts in Switzerland.) Even the Shah's hand-picked successor, Dr. Shapur Bakhtiar, was forced to announce (on January 3, 1979) that Iran would no longer serve as "the gendarme of the Persian Gulf."[49] The final ascendancy of the "revolutionary government" of Mehdi Bazargan on February 11, 1979, only signaled the *coup de grace* to the Surrogate Strategy.

Looking back, it is not hard to see how the U.S. arms program exacerbated, and in some cases created, the problems that led to the monarchy's collapse. As we have seen, a number of U.S. analysts warned that excessive arms spending was contributing to the regime's difficulties. The Senate Foreign Relations Committee study of 1976 (cited throughout this chapter) provided numerous indicators of the deteriorating situation. But Washington's hands had effectively become tied by its unwavering commitment to the Surrogate Strategy: once having contracted with the Shah to assume responsibility for policing the Gulf on America's behalf, it could take no action that would alienate the Shah or diminish his authority at home without threatening the survival of the strategy itself.

While there are many things that the Iranian experience can teach us, perhaps the greatest lesson to be learned is that arms transfers, improperly managed, can cause as much damage to U.S. interests as they ostensibly provide benefits. Indeed, the ultimate demise of U.S. policy in Iran can be attributed, in no small degree, to Washington's tendency to heap one mammoth expectation after another onto the arms transfer program. Of the ten "primal motives" for U.S. arms sales described in chapter 10, all were operant in the Iranian case—thus explaining the massive scale of U.S. transfers between 1970 and 1978. But if U.S. arms exports were expected to provide a multitude of benefits for the United States, they often proved, in practice, to produce the very opposite of their intended effect. Rather than improve Iran's security, they weakened the economy and thus diminished it; rather than strengthen the Shah's rule, they provoked discontent and thus weakened it; rather than enhance U.S. leverage, they tied U.S. policy so closely to the fate of the Shah that in the end he, and not Washington, called the shots on key issues.

In the final analysis, the Iranian case demonstrates that arms transfers cannot, by themselves, perform the many feats attributed to them in the absence of a supportive web of political and economic relationships. Had the Shah enjoyed the support of his people, and had he pursued a defense strategy that meshed with Iran's true economic and industrial capacities, then U.S. arms transfers, in modest quantity, could have contributed to Iran's security and stability. Lacking such props, Washington sought to fill the vacuum with arms—and then more arms. These ever more conspicuous transfers created an impression of strength, but in fact each new sale exacerbated Iran's internal frictions and thus weakened the regime rather than reinforced it. As Sen. Joseph R. Biden, Jr., of Delaware observed in a 1982 round table at the American Enterprise Institute, U.S. arms transfers have often given foreign leaders "a false sense of security"—and no one more than the Shah. "We kidded ourselves [in Iran], and we allowed the Shah to kid himself. We had $30 billion of the most sophisticated arms in the world in Iran [and] without a shot being fired, the Shah was marched out of the country." While one may argue with this analysis (as with Biden's assertion that the Shah was deposed without any shots being fired), few would question his parting observation that now "all those arms are lying dormant," or are being used "in a way that may be inimical to our interests."[50]

CHAPTER 7

After the Shah

U.S. Arms Sales to the Middle East in the 1980s

The collapse of the Pahlavi dynasty in January 1979 presented the Carter administration with a warning and an opportunity. The warning was unmistakable: U.S. reliance on surrogate gendarmes to protect vital overseas interests entails grave risks and consequences. Not only did the U.S. arms program help intensify the militarization of Iranian society and thereby contribute to the political isolation of the Shah, but it also, in the end, left a huge stockpile of modern arms in the hands of people with a pronounced anti-American bias. The opportunity was also unambiguous: with Iran no longer in a position to purchase American weapons, Washington could finally realize the significant reductions in U.S. military exports envisioned by President Carter's "arms restraint" policy of May 19, 1977. Because the Shah had accounted for such a large proportion of U.S. arms orders in the 1970s, the termination of Iranian sales—if not offset by increased purchases from other countries—would ensure the success of the presidential restrictions. However, Carter chose to ignore both the warning and the opportunity—thereby setting the stage for continuing crises over U.S. arms sales to the Middle East that have gripped Washington periodically ever since.

For nearly a decade, from 1970 to 1978, Iran was the principal customer for U.S. arms in the Third World and the principal defender of U.S. interests in the Persian Gulf. During the peak sales years of 1973 to 1978, Iranian arms orders averaged an impressive $3.2 billion per year (in current dollars), or about 28 percent of all FMS orders worldwide. And this was to be just the beginning: as part of the U.S. strategy of converting Iran into a surrogate gendarme, the Shah was invited to select a whole array of even more sophisticated American weapons in his next round of multi-billion-dollar purchases. According to some sources, Iranian purchases in 1979–80 would total as much as $15 billion—far more than had ever been spent by any Third World country on imported arms before. It is hardly surprising, therefore, that the Shah's downfall precipitated a major crisis in American foreign policy and reportedly sent "shock waves" through the arms export establishment.[1]

On a strategic level, the Shah's collapse called into question the entire policy of relying on surrogate gendarmes to protect American interests in critical Third World areas. Because a diminished U.S. military role in the Middle East was considered unthinkable by most policymakers, the defense establishment was given the urgent task of developing an alternative strategic design for the region. At the same time, U.S. arms officials were left with an estimated $8–$10 billion in outstanding Iranian orders—including several billion dollars' worth of advanced aircraft and ships already under construction—plus all of the issues raised by the sudden liquidation of the Shah's $15 billion shopping list.

Mindful of the warning conferred by the Shah's demise, some U.S. leaders counseled against any new military partnerships of the type previously undertaken with Iran. Speaking of an administration proposal regarding Egypt, for example, Sen. Frank Church warned that "the last thing we want to do is build up a new military colossus out there and then find it turning out like Iran with Sadat no longer president and the whole place in chaos."[2] But such restraint would have taken the wind out of the military export boom and threatened some Pentagon arms programs that had been undertaken with the assurance of future Iranian purchases of the items involved. Rather than risk a long-term decline in foreign sales, therefore, U.S. arms producers and their allies in the military establishment pressured the administration to seek new customers for all of the equipment originally destined for Iran. In doing so, they brandished all the justifications for arms sales described in chapter 2: military burden-sharing, political influence, access to bases, balance of payments, and the rest. Indeed, nowhere else have these justifications been advanced with such determination and persistence as in connection with sales to the Middle East.[3]

Besieged by all of these pressures, President Carter abandoned any hope he might have retained of reducing U.S. arms exports and endorsed the search for new arms customers in the Middle East. To facilitate the establishment of new arms-supply arrangements, Carter sent Secretary of Defense Harold Brown on an extended tour of the Middle East and dropped all remaining U.S. inhibitions on the export of high-tech hardware to the region. Within a year of the Shah's demise, major new arms agreements were signed with Morocco, North Yemen, Oman, Somalia, the Sudan, and Tunisia, and the existing U.S. supply relationships with Egypt, Israel, and Saudi Arabia were significantly expanded. When added together, these new orders canceled out the entire shortfall in Iranian purchases and also reconfirmed America's status as the leading supplier of arms and military equipment to the Middle East.

The United States had been a conspicuous supplier to other Middle Eastern countries before 1979, of course, but the loss of the Iranian market produced a profound shift in the pattern of U.S. arms exports. Prior to 1978, only Iran, Israel, and Saudi Arabia stood out as major U.S. clients in the region, and only Iran and Israel were permitted to buy any of America's more advanced hardware. In 1978, the Carter administration engineered a precedent-setting sale of combat aircraft to Egypt and Saudi Arabia (as part of the $5 billion "jet package" that also included significant sales to Israel), but this was viewed as an isolated transaction rather than as part of established arms-supply relationships. Only after Brown's extraordinary 1979 trip to the Middle East did the United States became a regular supplier of high-tech weaponry to a whole cluster of the region's major powers.

Today, as it has been for a decade, the Middle East is the number one market for American arms. As shown in table 6, Middle Eastern countries accounted for $57 billion in new FMS orders between 1970 and 1979, or exactly two-thirds of America's total world export business during that period.[4] This general pattern has not changed appreciably in the 1980s, with Middle Eastern orders continuing to account for a large percentage of FMS orders.[5] Total U.S. sales to the Middle East from 1955 to 1982 came to an astounding $84.1 billion, or eight times the total value of all U.S. arms exports to all countries during the quarter-century following World War II.[6]

The United States is not, of course, the only arms supplier to the Middle East. Prompted by many of the same motives that sustain U.S. sales, other major suppliers—including France, Great Britain, Italy, the Soviet Union, and West Germany—have also attempted to increase their exports to the region during the past decade. The successive OPEC price increases have proved an especially powerful motive for increased sales by the European countries, and the continuing competition between the superpowers for influence in the region has helped drive up Soviet sales. As a result, the Middle East has become the world's premier weapons market, accounting for approximately half of all arms transfers to the Third World between 1976 and 1980—a figure that does not reflect the very large number of weapons ordered but not delivered during this period (see table 7).[7] Even excluding undelivered items, however, the Middle East's net arms inflow was prodigious: between 1975 and 1982, these countries acquired 13,103 tanks and self-propelled guns, 23,115 armored per-

Table 6. U.S. Arms Sales to the Middle East, Fiscal 1955–82
(million current dollars)

Arms Transfer Agreements under the Foreign Military Sales Program

Recipient	1955–69	1970–79	1980–82	1955–82
Bahrain	—	$ 0.1	$ 12.4	$ 12.5
Egypt	0.4	1,630.5	4,732.7	6,363.6
Iran	656.8	14,015.5	—	14,672.3 ª
Iraq	13.2	—	—	13.2
Israel	534.8	8,540.1	1,360.8	10,435.7
Jordan	118.2	863.7	851.3	1,833.2
Kuwait	—	726.9	277.7	1,004.6
Lebanon	2.7	67.7	95.9	166.3
Libya	20.9	8.7	—	29.6
Morocco	24.4	464.4	326.0	814.8
Oman	—	2.7	97.8	100.5
Pakistan	76.4	381.2	1,613.3	2,070.9
Saudi Arabia	779.1	30,011.6	14,152.5	44,943.2
Sudan	—	320.5	136.8	457.3
Tunisia	2.9	83.5	384.4	470.8
United Arab Emirates	—	5.3	384.8	390.1
Yemen (North)	—	318.2	36.9	355.1
Total	2,229.8	57,440.6	24,463.3	84,133.7

SOURCE: U.S. Department of Defense, *Foreign Military Sales, Foreign Military Construction Sales and Military Assistance Facts*, 1979 and 1982 editions; includes military construction agreements.

ª Figures for Iran reflect cancellations by successors to the Shah.

sonnel carriers (APCs) and armored cars, 3,485 supersonic combat planes, and 23,421 surface-to-air missiles (see table 8).[8] When added to existing stockpiles, these acquisitions have made the Middle East a near-equal of the two European military blocks in total holdings of conventional weaponry and superior to NATO in such categories as numbers of tanks and tactical aircraft.[9]

Arms transfers on this scale would undoubtedly have immense political and military importance even if the weapons involved were not of the most recent vintage; what has made the Middle Eastern sales so profoundly significant, however, is the fact that so many are of the most advanced type available. Indeed, U.S. exports to the Middle East have involved some of America's most sophisticated weapons, including the McDonnell-Douglas F-15 Eagle interceptor (sold to Israel and Saudi Arabia), the General Dynamics F-16 multi-role fighter (sold to Egypt, Israel, and Pakistan), the Boeing E-3A AWACS surveillance plane (sold to Saudi Arabia), the M-60A3 tank (sold to Egypt, Israel, Jordan, and Morocco), and a wide selection of U.S. missiles, antiaircraft guns, and artillery systems. Similar equipment, such as late-model Mirage fighters and MiG interceptors, has been supplied by the other major arms suppliers.[10] As a result, the combined Middle Eastern arsenals are beginning to match those of NATO and the Warsaw Pact in quality as well as in quantity.

While the European arsenals have remained relatively untouched, however, the Middle Eastern stockpiles have been used in combat time and again since World War II. After each major war, moreover, these stockpiles have been replenished with larger supplies of even more sophisticated equipment. In the eight years following the Arab-Israeli War of 1973, for instance, the major Middle Eastern powers doubled their inventories of modern tanks, aircraft, and missiles.[11] The United States, which supplied the bulk of this new hardware, has claimed that such sales are intended to promote regional stability by rectifying any arms imbalances that might invite aggression. However, the $28 billion in U.S. arms delivered to these countries in the 1970s did not prevent the Iran-Iraq war of 1980–82, the 1982 Israeli invasion of Lebanon, or any of the lesser conflicts that have occurred in recent years. If anything, these deliveries exacerbated local tensions, encouraged preemptive action by the more aggressive powers, and ensured that such wars as did occur were fought at ever-increasing levels of violence and destructiveness.

Despite the awesome carnage of the Iran-Iraq war and the 1982 Lebanon conflict, there does not appear to be any diminution in the Middle East's quest for armaments. If the post-1973 war experience is any indication, the conflicts of the 1980s will be followed by another massive spurt in arms purchases. Indeed, the U.S. Department of Defense estimated in early 1982 that FMS sales to the Middle East would rise by 125 percent from 1980–81 to 1982–83, from $11.7 billion to a record two-year total of $26.5 billion.[12] Sales by the other major suppliers are likely to rise accordingly, leading to another doubling of Middle Eastern arms inventories by the end of the decade. As before, these sales will be justified on the grounds that they are needed to promote stability and peaceful change; but, as before, they are just as likely to produce new tensions and new incentives for war. No one can predict when and under what circumstances such conflicts will occur, but one can reasonably suppose that they will prove even more destructive than the wars of the early 1980s.

Table 7. Arms Transfers to the Middle East, 1976–80, by Major Supplier (million current dollars)

Recipient	All suppliers, Total	Soviet Union	United States	France	United Kingdom
Middle East, Total	38,600	12,500	14,200	3,500	2,700
Bahrain	40	—	5	20	—
Cyprus	10	—	—	—	—
Egypt	1,900	20	430	600	180
Iran	8,300	625	6,200	200	250
Iraq	7,800	5,000	—	950	90
Israel	4,300	—	4,300	—	60
Jordan	1,000	—	725	—	280
Kuwait	800	50	390	130	220
Lebanon	80	—	40	10	20
Oman	430	—	10	—	400
Qatar	170	—	5	70	90
Saudi Arabia	4,700	—	2,000	700	975
Syria	6,600	5,400	—	290	100
United Arab Emirates	575	—	20	450	60
Yemen (Aden)	775	775	—	—	—
Yemen (Sanaa)	1,100	625	170	80	—

SOURCE: U.S. Arms Control and Disarmament Agency, *World Military Expenditures and Arms Transfers, 1971–1980* (1983); indicates deliveries of arms, ammunition, and related equipment; excludes services and construction.

NOTE: Totals may not add due to rounding.

More than in any other region, the American public has a tremendous stake in the orientation of U.S. arms policy toward the Middle East. A rational, prudent policy can help promote peace in the region while ensuring a steady supply of petroleum to the United States and its allies; an irrational, imprudent policy can promote discord, intensify the violence of future conflicts, and jeopardize the steady flow of oil. Moreover, because the two superpowers are so deeply involved in the military affairs of this region, a future conflict in the Middle East could easily provide the fatal spark that would trigger World War III. It is obvious, therefore, that we need to take a very close look at the major U.S. arm-supply relationships in the Middle East and identify any policy initiatives that might conceivably reduce the risk of conflagration.

West Germany	Czecho-slovakia	Italy	Poland	Switzer-land	Yugo-slavia	Others
1,400	525	675	140	250	675	2,000
—	—	5	—	—	—	20
—	—	—	—	—	5	5
370	10	60	—	—	—	230
380	—	300	—	100	—	250
160	90	130	30	10	675	625
—	—	30	—	—	—	—
5	—	—	—	—	—	50
—	—	—	—	—	—	10
5	—	—	—	—	—	10
—	—	—	—	—	—	10
—	—	—	—	—	—	10
350	—	150	—	130	—	380
100	440	—	10	—	—	280
40	—	10	—	—	—	10
—	—	—	—	—	—	10
10	—	5	100	—	—	100

Harold Brown's Pilgrimage to the Middle East: The Search for Substitute Markets

The collapse of the Pahlavi dynasty on January 16, 1979, rocked the U.S. national security community as a whole, but proved especially traumatic for the arms export establishment. To begin with, U.S. firms were then at work on an estimated $8–$10 billion worth of advanced arms for Iran, including many custom-designed items that could not be easily diverted to other buyers. At first, U.S. officials entertained hopes that the successor government of Shapur Bakhtiar could be persuaded to reconfirm these orders, but all such hopes were dashed on February 11 when Bakhtiar was overthrown and the new government of Mehdi Bazargan—acting on orders of

Table 8. Deliveries of Major Weapons Systems to the Near East and South Asia, 1975–82

Weapons Category	Quantities delivered by:			
	United States	U.S.S.R.	"Big 4" W. Europe[a]	Total, U.S., U.S.S.R., Big 4
Tanks & self-propelled guns	4,933	7,040	1,130	13,103
Artillery pieces	1,967	7,670	1,050	10,687
APCs and armored cars[b]	11,015	9,450	2,650	23,115
Major surface combat ships	9	26	21	56
Minor surface combat ships	35	27	139	201
Submarines	1	6	5	12
Supersonic combat aircraft	785	2,330	370	3,485
Subsonic combat aircraft	179	190	50	419
Other aircraft	460	150	300	910
Helicopters	198	900	1,045	2,143
Guided missile boats	0	49	33	82
Surface-to-air missiles	6,311	15,000	2,110	23,421

SOURCE: Congressional Research Service, *Trends in Conventional Arms Transfers to the Third World by Major Supplier, 1975–82* (1983).

[a] France, United Kingdom, West Germany, Italy.

[b] APCS = armored personnel carriers.

the Ayatollah Ruhollah Khomeini—canceled all outstanding arms agreements with the United States. Beyond these existing orders, moreover, there were all those billions of dollars' worth of future orders that the U.S. arms industry had come to rely on to maintain a high level of productivity. These two problems—the status of the Shah's unfinished and undelivered merchandise and the loss of a major overseas market—combined to produce the greatest crisis in U.S. arms export policy since the onset of the sales program in the early 1950s.[13]

As suggested earlier, some U.S. policymakers urged caution in responding to this crisis, lest—in its rush to dispose of surplus arms—the United States helped create "another Iran." Such appeals were drowned out by all the voices calling for a vigorous export program, however, and President Carter ordered the secretary of defense to overcome the crisis as quickly and expediently as possible. Brown's first task was to dispose of all the equipment ordered by the Shah but not yet produced or delivered. According to U.S. officials, the $8–$10 billion in outstanding Iranian orders as of January

1979 included 160 F-16 fighters worth an estimated $3.5 billion (of which only 55 had as yet been formally contracted for); 4 Spruance-class guided missile destroyers worth $2 billion; 16 RF-4 reconnaissance planes worth $130 million; 400 Phoenix air-to-air missiles worth $300 million; and 208 Harpoon antiship missiles worth $117 million.[14]

Iran had made "progress payments" on some of these items, and an estimated $500 million in Iranian funds remained in the Foreign Military Sales Trust Fund as insurance against possible cancellations, but the problem of disposing of this hardware nonetheless appeared formidable. In theory, the administration could have used the money in the Trust Fund to make termination payments on all the projects and allowed the contractors to dispose of the leftover hardware as they saw fit, but this does not seem to have been seriously considered. Instead, Brown used these funds to continue production of the items involved while seeking alternative buyers for the finished products.[15]

To simplify this task, Brown invited the U.S. military services to bid on any of the equipment they wished for their own use. Thence ensued what columnist Jack Anderson called "the Great Iranian Fire Sale"—a stampede by military officials to pick up high-quality merchandise at bargain-basement prices.[16] The U.S. Navy set its sights on the four Spruance-class destroyers and the Phoenix missiles (to arm its F-14 Tomcat fighters), and the U.S. Army and U.S. Air Force picked out some of the remaining equipment. Before this hardware could be turned over to the services, however, Brown had something of a financial problem to overcome: the equipment in question had not been fully paid for by the Iranians, and Congress had never voted funds for the acquisition of these additional items. To get around this roadblock, Brown persuaded Carter to request a supplemental defense appropriation of $765 million from Congress—a move denounced by some lawmakers as a "bailout" of the arms industry by U.S. taxpayers.[17] Despite such criticism, Congress ultimately voted the extra funds and Brown had half of his problem solved.

To dispose of the remaining undelivered merchandise, Brown next looked abroad. Of greatest concern to the secretary was the order of 55 F-16 fighters then being assembled at General Dynamics' Fort Worth factories. Several other countries had expressed interest in buying F-16s, but the negotiation and review process (not to mention possible congressional debate) could take years rather than the months he had in which to come up with a buyer. However, there was one country—Israel—that had already signed up to buy F-16s and that had received the necessary congressional approval. Israel's first batch of F-16s was not due to be delivered (and fully paid for) until 1981, two years later, but Brown asked the Israelis to take over the Iranian contract and thereby receive their first F-16s two years early, in late 1979.[18] This offer was of obvious interest to the Israelis, who quickly agreed to Brown's proposal.* With the F-16s disposed of and other buyers found to absorb what remained of the leftover Iranian merchandise, Brown could now turn his attention to the second major problem resulting from the Shah's demise: how to cope with the loss of all those future orders which had promised steady work for America's arms industries.

In solving this problem, Brown adopted a novel approach: he went out "on the road" personally to sign up new customers for American arms. On February 9, 1979, he left Washington for a ten-day tour of the Middle East, the first ever by an American secretary of defense. While the ostensible aim of his journey was to reassure pro-Western governments that the United States remained a credible ally despite its inability to save the Shah, the secretary was accompanied by the nation's top arms export official, Lt. Gen. Ernest Graves of the Defense Security Assistance Agency, and future arms transactions were the principal topic of conversation in each of the four countries—Saudi Arabia, Jordan, Israel, and Egypt—he visited. And while most of these conversations took place behind the closed doors of ministerial conference rooms, Brown did on one occasion reveal the gist of his bargaining position: in a speech to cadets at Saudi Arabia's top military academy, he lauded the Arabs for assuming a more assertive role in world affairs and then declared, "We welcome your new role. We can provide the best training and equipment in the world. We will do so."[19]

Brown's first stop was Riyadh, and he wasted no time in bringing this message to the Saudis. The United States had already sold Saudi Arabia some advanced equipment, including 60 McDonnell-Douglas F-15 supersonic interceptors, but Brown now offered a much more comprehensive program of arms transfers. In essence, the secretary proposed that Saudi Arabia take over some of Iran's peacekeeping functions in the Gulf area in return for additional arms and military assistance from the United States. This would not involve

---

*In one of those recurring ironies of the arms trade, the Iranians' decision to cancel the F-16 commitment ultimately wound up aiding their newly sworn enemy, Israel. By taking up the Shah's order of 55 planes, the Israelis acquired a decisive edge in tactical airpower—an advantage that was amply demonstrated in the 1982 Lebanon war.

an active Saudi role in stopping a Soviet (or Soviet-backed) invasion—that would be the job of American forces—but rather a more modest role in combating local insurgencies and tribal conflicts that could threaten the oil flow. The Saudis, who had reasons of their own to assume such a role—the Islamic upheaval in Iran had sent off ripples of unrest throughout the Moslem world—wholeheartedly endorsed Brown's proposal.

Despite such agreement, the Saudis must also have pointed out the obvious: for Saudi Arabia to adopt a more activist role in the region, there would have to be a fundamental shift in the nature of the U.S. arms-supply relationship with their country. Previously, in deference to Israel and the pro-Israeli lobby in the United States, Washington had provided the Saudis with "defensive" equipment only; to perform the new role envisioned by Secretary Brown, however, the Saudis would require the supply of at least some offensive-type arms.* At a minimum, they would need long-range strike aircraft capable of penetrating enemy air defenses, plus some fully mechanized infantry forces and a limited naval capability. Such capabilities would enable Saudi Arabia to perform limited peacekeeping functions on the Arabian Peninsula and surrounding waters, but would also (and here was the basic pitfall in the new U.S. strategy) allow the Saudis to engage in offensive actions against Israel—a capability they did not have previously.

Given the inherent sensitivity of the whole subject, Brown did not disclose the results of his meeting with Saudi military leaders. On the basis of subsequent events, however, it is possible to infer that the Saudis gave Brown a list of the high-priority items on their military "wish list": external fuel tanks and bomb racks for their as yet undelivered F-15s (thereby converting the planes from mere interceptors into long-range strike aircraft with a close-support combat capability); more advanced air-to-air and air-to-surface guided missiles for their F-15s and F-5ES; aerial tankers for the refueling of Saudi combat planes; and sophisticated air defense systems, including an airborne radar platform of the AWACS type. So far as is known, Brown did not consent to any specific agreements for the sale of

---

*When the Carter administration asked Congress in 1978 to approve the sale of 60 F-15 jet fighters to Saudi Arabia, it emphatically stated that the aircraft would not be equipped with external fuel tanks, bomb racks, and other modifications that would permit the plane's use as a long-range ground-attack system. Other pre-1979 U.S. sales to Saudi Arabia involved internal-security hardware only or were similarly restricted to prevent their use as offensive weapons.

these items; but he must have told the Saudis that, in line with their upgraded role in the emerging U.S. security plan for the Gulf region, the United States would prove accommodating to requests for such hardware when they were presented through normal sales channels.[20] In any case, it was only a few months later that the Saudis presented the first of several requests for F-15 enhancement equipment and other sophisticated munitions—thereby touching off another crisis in U.S. arms export policy that was to persist well into the onset of the Reagan administration (see below).[21]

Although Brown and the Saudis did not come to any formal agreements on the sale of arms to Saudi Arabia itself, they did agree to a series of extraordinary deals involving sales to other countries. As part of its newly enhanced role in the promotion of regional stability, and to ensure the survival of friendly regimes, the Saudis agreed to finance the sale of advanced U.S. arms to several neighboring Moslem countries, including the Sudan and the Yemen Arab Republic (North Yemen).[22]

Earlier that year, South Yemeni forces had occupied some contested border areas of North Yemen, thereby provoking talk of a Soviet-inspired invasion. Although the "invasion" later turned out to be more of a border skirmish, and while no evidence was ever produced of Soviet prodding, the event was elevated by the Carter administration into a test of U.S. determination to combat Soviet intervention in the Gulf area; in consequence, Brown was instructed to tell the Saudis that Washington would furnish advanced arms to North Yemen if the Saudis were willing to pick up the bill. The Saudis, who feared a takeover of North Yemen by the Marxist-led South Yemenis (or, for that matter, by hostile factions of the North Yemeni leadership), agreed to finance the delivery of 12 F-5E fighters, 60 M-60 tanks, and 50 M-113 APCs for an estimated $383 million.[23]

For the Sudan, which was menaced by hostile forces in neighboring Ethiopia and Libya, the Saudis agreed to finance the delivery of 12 F-5E fighters and some related equipment in a package worth $188 million. As in the case of the North Yemeni agreement, this transaction was evidently designed to enhance Saudi Arabia's political influence in the region as much as to help defend a trusted ally against external attack.[24]

Having concluded these contracts of convenience with the Saudis, Brown flew on to Amman, where he met with King Hussein and other Jordanian officials. Here, too, there was much talk of U.S. concern for regional peace and stability, along with some hard bargaining behind closed doors. In Jordan's case, however, Brown had an added difficulty: because Israel opposed the sale to the Jordanians of any equipment that could be used in a combined Arab assault on their country (e.g., modern tanks, mobile air-defense systems, and long-range strike aircraft), he could not offer any of America's most advanced and capable systems with any assurance that Congress would go along with the sale. On the other hand, a failure to satisfy the Jordanians' desires for modern equipment could prompt Hussein to shop elsewhere—as he has often threatened and occasionally done—thereby diminishing U.S. influence. Accordingly, Brown tried to persuade Hussein to accept some of America's less-advanced hardware now with a promise of more advanced equipment later, when the political climate in the United States would be more amenable to such deliveries.[25] Hussein eventually extracted a tentative promise from Brown for the sale of 100 M-60A3 tanks and other ground combat equipment, but the problems raised by trying to balance conflicting Israeli and Jordanian security requirements persist to this day—as reflected in the flap produced in 1982 by Defense Secretary Weinberger's informal agreement to supply Jordan with F-16 fighters.*

From Jordan, Brown flew to Israel, where negotiations on new arms transactions were already well advanced. The secretary's first task was to work out the details of the accelerated F-16 delivery plan, a task that was evidently accomplished with no great difficulty. The Israelis then presented their latest shopping list for U.S. arms, and the real bargaining began. Included in the Israeli request were a wide variety of America's top-rated arms, including M-60A3 tanks, advanced-model AIM-9L Sidewinder air-to-air missiles, M-109 self-propelled 155-mm. howitzers, and a host of precision-guided munitions ("smart bombs"). These requests were anticipated by Brown, and while there may have been some haggling about costs and quantities, there was no real question about their ultimate delivery.[26]

---

*According to journalists who accompanied the secretary on his 1982 trip to the Middle East, Weinberger told government officials in Amman on February 13 that he would urge President Reagan to approve the sale of F-16s and other high-tech weaponry to Jordan. These reports provoked widespread alarm in Israel and considerable opposition in the U.S. Congress. Later, after Weinberger returned to Washington, administration officials indicated that it would only offer Jordan the less-advanced F-5G Tigershark.

The troubled U.S. arms-supply relationship with Jordan made headlines again in March 1984, when King Hussein declared that he would shop elsewhere if the terms of U.S. sales were demeaning to his country. "If the dignity of my country is in jeopardy, then thank you very much, we don't need the arms," he told the *New York Times*. "If the price is that the dignity of Jordan will be affected, then it's too big a price to pay."

The Israelis wanted more than arms, however. According to Pentagon officials who accompanied Brown on his visit, they asked for access to America's latest military technologies in order to modernize their domestic arms-making capabilities, as well as for formal recognition of Israel as America's leading strategic partner in the Middle East. The first request reflected Israel's desire to become more self-sufficient in the production of munitions and to reduce its outlays for imported arms. While this proposal clearly presented Washington with some potential economic and security problems (arising from Israel's stated ambition to become a major arms producer), its refusal would have diminished America's close ties to the Israeli military and so won grudging acceptance from Secretary Brown.[27] (See chapter 8 for discussion of the political, economic, and security implications of such technology transfers.) On the other matter, however, Brown was not so forthcoming. While the United States certainly viewed Israel as the most stable and reliable U.S. ally in the Middle East, American strategy called for the integration of the moderate Arab states into a regional security system of some sort, and this plan clearly precluded any sort of formal military alliance with Israel.[28] (In 1981, President Reagan agreed to a U.S.-Israeli accord of the type rejected by Brown in 1979.)

Secretary Brown's last and probably the most significant visit was to Cairo. Ever since President Sadat had ousted the Russians and Henry Kissinger had initiated his "shuttle diplomacy" between Israel and Egypt, the United States had been moving toward a closer political relationship with Sadat; not until the demise of the Shah, however, did that relationship acquire a significant military dimension. Sensing that Washington was avidly seeking new military partners to assure regional security in the wake of the Iranian upheaval, and believing that any country selected to perform such a role would be showered with modern weapons, Sadat literally pleaded with Brown to be chosen as the Shah's successor. "I don't want to see any foreign intervention in the Gulf," he later claimed to have told Brown, "I don't want to see any new threat to my brothers in the states of the Gulf."[29] Indeed, observers at the Cairo meetings reported that Sadat went much further, unveiling a sweeping plan whereby Egypt would serve as a regional gendarme in the vast area encompassing the Arabian Peninsula, the Horn of Africa, and the entire Saharan region. All this and more—if only the United States would agree to replace Egypt's aging Soviet military equipment with modern American weapons.[30]

Sadat's offer obviously had great attraction for the Carter administration. On one hand, the United States desperately sought new military partners to assume Iran's peacekeeping functions; on the other hand, it needed new arms markets to absorb all the future orders originally expected from the Shah. With certain limitations, Egypt fit the bill for both: it had a large, well-trained army with a staunch anti-Communist leadership and an almost limitless requirement for modern arms. It looked like an ideal arrangement, and Washington was quick to provide its blessing: upon learning of Sadat's offer, President Carter avowed that Egypt could provide "a legitimate stabilizing force in the area" and that Egyptian troops "might very well be used to preserve the peace" if another Middle Eastern country was threatened with aggression.[31] No doubt Brown made similar declarations in person.

But while Secretary Brown surely welcomed the Egyptian plan, he also recognized that there were some significant obstacles to its implementation. To begin with, Egypt was not a major oil producer like Iran and Saudi Arabia and thus lacked a steady source of cash with which to pay for its arms requirements. True, Kuwait and Saudi Arabia could be expected to subsidize some Egyptian purchases, as they had in the past, but this was not exactly an assured source of funds—especially if, as could easily happen, changing political positions produced a breach between Sadat and the other Arab governments. To make matters worse, Israel could be expected to oppose any significant improvement in Egyptian military capabilities, so Carter could anticipate considerable congressional resistance to any transfers of advanced equipment. As a result, Brown was forced to temper Sadat's expectations somewhat: the United States would begin to replace some of Egypt's obsolete Soviet arms with modern American arms, but not on the lavish scale proposed by Sadat, and not with the most advanced models available.[32] Later, when the new U.S.-Egyptian partnership had had a chance to mature, such advanced arms would be forthcoming; for the time being, however, Sadat would have to be content with second-best.

Not that second-best was all that meager: according to the Pentagon officials accompanying Brown on his visit to Cairo, the secretary promised Sadat that the United States would furnish Egypt with a vast array of U.S. weapons. The first priority would be basic combat gear to replace aging Soviet equipment: M-60 tanks, M-113 armored personnel carriers, TOW antitank missiles, Hawk air-defense missile systems, and assorted artillery pieces. To beef up the Egyptian air force, moreover, Washington would supply several dozen older-model fighters—presumably F-4 Phantoms.[33] This was far less than Sadat had hoped for, of course, but it was a substantial beginning, and, more important, it signaled the start of America's new role as Egypt's principal arms supplier. Formal ratification of this role would have to await the signing of a peace treaty with Israel (the final round of negotiations were then scheduled for mid-March, only one month away), but the groundwork for a new U.S.-Egyptian partnership had been established.

For Brown, the Cairo meetings climaxed an arduous but largely successful excursion to the Middle East. Not only had he laid the groundwork for a new military relationship with Saudi Arabia and Egypt, but he had also assured steady and reliable markets for all of the arms once intended for Iran. "I got done what I intended to do," he remarked upon arrival in Washington on February 19.[34] But while the White House was obviously pleased with the results of his journey, it soon became obvious that the various understandings and arrangements concluded by Brown created more problems for the United States than they had solved.

The Middle East Peace Treaty: Paving the Road to War

When Harold Brown returned to Washington from his Middle Eastern tour, he left behind the foundations for a qualitatively transformed U.S. arms-supply relationship with many of the nations of the area. Actual implementation of these arrangements, however, would require extensive bilateral negotiations with the governments involved, as well as exhaustive consultations with key members of Congress and the inevitable search for adequate financing. Most of all, however, it would require a new political framework that would confer popular legitimacy on these arrangements and thus elicit sufficient public support. That framework was provided by the Israeli-Egyptian peace treaty of March 26, 1979.

While the basic provisions of the peace treaty had already been worked out at Camp David before Brown left for the Middle East, the final details were not fully resolved until senior Israeli and Egyptian diplomats—accompanied by the defense ministers of the two nations—arrived in Washington in early March for a final round of negotiations. From what can be inferred today, these discussions centered on the scope and timing of the military aid to be provided by the United States as incentives for the treaty. On March 17 and 19, Secretary Brown met successively with Israeli Defense Minister Ezer Weizman and Egyptian Defense Minister Kamal Hassan Ali to negotiate the contents of the U.S. arms packages. Weizman was the first to emerge smiling from Brown's office on March 19, followed by Ali, who cheerfully announced the start of "a new military supply relationship" between his country and the United States.[35] With this issue settled, the stage was set for Prime Minister Begin and President Sadat to arrive in Washington for the final ceremonies.

The treaty was signed with appropriate fanfare on March 26, but it was not until several days later that the American public was informed of the full cost of the new U.S. aid commitments. On April 2, President Carter asked Congress to approve a special appropriation of $1.5 billion in order to finance nearly $5 billion in grants and loans to the treaty nations. These funds would be divided on an approximately 60/40 basis: Israel would receive $2.2 billion in new arms credits plus a direct grant of $800 million for the construction of new bases to replace those being relinquished in the Sinai, while Egypt would receive $1.5 billion in arms credits and a grant of $300 million for economic assistance.[36] This was no small amount, Secretary of State Cyrus Vance told the Senate Foreign Relations Committee on April 11, but it certainly did not compare with the cost of rearming Israel after each of its wars with the Arab states. "While peace is expensive," he declared, "war is more expensive."[37]

In the weeks that followed, Carter, Brown, and Vance lobbied Congress vigorously to endorse the $4.8 billion treaty package. In the process, they employed all the arguments normally used to justify arms sales abroad: that U.S. arms aid would promote regional peace and security, that it would enhance U.S. political leverage in Israel (and thus facilitate further Israeli concessions on other Middle Eastern issues), that it would ensure Egypt's loyalty to the West, that it would enable Egypt to help protect U.S. interests in the area, and so forth.[38] In justifying U.S. military aid to Egypt, for instance, Carter noted that the $41.5 billion in arms credits would help Cairo "to play a responsible role in promoting stability and modernization in the region."[39]

Although most U.S. lawmakers accepted the premise that some U.S. aid was needed to facilitate the peace process, not everyone agreed on the long-term benefits of such assistance. Noting that stepped-up U.S. aid to Israel and Egypt would undoubtedly generate insecurity in neighboring states, Sen. William Proxmire warned that the most likely result of the Middle East arms package would be an intensified arms race and a heightened risk of war. "This notion that we must provide military assistance to [these] nations," he declared, "is precisely what has led us down this long and bloody and reprehensible road of providing the weapons of death and destruction in the name of peace."[40] This theme was further developed by Sen. Jesse Helms of North Carolina, who challenged the administration's claim that increased U.S. aid would enhance Israeli confidence and thus reduce the risk of another Middle Eastern war. Suggesting that new U.S. arms transfers to Israel would surely provoke new Soviet deliveries to its allies in the region, Helms prophetically warned that "once the Israelis detect the buildup of Arab arms reaching a threatening point . . . they themselves will launch a surprise attack upon the Arabs, probably without warning even the United States."[41]

Despite these objections, Congress ultimately approved the treaty package, and U.S. officials began working out the details of the promised arms deliveries. On July 8, the administration announced that it had agreed to sell Egypt 35 F-4E Phantom fighter bombers, along with several hundred air-to-air and air-to-surface missiles, for an estimated $594 million.[42] Two weeks later, Washington unveiled another major package for Egypt, this one containing 550 M-113 APCS, 100 armored mortar carriers and command vehicles, and 12 batteries of Improved Hawk air-defense missiles. On this occasion, the Egyptian package was accompanied by a major sale to the Israelis: 200 M-60A3 tanks, 800 M-113 APCS, 200 M-109 howitzers, plus hundreds of air-to-air, air-to-surface, and surface-to-air missiles.[43]

As predicted by Proxmire, however, these transactions proved to be only the beginning of a continuing series of major arms transfers to Israel and Egypt. In September 1979, both Israel and Egypt presented U.S. authorities with new shopping lists for U.S. arms worth far more than the $3.7 billion in treaty-related arms credits.[44] The Israeli submission represented a predictable increment to earlier requests, but the Egyptian request was nothing short of amazing: according to some insiders, Sadat submitted a $10 billion "wish list" that included, among other items, 300 F-16 fighters, 600 tanks, and 2,000 armored personnel carriers.[45] At first, these requests were given a cool reception by administration officials; soon thereafter, however, events in Iran and Afghanistan inspired a new strategic turnaround in Washington, and thus the Israeli and Egyptian emissaries were called back for fresh talks on the proposed transactions.

The Iranian hostage seizure of November 1979, followed only six weeks later by the Soviet invasion of Afghanistan, had a traumatic impact on official Washington. Because these events underscored the decline of U.S. power in the region and posed a new threat to U.S. oil supplies, they induced a total transformation of U.S. strategy. The administration's new stance was first unveiled by the president in his State of the Union address of January 23, 1980, in which he affirmed that the United States was fully prepared to use military force to protect its Middle Eastern oil supplies. In what was quickly dubbed the Carter Doctrine, he declared that "an attempt by any outside force to gain control of the Persian Gulf region . . . will be repelled by any means necessary, including military force." But while ultimate responsibility for defense of the region would now fall on America's newly created Rapid Deployment Force (RDF), Washington would continue to rely on local powers to maintain regional stability. As part of the administration's new effort, Carter explained, additional arms aid would be provided to America's friends and allies in the region as part of a new "cooperative security framework" to be established by the United States.[46]

As many critics noted at the time, Carter's Mideast defense plan was a patchwork of pre-existing efforts (i.e., U.S. arms-supply programs with friendly countries in the area), as yet unproven military assets (the RDF), and hypothetical collaborative ventures (the so-called cooperative security framework).[47] But if there was anything about the plan that was certain, it was that it would involve additional arms transfers to the Middle East. As Assistant Secretary of State Harold H. Saunders observed in his testimony before the Senate Foreign Relations Committee on March 20, "our economic and security assistance programs are more important than ever" as the United States worked to "help governments in the area meet the threats to their security" arising from the events in Iran and Afghanistan.[48] U.S. arms were needed not only to buttress friendly governments, the White House explained, but also to ensure U.S. access to military bases in the area: in return for possible U.S. use of ports and airstrips in their country, Carter promised additional arms assistance to Egypt, Kenya, Oman, and Somalia.[49]

Implementation of the Carter Doctrine obviously implied a new U.S. arms-supply relationship with all friendly countries in the Middle East, but it had special meaning for the two treaty countries, and especially for Egypt. Desperately seeking new military partners in the region, administration strategists inevitably settled on Egypt as the only viable choice. To a large extent, this was simply due to the lack of credible alternatives: Saudi Arabia was too weak and preoccupied with internal Arab affairs to be of much help, and Israel— the most powerful country in the region—was viewed by friendly Arab states as a greater threat than Moscow.[50] Only Egypt had a potent military capability along with a leadership that was both Moslem and anti-Soviet. "You look around the region, and what else is there?" a senior U.S. official observed at the time. "There is Israel, but that presents all kinds of other problems; Egypt, after all, is an

Arab country."[51] On the basis of this sort of thinking, U.S. officials went back to the Egyptians with offers of an expanded military relationship.

The Egyptians, for their part, were more than willing to play a more vigorous role as America's agent in the area, but they also had their price: equality with Israel in the dissemination of U.S. arms. This demand emerged with considerable fervor in February 1980, when American officials flew to Cairo to discuss the sale of advanced U.S. combat planes to replace the aging MiGs in the Egyptian inventory. The U.S. negotiators offered the General Dynamics F-16 fighter, but Sadat insisted that he would be satisfied with nothing less than the F-15 Eagle—the most advanced aircraft in the U.S. arsenal, and a recent addition to the Israeli inventory.[52] In response, U.S. officials argued that the Egyptians were not ready to absorb anything as complex as the F-15, that it was extremely expensive ($20 million each for the F-15, compared to $12 million for the F-16), and that pro-Israeli forces in the American Congress would block the sale of anything so sophisticated to Egypt. Nevertheless, Sadat stood firm: no F-15, no military partnership with Egypt. Finally, after several days of intensive discussions, a compromise was worked out: the United States agreed "in principle" to sell Egypt the F-15, and Cairo agreed to decline this offer in favor of the more practical and economical F-16. This solution allowed Sadat to claim that Egypt had finally secured equality with Israel, while sparing Carter a grueling and possibly losing battle with Congress over the sale of F-15s.[53] And besides, the U.S. package (as finally prepared) was nothing to belittle: 40 F-16s worth an estimated $1 billion, along with 600 Maverick air-to-surface missiles, 244 M-60A3 tanks, 550 M-113 APCS, and a variety of other weapons.[54]

Although the F-15 solution provided substantially less than Sadat originally requested, it also contained significantly more than the United States had ever previously offered Cairo. As a result, it naturally provoked considerable disquiet in Israel, which had theretofore succeeded in persuading Washington to confine its Egyptian sales to second-string equipment. While the Israelis recognized that the United States owed Egypt some modern equipment as a reward for ejecting the Russians and signing the peace treaty, they were not prepared to countenance true equality when it came to the distribution of U.S. arms. Accordingly, the Begin government began efforts to block the sale of additional high-tech gear to the Egyptians. (When officially notified of the F-16 agreement, Begin told reporters in Tel Aviv that "we are having discussions with our American friends" about how to squelch the deal.)[55] When it was presented to the Congress, opponents brought out the now-familiar argument that Sadat could go the way of the Shah—thus leaving all that U.S. equipment in the hands of hostile forces. "Egypt could have F-16s under a new master," one congressional aide suggested.[56] In response, U.S. officials avowed that Sadat was a more reliable ally than the Shah because his pro-American policies enjoyed widespread popular support. "We're building here for the long haul," a senior U.S. diplomat observed, "on the assumption that we've got a firm foundation."[57]

On the basis of this assumption, Washington followed the F-16 transaction with one new arms package after another. Following the assassination of Anwar Sadat, for instance, the Reagan administration immediately promised the successor regime of Hosni Mubarek a wide variety of modern arms, including a second batch of 40 F-16s, plus 300 AIM-9L Sidewinder heat-seeking missiles and other sophisticated munitions.[58] These agreements have not, however, resolved the basic contradiction in the U.S.-Egyptian arms relationship. Whenever Washington indicates that it is prepared to supply the Egyptians with significantly upgraded military equipment, it encounters staunch resistance from those U.S. lawmakers who fear a potential theat to Israel; and any time such resistance compels Washington to downgrade its offer to Egypt, it encounters strong pressure from Cairo for a reaffirmation of the "equality" in arms deliveries promised by a succession of U.S. leaders.[59] The only solution that Washington has ever found to this dilemma is to balance each new delivery to Egypt with promises of future sales of even more advanced equipment to Israel. But this only perpetuates the conflict at ever-increasing cost to the United States—for each new sale of high-tech weaponry to Israel automatically produces fresh demands from Cairo in order to restore "equality" in the arms relationship.

In a sense, Washington has forced itself into a trap of its own making. Because the United States has hinged its Middle Eastern strategy on the cultivation of close military ties with Egypt, it is compelled to support the pro-Western leadership installed by Sadat and retained by Mubarek. To keep the support of the Egyptian military, however, the Sadat/Mubarek leadership must demonstrate that it can elicit a steady stream of high-tech arms from the United States. If it is to sustain Mubarek, therefore, Washington must be forthcoming with modern arms; both parties, in other words, have become dependent on an ever-expanding arms flow. And because the U.S.-Egyptian arms flow inevitably produces an even greater flow of modern weapons to Israel, the net result of this "Catch-22" policy is a self-sustaining arms race in the Middle East with all the attendant risks of explosive violence.[60]

The AWACS Sale to Saudi Arabia: What Price Friendship?

If the U.S. arms-supply relationship with Egypt appears unstable and ill-defined, then the U.S. arms link with Saudi Arabia can only appear more problematical. No U.S. sales program has aroused as much controversy as has the one with Saudi Arabia, and none has generated so many crises for U.S. policymakers. To some extent, of course, this is merely a consequence of scale: the Saudi arms program, now approaching $10 billion per year, is far and away the largest of its kind in the world today. There is also the issue of sophistication: although much of the U.S. effort is devoted to construction, training, and other noncombat programs, the Saudis have bought some of the most advanced and capable arms in the U.S. inventory. But most of all, the controversy is a reflection of the high stakes involved: the arms transfer program is the single most important U.S. link with the richest and most influential nation in the Arab world.

Ultimately, U.S. arms sales to Saudi Arabia are so controversial because nowhere else are military sales expected to accomplish so much. On the political-military side of the equation, U.S. arms exports are intended to promote regional security, to help ensure the safety of U.S. oil supplies, to enhance U.S. political leverage in Riyadh, and to guarantee the security of the present Saudi leadership. On the economic side, they are intended to help redress America's balance-of-payments problem, to absorb the surplus output of U.S. arms firms, and to assimilate some of the research and development costs of new U.S. weapons systems.[61] That is a lot to expect from any arms effort, even one of this magnitude.

If the U.S.-Saudi arms relationship has been credited with all of the advantages supposedly generated by military sales, it has also provoked the most skepticism about these very benefits. Considerable doubt has been voiced over the effectiveness of U.S. arms transfers in promoting regional stability, in gaining political leverage, in protecting U.S. oil, and so forth. "Massive weapons transfers to Saudi Arabia are worse than useless," Charles Krauthammer noted in the *New Republic*. "The fall of the Shah and the Iran-Iraq war made clear that the megalomaniac acquisition of advanced weapons threatens both internal and external stability in the region."[62] Indeed, given the perceived instability of the Saudi regime, it is hardly surprising that so many U.S. leaders have warned that the present U.S. arms policy risks another Iran. In a characteristic expression of this outlook, Rep. Richard Ottinger observed in 1981, "the United States should not repeat the errors it made in Iran by selling too much advanced weaponry to an unstable client faced with internal rather than external threats."[63]

While there had always been some high-level apprehension over U.S. arms exports to Saudi Arabia, all these doubts came to a head during the 1981 battle over the sale of five AWACS radar surveillance planes and other sophisticated military equipment. On the basis of scale alone—the total package was estimated to be worth $8.5 billion, far more than any other previous U.S. arms transaction—the AWACS sale was destined to provoke some controversy; the fact that it involved America's most advanced and sophisticated airborne defense system absolutely guaranteed that it would be the focus of intense national debate. Indeed, the AWACS battle occupied Congress for most of the summer and fall of 1981 and triggered the first major foreign policy crisis of the Reagan administration. It also provoked the most serious congressional challenge to date of a proposed U.S. weapons sale, leading many American policymakers to question the basic premises of the arms export program as a whole.[64]

Although the AWACS conflict did not erupt until April 1981, its roots can be traced back to 1978, when the United States agreed to sell the Saudis 60 F-15 fighters as part of the three-nation "jet package" arranged by the Carter administration.[65] In order to soften congressional opposition to the Saudi sale—by far the most controversial component of the package—the White House promised to impose a number of operational restrictions on the F-15 model sold to the Saudis. These restrictions, which were intended to prevent the Saudi F-15s from being used in an offensive mode against Israel, included a ban on the sale of external fuel tanks and bomb racks that would have increased the operating range of the aircraft and permitted them to be used in attacks on ground positions.[66] The administration's assurances were explicitly detailed in a letter from Defense Secretary Brown to the Senate Foreign Relations Committee, dated May 9, 1978, in which it was stated that "Saudi Arabia has not requested *nor do we intend to sell* any other systems that would increase the range or enhance the ground attack capability of the F-15" (emphasis added).[67] According to many observers, Brown's letter was critical in persuading several undecided senators to approve the package.[68]

However strongly the Saudis and their American associates may have been committed to these promises, by 1980 the situation in the Middle East had changed to the point where both felt obliged to consider breaking them. As the Saudis saw things, the fall of the Shah, the Soviet invasion of Afghanistan, and the war between Iran and Iraq had made their immediate security position far more perilous than it had been only two years earlier; from the administration's perspective, the burgeoning military partnership with Riyadh— forged in response to just such developments—entailed an expanded U.S. responsibility to strengthen Saudi defense capabilities. Shortly after the promulgation of the Carter Doctrine, therefore, the administration announced that it was giving sympathetic consideration to a Saudi request for external fuel tanks and bomb racks for its F-15s (which at that point were still being assembled in the United States).[69] Arguing that "changes in the regional security atmosphere such as the increased threat which was posed by the invasion of Afghanistan" provided a justification, the State Department suggested that it was in America's interest to supply the Saudis with the requested equipment.[70]

The Saudi request—and apparent administration approval— triggered a major foreign policy crisis for the Carter administration. On one hand, the administration had repeatedly expressed Washington's desire for a closer U.S.-Saudi military partnership in the wake of events in Iran and Afghanistan; on the other, Carter was eager to avoid a major confrontation with Congress at a time when he was seeking to mobilize support for his troubled reelection bid. "A replay of the 1978 Saudi-versus-Israel struggle over the F-15 would pit the pride, prestige, and power of America's top overseas oil supplier against that of America's most politically potent ally," Don Oberdorfer of the *Washington Post* observed at the time. "That is just the kind of conflict that a U.S. administration would like to avoid in an election year."[71] Given this sort of reasoning, and what was described as "a firestorm of opposition" in Congress over the proposed sales (at one point, sixty-eight senators signed a letter urging Carter to reject the Saudi request), Carter decided to reject the counsel of his foreign policy advisors and refused the Saudi request.[72] As a result, Secretary Brown was sent to Geneva to meet with the Saudi defense minister, Prince Sultan, with a plea that he withdraw the request until after the presidential election in November; in return for cooperation, Brown reportedly promised to speed up consideration of Saudi requests for other military equipment, including a variety of early-warning and air defense systems.[73]

Following the 1980 election, outgoing Carter officials discussed the F-15 proposal with incoming Secretary of State Alexander Haig and even, according to some accounts, agreed to reintroduce the matter in Congress during the "lame duck" session so as to spare Reagan the embarrassment of association with such a patently controversial issue.[74] Nothing came of these overtures, however, and thus when President Reagan took office in January, he found himself

saddled with the same dilemma faced by Carter eight months earlier: the Saudis were continuing to press for action on their request
for F-15 enhancements, while opposition in Congress remained
strong. Believing that such opposition could be overcome, and eager
to establish close working relations with the Saudis, Reagan decided
to bite the bullet: on February 25, the White House announced that
the president had approved the sale of fuel pods and bomb racks for
the F-15s plus late-model Sidewinder missiles and other unspecified
air defense equipment to Saudi Arabia.[75]

Much to his surprise, Reagan discovered that resistance to the
Saudi sale in Congress was stronger than ever. Confronted by the
same storm of opposition that had greeted Carter a year earlier, Reagan at first decided to scale down the Saudi F-15 proposal by with-
drawing the offer of external bomb racks and some air-refueling
equipment. To mollify supporters of Israel, moreover, he promised
to sell that country additional quantities of F-15s and other sophisticated arms.[76] These concessions did not, however, quiet the outcry
in Congress, and Reagan therefore announced that he would temporarily shelve the F-15 proposal while his advisors studied the whole
question of Saudi arms purchases.[77]

Once again, the F-15 issue dropped out of public view as administration officials considered the relative advantages of various policy options; while there were rumors that the administration was
considering other Saudi arms requests, most of the talk continued to
focus on the F-15 enhancement package. Then, on April 21, came
the biggest bombshell of them all: the White House announced that
Reagan had agreed to supply not only the F-15 package and the Side-
winders, but also 5 AWACS patrol planes, 7 KC-135 tankers, 22 ground
radar stations, and other sophisticated air defense equipment. In explaining the president's extraordinary decision, White House spokes-
person Larry Speakes indicated that Reagan believed that this sale
was essential in light of "a serious deterioration over the last year or
so of security conditions in the Middle East and Persian Gulf region
and the growing threats there to our friends from the Soviets and
other pressures."[78]

If the original F-15 enhancement package produced a storm of
controversy, Reagan's AWACS proposal triggered a veritable typhoon.
Profound shock and outrage was voiced by prominent leaders of both
major parties, and a total of fifty senators—including eighteen Republicans—introduced a resolution of disapproval in accordance
with the veto provisions of the Arms Export Control Act. So strong
was the outburst of opposition that many observers predicted that
the sale would be vetoed—thereby presenting Reagan with a major

foreign policy crisis as well as a stunning political defeat.[79] Not pre-pared for the outburst of opposition that greeted his AWACS an-nouncement, Reagan decided to postpone formal submission of the proposal until later in the year. This postponement enabled the ad-ministration to rally support for the package, but also initiated an extraordinary public debate on U.S. arms sales that permitted both opponents and supporters to examine every facet of the AWACS proposal.[80]

The primary issue, of course, was the potential impact of the sale on Israeli security. Opponents of the sale argued that the partic-ular technology involved represented an unprecedented threat to Is-rael, and that the Saudis, whatever their assurances, might someday be tempted to use it for just such a purpose. By extending the range of the F-15s, it was charged, the U.S. package would enable the Sau-dis to mount attacks on Israeli territory, while possession of the AWACS would permit the Saudis to mount a coordinated Arab air de-fense against future Israeli punitive strikes.[81] The Saudi package, Sen. Edward Kennedy avowed, contained "offensive weapons that can easily be used to threaten the security of Israel, our closest ally in the Middle East."[82]

In response, supporters of the AWACS deal claimed that the weapons involved were largely defensive and that, in any case, Saudi Arabia was too backward technologically to operate the planes with-out U.S. technical assistance—which would be halted if the Saudis used the equipment for any purposes other than those authorized by Washington. The AWACS "is not offensive," Sen. Barry Goldwater sug-gested. "It's designed to give Saudi Arabia information of what po-tential enemy forces are up to." Moreover, "the Israelis could send jets up to shoot down the AWACS anytime it wants. They're unarmed. AWACS would not stop Israel if it were determined to strike."[83]

Although the question of Israeli security dominated the AWACS debate, other issues inevitably entered into the discussion. Many critics claimed that the possession of high-tech weapons would blind the Saudi leadership to internal threats, thereby inviting rebellion and the possible loss of U.S. technology to radical Arabs and/or the Russians. "If they do get the AWACS," author Ronald Steel noted in the *New York Times*, "within a few years, following the Saudis' own Iran-style revolution, the planes will no doubt fall into the hands of Col. Muammar el-Qaddafi or even the Russians."[84] Other critics warned that the U.S. sale would significantly alter the balance of power in the region, prompting neighboring states to seek additional arms of their own—in many cases from the U.S.S.R.—thereby provoking a dangerous new arms race in the region. "The introduction of these sophisticated new weapons in the Middle East," Sen. Alan Cranston of California observed, "can only escalate the arms race."[85] Critics of the AWACS transaction also noted that the sale to the Saudis would produce a long-term requirement for U.S. technical support on the ground in Saudi Arabia—thereby creating a significant U.S. presence that could become the target for future enemy strikes against Saudi Arabia and thereby trigger U.S. military involvement in a regional conflict. (Secretary of State Alexander Haig subsequently reported that at least 480 civilian contractor personnel and 30 U.S. Air Force officers would have to be stationed in Saudi Arabia until "well into the 1990s" to assist with AWACS operations.)[86] The U.S. technicians at these facilities would be "sitting ducks," Charles Krauthammer wrote in the *New Republic*, "and the United States would become hostage to Saudi politics." If the Saudis became involved in a local conflict, "that would necessarily involve American servicemen and draw in the United States against its will and against its interests."[87]

Eventually, the debate over the AWACS sale evolved into a debate over the conduct of arms sales itself. Critics charged that the administration had failed to weigh America's true security interests in its haste to please the Saudis. "For sheer bloody incompetence," columnist Anthony Lewis wrote in the *New York Times*, "there has been nothing in recent memory to equal the handling of the AWACS sale."[88] Recognizing that such criticism threatened the fundamental authority of the U.S. foreign policy establishment, even critics of the sale, including Henry Kissinger, ultimately counseled its passage in order to preserve the integrity of presidential decisionmaking. For Reagan to have rejected the AWACS request "would have involved unacceptable costs in the relationship to Saudi Arabia," Kissinger wrote in the *Washington Post*, "and for Congress now to overturn a new president's recommendation on a matter of such magnitude would magnify these dangers and jeopardize the entire design of our foreign policy."[89]

Perhaps it was this argument, more than any other, that prevailed in the end. When it appeared that the sale might actually be defeated in the Senate after the House, as expected, voted to veto the sale, Reagan mounted a last-minute, all-out personal campaign to win over undecided lawmakers. "If you [defeat this sale]," he told a group of Senate Republicans at a White House meeting, "you're going to cut me off at the knees on foreign policy."[90] Backed by such arguments and all the persuasiveness at this command, Reagan ultimately succeeded in winning over the minds of sufficient senators to give him a narrow 52 to 48 victory when the sale was finally brought to a vote on October 28, 1981.

The AWACS victory was widely regarded as a major victory for Reagan and a vote of confidence in the administration's Mideast policy. "President Reagan's startling catch-up victory in the Senate on the arms package for Saudi Arabia will bolster his credibility and influence with the moderate Arab countries," Hedrick Smith of the *New York Times* observed after the vote.[91] But the president's victory did not please the many supporters of Israel, who promised to lobby for increased U.S. aid to that nation, nor did it silence opponents of the U.S.-Saudi arms relationship, who continue to voice their doubts over U.S. policy. "We're putting all our eggs in one basket, the Saudi basket," Sen. Robert Packwood of Oregon lamented after the Senate vote, "and it's the wrong basket."[92]

While the AWACS vote may have reaffirmed the primacy of presidential authority in the foreign policy arena, it can hardly be said to have demonstrated the utility of arms sales as an instrument of U.S. influence. Long before Reagan approved the AWACS sale, top Saudi officials warned that increased U.S. sales would not translate into automatic support for U.S. initiatives. "Ronald Reagan will offer us weapons in return for bases and ports in Saudi Arabia," a Saudi prince observed in 1980. "We will say no, and he will be disappointed because he expects too much."[93] Similar comments were made by other Saudi officials during the AWACS debate, and even after its approval by Congress there has been no noticeable shift in the Saudis' position on the Camp David accords or other key issues. "You are just arms salesmen and we pay cash," is the way one top Saudi official summed up the long-term significance of the AWACS transaction.[94]

If any expectations remained in Washington about the political benefits conferred by arms sales, they were brutally dispelled during Defense Secretary Caspar Weinberger's 1982 trip to Saudi Arabia. Arriving in Riyadh three years to the day after Harold Brown concluded his pioneering 1979 visit, Weinberger sought unsuccessfully to enlist Saudi support for the Reagan administration's Mideast policies. After three days of grueling talks, Weinberger failed to spark any Saudi interest in an Arab-Israeli rapprochement based on the administration's proposal for a "strategic consensus" of regional powers opposed to the expansion of Soviet influence in the area. To make matters worse, the Saudis flatly refused to discuss any further limitations on the use of AWACS aircraft, despite Reagan's plea for assurances that they would not be used against Israel. Noting that

Weinberger had "achieved scant results" during his visit to Riyadh, *New York Times* analyst Richard Halloran suggested that the whole U.S. strategy of courting Saudi Arabia through arms transfers "has been built on wishful thinking."[95] Indeed, there is little evidence that U.S. sales of increasingly sophisticated weaponry to Saudi Arabia have produced a significant increase in political influence, regional stability, or any other political-military benefits normally ascribed to military exports.[96]

The Inadequacy of Safeguards: U.S. Arms Restraints and Israeli Defiance

If U.S. arms sales to Saudi Arabia cast doubt on the supposed utility of military exports in promoting U.S. security interests, arms sales to Israel cast doubt on an equally critical matter: the ability of the United States to prevent the misuse of its weapons once they have been delivered to another country. Legally, American arms can only be sold to foreign governments for essentially defensive purposes, and various penalties—including a complete cutoff of military supplies—are prescribed for governments which violate these restrictions by employing their U.S.-supplied weapons for other, aggressive purposes. Any failure to enforce this requirement in the case of flagrant violations would obviously invalidate the most basic rationale for arms transfers: namely, that they promote peace and stability by enhancing the self-defense capabilities of otherwise vulnerable countries. Nevertheless, Washington has persistently declined to penalize Israel for acknowledged transgressions of U.S. arms regulations, thereby inviting further Israeli violations and jeopardizing ultimate U.S. interests in the Middle East.

Clearly, U.S. laxity in policing an arms-supply relationship of the magnitude of that with Israel is no trivial matter. After Saudi Arabia (and Iran under the Shah), Israel is the leading recipient of U.S. arms, with $9.3 billion in FMS orders placed between 1950 and 1980 and another $3.2 billion recorded in 1981–83.[97] Israeli imports are significant not only from the quantitative point of view, but also from the qualitative perspective: usually the first Third World nation to be offered the latest U.S. arms (the AWACS sale to Saudi Arabia being a notable exception), Israel is the possessor of some of America's most advanced aircraft and missiles, including the top-rated F-15 and F-16 jet fighters and the E-2C Hawkeye electronic spy plane. More importantly, perhaps, Israel has been the most frequent user of American weapons, employing them repeatedly in regional conflicts and punitive raids against neighboring Arab countries.[98]

As in the case of all other U.S. arms-supply programs, American exports to Israel are supposedly intended to enhance the latter's self-defense capabilities and thereby promote regional security. Because of Israel's perceived vulnerability to superior Arab forces, however, U.S. and Israeli officials have always interpreted Israel's defense needs as requiring qualitative if not quantitative superiority over its hostile neighbors. For this reason, Washington has always acknowledged a "special relationship" with Israel that transcends all other U.S. supply programs with Third World countries. Thus, in announcing President Reagan's 1981 decision to proceed with the AWACS sale to Saudi Arabia, Under Secretary of State James L. Buckley affirmed that "this Administration remains committed to the security of Israel and will insure that Israel maintains its substantial military advantage over potential adversaries."[99]

While most U.S. officials maintain that such superiority is needed as a deterrent, however, Israeli officials and their American supporters have consistently argued that Israel must periodically use its military might to disrupt impending invasions and to diminish future Arab capabilities. Indeed, Senator Cranston opposed the AWACS sales to Saudi Arabia precisely because—by providing advance warning of Israeli attack—it might preclude such action. "Because of its small size," he argued in 1981, "Israel . . . must have the ability to make *a pre-emptive strike* against an aggressor" (emphasis added).[100] On the basis of this logic, Israel has mounted a succession of preemptive strikes against neighboring Arab countries, most of which involved extensive use of U.S.-supplied weapons. But while such moves may appear to conform with Israeli definitions of national security, they conflict with most established notions of self-defense, including those incorporated into U.S. arms export regulations.

Of the various legal constraints imposed on the sale of U.S. arms to foreign governments, none is more emphatic than the ban on their use for nondefense purposes. Thus, the 1952 U.S. security assistance pact with Israel states that American-supplied equipment can be used by Israel "solely to maintain its internal security [and for the] legitimate self-defense of areas of which it is a part."[101] Similarly, the Arms Export Control Act of 1976 decrees that U.S. arms can be sold to foreign governments "solely for internal security, legitimate self-defense, [and] to permit the recipient country to participate in regional or collective arrangements for or measures consistent with the Charter of the United Nations."

Such provisions can be interpreted in a multitude of ways, of course, but only through the most extreme distortion of logic can they be stretched to cover such acts as the 1981 Israeli attack on a nuclear reactor in Baghdad or the 1982 Israeli invasion of Lebanon. While Israeli officials and some U.S. lawmakers have attempted to portray these acts as essentially defensive in nature—the Baghdad raid because it set back purported Iraqi efforts to construct an atomic bomb, and the Lebanon invasion because it precluded future PLO artillery attacks on northern Israeli settlements—most U.S. officials (including many who were otherwise in sympathy with Israel's security policies) contended that they violated U.S. prohibitions against the use of American-supplied weapons for offensive purposes. Thus, following the 1981 Baghdad raid (which was conducted by U.S.-supplied F-15 and F-16 aircraft), President Reagan notified Congress that "a substantial violation" of U.S. arms regulations had apparently occurred and punished Israel by temporarily suspending deliveries of F-16 aircraft.[102] Similarly, Reagan condemned the 1982 Israeli attack on Lebanon (which also made extensive use of American equipment) and again ordered a delay in the delivery of U.S. aircraft to Israel.[103]

Charges of Israeli misuse of American-supplied equipment have also occurred with respect to the mode of employment of certain weapons—specifically, the "cluster bombs" periodically used by Israel in attacks on guerrilla strongholds in Lebanon. Cluster Bomb Units, or CBUS, are composed of a canister that splits open when dropped over the target zone, plus hundreds of antipersonnel grenades or "bomblets" that are then strewn over a very wide area. First used extensively by the United States during the Vietnam War, CBUS are considered by many humanitarian organizations to be proscribed by the Geneva Conventions because they can be used to slaughter large numbers of people indiscriminately, and because of the high risk of civilian casualties when used anywhere near populated areas. For this reason, Washington has directed foreign customers to limit their use of CBUS to operations against clearly defined military targets, such as artillery emplacements or infantry units. Despite such restrictions, however, Israeli forces have repeatedly used their U.S.-supplied cluster bombs in attacks against civilian targets, notably Palestinian refugee camps in Lebanon. The first confirmed Israeli use of CBUS occurred in 1978, when Israel attacked Palestinian strongholds in southern Lebanon, and the second in 1982, during the Israeli invasion of that country. In both cases, Israel insisted that the cluster bombs were used exclusively against guerrilla formations, but each time witnesses and survivors reported that the target population included many civilians.[104]

Despite widespread evidence of Israeli CBU violations, however,

U.S. authorities have consistently refused to punish Israel or to prevent the repetition of such transgressions in the future. Following the 1978 attacks, a State Department official conceded that Israel's use of cluster bombs against civilian targets "was contrary to [U.S.] restrictions," but assured angry members of Congress that U.S. officials "are having discussions with the Israeli government with a view to assuring that these restrictions will be observed in the future."[105] As a result of these talks, the Israelis reaffirmed an earlier agreement in which they pledged, "These weapons . . . will not be used against targets located in, or in close proximity to, civilian population centers."[106] On this basis, the Carter administration dropped any thoughts it might have had of punishing Israel for its CBU violations in Lebanon, and instead agreed to provide fresh supplies of these deadly weapons. Indeed, the very willingness of the United States to supply such weapons—despite flagrant evidence of their repeated misuse—must have convinced Israel that Washington had no real objection to such action: for, after pledging in 1978 to confine CBU use to military targets, the Israelis again employed them against civilian populations in Lebanon four years later.

In many respects, U.S. behavior regarding the CBU violations is symptomatic of the whole U.S. approach to rifts in the U.S.-Israeli arms relationship. Typically, Israel agrees to a certain set of conditions regarding the use of U.S.-supplied military equipment and then proceeds to violate these restrictions in some minor incident. Washington responds to these infractions by issuing a stern protest and temporarily halting deliveries of the U.S. arms. Then, after a suitable cooling-off period, Israel promises to abide by the restrictions in the future and the United States resumes deliveries as if nothing untoward has occurred. No doubt regarding the feeble U.S. response as a sign of inverted acquiescence, the Israelis subsequently commit a similar violation on an even larger scale. Indeed, the record of U.S. and Israeli behavior regarding the misuse of American-supplied weaponry can only lead to one conclusion: America's failure to punish earlier instances of arms misuse by Israel often leads to further abuse on later occasions. Certainly, there is ample evidence for this in the events leading up to the 1982 invasion of Lebanon.

In late 1981, Israel annexed the Golan Heights in defiance of stated U.S. policy, thereby causing an angry President Reagan to suspend a "strategic cooperation agreement" that had just been concluded with the Begin government. As on other occasions, however, U.S. authorities allowed things to cool down a bit and then resumed discussions with Israel on the sale of additional arms. By early May, these discussions had proceeded far enough for Reagan to announce a major new sale to the Israelis: 75 additional F-16 fighters worth an estimated $2.5 billion. To finalize this transaction, Israeli Defense Minister Ariel Sharon was invited to Washington on May 25 for talks with Secretary of State Haig and Secretary of Defense Weinberger—talks that were widely regarded as a sign that the United States had overcome its objections to the Golan seizure and was prepared to resume its normal, high-tempo arms relationship with Israel.[107] Less than two weeks later, Sharon led the massive Israeli attack into Lebanon.

Even if, as U.S. authorities insist, Sharon did not discuss the impending invasion with Haig and Weinberger while in Washington, it is hard not to conclude that the administration's action on the F-16s and its reaffirmation of the U.S. arms link was not seen by the Begin government as an implicit U.S. endorsement of its aggressive design. Certainly, Washington had ample warning of Israel's military intentions: aside from the data presumably supplied by U.S. intelligence officials, many observers of Middle Eastern affairs warned of a possible Israeli move—among them Jordan's King Hussein, who declared in March that the situation in the Middle East "is far more serious than it has ever been."[108] Given these warnings, and what we have learned of the U.S.-Israeli arms relationship, one cannot help wondering what would have happened if, instead of promising more weapons, Haig and Weinberger had told Sharon on May 25 that the United States would respond to any future Israeli preemptive strikes with a complete cutoff in U.S. arms deliveries in accordance with U.S. law. Although no one can predict what might have ensued, logic suggests that such an announcement would have forced the Israelis to cancel or at least scale down their planned invasion—and possibly saved the lives of an estimated 20,000 human beings.[109]

Much has been written about Israeli security policy, and no doubt debate will continue to erupt on the validity of Israel's preemptive strategy. But while many Israeli and American strategists may persist in the belief that such action is the only sure way to guarantee Israel's survival, it does not automatically follow that the United States should endorse this approach or facilitate it by supplying Israel with the weapons necessary to carry it out. Indeed, we are compelled by both humanitarian considerations and our own strategic interests to seek a peaceful solution to the Arab-Israeli conflict. It appears obvious, moreover, that such a solution cannot be achieved unless both sides are deterred from the preemptive use of military force. This means, in turn, that the United States must take concrete steps to prevent the misuse of American-supplied weaponry and punish transgressions when they occur.

The enforcement of U.S. arms restrictions is essential not only to the Middle East peace process, but to the integrity of the U.S. arms program as a whole. If Washington does not take visible and meaningful action to curb the abuse of American weapons sold abroad, we can have no assurance that such arms will not be used again and again for purposes wholly inconsistent with both international law and U.S. national security. U.S. statutes state unequivocally that American arms shall be exported for defensive purposes only, and however one defines that limitation, it obviously has no impact whatsoever if foreign buyers believe that they can ignore U.S. restrictions on the use of American-supplied weapons with impunity.

Conclusion: Toward a Sane Arms Policy in the Middle East

Because the stakes are so high in the Middle East—involving nothing less than global war or peace—and because, more than anywhere else, U.S. strategy in the Middle East is defined by arms transfer decisions, it is obvious that America must seek to adopt the most prudent policy possible regarding military exports to this highly volatile region. Such a policy must address the legitimate self-defense needs of individual nations, but give highest priority to the promotion of peace and stability in the region as a whole. Treading a path between these competing interests will not be easy, of course, but hopefully we have learned some things in our exploration of past U.S. arms export patterns that might be helpful in shaping a more judicious approach.

To begin with, it should be obvious by now that all the benefits supposedly provided by arms sales—especially those aimed at the Middle East—rarely materialize in practice. Massive sales to Iran did not produce long-term stability in the Persian Gulf, nor did they immunize the Shah against internal revolt; sales to Saudi Arabia have not enhanced U.S. political leverage in the kingdom, nor have they furthered U.S. strategic designs in the region; sales to Israel have not ensured the peace, nor have they inspired greater Israeli support for U.S. peace initiatives. One could argue, of course, that U.S. interests would have also suffered in the absence of such sales, but the available evidence argues rather persuasively that arms transfers have been oversold as an instrument of U.S. policy in the Middle East.

This is far more significant than it might seem, because it tells us that arms exports to the Middle East can be greatly scaled down without causing automatic harm to U.S. interests.[110] Indeed, it is often likely that U.S. restraint will promote rather than damage U.S. interests. When it can be shown, without doubt, that a particular

sale will help advance U.S. efforts to promote regional peace and stability, then it should be considered for approval (if all other U.S. requirements are satisfied); in the absence of such certainty, it should
be assumed that a proposed sale is just as likely to have negative
as positive consequences for U.S. security. From this perspective, it
should be much easier to scale down or reject dubious transactions.

It will be argued, of course, that U.S. restraint will invite aggressive marketing by America's principal competitors—especially
the Soviet Union. This may be true. But it does not mean, as has so
often been prophesied, that this will result in increased Soviet influence in the region; indeed, the record shows that high levels of Soviet exports in the 1950s and 1960s did not produce lasting Soviet
influence in the region, and, in the case of Egypt especially, left a
residue of resentment that has not been erased to this day (see chapter 10). Nor, on the other hand, is there any evidence that increased
U.S. arms exports will result in decreased Soviet influence. In fact,
just the opposite is likely to be the case: by providing U.S. clients
like Egypt, Israel, and Morocco with large quantities of high-tech
weaponry, we automatically generate fresh insecurities in neighboring countries like Algeria, Libya, and Syria—thereby stimulating an
increased market for Soviet (and, in some cases, Western European)
arms. Nor should we assume that the Soviets are blind to the risks
entailed by an uncontrolled arms race in the Middle East: they are
much closer geographically to the region and have as much to lose as
we do from a local conflict that explodes out of control. If the necessary safeguards and assurances can be agreed upon, therefore, it
should be possible at some point to enlist Soviet cooperation in a
policy of mutual arms restraint in the Middle East—and this, in the
final analysis, must be the ultimate aim of U.S. policy.

This still leaves the question of the economic benefits supposedly generated by high-volume arms sales. The loss of some high-
priced arms transactions would, undoubtedly, complicate the U.S.
balance-of-payments situation and cause difficulties for some U.S.
arms firms. But these losses have to be measured against the net
gain in national security—and the even greater losses we would suf-
fer if the Middle East goes up in flames as a result of a U.S.-fueled
arms race. These potential costs are rarely factored into the policy
equation, but they are nonetheless germane.

On the basis of these considerations, and all that we have learned
about past U.S. experience in supplying arms, it would appear that a
sane export policy to the Middle East would best rest on the following basic principles:

   1. A *general reluctance to provide arms* to any country unless

it can be convincingly shown that a given sale will be used for defensive purposes only and will enhance rather than frustrate U.S. efforts to promote regional peace and security.

2. A *ban on sales of new high-tech weapons* whose delivery to the Middle East will automatically set off a chain reaction of similar acquisitions by other countries.

3. The adoption of *strict guidelines on the use* of American-supplied weapons, with a vigorous policy of enforcement involving substantial penalties for any government found in violation of U.S. regulations.

4. The initiation of a concerted effort to negotiate *multilateral constraints on conventional arms transfers* to the Middle East.

The adoption of these guidelines will not automatically produce peace in the Middle East, nor will they necessarily guarantee the attainment of other U.S. objectives. But they will help slacken the outpouring of arms that has made the Middle East such a potential threat to world peace. Furthermore, by suggesting that U.S. arms will not always be available to allies that engage in aggressive behavior, they may help promote the search for peaceful solutions to regional problems. By slowing the influx of high-tech weapons, moreover, they will reduce the risk that conflicts which do occur will explode into regional conflagrations that threaten global security. Finally, even if we cannot be assured that these guidelines will automatically produce peace, it is hard to imagine how peace will ever be achieved in the absence of such restraints.

CHAPTER 8

Coproduction and Licensing

The Export of America's Arms-Making Technology

Until now, we have spoken of the weapons trade strictly in terms of *arms* transfers—specifically, the transfer of complete, ready-to-use weapons systems from one country to another. Such transfers have always constituted a mainstay of the arms business and no doubt will continue to do so for a long time to come. Increasingly, however, such sales are being accompanied or even supplanted by another type of transfer: the sale of arms-making *technology*. Such transfers have become an expanding feature of the arms trade as more and more Third World nations seek to establish domestic arms industries of their own. In order to acquire the "know-how" to produce modern arms, these nations often demand that such technology transfers accompany any major purchase of completed weapons systems. Thus, South Korea and Taiwan have both acquired production know-how for the manufacture of F-5E aircraft in conjunction with their recent purchases of the plane, and both produce a variety of other U.S. arms under license from American firms. Technology transfers have also figured in recent U.S. military sales to the NATO powers and Japan—countries which often compete with the United States in the production and sale of advanced military hardware. Because such transfers contribute to the arms-making potential of other nations, and because they enhance the competitive position of other industrial powers, they obviously raise important questions for U.S. foreign policy. Technology transfers have not, however, received as much attention from Congress and the press as have sales of completed weapons systems, so it is important that we address these questions here.[1]

When applied to military systems, the term "technology transfer" can refer to a wide variety of transactions: the sale of blueprints and technical data for the production of complete weapons by another country; the sale of components, machine tools, and manufacturing know-how for the assembly of such items; the provision of training and technical assistance in the introduction of new production processes; and the sale of complete factories or production lines

with all the parts and machines needed to operate them. Such transactions can also involve one-way transfers, whereby the U.S. government (and/or U.S. firms) provides another government (or foreign
firms) with the technology to produce a given weapon or component
for its own use, or collaborative ventures, wherein the U.S. government (and/or U.S. firms) provides such expertise as part of an agreement for the joint production of a given item for the use of both. For
regulatory purposes, the U.S. government further distinguishes between *licensing* agreements, wherein a U.S. company sells a foreign
firm the blueprints and the manufacturing know-how for a particular item along with the rights to market that item within a specified
sales territory, and coproduction agreements, wherein the U.S. government actively participates in the transfer of military technology
to another country (usually in conjunction with military aid agreements or as part of collaborative ventures involving the multinational
production of U.S.-designed weapons).[2]

Given the multiplicity of possible arrangements and the inherent complexity of such transactions, it is difficult to compile a stan-
dardized list of all major U.S. technology-export programs in the
military field. Nevertheless, there is no disputing the fact that such
programs are already numerous and will become more so in the future. In 1977, the Congressional Research Service estimated that the
United States was then involved in some 400 manufacturing license
agreements and 30 major coproduction projects.[3] Another study, by
the Office of Munitions Control, indicated that a total of 377 new
licensing agreements were approved by the State Department between January 1, 1976, and June 15, 1980.[4] And, while more recent
figures on licensing agreements are not available, the existing information suggests a continuing increase in both these and coproduction programs.[5] (See tables 9 and 10 for tallies of current coproduction programs.)

The increase in licensing and coproduction projects is attribut-
able to several factors: the desire of foreign producers (especially in
Europe and Japan) to acquire advanced manufacturing technologies;
the desire of Third World countries to obtain external assistance in
the development of modern high-tech industries; the desire of some
countries to become self-sufficient in weapons production in order
to frustrate possible arms embargoes; and the desire of many weap-
ons-buying countries to compensate for heavy arms outlays by com-
pelling the seller to award at least some subcontracting work to their
own firms. These motives have become increasingly pronounced
since the 1960s and are likely to become more so in the future—

Table 9. Major U.S. Coproduction Programs with Europe and Japan, 1982

Item	U.S. producer	Overseas producer
F-15 aircraft	McDonnell-Douglas	Japan
F-100 jet engine	Pratt and Whitney	Japan
AIM-9L Sidewinder air-to-air missile	Raytheon/Ford-Aeronutronic	NATO consortium (Italy, W. Germany, Norway, U.K.); Japan
MK-46 torpedo	Honeywell	Japan
P-3C aircraft	Lockheed	Canada; Japan
FFG-7 frigate components	n.a.	Australia
F-5E aircraft	Northrop	Switzerland
F-16 aircraft and components	General Dynamics	NATO consortium (Norway, Belgium, Denmark, Netherlands)
Harpoon antiship missile	McDonnell-Douglas	United Kingdom
XM-712 Cannon-Launched Guided Projectile	Martin Marietta	NATO consortium (U.K., W. Germany, Italy)
Improved Hawk surface-to-air missile	Raytheon	NATO consortium (Belgium, Denmark, W. Germany, Italy, Norway, Netherlands)
AN/TSQ-73 radar	Litton Data Systems	France; Italy
AWACS components	Boeing, Westinghouse, IBM	All NATO nations
M-113 Armored personnel carrier	FMC Corp.	Italy
M-109 Self-propelled howitzer	GMC-Allison	Italy; Netherlands; Switzerland
81-mm. mortar	n.a.	United Kingdom
8-inch howitzer	n.a.	Japan
Dragon antitank missile	Raytheon/Kollman	All NATO nations
M-483 artillery ammunition	n.a.	NATO consortium (Italy, W. Germany, Netherlands, U.K.)
Maverick air-to-surface missile	Hughes	W. Germany; Italy
JTIDS (Joint Tactical Information Distribution System)	ITT/Hughes	France; W. Germany; U.K.

SOURCE: Office of the Undersecretary of Defense (Research and Engineering).
n.a. = not available.

Table 10. Major U.S. Coproduction Programs with the Third World, 1982

Item	U.S. producer	Overseas producer
F-5E aircraft	Northrop	Taiwan
F-5E aircraft	Northrop	South Korea
500-MD helicopter	Hughes	South Korea
2.75-inch rocket	n.a.	Turkey
F-16 aircraft components	General Dynamics	Israel
Type-1120 turbojet engine	Pratt and Whitney	Israel
M-48 and M-60 tank components	Chrysler	Israel
AN/TPS-63 radar	Westinghouse	Egypt
M-456, M-735 artillery ammunition	n.a.	Egypt

SOURCE: Office of the Undersecretary of Defense (Research and Engineering).
n.a. = not available.

thus ensuring a continuing increase in the scope and number of overseas arms-production programs. As Under Secretary of State Matthew Nimitz observed in 1980, "this trend toward more widespread coproduction is likely to continue and intensify in the years ahead, for the simple reason that the motivation behind it is likely to be greater rather than less."[6]

On the whole, U.S. law and policy stress the sale of completed weapons systems rather than of the technology to produce them. Thus, the Arms Export Control Act of 1976 states that, in implementation of the Foreign Military Sales program, "special emphasis" shall be placed on procurements of finished weapons in the United States. In order to improve the combat efficiency of NATO forces, however, U.S. leaders have called for the increased standardization of weapons used by member armies—an objective that can most readily be attained through the joint production and procurement of key systems. Furthermore, as competition among the major arms suppliers increases—thereby enhancing the bargaining position of potential buyers—U.S. producers have come to regard technology transfers as an inescapable "fact of life" of the arms business. While U.S. officials may prefer to inhibit the export of U.S. arms technology, the CRS reported in 1977, when faced with adamant clients they will usually "agree to coproduce the item rather than lose the entire sale to another country."[7]

Although U.S. officials have tended to ignore the policy implications of arms-technology exports (except insofar as they relate to the acquisition of advanced military technology by the U.S.S.R.), the growing scale of such programs will make it increasingly difficult to do so in the future. Already, many economists are worried that past or present transfers of U.S. arms-making know-how have diminished the technological lead of U.S. industries and enhanced the competitive position of foreign producers. Thus, a 1982 report by the GAO found that U.S. military coproduction projects with Japan had produced a one-way flow of technology to Japanese aerospace firms, thereby enhancing their ability to compete with American firms in the development of new products for the civilian aircraft market.[8] The economic risks engendered by such programs tend, moreover, to increase with time and with the degree of sophistication involved. As noted by J. Fred Bucy of Texas Instruments in a 1976 Defense Science Board report, "The release of technology is an irreversible decision. Once released, it can neither be taken back nor controlled. The receiver of know-how gains a competence which serves as a base for many subsequent gains."[9]

The growing trade in arms-making technology has also produced considerable concern in the arms control community. Because such transfers will increase the number of countries capable of producing modern weapons, they automatically make it easier for potential belligerents to stockpile arms while at the same time making it harder to impose embargoes or negotiate arms control agreements. Indeed, many specialists believe that technology transfers are potentially far more destabilizing than regular arms transfers, since many recipients of such technology are beginning to export arms on their own—Brazil and Israel, for instance, have become major suppliers of unsophisticated weapons to other Third World countries—thus producing a geometric increase in the world's total supply of war-making capabilities.[10]

Given the obvious importance of these issues and the lack of a coherent U.S. policy to deal with them, the whole problem of arms-technology exports should be examined more closely. In this chapter, we shall review the origins of U.S. licensing and coproduction programs, the current status of these programs, and the motives which prompt both supplier and recipient to conduct such transfers. Then, following a review of the policy implications of rising technology exports, we shall consider possible approaches for the control of this trade.

Coproduction in Europe: The Conflicting Goals of U.S. Policy

The American government first authorized the export of U.S. arms-making technology in the early 1950s when, as part of the global struggle against Communism, the United States sought to enhance the military-industrial capacities of its closest allies in Europe and the Far East. At first, these countries were invited to provide maintenance and servicing for U.S. ships and planes based abroad, and then, as they became more familiar with modern military technologies, to produce U.S. weapons under license. By helping to modernize these countries' arms industries, it was believed, the United States was contributing to the military strength of the West as a whole. That such projects would ultimately contribute to the domestic economic vitality of these countries—to the possible detriment of the U.S. economy—did not, at the time, appear significant.

As part of this Cold War effort, U.S. firms established coproduction and licensing programs in most of the major Western countries. But because France and Great Britain emerged from World War II with their military industries largely intact, the greatest effort was undertaken in those countries which had experienced the greatest wartime damage: Italy, Japan, and West Germany. Thus, in its overriding commitment to anti-Communism, Washington disavowed one of the Allies' principal wartime aims: the demilitarization of the Axis powers. Military factories that had been dismantled by the Occupation authorities were now set back in operation, and U.S. companies were encouraged to collaborate in the resuscitation of firms like Messerschmitt and Mitsubishi which had once churned out the warplanes most dreaded by American soldiers. Perhaps no greater irony has emerged from the Cold War era than this pattern of collaboration between firms that had only recently been supplying arms to contending forces.

Because U.S. firms were so intimately involved in the reestablishment of the military industries of the former Axis powers, arms companies in these countries have developed especially close ties with U.S. industry and have consistently accounted for a large percentage of U.S. coproduction and licensing agreements.[11] Indeed, these three countries accounted for half of all U.S. coproduction projects in 1977 (in dollar terms), and, with the recent decision to coproduce the F-15 and P-3C aircraft in Japan, continue to account for a large percentage of such projects today (see table 9).

Although rooted in the policies of the Cold War era, U.S. arms technology exports to Germany, Italy, and Japan continue to raise important and sometimes difficult issues for U.S. policymakers.

Given their role in the Western alliance system, the United States can hardly sever its existing technological links with these countries without in some sense degrading the military potential of the West as a whole; on the other hand, the continued transfer of U.S. technical know-how will almost certainly contribute to the competitive advantage of these countries' civilian aerospace industries and thus further erode the economic position of U.S. firms. This problem is becoming especially acute, moreover, as these countries become self-sufficient in the production of basic weapons—tanks, artillery, fighters, and so forth—and thus seek U.S. cooperation only when developing the most advanced and sophisticated systems.

U.S. policy regarding coproduction programs in Europe has always wavered uncertainly between enthusiasm and reluctance, but by 1980 it was being pulled apart by seemingly irreconcilable goals. On one hand, U.S. leaders sought to promote political cohesion and military standardization within NATO through collaborative arms programs; on the other hand, they wished to prevent further erosion of America's technological leadership through curbs on technology exports. These contrary impulses had long been latent in U.S. coproduction policy, but they became increasingly incompatible in the late 1970s when it became apparent that European producers were interested in importing only the most advanced U.S. technologies. Despite this, President Carter approved a number of major coproduction programs as part of the U.S. effort to promote arms standardization in Europe; these initiatives did not, however, resolve the inconsistencies in U.S. policy, and thus the Reagan administration was forced to grapple anew with the coproduction issue. While some progress has been made toward defining U.S. objectives, the coproduction issue is likely to provoke debate for the indefinite future.[12]

On one side of this debate is the drive toward increased arms standardization within NATO. Unlike the Warsaw Pact forces, which are generally armed with standard-issue Soviet equipment (or Soviet-design hardware produced under license), each individual NATO army is equipped with its own guns, vehicles, and aircraft. Such individualism is highly wasteful, since each country maintains separate research and development and production facilities (which often operate at less-than-economic scale); it is also militarily hazardous, since the parts and ammunition of one country cannot be used in the weapons of another. For this reason, U.S. strategists have long sought to promote joint arms procurement within the Alliance.[13] Noting that at least $10 billion of the $140 billion spent annually by the NATO countries on European defense is wasted through duplication, Under Secretary of Defense William J. Perry complained in

1979 that "the lack of effective coordination and cooperation within the Alliance causes the whole of our defense output to be less than the sum of the contributing national inputs."[14] This waste and duplication is especially dangerous, Perry argued, because of a continuing buildup of Soviet forces. The NATO Alliance can "readily maintain defense superiority over the Warsaw Pact," he avowed, "only . . . if each ally rises above the national parochialism which has crippled cooperation in the past."[15]

Although European leaders have long acknowledged the value of standardization, they have often complained that most of the time it translates into the blanket purchase of American hardware by the other NATO countries. Because the arms factories of the individual European countries are generally smaller than their American counterparts, they cannot achieve the economies of scale that are possible in the United States and cannot always afford to employ the most advanced (and costly) production techniques. Consequently, U.S. producers can often offer superior equipment at less cost than European producers, and this has naturally resulted in high-volume U.S. arms sales to Europe. At the same time, congressional resistance to American acquisition of foreign-produced arms, as expressed in such measures as the Buy America Act, has narrowed the market for European arms in the United States. This imbalance— the United States sold $5.2 billion worth of arms to Europe in 1976– 80, compared to only $800 million worth of arms sold by Europe to the United States—has long rankled European officials.[16] Noting that domestic arms industries are an important source of foreign trade and national prestige for many European nations, G. R. Jefferson of the British Aerospace Dynamics Group told American arms officials in 1978 that "we must try to move away from a situation in which standardization has largely been achieved, if at all, by de facto standardization on weapons conceived and developed in the U.S."[17]

One way to overcome these objections, of course, would be for the United States to buy more of its arms in Europe. Such a "two-way street" in arms procurement has long been a stated goal of NATO officials, but has proved largely ephemeral in practice. Under the banner of Alliance solidarity, the White House in 1975 persuaded the U.S. Army and Congress to produce the Franco-German Roland antiaircraft missile system in U.S. factories, but few other large buys of European equipment have followed. (The Roland program was terminated, moreover, when only 27 fire units out of a planned force of 180 had been produced.)[18] Some new transactions may be approved by the Reagan administration—particularly in light of the pending sale of 18 AWACS radar planes to NATO—but the White House has generally expressed a preference for American products when acquiring major new weapons systems.

Given the resistance on both sides of the Atlantic to the outright purchase of each side's arms, the surest way to promote standardization within the Alliance is through U.S./European coproduction of common systems. If factories in all participating countries are given a share of the work, each nation theoretically shares in the economic employment benefits of the project while the Alliance as a whole benefits through the joint procurement and deployment of a common item. An important model for such efforts was the F-16 fighter program, which united major contractors in five nations— Belgium, Denmark, Holland, Norway, and the United States—in the joint assembly and production of a major weapons system. Although described as a "management nightmare" by Pentagon officials, the F-16 program was widely cited as evidence that such multinational ventures can be successfully organized.[19]

On the basis of the F-16 precedent, the NATO countries agreed in 1978 to facilitate the coproduction of other major systems. Under the NATO plan, various "families" of weapons—for example, air-to-air missiles, antitank munitions, air defense systems—will be identified, and then individual countries (or combinations of countries) will be given the task of developing various members of the "family" on behalf of the Alliance as a whole. (Thus, one nation may develop short-range systems, another medium-range, and still another long-range weapons.) In accordance with this plan, European companies will be invited to coproduce several new American weapons systems—including the advanced AIM-9L Sidewinder air-to-air missile, the Multiple-Launch Rocket System, and the Patriot air-defense missile system—while the United States will procure selected European systems which fall into the same weapons "families."[20]

This renewed commitment to coproduction will, if fully implemented, promote greater cooperation within NATO while enhancing the "interoperability" of allied weapons. It will also, according to Under Secretary Perry, reduce the waste and duplication in arms development. (Exactly how much waste is eliminated is a matter of some debate, however; because many of these programs—such as the F-16 aircraft project—involve the establishment of duplicate production facilities, they may increase costs rather than reduce them.) But while U.S. strategists continue to emphasize the advantages of coproduction, other policymakers are becoming increasingly concerned about its long-term impact on U.S. economic and military security. Thus some economists and engineers argue that these programs can damage America's economic health by providing competitors with advanced technologies that are applicable to civilian as well as military production. Speaking of the F-16 project, for instance, a U.S. corporate official told *Aviation Week* that "some of these countries didn't even have an aerospace industry before this program. Now they are developing a capability that can match a lot of [U.S.] companies."[21]

These economic and trade considerations arise in all coproduction programs, of course, but they are particularly acute in programs involving Europe and Japan, as these countries are only interested in procuring the latest and most sophisticated U.S. equipment. As a result, participating U.S. firms are no longer providing well-established technologies—as they did in the coproduction efforts of the 1950s and 1960s—but rather their most advanced designs and production techniques.[22] This means, as Jack Baranson noted in *Foreign Policy*, that these programs are contributing to the technological advance of America's most powerful trade competitors:

> It is no longer merely mature products and standardized technologies that are moving abroad. Certain U.S. firms . . . now feel compelled to release to foreign enterprises their most recently developed technology (in terms of product designs, process engineering, and production systems). In some instances, the "product" has become the implanting of design and engineering capabilities which are the spawning grounds of future industrial competitors.

Many economists contend, he noted, that this phenomenon "has resulted in the outward shift of comparative advantages from the U.S. economy and that this is occurring at a rate and to an extent that is increasingly threatening and disruptive to the U.S. industrial position in the world economy."[23]

The export of sophisticated military know-how also magnifies the risk of industrial espionage, since it is known that Moscow avidly seeks the latest Western technologies in order to compensate for its own backwardness in many technical areas. Secretary Perry admitted in 1979 that "we are concerned that advanced technology may fall into the hands of our adversaries" through coproduction of sophisticated weapons.[24]

Concern over the loss of technological secrets has been a particular concern of the Reagan administration, resulting in some fresh attempts to tighten U.S. procedures for the review of pending coproduction and licensing agreements. "Transfers of technologically sensitive materials," Under Secretary of State for Security Assistance James L. Buckley promised in 1981, "will not be approved if a signifi-

cant possibility of compromise of sensitive information or equipment exists, or if justification on the basis of overriding U.S. interest
cannot be made."[25] In line with this principle, the Defense Department in 1982 proposed a number of measures for ensuring high-level
review of all coproduction and licensing agreements involving the
transfer of advanced technologies.[26]

While the Reagan administration appears committed to increased arms coordination within NATO, it is obvious that the current emphasis on domestic production and the safeguarding of U.S.
technological secrets are inconsistent with an expanded coproduction effort abroad. No doubt some high-visibility projects—Sidewinder and Patriot, for instance—will be allowed to proceed, but it
is unlikely that these will be followed by a large number of similar
programs. Given the symbolic importance of the standardization issue, however, it is unlikely that U.S. officials will adopt clear-cut
guidelines on coproduction to replace the current ambiguous approach. The problem of defining a comprehensive U.S. policy on this
issue will, therefore, remain with us for the foreseeable future.[27]

Coproduction in the Third World: The Proliferation of Conventional Arms-Making Capabilities

For most of the post-World War II era, U.S. coproduction and licensing agreements were largely concentrated in Japan and the major NATO powers, with only a few programs—involving relatively
unsophisticated hardware—underway in the less-developed areas. In
the past few years, however, Third World countries have accounted
for a significant portion of new arms-production agreements, including many of those involving sophisticated equipment. Given the
Third World's growing appetite for modern technology, moreover, it
is likely that such projects will play an ever-growing role in the U.S.
military trade with these countries. And because such exports raise
all of the problems associated with U.S. technology transfers to Europe plus a host of other problems, it is essential that we examine
this phenomenon closely.

As recently as 1978, U.S. coproduction and licensing agreements in the Third World were limited to a handful of programs in a
relatively small number of countries. A tally of major current coproduction operations prepared by the Department of Defense in that
year listed only eight projects in four countries: three in Taiwan
(F-5E aircraft, M-14 and M-60 infantry weapons, and army vehicles),
three in South Korea (M-16 rifle, AN/PRC-77 radio, and infantry ammunition), one in the Philippines (M-1 rifle), and one in Turkey

(2.75-in. rockets).[28] Another three or four countries (including Argentina, Brazil, and Israel) held licenses for the manufacture of American light planes or aircraft parts. By 1982, the list of current or pending coproduction/licensing countries had swelled to include Egypt, Greece, Pakistan, Saudi Arabia, Singapore, and Thailand, and the equipment involved had become steadily more sophisticated. South Korea, for instance, is now producing Northrop F-5E aircraft, Hughes 500-MD helicopters, and a variety of other U.S. weapons in addition to the systems listed earlier (see table 10).[29]

The Third World's growing appetite for modern arms-making technology appears to be motivated by a number of key factors. The first, undoubtedly, is nationalism, in the sense that possession of a domestic arms-making capability is thought to provide a degree of political independence and status in a world dominated by a handful of major military-industrial powers. "The time has come to free ourselves from the United States and countries of Europe," Brazilian Air Force Minister Joelmir Campos de Araripe Macedo declared in 1977. "It is a condition of security that each nation manufacture its own armaments."[30] And not just any armaments: because modern weapons are widely considered the apotheosis of industrial might, many aspiring Third World countries have attempted to develop elaborate arms facilities capable of producing a wide range of relatively sophisticated armaments. Argentina, for instance, produces the twin-turboprop Pucara attack plane (which was widely used during the Falklands conflict), while Brazil manufactures the Xavante counterinsurgency plane, the Bandeirante troop-transport plane, and the Italian-designed AMC supersonic fighter; both countries also produce a variety of light armored vehicles, antitank missiles, and modern frigates.[31] While few other Third World countries are likely to match the varied output of these two countries or Israel (another major producer) in the immediate future, it is evident that their model of a diversified, modern arms industry is being followed by a number of other rising powers, including India, Indonesia, Pakistan, South Korea, and Turkey.[32]

Linked to the issue of nationalism is the quest for technological "spinoffs." In obvious emulation of the American experience, several Third World governments have launched ambitious arms-production projects in the expectation that they will benefit the national economy as a whole through the acquisition and dissemination of modern technology. Such efforts stem from the belief that high-tech arms industries stimulate the growth of a wide range of other modern enterprises—especially in the areas of telecommunications, electronics, and metallurgy—while also serving as the primary training grounds for future generations of scientists and engineers.[33] It was these assumptions, more than any other factors, which apparently motivated the late Shah of Iran to launch a multibillion-dollar program to establish a modern arms industry in his country.[34]

For some countries, the quest for a domestic arms-making capability is motivated largely by a need for protection against embargoes. Several of the more prolific Third World arms producers—in particular Israel, South Africa, and Taiwan—began their production programs in response to existing or anticipated arms embargoes. South Africa, for instance, began work on its elaborate arms infrastructure in 1965, after the United Nations imposed an embargo on weapons deliveries to that country, while Taiwan recently stepped up its domestic production efforts in expectation of an eventual U.S. ban on arms transfers.[35] In some cases, these so-called pariah states have agreed to cooperate in each other's arms-production efforts in order to frustrate such embargoes.[36] Other countries, having been subjected to temporary embargoes while they were at war, subsequently established domestic armaments industries in order to protect themselves against any repetition of such action. Thus, India and Pakistan both launched large-scale arms programs in 1966, following their war over the Kashmir and the resulting Anglo-American arms cutoff.

Finally, many arms-importing countries view the development of domestic production facilities as a way of reducing hard-currency outlays and promoting exports. In recent years, the price of armaments has risen faster than that of most other commodities, placing a heavy burden on the arms-importing countries and motivating some to establish domestic arms-making facilities. Thus Brazil, with foreign debts totaling many billions of dollars, has imposed tight restrictions on aerospace imports while accelerating production at state-owned aircraft factories.[37] As these programs have come on line, moreover, several Third World nations have begun to export arms in order to further improve their balance-of-payments situation. Generally, these fledgling suppliers have specialized in the production of low-cost, relatively unsophisticated hardware that can compete effectively with more costly American and European products in the Third World market. Brazil, for instance, has sold its Bandeirante turboprop to several countries in South America, while Israel has successfully marketed its Arava transport plane in Central America and other Third World areas.[38]

For these reasons, many of the more affluent Third World countries have already launched elaborate programs for the development of modern arms industries, or are likely to do so in the coming decade. Despite their sometimes lofty ambitions, however, these countries generally cannot establish a sophisticated arms-making capability without substantial external support. Most modern weapons incorporate complex parts and materials whose fabrication exceeds the technical capacity of even the more advanced Third World countries, so at least some components must be imported from the industrialized powers. Many of these countries also lack experience in the introduction of new production techniques, and so must acquire foreign know-how and technical support. This dependency on imported techniques and materials tends to increase, moreover, with the degree of sophistication being sought.[39] Thus Brazil, which has consistently stressed self-sufficiency in domestic arms production, has repeatedly turned to foreign producers for assistance in developing new weapons (e.g., it is using Italian technology in its new AMX fighter program) and continues to install imported engines and electronic gear in domestically produced aircraft like the Xavante and Bandeirante.[40]

Given this continuing requirement for imported technology, the Third World's domestic arms-production programs are slowly but surely transforming the international arms trade. Whereas buying countries were once content to acquire finished merchandise only, today they seek technical expertise as well as fully assembled products. Indeed, many Third World governments now require that all major arms-import transactions allow for at least some coproduction or assembly work in domestic factories. Brazil, for instance, insisted on producing some F-5E subsystems before agreeing to purchase 42 of the aircraft in 1975, while Greece and Turkey are both demanding substantial coproduction work as part of major forthcoming aircraft buys.[41] Such demands can only multiply, moreover, as more Third World governments embark upon full-fledged arms-production programs. As Northrop President Thomas V. Jones has acknowledged, the days are gone when "you could walk into their office with a package under your arm, unwrap it and wave it in the air" with little fear of rejection. Nowadays, "they want to share technology, not just buy a piece of equipment." And if American firms want to continue doing business with them, "we'll have to stop talking for awhile and listen."[42]

The growing sale of U.S. arms-making technology to Third World governments raises a variety of obvious problems for U.S. policymakers. One of these problems has already been encountered in our discussion of European arms programs: the danger that U.S. technology transfers will contribute to the industrial modernization of potential competitors, thereby diminishing the U.S. technological lead in both the military and civilian marketplace. While Third World producers do not present the same economic challenge as do the Europeans, the threat of increased competition is no longer insignificant and can only grow larger in the years ahead. Indeed, U.S. arms firms have already complained that Israeli producers have incorporated U.S.-origin technology into weapons sold to Third World countries that normally do their arms shopping in the United States.[43] This pattern is likely to be repeated with other Third World suppliers, especially those like Argentina, Brazil, and South Korea which seek to develop a broad-based arms industry. In anticipation of just such competition, U.S. officials have imposed tight restrictions on foreign sales of American arms being coproduced in South Korea.[44]

But competition is not the only problem; transfers of military technologies to Third World countries also raise significant issues of foreign policy, military security, and arms control. To begin with, transactions of this sort often lead to deep and lasting American involvement in the armaments industry of the recipient, implying a U.S. commitment to that country far exceeding that represented by regular arms transfers. Such a commitment may be an appropriate form of assistance for very close allies, but could also result in excessive U.S. support for regimes of dubious stability or questionable intentions. It is now obvious, for instance, that the U.S.-backed armaments program of the late Shah of Iran produced economic dislocations and popular resentments that ultimately contributed to his downfall. Many other current recipients of U.S. technology, including Argentina and Brazil, have territorial and political ambitions which may prove incompatible with U.S. foreign policy objectives. And the continuing American involvement in Taiwan's arms-making infrastructure has become a significant obstacle to improved U.S. relations with China.

Arms-technology transfers can frustrate U.S. foreign policy in another important way: by routing U.S.-designed or U.S.-equipped military hardware to governments deemed ineligible for direct U.S. arms purchases because of their human rights behavior or their support for terrorism. In the 1970s, restrictions were placed on the transfer of U.S. arms to a number of Third World countries cited for persistent human rights violations, including Argentina, Chile, and Uruguay. The United States has also adhered to the U.N. arms embargo on South Africa because of the apartheid policies of the Pretoria regime and banned sales to Iraq and Libya because of their support for terrorist organizations. But while U.S. enforcement of these measures has been relatively effective when applied to direct exports from the United States to these countries, it has proven to be much more difficult to prevent the transfer of U.S.-designed and U.S.-equipped hardware produced in other countries. Thus U.S. components—including sophisticated radar systems—have been installed on Brazilian aircraft shipped to Chile, and U.S.-origin technology has been incorporated into weapons systems sold to both Chile and South Africa by Israel.[45] While such violations may appear relatively insignificant, they suggest how much more difficult it will become to enforce such measures when a larger number of Third World countries become producers and exporters of modern arms.

National security considerations can arise in two ways: first, through the loss of U.S. technological secrets to hostile powers due to inadequate security procedures in the recipient country or the overthrow of pro-U.S. regimes; and second, through the use of U.S.-designed weapons for purposes inconsistent with American security interests. An instance of the first is believed to have occurred in Iran in 1979, when U.S. military equipment and documents disappeared during the chaotic upheaval that followed the flight of the late Shah; an example of the second (or at least a prototype) occurred in the Falklands in 1982, when Argentina used its indigenously produced Pucaras in attacks on British warships, most of which were committed to NATO fleets. (Although Argentina's arms industry relies mostly on European technology, at least some American components were incorporated into Argentine-made equipment used in the Falklands war; even if the usage of American technology was relatively minimal, the Falklands crisis represents a model for other possible encounters between two allies of the United States.) These problems can also arise in the case of U.S. technology transfers to Europe and Japan, of course, but are more likely to emerge in the Third World because of growing political instability and the attendant risk that U.S. clients will engage in military adventures that conflict with U.S. security interests.

U.S. security or that of its allies can also be undermined by expensive arms-production schemes that divert resources from other development programs, thereby contributing to economic irregularities and political disorders. The development of modern arms industries obviously requires great concentrations of capital and technical expertise—both of which are normally in short supply in most Third World countries and can therefore only be secured through the cancellation or postponement of other essential projects. Armaments programs also tend to involve heavy borrowing from foreign banks to pay for the importation of expensive machinery, parts, and raw materials, thus further limiting the development potential of the nations involved.[46] Such sacrifice may be considered legitimate in some countries faced with possible aggression, such as Israel, but could also be considered frivolous in countries with a less menacing strategic environment. When coupled with other grievances, such apparent waste could contribute to popular antagonism to the regime in power—as occurred in Iran, where the late Shah's grandiose arms schemes consumed funds earmarked for other development projects (see chapter 6).

Ultimately, however, the greatest threat to U.S. security probably arises from the fact of technology diffusion itself. By contributing to the arms-making capabilities of foreign powers, the United States automatically contributes to the war-making potential of those countries—as well as that of any third countries they supply with U.S.-designed or U.S.-equipped weaponry—and thus inevitably increases the world's total capacity for military violence. This is not to say that any specific technology transfer will produce an increased risk of war, but rather that cumulative U.S. transfers—along with all those of the other major industrial powers—are steadily adding to the world's gross capacity for initiating and sustaining warfare. In this sense, the problem of conventional arms-technology exports is similar to the problem of nuclear-technology exports: we cannot always predict that a specific transfer of nuclear technology will eventually result in nuclear weapons programs, but there is widespread agreement that the general diffusion of certain nuclear technologies *per se* increases the likelihood of nuclear arms proliferation and thus, ultimately, the risk of a nuclear war.[47]

Also as in the case of nuclear proliferation, the export of conventional military technology raises significant issues of arms control. Obviously, the greater the number of nations in possession of such technology, the more difficult it becomes to negotiate restraints on conventional arms transfers. Although President Carter's efforts to negotiate such restraints met with failure, and while it may be some time before the world is again ready to consider such proposals, there is a growing international perception that controls of some sort are needed to defuse local arms races and to reduce the risk of conflict in unstable areas. Such controls can only work, however, if all major suppliers agree to participate—an arrangement that would be hard enough to negotiate if there were only five or six major suppliers, but one that becomes much, much harder when the number reaches a dozen or more. The same principle applies to embargoes in times of crisis: while the traditional suppliers may agree to a suspension in arms deliveries to all parties in a conflict—hoping thereby to spur negotiations, or at least to limit the extent of the violence—such measures would obviously prove fruitless if the belligerents could turn to alternative suppliers (some of which may be ideologically opposed to such forms of coercion) for their military needs. By contributing to the arms-production programs of foreign powers, therefore, the United States is making the attainment of its own stated arms control objectives more difficult.

The Imperative of Control:
Toward a Policy on Arms-Technology Exports

From all of the above, it is evident that the export of arms-making technology to foreign powers poses some difficult and important issues for American policymakers. While tightly controlled transfers may serve U.S. interests in some cases, they can also do great damage to U.S.—and global—interests in others. Thus, while coproduction in Europe may promote standardization within NATO, it can also lead to lasting economic harm for U.S. producers of high-tech products; similarly, while technology transfers to friendly Third World countries may contribute to their self-defense capabilities, they can also stimulate local arms races and military adventurism. Given these potential hazards, and the likelihood of a continuing proliferation of conventional arms-making capabilities, the United States clearly requires a strict, comprehensive policy on arms coproduction and licensing.

Unfortunately, existing legislation considers technology transfers as a variety of arms exports, rather than as a separate phenomenon with distinctive policy issues of its own. Thus, while the Arms Export Control Act sets elaborate procedures for the conduct of weapons sales, it addresses technology transfers only rarely. The AECA, as noted earlier, proclaims that "special emphasis" shall be placed on direct sales of U.S. military equipment, but notes that "consideration shall also be given to coproduction or licensed production [of U.S.-designed arms] outside the United States" when such production "best serves the foreign policy, national security, and economy of the United States." No guidelines are provided for making these determinations, however, and thus interpretation of this provision is left entirely to the secretary of state.

In another passage of the AECA, the secretary is enjoined to consult with the director of the Arms Control and Disarmament Agency as to whether proposed coproduction/licensing programs "might contribute to an arms race, or increase the possibility of outbreak or escalation of conflict, or prejudice the development of bilateral or multinational arms control agreements." Here again, however, no guidance is provided on how such findings should be weighed when deciding on these programs. (In any case, it is impossible to determine how thorough an assessment of these problems the ACDA actually makes, since the State Department refuses to release copies of these studies.)[48]

The executive branch has been equally taciturn on the subject of arms-technology transfers. President Carter, in his "arms restraint" directive of May 1977, banned the initiation of new coproduction agreements involving major weapons systems in the nonexempt countries (i.e., all countries except the NATO powers, Australia, Japan, and New Zealand), but permitted coproduction of components and subsystems when intended for the recipient's exclusive use. (As in other provisions of the Carter policy, this ban could be relaxed if the president determined that "extraordinary circumstances" necessitated a presidential exception—an event that occurred more frequently with coproduction programs than with any other provision.)[49] The Carter policy was subsequently revoked by President Reagan, who declined to offer any substitute language on the control of military coproduction and licensing agreements. In the sole reference to this issue in his Arms Transfer Policy directive of July 8, 1981, Reagan simply noted that proposed arms-technology transfers "will receive special scrutiny," taking into account such issues as the "economic and industrial factors for both the United States and other participating countries, the importance of arms cooperation with NATO and other close friends and allies, potential third party transfers, and the protection of sensitive technology and military capabilities." Interpretation of this edict, however, was left entirely to the president's discretion.

Clearly, existing congressional and presidential policies on arms-technology exports are woefully inadequate. What is needed, in their place, is a comprehensive policy on coproduction and licensing that provides clear and precise guidelines on when, under what specified circumstances, agreements of this type should be concluded. Such a policy should view technology exports as distinct from regular arms transfers, requiring separate guidance and review procedures and tight follow-up supervision. These measures should be contained in a new section of the Arms Export Control Act, or in an entirely new piece of legislation.

In drawing up such an ordinance, U.S. legislators should give careful consideration to the liabilities as well as the benefits of technology transfers. To protect the long-term economic, political, and military interests of the United States, and to advance the cause of world stability, no coproduction or licensing agreement should be permitted that has the potential to seriously damage the economic health of U.S. industries; undermine U.S. foreign policy objectives in the area of arms control, human rights, or economic development; or contribute to regional arms races or an increased risk of military conflict.

To ensure that these considerations are properly examined, all proposed agreements of this type should be subjected to thorough study by senior State, Defense, and ACDA officials and should require the preparation of an "arms control impact statement" covering all possible consequences of any given transfer. This statement, plus additional documentation, should then be submitted to Congress for review and possible veto. Finally, all those projects that are approved should be subjected to continuous U.S. monitoring to ensure that all restrictions on the utilization of U.S. technology are fully adhered to; nations that violate U.S. regulations by selling U.S.-designed or U.S.-equipped weaponry to unauthorized third countries (e.g., Libya and South Africa) should be barred from future transfers of U.S. technology.

Such a policy, if fully implemented, would greatly reduce the risk of inappropriate or imprudent technology transfers. Ultimately, however, unilateral restraints of this sort will prove futile if other powers continue to export sophisticated technology to fledgling producers—who can then collaborate with other nations in the further diffusion of arms-making capabilities. It is essential, therefore, that U.S. policymakers include technology transfers in any future negotiations aimed at imposing multilateral restraints on the international arms traffic. The U.S.-Soviet Conventional Arms Talks could, if reconvened by Washington and Moscow, provide a framework for such efforts. Steps will also have to be taken to include the other major arms suppliers in such talks and to provide adequate security guarantees for all Third World countries affected by such measures. None of this will be easy. Nevertheless, many similar problems were overcome when negotiating the Nuclear Non-Proliferation Treaty, and, hopefully, the growing costs of the technological arms race will motivate world leaders to negotiate similar controls on the proliferation of conventional arms technology.

CHAPTER 9

Arms Sales and Human Rights

The Merchants of Repression

Shortly after taking office as president, Jimmy Carter pledged that the advancement of human rights abroad would be a major objective of his administration. "Our values," he told the Organization of American States on April 14, 1977, "require us to combat abuses of individual freedom, including those caused by political, social, and economic injustice."[1] This stance would be reflected not only in words, he further affirmed, but also in deeds. Henceforth, any governments that were cited for persistent human rights violations would be subjected to various penalties by Washington, including cutbacks in military assistance and arms transfers. This linkage between arms sales and human rights was subsequently formalized in Carter's "arms restraint" policy of May 19, 1977 (see chapter 3). And while President Reagan has since rescinded the Carter policy and adopted a new set of priorities to govern arms export decisionmaking, the link between military sales and human rights remains fixed in public opinion and U.S. law. Because this linkage will undoubtedly influence government debate on these issues for a long time to come, it is important that we examine this relationship closely and consider how it should contribute to the development of U.S. arms export policy.[2]

Of all major "implements" of U.S. foreign policy, none appears to bear more heavily on human rights considerations than arms exports. This is true for two key reasons.

First, through the bestowal of legitimacy: arms transfers are widely perceived as a major indicator of government-to-government relations, signifying, in some sense, a "vote of confidence" in the recipient by the supplier. Thus, when newly inaugurated President Reagan promised South Korean strongman Chun Doo Hwan a big increase in U.S. arms deliveries during a visit to Washington in 1981, this was widely viewed as a significant expression of support for the Chun regime, particularly since earlier South Korean requests for new arms had been rebuffed by the Carter administration.[3] Subsequent announcements of stepped-up U.S. military sales to Pakistan and the Philippines were also seen in this light, as were administration efforts to weaken the embargo on arms transfers to South Africa.[4]

Second, through direct application to internal repression: in many cases, U.S. arms have been used by military juntas to topple democratic governments and to silence domestic opposition to their continued rule. The present rulers of Argentina, Chile, and Uruguay, for instance, used their U.S.-supplied weapons in the bloody coups that brought them to power and in the reign of terror that followed.[5] In many such countries, moreover, U.S. arms and equipment have been sold to the police and paramilitary organizations most directly involved in internal repression, such as the DINA in Chile, SAVAK in Iran, and the KCIA in South Korea. In these cases, U.S. arms transfers can be said to constitute a direct contribution to the repressive capabilities of the regimes in question.[6]

For these reasons, U.S. lawmakers have explicitly linked the provision of U.S. arms aid to the recipient's human rights behavior. Under section 502B of the Foreign Assistance Act (FAA) of 1961, as amended in 1976, the president is obliged to terminate security assistance "to any government which engages in a consistent pattern of gross violations of internationally recognized human rights." In line with this principle, Congress has on occasion outlawed military aid and/or arms sales to certain foreign countries, including Argentina, Brazil, Chile, El Salvador, Guatemala, and Uruguay.* Human rights behavior was also a critical consideration in the 1981–82 debate over military aid to El Salvador, resulting in a congressional stipulation that the president "certify" that substantial progress was being made by the Salvadoran government in curbing abuses by the armed forces.† And, of course, human rights considerations are the principal justification for the continuing embargo on arms transfers to the apartheid regime in South Africa.[7]

*Thus section 406 of the International Security Assistance Act of 1976 banned all forms of security assistance (including FMS and licensed Commercial Sales) to Chile, while section 602B of the FAA of 1961 (as amended in 1977) outlawed all security aid to Argentina; similarly, section 503A of the FAA of 1978 banned military aid and arms credits to Uruguay, and section 503B of that act made Brazil, El Salvador, and Guatemala ineligible for arms credits under the FMS program.

†Under section 728B and D of the International Security and Development Act of 1981, Congress ruled that no U.S. aid may be provided to El Salvador unless the president can provide detailed "certification" every six months that the Salvadoran government "is making a concerted and significant effort to comply with internationally-recognized human rights." A similar measure was vetoed by President Reagan in 1983, but again inserted into proposed legislation the following year.

The Reagan administration has attempted to dilute or rescind these restrictions, arguing that arms transfers contribute to the self-defense capabilities of America's allies and thereby strengthen our own national security—a goal that is considered to take priority over the promotion of human rights. Thus, in a critique of congressional restraints on arms transfers, Under Secretary of State for Security Assistance James L. Buckley contended in 1981 that "while these well-intentioned efforts have had little detectable impact on [the affected countries'] behavior . . . they did lead at times to the awkward result of undercutting the capabilities of strategically-located nations in whose ability to defend themselves we have the most immediate and urgent self-interest."[8] This argument succeeded in persuading Congress to lift the human rights restriction on military exports to some countries—most notably in the case of Argentina—but not to abandon the basic premise that arms sales and human rights are closely linked issues.

In principle, this linkage suggests that human rights considerations are raised whenever the United States sells arms to undemocratic regimes abroad. As suggested earlier, however, some arms transfers appear to bear more heavily on human rights issues than others. Thus, while sales of advanced fighters and other sophisticated weapons may confer a certain amount of legitimacy and political support on a particular regime, they rarely impact directly on the human rights situation within the recipient country. Sales of counter-insurgency and police equipment, on the other hand, may not have as much symbolic significance (because of the low cost and reduced visibility of the systems involved), but often do have a very substantial impact on human rights, by endowing government security forces with enhanced repressive capabilities. Clearly, transfers of internal security equipment can raise significant human rights considerations even when the recipient has a relatively unblemished record in this regard; when sold to undemocratic governments, however, they almost always impact on the human rights situation because of the likelihood that they will be used to silence dissent. In such cases, U.S. sales of police and paramilitary gear can be said to constitute a special component of the arms business that can best be described as the "repression trade."[9] Because such transactions are rarely discussed in Congress, and because of their obvious relevance to human rights, we shall concentrate here on this particular aspect of the arms trade.

American exports of police and security gear are conducted through three separate export channels, each of which is processed separately by the arms export establishment:

Sales of Military and Paramilitary Gear through the Foreign Military Sales Program. Although most publicly announced FMS transactions involve sales of advanced aircraft, ships, and armored vehicles intended for external defense purposes, a very large percentage of routine FMS transactions involve infantry weapons equally applicable to external or internal security operations (small arms, jeeps, radios, etc.) or intended exclusively for internal security use (armored cars, tear gas grenades, counterinsurgency planes). In many cases, such mixed-use and paramilitary hardware has been sold to countries where the armed forces perform a civil police function under martial law decree or are engaged in a counterinsurgency war against domestic insurgents.[10] And while U.S. law (specifically, section 660 of the Foreign Assistance Act of 1974) bans the use of FMS channels for sales to foreign police and intelligence agencies, the FMS program has been used to supply paramilitary organizations with an exclusive internal security mission, such as the Imperial Iranian Gendarmerie, the Philippines Constabulary, and the Saudi Arabian National Guard.[11]

Sales of Police and Security Gear through the Commercial Sales Program. Under the Arms Export Control Act, U.S. arms firms are permitted to sell firearms, tear gas, and other Munitions List items directly to foreign police and security agencies through the Commercial Sales program. When conducting such sales, the seller must obtain an export license from the State Department's Office of Munitions Control. Documents I acquired through the Freedom of Information Act indicate that U.S. firms exported such gear to police and security agencies in 82 Third World countries between 1976 and 1979, including many with a conspicuously poor record in the human rights area (see appendix 2).[12]

Sales of Computers, Anti-Riot Equipment, and Other "Nonmilitary" Systems through Commerce Department Channels. U.S. firms can also supply foreign governments with a wide range of police and security devices through Commerce Department channels. Such equipment, which by definition excludes items on the Munitions List (which must be exported through the Commercial Sales program), can range from computers and transport planes to truncheons and electronic "shock batons." Export of such gear to most non-Communist nations is essentially unregulated, but sales to Libya, South Africa, and all Communist countries require a "validated" license from the Commerce Department and are thus subjected to closer government scrutiny. Nevertheless, because these items are not listed on the Munitions List, they are considered exempt from section 502B of the Foreign Assistance Act and thus are routinely sold to countries barred from FMS and Commercial Sales for human rights reasons.[13]

Because of the secrecy involved in many of these transactions (the Commerce Department, for instance, refuses to divulge any information on sales of computers to foreign police and intelligence agencies) and the variety of export channels involved, it is difficult to compile an accurate annual tally of all such sales. It seems reasonable, however, to venture an estimate of $2 billion per year (including counterinsurgency equipment and mixed-use items sold to countries ruled under martial law), or about 10 percent of total U.S. military exports. Such a figure reflects the relatively low cost of the items involved (compared to front-line systems like jet fighters and missiles), but also takes account of the fact that a large percentage of the individual FMS and Commercial Sales cases processed each year are composed of such equipment.[14]

Although $2 billion may not seem like much when compared to the $20 billion spent each year by foreign governments on U.S. arms, sales of police and paramilitary equipment of this sort probably have as much long-term political significance—for both the supplier and the recipient—as do sales of more costly planes and missiles. Paramilitary weapons are more likely to prove decisive in internal conflicts and power struggles than sophisticated armaments and are also far more likely to be seen on a day-to-day basis in the streets and villages of military-ruled societies. It is not surprising, therefore, that dissidents and insurgents often harbor particular resentment toward the suppliers of internal security gear to the regime in power—a phenomenon that can significantly affect government-to-government relations when, as in the case of Iran and Nicaragua, the one-time rebels and dissidents become the new reigning powers.

Despite the obvious significance of police and paramilitary exports, such sales rarely come to the attention of Congress or the public. To some extent, this reflects the emphasis on costly and sophisticated weapons built into the reporting requirements of the Arms Export Control Act, for few FMS sales of security systems reach the $50 million level required to trigger advance notification to Congress. Commercial Sales and Commerce Department transactions are subject to even less scrutiny: CS sales of $1 million or more must be reported to Congress, but only after the sale has been consummated; Commerce Department exports of this type need not be reported at all. Furthermore, both the State and Commerce departments have resisted efforts to provide such information through the Freedom of Information Act.[15] Nevertheless, it is possible to produce a relatively complete picture of the trade in police and security hardware using industry sources, interviews, and the available government statistics. In the pages that follow, we shall look at each of the three export channels identified above and then conclude with recommendations for tightened controls over the repression trade.

The Foreign Military Sales Program

Although the FMS program is usually described as a vehicle for strengthening the capacity of friendly countries to defend themselves against external aggression, a significant proportion of FMS transactions involve mixed-use systems (i.e., equipment that is usable for both external and internal security operations) or weapons intended exclusively for paramilitary purposes. Such equipment is often sold, moreover, to military forces which perform civil security functions under martial law decree, or to paramilitary organizations with an exclusive internal security function. The use of FMS channels for sales of this sort is permitted under section 4 of the AECA, which states that "defense articles and defense services shall be sold by the United States Government . . . for internal security [and] legitimate self-defense. . . ." On this basis, the United States has long supplied friendly foreign governments with a vast array of counterinsurgency and paramilitary gear through FMS channels. Indeed, this sort of equipment constitutes the bulk of U.S. equipment supplied to countries such as Colombia, El Salvador, Honduras, Indonesia, Morocco, the Philippines, and Thailand that are now or have periodically been engaged in major anti-guerrilla campaigns.[16]

Although U.S. officials tend to stress the external defense role when defending the FMS program, they are not unmindful of the primacy of internal security considerations when considering requests from the countries described above. Thus, in the *Congressional Presentation Document* on the Security Assistance Program for Fiscal Year 1983, the Pentagon contended that military sales to the Philippines were justified because "they are likely to have a positive impact on internal stability." Similarly, in justifying sales to Colombia, the document noted that the government of Colombia (GOC) is "heavily involved in curbing armed guerrilla groups," and that U.S. arms aid "is tailored to provide the GOC with the material and resources it must have to counter" these groups.[17]

To a great extent, sales of this sort are viewed as a continuation of supply patterns established under the Military Assistance Program in the 1950s and 1960s, when internal security was a more conspicuous function of U.S. arms export policy. Indeed, during the

Kennedy and Johnson periods, internal security was considered the principal goal of MAP assistance to many Third World areas.[18] Later, under the Nixon Doctrine, internal security was again seen as a critical MAP goal when Washington sought to reduce direct U.S. military involvement in anti-guerrilla wars by building up the defense capabilities of pro-U.S. regimes in the Third World (see chapter 5).[19]

Although Congress generally concurred with the basic goals of the Nixon Doctrine, it became increasingly disinclined to vote the increased aid funds needed to carry it out. To some extent, this reluctance reflected public antipathy to the lingering Vietnam War— and to anything as closely associated with it as the MAP program had become. In just three years, from fiscal 1973 to fiscal 1976, Congress cut MAP spending by 94 percent—from $4.2 billion to a mere $264 million. Faced with the potential collapse of their strategic design, Nixon administration officials took the only recourse available: they persuaded Congress to vote additional FMS credits and persuaded U.S. allies to buy the items they had previously obtained at no cost. As a result, FMS sales jumped from about $2 billion per year in the early 1970s to $12–$14 billion by the end of the decade. And, as indicated by FMS transaction records, counterinsurgency and internal security hardware have constituted a significant portion of the increased sales.[20]

Turning to these records, we find that some of the most popular items sold to FMS customers in the Third World are counterinsurgency planes, such as the Rockwell OV-10 Bronco, the Fairchild AU-23A Peacemaker, and the Cessna A-37B Dragonfly; troop-carrying helicopters, especially the Bell/Textron UH-1 Iroquois (more popularly known by its Vietnam nickname, the "Huey"); and armored cars, such as the Cadillac-Gage V-150 Commando. Although these systems could conceivably be used in an all-out conflict between the regular armies of two or more nations, they are primarily intended for rural counterinsurgency warfare or, in the case of the V-150, for urban security operations.[21] Not surprisingly, therefore, many of the prominent customers for these items are militarized regimes that have recently engaged in anti-guerrilla campaigns or that anticipate major flare-ups of domestic violence. Thailand, for instance, has ordered 46 OV-10s, 20 AU-23As, 14 UH-1s, and 164 V-150s in recent years, while Indonesia has ordered 16 OV-10s, 16 UH-1s, and 60 V-150s, and the Philippines has ordered 18 OV-10s, 35 UH-1s, and 20 V-150s. Other recent customers for these items have included Malaysia (200 V-150s), Singapore (250 V-150s), Chile (34 A-37Bs), and Saudi Arabia (729 V-150s).[22] These are not, by any means, the only prominent sales of these or similar counterinsurgency weapons to overseas customers through the FMS program, but they are suggestive of the popularity of such systems.

Exports of these and all other items supplied through the FMS program are of course subject to blockage under section 502B of the FAA or similar measures. As we have seen, these provisions have on occasion been used to bar such exports to particular Latin American countries. In recent years, however, Congress has been reluctant to extend such restrictions to other countries with a similar human rights record, and since 1981 the Reagan administration has lobbied to eliminate such curbs altogether. Given the administration's emphasis on aiding U.S. allies threatened by Soviet- or Cuban-sponsored insurgency, moreover, it is likely that sales of paramilitary hardware will be stepped up in the years ahead.

The Commercial Sales Program

While FMS channels are normally used to supply foreign military forces, all sales of Munitions List items to foreign police and intelligence organizations must be processed through the Commercial Sales program. Through this program, U.S. arms firms sell millions of dollars' worth of firearms, chemical munitions, vehicles, and helicopters to foreign security agencies every year. These sales are particularly relevant to human rights concerns, since in many cases this equipment is going directly to the police and intelligence agencies that have been identified by investigators as being responsible for the arrest, torture, and assassination of political dissidents.[23] Despite such charges, U.S. officials tend to subject such sales to much less scrutiny than is paid to the sale of other, more conventional military systems.

Under existing law, firms wishing to export items on the U.S. Munitions List must obtain an export license from the State Department's Office of Munitions Control. (While there have been periodic revisions of the Munitions List, licenses are generally required for such hardware as pistols and revolvers, carbines and submachine guns, armored vehicles of all kinds, chemical munitions, and ammunition for the above.)[24]

Theoretically, when a company submits a license application to the OMC, the State Department can investigate the human rights implications of the proposed sale and, in accordance with section 502B of the FAA, deny approval for the license. In practice, however, this is rarely done. This is partly due to the very large numbers of license applications received each year by the OMC staff—most of which involve relatively small quantities of arms and equipment—and partly because Congress and the executive branch have adopted a relatively permissive attitude toward such sales. Thus, Congress does not require advanced notification of proposed cs sales (as it does in the case of major FMS transactions) and only requires after-the-fact notification of sales totaling $1 million and above (a rarity for sales of police-type equipment). The State Department, for its part, rarely intercedes in cs transactions unless pressured to do so by Congress (as in the case of El Salvador) or if the president has ordered a temporary ban on U.S. arms transfers to the country in question (such as Jimmy Carter's ban on Nicaragua during the final months of the Somoza regime). Most of the time, therefore, cs transactions are processed with relatively little policy oversight by the U.S. government.*

The government's apparent disinterest in the policy implications of cs transactions should not lead us to conclude that such sales are lacking in political significance. While it is true that most individual cs transactions involve relatively small quantities of equipment—several hundred revolvers, say, or a few thousand dollars' worth of tear gas—their collective proportions are decidedly impressive. According to export licenses I acquired from the OMC under the Freedom of Information Act, U.S. firms sold police forces in the Third World a total of 615,612 gas grenades and 126,622 pistols and revolvers between September 1976 and May 1979, along with 51,906 rifles and submachine guns, 12,605 canisters of chemical Mace, and 56 million rounds of ammunition (see table 11).[25] And this represents sales to the police only; much larger quantities of such items are sold every year to military and paramilitary organizations in these countries through the cs program. When combined with FMS shipments and Commerce Department transactions, therefore, these sales represent a very significant transfer of internal security capabilities to Third World governments—many of which have been cited in U.S. government publications for persistent violations of individual human rights.[26]

Even where the quantities of cs sales are relatively small, however, the net impact on human rights conditions in the recipient country can be quite significant. This is true for two reasons: first,

_____

*Evidence of the government's laxity in processing cs transactions surfaced in the 1978 proceedings against the Olin-Winchester Corporation, which was charged with smuggling $20 million worth of guns and ammunition to South Africa in violation of U.S. arms export regulations. During the trial, lawyers for Olin argued that company officials believed that the State Department was "winking" at such sales because of its consistent failure to block patently suspicious transactions over a several year period.

many of these items are specifically designed for crowd control and civil security operations, and thus are especially useful in suppressing popular resistance to government policy; and second, such equipment is often sold directly to the government agencies that are specifically charged with responsibility for monitoring and silencing political dissent, such as the DINA in Chile, SAVAK in Iran (under the Shah), and the KCIA in South Korea.[27] In such cases, U.S. arms transfers often contribute directly to the violation of human rights in these countries.

Given this potential, it is not surprising that information on the sales of U.S. security gear to foreign police agencies is normally concealed by the U.S. government. However, the export licenses I obtained under the Freedom of Information Act provide graphic evidence of U.S. involvement in the repression trade. Of the eighty-two countries which acquired at least some U.S. equipment during this period, at least a third—including El Salvador, Guatemala, Haiti, Indonesia, Iran, Nicaragua, Pakistan, Paraguay, the Philippines, and South Korea—have been repeatedly cited by Amnesty International and other humanitarian organizations for persistent abuses of basic human rights.[28] Several others, including Afghanistan, Iraq, and Syria, are allies of the Soviet Union and are ineligible for purchases of regular U.S. military gear. The OMC documents also indicate that some of this equipment has been delivered to specific security agencies in those countries that have been directly linked to human rights abuses, including the Carabineros of Chile, the paramilitary police of Paraguay, and the Border Patrol Police of Thailand.

The OMC documents also provide considerable information on the suppliers of police and security hardware and on the types of

Table 11. U.S. Arms Transfers to Third World Police and Security Forces by Region, 1976–79

Region	Tear gas grenades	Tear gas guns	Canisters of Mace
Latin America	139,100	1,188	1,623
East Asia & Pacific	135,748	914	6,295
Africa	106,792	377	650
Near East & South Asia	233,972	681	302
World, Total	615,612	3,160	8,870

SOURCE: Export licenses issued to major U.S. arms firms by Office of Munitions Control, U.S. Department of State.

equipment most in demand abroad. Unlike the FMS program, which tends to be dominated by a few large aerospace firms with close ties to the U.S. military establishment, the CS program is used by a larger corps of generally smaller firms, many of which produce only a handful of specialized items. Among the major CS producers are well-known gun firms such as Colt, Winchester, and Remington that dominated the U.S. arms business until being overtaken by the high-tech aerospace combines. Other prominent CS suppliers include smaller companies like Federal Laboratories that produce specialized police and security gear for the U.S. and foreign markets, and export firms like Fargo International and Jonas Aircraft that market the products of several specialty producers.[29] Together, these companies comprise what has been called the "police-industrial complex," and, when selling to totalitarian governments abroad, the "merchants of repression."[30]

Table 12 lists some of the principal suppliers of police gear to police agencies in the Third World, and the commodities they normally export through the CS program. (Some of these companies also export other types of security hardware through Commerce Department channels, but the OMC documents only list exports of items that are entered on the Munitions List.)

Of the Munitions List items normally acquired by foreign police and security organizations, the most prominent are:[31]

Handguns. The most popular police sidearm is the .38-calibre revolver, of which Smith & Wesson and Colt (the leading producers) sold over 100,000 between 1976 and 1979. Other popular handguns include .357- and .32-calibre revolvers. The OMC documents indicate that almost every country in the world has acquired at least some

Carbines, rifles, sub-machine guns	Pistols & revolvers	Small arms ammunition (1,000 rounds)
8,009	41,602	19,772
43,658	33,247	30,303
100	17,847	325
139	33,926	5,434
51,906	126,622	55,834

U.S. handguns, and in some cases entire police forces have been re-armed with U.S. weapons. In 1978, for instance, the Royal Malay Police bought 16,000 Smith & Wesson .38s and the Peruvian Civil Guard bought 10,000 Colt .38s.

Other Firearms. These include rifles, submachine guns, and shotguns. The most popular export types are the Colt M-16 automatic rifle, the Military Armament Corporation's .380-calibre and 9-mm. submachine guns, and the High Standard Model #10, 12-gauge shotgun. Major sales have included 15,000 Colt M-16s to Indonesia in 1979, and 5,000 M-16s to the Nicaraguan National Guard in 1976.

Chemical Agents. U.S. firms export two types of anti-riot chemical agents: CN (chloroacetophenone) and CS (orthochlorobenzal-malononitrile). Both are popularly known as "tear gas," although they are not really gases but powdery substances, and CS (also known as "pepper gas") produces breathing difficulties and burning sensations rather than tearing. The major U.S. suppliers of CN and CS are Smith & Wesson and Federal Laboratories, both of which produce a wide range of grenades, projectiles, and dispensing systems. Both firms also produce an aerosol spray containing CN and kerosene known generically as Mace. (Mace is in fact the trademark for Smith & Wesson's version of this product; other companies are required to use different names—hence Federal Laboratories' version is called the "Federal Streamer.") Among the more prominent Third World customers for these products are Egypt, which ordered 154,000 CN

Table 12. Sales to Third World Police and Security Forces by Selected U.S. Companies, September 1976–79

Manufacturer	Gas grenades & projectiles	Gas guns	Canisters Mace[b]
AAI Corp.	5,100	—	—
Browning Arms	—	—	—
Colt Industries	—	—	—
Federal Cartridge	1,770	—	—
Federal Labs	585,551	3,021	3,910
Remington Arms	—	—	—
Smith & Wesson[a]	25,316	119	8,695
Winchester International	—	284	—

SOURCE: Licenses issued by the Office of Munitions Control, U.S. Department of State.
[a]Includes sales by the General Ordnance Equipment Co., a subsidiary.
[b]Includes Federal Streamer, a derivative product.

and cs projectiles between 1976 and 1979, and Malaysia, which bought 102,000.

Armored Cars. The only armored police vehicle currently produced for export in the United States is the v-150 Commando, manufactured by the Cadillac-Gage Corporation of Warren, Michigan, a subsidiary of the Ex-Cell-O Corporation. These vehicles normally come equipped with radios, anti-riot equipment, and gun turrets and can carry up to twelve police or soldiers. Over 5,000 have been sold abroad over the past ten years, at an average cost of about $150,000. v-150s are exported both through the cs program (when sold to police agencies) and the fms program (when sold to military forces).

Other items sold to foreign police and intelligence agencies through the cs program include surveillance and night-vision devices (such as Smith & Wesson's "Star-tron" system), jeeps and other military vehicles, communications systems, and helicopters (such as the Hughes Model #500 scout helicopter). Although cs sales of this type represent a very small portion of the total U.S. arms trade with the Third World, they often have, as suggested above, a very significant bearing on the human rights situation in recipient countries. Indeed, there are a number of documented cases in which that connection can be explicitly demonstrated, including the following.

During the January 1977 "food riots" in Egypt (a spontaneous protest against price increases for government-subsidized staples

Rifles & carbines	Pistols & revolvers	Ammunition (1,000 rounds)
—	—	—
—	15,000	20
49,469	22,691	52
—	—	1,441
—	—	26
856	—	8,691
—	90,854	3,427
284	—	41,895

which resulted in seventy-five deaths), Robert Fisk of the *London Times* filed this report from Cairo:

> One after another, young policemen wearing gas masks ran forward, knelt on one knee and fired cannisters into the crowd. . . . Behind them ran three perspiring soldiers carrying dustbins full of replacement gas cartridges. As the crowds noticed with interest, these came not from the country's former military suppliers—the Soviet Union—but from the United States. One group of demonstrators chanted anti-American slogans, charging that all the tear gas came from the United States. Indeed, this appeared to be true. Every empty gas cannister which I picked up bore the words "CS #518—Federal Laboratories, Inc., Saltsburg, PA."[32]

During the military coup in Thailand on October 6, 1976, Thai police and paramilitary forces stormed the campus of Thammasat University in Bangkok, killing or wounding several hundred unarmed students who had barricaded themselves inside. In photographs taken at the scene and later published in Western journals, one can easily make out the U.S.-supplied small arms, recoilless rifles, and other weapons used by Thai forces during their bloody assault.[33]

Following a 1978 antigovernment demonstration in São Paulo, Brazilian journalists reported that several students had been badly burned by a chemical spray fired by government security forces. The spray was reportedly produced by canisters (some of which were dropped by the police during the melee) which were clearly marked "No. 502 CS Irritant Agent—Federal Laboratories, Saltsburg, PA, USA."[34]

These are just a few of the cases which demonstrate the high potential for abuse inherent in cs sales of police and paramilitary hardware. Despite this potential, Congress has not subjected this program to as much scrutiny as that accorded to major FMS transactions. If the United States is to retain its commitment to human rights, therefore, it is obvious that greater oversight of cs transactions is needed to reduce the likelihood of abuse.

Commerce Department Channels

In addition to selling through the State Department's cs program, many U.S. firms export police and security equipment to foreign governments through normal trade channels. Such exports, which by definition exclude items found on the Munitions List, include a wide variety of security systems, among them: computers and related data-processing equipment; police and prison hardware (e.g., helmets, handcuffs, shackles, sirens, etc.); "nonmilitary" weapons such as clubs, truncheons, and electric-shock devices; and assorted "crime control" equipment (e.g., polygraph systems, fingerprint-taking equipment, etc.). These exports are theoretically supervised by the Department of Commerce, but in practice are conducted with little or no regard for the possible human rights implications of proposed sales—despite the fact that such equipment can easily be used to apprehend dissidents or to abuse political prisoners.

Under current regulations, U.S. firms can export most of the products described above to most non-Communist countries without prior approval by the Department of Commerce. (In such cases, these exports are said to be conducted under a "general" license, which merely requires periodic notification to Commerce of completed transactions.) However, firms wishing to export items that incorporate sensitive technology, or that involve sales to Libya, South Africa, Syria, and other nations that are subject to stiffer export controls, must first obtain a "validated" license from the Office of Export Administration. The Commerce Department has reportedly tightened the licensing process to prevent the transfer of advanced technology to potential adversaries, but evidently very little effort has been made to prevent the transfer of repressive technology to known human rights violators abroad. Indeed, statistics provided by the Bureau of the Census (which monitors U.S. exports for the Commerce Department) indicate that many of the security systems described above are being sold to governments that have been cited for persistent human rights violations.[35]

Among the many categories of manufactured goods listed in the Commerce Department's directory of trade classifications, one finds "Crime Control and Detection Equipment." According to the Census Bureau, this category encompasses "non-military arms such as shotguns, stun guns, dart guns, riot guns, and shock batons." Also included are "straight-jackets, non-military gas masks, bullet-proof vests and shields," and "non-military protective vests, leg irons, shackles, handcuffs, thumbscrews, and other manufactures of metal."[36] Just how many of any particular items in this category are sold to any particular government is difficult to determine, both because of the incomplete and inconsistent reporting procedures involved and because of the pervasive secrecy that enshrouds most Commerce Department operations. Compounding the lack of formal documentation (such as the export licenses issued by the Office of Munitions Control), the Census Bureau lumps police hardware together with meat hooks and other miscellaneous items under the heading "Articles, not elsewhere classified, of iron and steel." Accordingly, one can only speculate as to how many thumbscrews were included in the $1.7 million worth of hardware Chile purchased in this category between 1974 and 1976, or how many leg irons and shackles South Africa acquired among its purchases of $2.4 million.[37]

Sales of "non-military arms and ammunition" are somewhat easier to track, since the Census Bureau maintains a separate category for such equipment in its monthly statistics reports on U.S. trade. According to these reports, U.S. firms sold 69,776 "non-military shotguns" to customers in Thailand during the year preceding the bloody coup of October 1976, and another 2,435 firearms to Nicaragua during the last two years of Somoza's dictatorship. Other customers for such weapons include Uruguay, which bought 400 shotguns in the first few months of 1977 alone (despite a total congressional ban on military aid and FMS sales), and South Africa, which bought more than 1,000 shotguns over the eighteen-month period ending in September 1977.

Another troubling category of hardware listed by the Census Bureau is "non-military arms, not elsewhere specified." This category includes such things as blackjacks, truncheons, billy clubs, and similar items. Recipients of such equipment, according to Census Bureau trade reports, include Brazil, the Dominican Republic, Indonesia, Iran (under the Shah), and Saudi Arabia. And despite the arms embargo on South Africa, U.S. firms sold $300,000 worth of such weapons to that country between January 1976 and September 1977.[38]

When these statistics were first revealed by Cynthia Arnson of the Institute for Policy Studies in the *Los Angeles Times* in 1978,[39] many readers were understandably skeptical that any U.S. companies produced—let alone exported—items like thumbscrews, leg irons, truncheons, and shock-batons which could so easily be used for torture. Yet, by examining the catalogs issued by U.S. security firms, one can find examples of virtually all of these goods. Thus the Technipol International Corporation of Foster City, California, for instance, freely advertises a wide selection of "restraint equipment" including leg irons, shackles, and "thumbcuffs." Several other suppliers, including Smith & Wesson, produce a variety of clubs, billies, and truncheons for export. The Shok Baton Company of Savage, Minnesota—also home of the Hot-Shot Company, producers of cattle prods—produces the Electric "Shok-Baton," a billy club fitted with an electric shock device that can deliver up to 600 volts on contact. A rival firm, Universal Safety Corporation, sold 2,500 shock-batons to South Africa in 1982.[40]

Following the publication of the 1978 article in the *Los Angeles Times*, Congress adopted an amendment to the Foreign Assistance Act tightening the regulations governing the export of nonmilitary weapons and equipment to the Third World. Known as the "thumbscrew amendment," the measure required that all crime control and detection equipment exports to Third World countries be fully licensed and reviewed in advance by the State Department's Office of Human Rights and Humanitarian Affairs. Shortly after its passage, however, the measure was undermined by an amendment to the Export Administration Act of 1979, which gave the executive branch broad authority to exempt friendly countries from the special licensing procedures.

Commerce Department channels have also been used to supply "gray-area" hardware to police and military forces in South Africa. This trade encompasses noncombat equipment (jeeps and trucks, transport planes, communication gear, computers, and so forth) that can be used for both civilian and military/police purposes. In compliance with the U.N. arms embargo, the United States has consistently banned the sale of weapons and other Munitions List items to South African police and military forces; sales of gray-area equipment, however, have not been uniformly proscribed, with some administrations favoring a looser interpretation of the embargo and others a more stringent approach. Such fluctuation has been possible because of the inherent difficulty in categorizing dual-use equipment of this sort: while a tank or howitzer obviously constitutes an "implement of war" as construed by the Munitions List, it is not possible to describe a truck or computer in this way unless one knows to what use it will eventually be put. This ambiguity has permitted some U.S. presidents to authorize sales of support-type gear to South African forces while nevertheless professing adherence to the U.N. embargo.[41]

During the Kennedy and Johnson administrations—the first to affirm U.S. compliance with the embargo—few sales of gray-area equipment were permitted. When Richard Nixon took office, however, the dual-use provision was reinterpreted to permit sales of a much wider array of support equipment to South African forces. This new interpretation resulted from a review of U.S. policy in the region conducted by Henry Kissinger, then the assistant to the president for national security affairs. According to published versions of the review, officially known as National Security Study Memorandum 39 (NSSM-39), Kissinger suggested that the United States "enforce [the] arms embargo against South Africa but with liberal treatment of equipment which could serve either military or civilian purposes."[42] As a result of this modification, exports of U.S. aircraft and aviation equipment to South Africa soared, with annual sales rising from $30 million per year in the 1960s to $60 million per year in 1970–73 and $170 million in 1974–76.[43]

To appreciate the significance of the Nixon/Kissinger decision on gray-area sales, one need only examine the current inventory of the South African Air Force (SAAF). According to the International Institute for Strategic Studies, no less than 144 out of the 349 fixed-wing aircraft in SAAF hands in 1982 (excluding trainers) were fully or partly of American origin. Of these, 36 were obtained prior to 1963; all the rest were acquired after the embargo was imposed. Among this second group were 15 Lockheed L-100 cargo planes, five Swearingen Merlin transports, and 20 Cessna Skywagon utility planes delivered during the Nixon period. Also included are a large number of Italian aircraft—Piaggio P-166s patrol planes and AerMacchi AM-3C transports—powered by American-supplied engines.[44] Although none of these aircraft can be considered front-line combat planes, they nevertheless represent a significant contribution to South Africa's logistical and surveillance capabilities.[45]

U.S. sales of gray-area equipment were severely curtailed in 1978 when, in the wake of the Soweto uprising and the death (while in government custody) of Black Consciousness leader Steve Biko, President Carter banned the sale of any type of equipment to South African police and military agencies. When President Reagan took office, however, the restrictions on gray-area sales were again loosened in accordance with shifting political priorities. Citing a desire to improve U.S. ties with Pretoria and to foster U.N.-sponsored negotiations on the status of South African-ruled Namibia, the Reagan administration approved sales of sophisticated computers and electronic systems to South African scientific and technical agencies—many of which have close links to the military establishment.[46] In 1982, for instance, the Commerce Department authorized the export of a powerful Control Data Corporation Cyber-170/750 computer to the Council for Scientific and Industrial Research (CSIR), a government agency that performs critical data-processing services for the South African military.[47] Other U.S. computers have been sold to subsidiaries of ARMSCOR, the state-owned munitions conglomerate, and to the National Institute for Telecommunications Research, a branch of CSIR with responsibility for the development of military radars and communications systems.[48] These sales have generated considerable controversy in Washington both because of their potential contribution to South Africa's military capabilities, and because they implied a more sympathetic U.S. attitude to the white-ruled regime[49]

All this suggests that the Commerce Department—no less than State and Defense—plays an important role in the transfer of military and paramilitary hardware to governments with a history of persistent human rights abuses. While the specific items involved may not be as immediately lethal as ordinary weapons, they can contribute significantly to the net repressive capabilities of authoritarian and undemocratic regimes. This is particularly true in the case of computers, which can be (and have been) used by government security agencies to locate, identify, and track dissidents for possible arrest, harassment, and assassination.[50] This being the case, it is only just and logical that such exports be subjected to the same human rights criteria as other types of military and paramilitary equipment.

Conclusion and Recommendations

It is evident from all of the above that U.S. arms firms and the U.S. government are deeply involved in the sale or transfer of police and paramilitary equipment—much of it directly applicable to social control and antidissident operations—to state security agencies in many undemocratic regimes in the Third World. The United States is not, of course, the only supplier of such equipment, as France, Great Britain, and the Soviet Union also enjoy a brisk trade in repression hardware.[51] But this competition notwithstanding, America's involvement in the repression trade would appear to constitute a clear violation of U.S. law and America's historic commitments to the advancement of human rights abroad.

In responding to charges that U.S. arms exports have conflicted with American efforts to promote human rights, government officials normally argue that such transfers are needed to combat terrorism, or to enhance U.S. national security by strengthening the self-defense capabilities of friendly countries. These, indeed, are the reasons given by the Reagan administration for repealing all remaining congressional restraints on arms transfers to authoritarian governments abroad. But while the president has found some support for this position in Washington, there are a number of grounds upon which the administration's logic has been challenged.

First, many of the security systems being sold (e.g., chemical munitions, armored cars, clubs and truncheons) are primarily intended for use against unarmed demonstrators, not hardcore terrorists. Moreover, many recipients of U.S. security systems have used them to terrorize the public at large, rather than to seek out and isolate individual terrorist cells. Thus, while perhaps a few of the thousands of Argentinians who have "disappeared" over the past few years were members of genuine underground movements, the overwhelming majority were students, professors, labor leaders, journalists, lawyers, and others who protested government policies.[52] Similarly, the governments of El Salvador and Guatemala have been charged with practicing "state terrorism" by many observers, including former State Department official Charles Maechling, Jr., because of the many "SS-type" executions of civilian dissidents attributed to the security forces of these countries.[53]

Second, while sales of regular military equipment to authoritarian regimes may enhance U.S. security in the short run, sales of police and internal security systems can damage it in the long run by imbuing dissidents and insurgent forces with an abiding resentment toward the suppliers of such hardware. This was clearly the case in Iran and Nicaragua, where sustained U.S. assistance to the Shah and Somoza helps explain the antagonistic attitude of Khomeini and the Sandinistas. Furthermore, by helping such regimes to suppress nonviolent forms of dissent in their countries, these exports help ensure that such dissent will ultimately take violent forms—often to the detriment of U.S. interests.

For these reasons, it should be obvious that the United States has both a moral and a practical interest in curbing the flow of repressive technology to undemocratic regimes abroad. As noted by former Secretary of State Cyrus Vance in his 1980 commencement address at Harvard University, "we must ultimately recognize that the demand for individual freedom and economic progress cannot be long repressed without sowing the seeds of violent convulsion. Thus . . . we have a stake in the stability that comes when people can express their hopes and build their futures freely."[54]

Unfortunately, while most U.S. lawmakers would probably agree with this premise, Congress has not, as yet, adopted the sort of measures that would effectively inhibit the flow of repressive technology to authoritarian governments abroad. A sound basis for such action does exist in the form of section 502B of the Foreign Assistance Act, but this provision does not cover all of the export channels described above, nor does it embody adequate enforcement measures. Accordingly, some modification of existing legislation appears essential. Specifically, amendments are needed to:
• Outlaw any sales or transfers of torture equipment, or devices

whose use would violate international standards regarding the apprehension and treatment of prisoners;

• Require mandatory prior notification to Congress of any sales of police and security equipment (including computers) to any foreign governments that have been cited for persistent human rights violations by Amnesty International or other humanitarian organizations;

• Permit congressional disapproval of any sales of arms or security systems to foreign police or paramilitary organizations;

• Prohibit transfers of arms and security systems to the military and paramilitary forces of nations ruled under martial law, unless the president certifies that such transfers are not contributing to the abuse of individual human rights in the recipient country;

• Require the automatic cutoff of all types of Security Assistance to any nation that has been cited two years in a row for significant human rights violations in the report compiled by the U.S. Department of State in accordance with section 502B, with this cutoff to remain in effect until the president certifies to Congress that the government involved has made significant progress in the human rights area.

• Prohibit sales of computers and other support-type hardware (vehicles, communications and electronic gear, aviation equipment) to government agencies in South Africa.

These steps will not, of course, halt the abuse of human rights abroad. Nor will they halt all forms of U.S. assistance to the police and paramilitary organizations of authoritarian governments. But they will hinder the efforts of such governments to enhance their repressive capabilities and will greatly diminish the risk that U.S. equipment will be used to silence dissent or otherwise contribute to the suppression of human rights. More importantly, they will invest existing human rights legislation—particularly section 502B of the FAA—with an enforcement capacity it has heretofore lacked. And while they would produce some inconvenience for U.S. firms, they would demonstrate that the United States is firmly committed to the curtailment of human rights abuses in all countries that receive U.S. arms and military assistance.

CHAPTER 10

A Look at the Competition

Soviet and European Arms Sales to the Third World

In March 1979, President Jimmy Carter invoked emergency provisions of the Arms Export Control Act to permit the Department of Defense to deliver arms and ammunition to North Yemen without first obtaining the approval of Congress. Invocation of this measure was necessary, Carter affirmed, in order to demonstrate America's determination to help defend North Yemen against an imminent invasion by the Soviet-equipped forces of South Yemen. By the time the U.S. arms package was in transit, however, the expected invasion had evaporated, and the two Yemens had agreed to discuss the possibility of a merger. Despite this, the Pentagon went ahead with the delivery and accompanying training program, only to experience a second shock: the North Yemenis, who had requested the U.S. aid to repel what had been described as a Soviet-inspired invasion, had turned around and ordered $500 million worth of arms from Moscow.[1] While Washington fumed over this apparent betrayal, North Yemeni officials defended their arms-buying policies. "We have our own interests," Foreign Minister Hassan Makki observed. "I will never [tell] the Soviets not to come because somebody is not happy that they are here. I will never accept that someone tells us how to deal with other countries."[2]

This incident, which is hardly the only example of its kind, boldly illustrates what has long been apparent in our study of arms exports: the weapons trade is a truly international business, with many nations competing for an ever-larger share of a complex and often unpredictable market. The United States clearly enjoys many advantages in this competition, but has nevertheless lost ground over the past decade to some aggressive competitors—notably the Soviet Union, France, West Germany, Israel, and Brazil.[3] According to the Congressional Research Service, the U.S. share of the Third World arms market dropped from approximately 48 percent in 1974–76 to 26 percent in 1980–82, while the Soviet share rose from 25 percent to 28 percent and the French share from 9 percent to 15 percent (see table 13). These figures are admittedly imprecise, given the erratic year-to-year shifts in sales volume, but nonetheless indicate the growing prominence of non-U.S. suppliers in the global marketplace. All told, the Soviet Union sold $65 billion worth of arms to the Third World between 1975 and 1982 and other non-U.S. suppliers sold $98 billion worth, compared to $74 billion for the United States.[4]

Not only have the Soviet Union and other competitors succeeded in capturing a larger share of the Third World arms market, but they have also, in some cases, followed the American example by establishing durable arms-supply relationships with individual countries. As noted in table 14, the Soviet Union is the principal supplier to a dozen or so Third World countries, including Algeria, Angola, Cuba, Ethiopia, India, Iraq, Libya, South Yemen, and Syria. The major European suppliers (France, Great Britain, West Germany, and Italy) singly or jointly dominate the trade with another dozen countries, including Argentina, Brazil, Ecuador, Morocco, Oman, and South Africa.[5] Even in those cases where the United States remains the major supplier, moreover, other sellers have carved out a large piece of what was once an exclusive American domain.

Needless to say, these developments have caused considerable concern in Washington, where arms transfers have long been viewed as a key instrument of foreign policy. The growing Soviet arms effort has been a source of particular concern, since in many instances it has been accompanied by other forms of Soviet political and military involvement—the deployment of advisors and technicians, the establishment of basing facilities, and so forth. Indeed, some analysts have argued that arms transfers are the opening wedge of a long-term Soviet campaign to erode Western power and influence by establishing military alliances with hostile Third World countries and by arming guerrilla forces committed to the overthrow of pro-Western regimes. The growing worldwide demand for arms, former Pentagon official Anthony Cordesman wrote in *Armed Forces Journal*, is "nearly certain to give the U.S.S.R. new opportunities to use its arms sales to play a 'spoiler role,' to threaten key Western interests in the developing world, to seek control of developing nations in sub-Saharan Africa, and to exploit opportunities in the Middle East and Latin America."[6] These arguments were echoed by the Department of Defense in its 1981 study on *Soviet Military Power*, which describes arms sales as "the basis for Soviet penetration of a number of Third World countries, providing Moscow access to nations and regions where it previously had little or no influence."[7]

These arguments have been accompanied by an intense debate

over the relative standing of the U.S.S.R. and the United States in the arms export competition. In his "arms restraint" policy directive of May 19, 1977, President Carter stated that "because of the special responsibilities we bear as the *largest arms seller*," the United States must take the initiative in curbing military sales (emphasis added). However, the assertion of U.S. supremacy in the arms trade—and thus the requirement for U.S. initiative in controlling it—was soon challenged by other authorities, who regarded the U.S.S.R. as the leading seller.

Arguing that official U.S. statistics tend to overstate exports (by including sales of services and military construction along with sales of combat equipment) and to understate Soviet exports (by underestimating the price of Soviet military hardware), these critics maintained that a truly accurate tally would show the U.S.S.R. ahead of the United States in sales of combat equipment to the Third World.[8] This assessment was given further credence by the Stockholm International Peace Research Institute, which in 1981 reported that the Soviet Union had overtaken the United States as the leading supplier of "major weapons systems" to the Third World.[9] (The SIPRI

Table 13. Arms Transfer Agreements with the Third World by Supplier, 1974–82 (million current dollars)

		Free World Suppliers				
Year	U.S.A.	France	U.K.	West Germany	Italy	Other Free World
1974	8,723	2,060	750	620	410	760
1975	9,617	2,625	495	630	1,040	895
1976	12,574	1,040	500	725	360	1,380
1977	6,042	3,065	1,410	1,225	980	1,265
1978	6,714	1,965	2,535	2,510	1,390	1,420
1979	9,077	4,130	1,270	875	345	2,110
1980	9,660	8,700	2,140	780	2,875	3,685
1981	4,589	1,555	1,835	1,640	345	6,020
1982	15,307	7,670	1,485	430	1,405	2,995
1974–82	82,303	32,810	12,420	9,435	9,150	20,530

SOURCE: Congressional Research Service, *Trends in Conventional Arms Transfers to the Third World by Major Supplier, 1975–1982* (1983), and edition for 1974–81 (published 1982); includes arms, ammunition, services, and construction; excludes cancelled Iranian contracts and U.S. sales under the Commercial Sales program. U.S. data are for fiscal year indicated; all other countries are by calendar year.

tally included such equipment as tanks, aircraft, ships, and missiles, but excluded small arms, services, and construction.) Similarly, in 1982, the U.S. Department of State released a report on *Conventional Arms Transfers in the Third World* that listed the Soviet Union as the number one supplier of weapons, with $64.9 billion in sales for 1972–81 compared to $48.1 billion for the United States.[10] This mode of accounting has been challenged, however, by other U.S. government analysts, who believe that military construction (e.g., air bases, communications facilities, etc.) and technical services are an essential component of total military effectiveness and thus should be counted along with hardware sales. On this basis, the United States jumps back ahead of the U.S.S.R., with total sales of $73.6 billion to the Third World in 1972–82, compared to $65.2 billion for the Soviets (see table 15).[11]

But while these statistics—however tallied—show a substantial Soviet gain in arms transfers to the Third World, there is no clear-cut evidence of a corresponding gain in Soviet political and military influence. Certainly, the record shows a string of Soviet successes in establishing arms-supply relationships with a number of

Free World total	U.S.S.R.	Communist Bloc Suppliers		World Total
		Other Communist	Communist total	
13,323	5,970	970	6,940	20,263
15,302	3,655	760	4,415	19,717
16,579	6,550	1,210	7,760	24,339
13,987	10,155	935	11,090	25,077
16,534	2,875	1,025	3,900	20,434
17,807	8,925	1,480	10,405	28,212
27,840	15,485	2,295	17,780	45,620
15,984	7,380	6,845	14,225	30,209
29,292	10,205	3,700	13,905	43,197
166,648	71,200	19,220	90,420	257,068

Table 14. Major Third World Recipients of U.S., Soviet, and Western European Arms, 1975–79 (Countries with total deliveries in excess of $150 million in current U.S. dollars)

Recipient	Total, all suppliers[a]	U.S.S.R.	U.S.A.
Africa, Total[b]	17,200	9,900	725
Algeria	1,900	1,500	—
Angola	850	500	—
Ethiopia	1,800	1,500	90
Ivory Coast	160	—	—
Libya	6,900	5,000	—
Morocco	1,400	20	310
Mozambique	240	170	—
Nigeria	300	150	30
Somalia	440	210	—
South Africa	525	—	20
Sudan	400	10	120
Tanzania	440	300	—
Tunisia	170	—	50
Zaire	250	—	30
East Asia, Total[b]	9,500	2,000	5,400
China	625	210	—
Indonesia	440	—	120
Kampuchea	380	20	300
Korea, No.	575	280	—
Korea, So.	1,900	—	1,700
Malaysia	420	—	180
Philippines	250	—	190
Singapore	270	—	150
Taiwan	1,000	—	900
Thailand	430	—	320
Vietnam, No.	1,300	1,300	—
Vietnam, So.	850	—	850
Latin America, Total[b]	5,500	1,500	725
Argentina	975	—	90
Brazil	725	—	160
Chile	380	—	110
Cuba	875	875	—
Ecuador	575	—	40
Peru	1,100	650	100
Venezuela	410	—	110

France	U.K.	West Germany	Italy
1,800	150	925	700
10	—	350	10
5	10	10	—
10	—	5	30
100	—	—	—
310	10	160	450
725	5	50	50
—	—	—	—
40	50	10	—
20	5	10	30
310	—	—	50
—	—	230	—
—	5	—	10
10	5	10	30
120	—	5	10
120	440	140	90
50	350	—	—
20	—	10	—
—	—	—	—
—	—	10	—
10	5	80	50
10	30	—	—
5	20	10	5
10	10	—	—
—	—	—	5
—	5	—	30
—	—	—	—
—	—	—	—
775	675	440	350
270	60	110	80
50	400	20	80
5	40	30	—
—	—	—	—
280	70	110	5
110	10	40	80
10	60	80	110

Table 14 (continued)

Recipient	Total, all suppliers[a]	U.S.S.R.	U.S.A.
Middle East, Total[b]	32,900	10,300	13,700
Egypt	1,500	250	250
Iran	8,700	650	6,600
Iraq	6,800	4,900	—
Israel	4,200	—	4,100
Jordan	600	—	500
Kuwait	800	50	350
Oman	370	—	10
Saudi Arabia	3,600	—	1,800
Syria	4,500	3,600	—
United Arab Emirates	410	—	10
Yemen, No.	625	210	110
Yemen, So.	600	575	—
South Asia, Total[b]	3,600	2,300	220
Afghanistan	470	450	—
India	2,200	1,800	40
Pakistan	875	20	180

SOURCE: U.S. Arms Control and Disarmament Agency, *World Military Expenditures and Arms Transfers, 1970–1979* (1982); indicates deliveries of arms, ammunition, and related equipment; excludes services and construction.

[a]Includes transfers by six listed countries plus all other suppliers.

[b]Includes recipients listed plus all other recipients in region.

key Third World nations—Algeria, India, Iraq, Libya, and Syria, to mention a few—but the record also shows a string of Soviet failures in perpetuating such relationships and converting them into meaningful political leverage. Thus a 1973 list of major Soviet clients would have included such countries as Egypt, Nigeria, Peru, and Somalia—all of which have since indicated a preference for Western arms. Furthermore, many long-time Soviet customers, including Algeria, Iraq, and Libya, have consistently sought to diversify their arsenals by acquiring Western (especially European) equipment. "The Soviet position in the Third World may seem secure," the Center for Defense Information (CDI) noted in a 1979 study, "but many of their relationships have proved unstable and impermanent."[12] And even where the arms relationship has been relatively durable, as in the case of India and Syria, there is ample evidence to demonstrate that

France	U.K.	West Germany	Italy
2,200	2,100	925	650
490	110	180	60
200	310	430	340
410	20	160	70
10	60	—	30
—	20	5	—
150	210	20	—
—	330	—	—
290	900	20	130
190	30	100	—
350	30	—	20
80	—	5	5
—	—	—	—
360	130	10	20
—	—	—	—
40	100	10	20
320	20	—	—

the recipients in question pursue their own foreign policies whether or not they accord with those of Moscow.

In this respect, the Soviet experience appears to parallel that of the United States. As the 1979 North Yemen incident demonstrates, Washington has also established arms-supply relationships with nations that subsequently sought new partners. Indeed, there are many other striking parallels between the American and the Soviet arms export programs: both countries shifted their emphasis from grants to cash sales in the mid-1970s to help shore up their balance-of-payments situation, and both have offered increasingly sophisticated arms in order to satisfy the desires of newly affluent (and thus more demanding) Third World clients. An analysis of Soviet military exports would therefore provide us with a double benefit: on one hand, it would allow us to evaluate the validity of competing claims over

Table 15. Comparative Statistics on U.S. and Soviet Arms Transfers (U.S. dollars in millions)

Year	ACDA: Deliveries, all countries, current dollars[a]		DOS: Orders, Third World, current dollars[b]	
	U.S.A.	U.S.S.R.	U.S.A. (arms)	U.S.S.R.
1973	4,900	5,300	5,390	3,320
1974	4,600	4,100	7,700	5,970
1975	4,800	4,000	4,420	3,670
1976	5,900	5,300	5,420	6,610
1977	6,800	6,600	3,720	9,750
1978	6,400	7,700	4,520	2,920
1979	6,300	11,300	4,910	8,880
1980	6,500	10,000	5,040	14,770
1981	8,300	9,900	3,310	6,630
1973–81	54,500	64,200	44,430	62,520
1982	9,500	10,900	n.a.	n.a.
1983	n.a.	n.a.	n.a.	n.a.

[a]U.S. Arms Control and Disarmament Agency, *World Military Expenditures and Arms Transfers, 1972–1982* (1984); excludes services and construction.

[b]U.S. Department of State, *Conventional Arms Transfers in the Third World, 1972–81* (1982). Figures for the U.S.A. represent sales of weapons only; figures for the U.S.S.R. include all military exports (including construction and services).

[c]Stockholm International Peace Research Institute, *SIPRI Yearbook 1983* (1983); includes sales of major weapons systems only; excludes small arms and ammunition, services, and construction.

[d]Richard F. Grimmett, *Trends in Conventional Arms Transfers to the Third World, 1976–1983* (Congressional Research Service, 1984), and earlier editions; includes services and construction.

the political-military significance of the Soviet arms program; on the other, it could help verify some of the conclusions we have drawn about the effectiveness of the American program.

An analysis of non-U.S. sales is important for another critical reason: given the growing prominence of such sales in the Third World market, it is obvious that no effort to control the international arms traffic will prove effective without the participation of the other major suppliers—and obtaining that will require a thorough knowledge of their arms export programs and policies. It is appropriate, therefore, that we augment our study of U.S. arms programs with "a look at the competition"—an analysis of Soviet and European arms exports to the Third World.

SIPRI: Deliveries, Third World, constant 1975 dollars[c]		CRS: Third World, current dollars[d] Orders		Deliveries	
U.S.A.	U.S.S.R.	U.S.A.	U.S.S.R.	U.S.A.	U.S.S.R.
1,061	1,537	4,412	3,320	1,319	3,550
1,404	1,930	8,723	5,970	2,793	2,530
2,343	2,160	9,617	3,655	3,084	2,390
3,892	1,554	12,574	6,550	4,646	3,445
4,826	2,156	6,042	10,155	5,932	5,060
5,244	3,682	6,714	2,875	6,382	6,410
2,046	3,631	9,077	8,925	6,463	9,720
2,794	3,774	9,660	15,485	5,079	8,260
2,547	3,172	4,589	7,380	6,008	7,570
26,157	23,596	71,408	64,315	41,706	48,935
2,836	2,390	14,901	12,575	7,547	9,945
n.a.	n.a.	9,528	4,165	9,684	7,825

Parameters of the Export Trade

In conducting our study of Soviet and European arms exports, it makes sense to begin with the same sort of "briefing" on basic trends that began our study of American programs. Accordingly, we shall discuss here some of the basic parameters of the non-U.S. export trade, concentrating largely on the Soviet effort, but examining European and Third World sales where appropriate.

Suppliers. According to the CRS, six nations—the United States, the Soviet Union, France, Great Britain, West Germany, and Italy—dominate the arms trade with the Third World, accounting for 84 percent of all orders placed between 1975 and 1982 (in dollar terms). Of the $237 billion worth of arms ordered by less-developed countries during this period, the U.S.S.R. alone supplied $65.2 billion (28 percent of the total), while the United States supplied $73.6 billion (31 percent) and the "big four" European countries together supplied $60 billion—($30.8 billion from France, $11.7 billion from Great Britain, $8.8 billion from West Germany, and $8.7 billion from Italy, giving them a combined 25 percent share of the Third World market (see table 13).[13] The remaining $38 billion was provided by a number of less prominent suppliers, including Canada, Czechoslovakia, East

Germany, the Netherlands, Poland, Sweden, Switzerland, and Yugoslavia. A number of Third World countries have also entered the ranks of arms exporters, among them Argentina, Brazil, China, and Israel.[14]

While the same six major suppliers are expected to continue dominating the Third World market in the 1980s, many experts believe that we can expect at least some shifts in the relative distribution of sales among them, as well as between the combined shar-- held by all six and that of all remaining suppliers. Thus, the relaxed export policies adopted by the Reagan administration are expected to result in a significant increase in U.S. sales, while the Soviet Union is likely to experience a slackening in sales due to the saturation of its principal markets and a failure to line up new customers. France is also likely to encounter difficulty in sustaining the rapid growth of the 1970s, while Great Britain may benefit from the performance of its equipment during the Falklands conflict. At the same time, the combined market share enjoyed by all six suppliers is likely to contract as other suppliers—led by aggressive new producers in the Third World—intensify their marketing efforts.

Recipients. According to the ACDA, the Soviet Union transferred at least some arms to forty-two Third World countries in 1975–79, while the "big four" European suppliers sold to sixty-eight countries and the United States to fifty-one countries. The U.S.S.R.'s recipients were mostly concentrated in Africa (twenty-two countries) and the Middle East (seven countries), with only two located in Latin America (Cuba and Peru), five in South Asia, and six in East Asia. The Europeans' recipients were more or less evenly distributed throughout all regions, although they, too, had a particularly heavy concentration in the Middle East and Africa. The United States also enjoyed fairly solid representation in all regions, but was particularly active in Latin America (seventeen countries) and the Far East (eleven countries).[15]

Looking at the ACDA figures on the dollar value of arms transfers, we find that the Soviet Union is the dominant supplier to Africa ($9.9 billion in sales) and South Asia ($2.3 billion), while the United States is dominant in the Middle East ($13.7 billion) and East Asia ($5.4 billion), and the four European suppliers are dominant in Latin America ($2.2 billion). These figures also tell us that the U.S.S.R.—like the United States—tends to concentrate its export activity in a number of key client nations, which together account for a very large proportion of total transfers. Thus the top seven recipients of Soviet arms—Algeria, Cuba, Ethiopia, India, Iraq, Libya, and Syria—together accounted for about 70 percent of all Soviet transfers in 1975–79. Approximately the same percentage is absorbed by America's top six or seven recipients. The Europeans, on the other hand, tend to distribute their exports more evenly over a larger field of countries (see table 14). [16]

Although there is considerable variety in the types of arms-supply relationships among all these countries, some basic patterns can be discerned. Several of the U.S.S.R.'s key customers are nationalistic Arab nations that originally turned to Moscow for assistance in the late 1950s and 1960s when denied military aid by the West and continue to rely on Soviet supplies to counter U.S. transfers to Israel. Other Soviet clients are former colonial states that received Soviet aid during their independence struggle (e.g., Angola and Mozambique), or countries that shop in Moscow in order to emphasize their "nonaligned" status (e.g., India, Kuwait, Peru); still others are not really "customers" at all, but rather aid recipients that have become totally dependent on Soviet assistance (Cuba, Ethiopia, Vietnam). [17]

Recipients of European arms tend to fall into two categories: former colonies that choose to retain close political-military ties with their former rulers and self-consciously "nonaligned" states that seek to avoid a close military relationship with either superpower. Included in the former category are many of the French-speaking nations of North and West Africa, while the latter includes several countries in Latin America (e.g., Argentina, Brazil, Ecuador, Peru) that seek to affirm their independence from the United States. [18]

Commodities. Like the United States, the Soviet Union and the "big four" European suppliers offer a wide range of military hardware for sale to Third World countries. [19] Among the most popular Soviet export items are: MiG-21, MiG-23, and MiG-25 fighters; Tu-22 medium bombers; MI-8 and MI-24 helicopters; T-54, T-55, T-62, and T-72 tanks; ZSU-23-4 mobile antiaircraft guns; BMP-1 and BTR-60 armored personnel carriers (APCs); Osa-class missile patrol boats; and SA-2, SA-3, SA-6, SA-7, SA-8, and SA-9 surface-to-air missiles (SAMS).* Ac-

---

*These are the standard international designations for these items, largely based on Soviet abbreviations. Thus most Soviet aircraft are identified by the design bureau responsible for their development (hence "MiG" signifies the Mikoyan/Gurevich bureau, founded by Gen. Artem I. Mikoyan and mathematician Mikhail I. Gurevich, while "Tu" signifies the Tupolev bureau, founded by Alexei A. Tupolev). Many of these items have also been given code names by NATO, and it is common to encounter these names in the Western press. Thus the MiG-21 is known as "Fishbed," the MiG-23 as "Flogger," the MiG-25 as "Foxbat," and so forth. In this text, however, I generally employ the standard international designations.

cording to the CRS, between 1975 and 1982, the Soviet Union sold Third World nations a total of 10,080 tanks and self-propelled guns, 12,600 artillery pieces, 12,475 APCS and armored cars, 3,160 supersonic aircraft, 41 major and 175 minor surface warships, 1,250 helicopters, and 18,300 SAM missiles (see table 16).[20] The Soviets have also provided very large quantities of other basic military hardware, including rifles, machine guns, mortars, trucks, and the like.

The Europeans, while supplying the same mix of equipment as the Americans and the Soviets, have tended to specialize in certain types of equipment that are especially suited to Third World countries with limited technical capabilities, such as patrol boats and frigates, light strike aircraft and trainers, helicopters, light armored vehicles, and small diesel-powered submarines. Thus, while the "big four" trail the U.S.S.R. and the United States in such categories as tanks and supersonic aircraft, they exceed or match the superpowers in sales of minor surface warships (313 for the Europeans vs. 175 for the U.S.S.R. and 124 for the U.S.A.), submarines (21 vs. 9 for the U.S.S.R. and 6 for the U.S.A.), and helicopters (1,610 vs. 1,250 for the U.S.S.R. and 542 for the U.S.A.) (see table 16).[21] The smaller European producers tend to specialize in just one or two types of weapons systems (Sweden, for instance, is noted for its Bofors antiaircraft guns) or in the production of small arms and counterinsurgency gear aimed specifically at the Third World market.[22]

One feature common to all export programs is the trend toward increasingly sophisticated hardware. In order to improve their competitive position in the Third World market, all major suppliers have offered potential Third World customers their most advanced and capable systems. Thus the Soviet Union, which once limited its Third World sales to stripped-down, obsolete equipment, is now supplying the same types of weapons provided to its front-line forces in Europe. As a result, the MiG-17s and MiG-21s of earlier Soviet transactions are being replaced by late-model MiG-23s and MiG-25s, while T-54s and T-55s of Korean War vintage are being replaced by more modern T-62s and T-72s. Similarly, the Europeans have begun to export a wide range of modern combat systems, including a wide range of tactical missiles. Among their most popular export items are antiship missiles like the French Exocet used by Argentina during the Falklands war and antitank missiles like the Franco-German Milan.[23]

Advisors and Technical Support. Just as American exports of high-tech weaponry have often been accompanied by sales of technical military services, the Soviet Union has provided such services

Table 16. Deliveries of Major Weapons Systems to the Third
World, 1975–82

Weapons category	United States	U.S.S.R.	"Big 4" Western Europe[a]
Tanks & self-propelled guns	6,188	10,080	1,420
Artillery pieces	5,519	12,600	1,670
APCs and armored cars[b]	12,711	12,475	4,500
Major surface combat ships	63	41	66
Minor surface combat ships	124	175	313
Submarines	6	9	21
Supersonic combat aircraft	1,254	3,160	470
Subsonic combat aircraft	579	380	120
Other aircraft	1,062	480	830
Helicopters	542	1,250	1,610
Guided missiles boats	0	78	39
Surface-to-air missiles	8,007	18,300	2,950

SOURCE: Congressional Research Service, Trends in Conventional Arms Transfers
to the Third World by Major Supplier, 1975–82 (1983).
[a] France, United Kingdom, West Germany, Italy.
[b] APCS = armored personnel carriers.

as part of its arms programs in the Third World. And, just as U.S.
sales of technical services tend to expand as the equipment provided
becomes more sophisticated, Soviet exports of such services have
expanded in step with the transfer of progressively more advanced
hardware. But while most American military technicians are civilians or retired military personnel in the employ of private aerospace
corporations, Soviet advisors are almost always regular officers in
the Soviet and Eastern European military establishments. According
to the CIA, some 16,280 Soviet and 1,925 Eastern European military
technicians and advisors were present in Third World countries in
1981, with the largest Soviet-bloc contingents (over 1,000 technicians each) in Afghanistan, Algeria, Angola, Ethiopia, Iraq, Libya,
South Yemen, and Syria.[24]

    These advisors and technicians perform basically the same type
of functions as their American counterparts: assistance in the delivery, assembly, and maintenance of military equipment; training of
indigenous personnel in the operation and upkeep of such equipment; and advisory support for military commands and headquarters

organizations. In some cases, Soviet (or Cuban, Eastern European, or North Korean) personnel have piloted aircraft sold to Third World countries (especially in countries like Libya that have a shortage of flight-trained officers) or operated other systems considered too complex or too sensitive for use by indigenous personnel (as in the case of the sa-5 antiaircraft missiles deployed in Syria following the 1982 conflict in Lebanon). The U.S.S.R. has also provided technical assistance to a few countries (most notably India) for the development of domestic arms industries.[25]

The major European suppliers also provide technical military services to arms-importing countries, although not on the same scale as the United States and the Soviet Union. Typically, such services are provided to ex-colonial states that retain the language of their former imperial rulers. Hence French advisors tend to be employed in the Francophone nations of North and West Africa, while British advisors are employed in East Africa and in the former British protectorates in the Persian Gulf area (especially in Oman and the United Arab Emirates, where British officers still command some combat units).

Although this is but a brief sketch of Soviet and European arms transfer dynamics, it is sufficient to indicate that such exports are significant in both quantity and sophistication. When combined with American deliveries, they represent a very substantial transfer of military capabilities to the Third World. Indeed, because the major suppliers tend to vie with one another in providing ever more sophisticated hardware, this dynamic is stimulating and sustaining local arms races in many areas of the Third World. Clearly, the United States cannot hope to end these races by reducing its arms transfers unilaterally; only multilateral restraint by all major suppliers will result in a significant reduction in Third World arms stockpiling. And because we cannot hope to inspire such cooperation unless we offer other suppliers some incentives for curbing their own sales, it is important that we look next at the "primal motives" that propel Soviet and European arms transfers to the Third World.

A Constellation of Motives: The Political Economy of Soviet and European Arms Transfers to the Third World

Although it is common for American commentators to explain Soviet and European arms transfers in terms of one or two basic motives—political influence in the case of the U.S.S.R. and economic gain in the case of the Europeans—analysis suggests that a much wider range of motives are at work. As in the United States, a constellation of political, military, and economic factors are responsible for the steady growth in arms exports to the Third World. As we shall see, some of these are rather similar to the motives that propel American sales (see chapter 2), while others are rather different.

Described below are the principal motives that drive Soviet arms exports to the Third World; later we shall look at some of the European motives.[26] Because, for the Soviet Union, political-military factors tend to outweigh economic factors, we shall begin with the former; within this grouping, however, the factors are listed in conceptual sequence rather than in any presumed order of importance (as this may vary widely in any given case).

Political Presence. Although hardly the only motive for Soviet arms transfers, this has long been one of the most important. In many cases, Soviet ties with Third World nations were first developed through the initiation of arms-supply arrangements (particularly in the 1950s and 1960s, when U.S.-sponsored collective security systems like SEATO and CENTO effectively blocked Moscow's access to the Third World), and such arrangements continue to underlie Soviet links with many of these countries. As Roger Pajak of the Treasury Department's national security staff has written, arms aid "has served as the primary Soviet vehicle for establishing a presence in regions important to Western interests, often providing the USSR with political entree." In many cases, moreover, such entree has led to other forms of presence: "Military assistance and sales," Pajak noted, "have often provided the opening wedge for a variety of diplomatic, trade, and other contacts that would have been difficult to achieve otherwise."[27] Although Moscow's reliance on arms transfers as an "opening wedge" has often been ascribed to cold calculation, it generally reflects a lack of viable alternatives. "Moscow has comparatively little to offer in the way of trade, investment, and the transfer of technology," Andrew Pierre observed in *Foreign Affairs*, and "its development assistance has been kept low." Weapons, on the other hand, can "be provided cheaply and abundantly."[28] Given the present stagnation of the Soviet economy, moreover, it is likely that this condition will continue to prevail for the foreseeable future.

Superpower Competition. As America's principal rival for world power and influence, the U.S.S.R. has followed Washington's example by using arms transfers to establish military alliances with key Third World nations and to woo other countries away from the U.S. orbit. When the West has refused to supply nationalistic Third

World leaders with modern arms, as in the case of President Nasser of Egypt in 1956, Moscow has been quick to offer the desired hardware; when Western suppliers try to sell sophisticated equipment at high prices, as occurred in Peru in the mid-1970s, Moscow has offered to supply similar gear at greatly reduced prices. "Moscow's arms sales have been carefully calibrated to serve its political purposes," Pierre noted in *Foreign Affairs*. Arms have been sold to countries "whose favor the Soviets have wanted to court, or whose political leanings they have wanted to influence."[29] But such superpower competition is a two-way street: just as Washington has been forced on occasion to respond to such Soviet initiatives by enhancing the defensive capabilities of its pro-Western regimes, the U.S.S.R. has been forced to respond to U.S. initiatives by strengthening the defenses of pro-Soviet regimes. Thus a large share of Soviet arms transfers continue to flow to nations such as Angola, Cuba, North Korea, and Vietnam that are threatened by U.S.-backed regimes or by the United States itself.

Sino-Soviet Competition. Although most Soviet arms programs in the Third World have been motivated largely by competition with the West, some have also been motivated by competition with the East—namely, with the People's Republic of China. Ever since the Sino-Soviet split of 1960, Peking has vied with Moscow for the loyalty of national liberation movements and nonaligned Third World regimes, and arms transfers have played a key role in this competition. This Sino-Soviet contest has been particularly intense in Africa and Southeast Asia, where both China and the U.S.S.R. have long been active in supporting national liberation movements and the anti-Western regimes they spawned.[30]

Establishing Secure Borders. Just as Washington views Central America and the Caribbean as a "border" region whose stability is considered essential to U.S. security, Moscow views much of South and Southwest Asia as a vital security zone. For this reason, the U.S.S.R. has long sought to enhance the stability of friendly nations, such as Afghanistan and Iraq, or at least to promote neutralism and nonalignment in those that were not, such as India and Iran. "In addition to the broader objective of undermining Western influence," Roger Pajak noted in 1981, "Soviet policymakers have used arms transfers to eliminate Western military facilities and alliances adjacent to Soviet borders."[31] Thus the prices of arms offered to India—Moscow's number four arms customer—have always been held low in order to stimulate sales and thereby diminish India's reliance on the West, and significant sales were arranged with the late Shah of Iran in the hope of moderating his hostility to the U.S.S.R.

The Acquisition of Basing Facilities. As the U.S.S.R.'s activities and commitments in the Third World have expanded, it has sought to establish basing facilities of its own in strategic areas. Lacking the sort of historical basing rights enjoyed by the United States in such countries as Cuba (Guantanamo Bay) and the Philippines (Subic Bay), the U.S.S.R. has often used arms transfers as "payment" for access to the military facilities of its clients. "In return for their arms shipments," CDI observed in 1979, "the Soviets have sought a variety of rewards from their customers, [including] naval or aircraft visitation rights and [the use of] repair and replenishment facilities."[32] Such "rewards" were a primary motive for the large-scale Soviet transfers to Egypt and Somalia (both of which granted Moscow access to their port facilities), and continue to motivate Soviet transfers to Libya and South Yemen (both of which have been used as staging areas for Soviet transport and reconnaissance aircraft). These facilities are normally described in the West as "bases," comparable to the permanent U.S. facilities at Subic Bay and Diego Garcia in the Indian Ocean, but it is important to note that they actually represent access agreements rather than bases, and as such can be (and have been) revoked by the host country.[33]

Access to Military Elites. Like their counterparts in the United States, Soviet strategists view Third World military elites as an especially critical force in national politics and accordingly employ arms transfers to cultivate relations with this constituency. Indeed, the Soviets place special emphasis on such linkages, since in many traditional societies the military has proven particularly susceptible to Marxist ideas and has, on occasion, overthrown pro-U.S. regimes. It is not surprising, therefore, that some of the U.S.S.R.'s most important arms customers—notably Ethiopia, Iraq, and Libya—are ruled by nationalistic military regimes that turned to Moscow after deposing Western-backed monarchies.[34]

Political Insurance. Although Western commentators tend to view Soviet arms programs in the Third World as a consistent gain for Soviet policies, the leadership in Moscow knows better: such programs have often soured (as in the case of Egypt and Somalia), or have been used for adventuristic purposes (as in the 1976 Syrian occupation of Lebanon and the 1980 Iraqi invasion of Iran), thereby threatening other Soviet objectives or risking Soviet involvement in an unwanted regional conflagration. Despite significant Soviet gains, Roger Rajak noted in 1981, "the Soviet Union has discovered that the expansion of her involvement in the international arena has led to conflicting commitments, thus complicating her bilateral relations and limiting her options."[35] Given this dilemma, Moscow—

like Washington—has often felt compelled to expand an arms-supply relationship it would rather curtail in order to retain some influence over the behavior of its client or to prevent the defection of the client altogether. This appears to be especially true in the case of Iraq and Syria, which continue to receive large quantities of Russian arms despite considerable Soviet discontent with the policies of their present leaders.[36]

Source of Hard Currency. Although Soviet leaders have been largely motivated by political-military considerations in undertaking arms-supply programs in the Third World, they are not entirely unmindful of the economic benefits of such transfers. Indeed, since 1970, they have placed increasing emphasis on strictly cash transactions while cutting back on grant aid programs. In the view of Western analysts, this shift reflects Moscow's concern over its growing trade imbalance with Third World countries (partly caused by large-scale purchases of grain and other foodstuffs), as well as its need for hard currency with which to purchase Western technology. According to the CIA, arms transfers "now cover large annual deficits in Soviet nonmilitary trade with LDCs, and significantly supplement Moscow's hard currency earnings."[37] Indeed, the Joint Economic Committee of Congress estimates that arms sales represent Moscow's third principal source of hard currency (after nonmilitary exports and gold sales), providing over $1.5 billion per year in the late 1970s.[38] Many analysts believe, moreover, that this motive is becoming more important as a result of the sluggish performance of the Soviet economy (especially its agricultural sector), and the resulting need for imported food and technology.

These eight factors appear to be the principal motives underlying Soviet arms transfers in the Third World. As in the American case, political motives tend to play a more decisive role than economic motives (even though, in certain particular cases, economic motives may predominate). For the Europeans, the priorities tend to be reversed: economic factors rather than political factors tend to motivate arms exports to the Third World. This is not to say that political motives are insignificant; as we shall see, political factors are often closely intertwined with economic factors in driving European exports.[39] Here, then, are the principal European motives.

Balance of Trade. The highly industrialized nations of Western Europe must export manufactured goods to other countries in order to finance imports of food and raw materials (especially energy sources), and few products have encountered as much demand as modern arms. Because, moreover, the internal U.S. and Soviet markets are almost totally dominated by indigenous producers, the Third World has become the major outlet for European arms. France, in particular, has come to rely on military exports as a source of revenue and has been especially conspicuous in the Middle Eastern market since the OPEC oil price increase of 1974.[40]

Sustaining Employment. Given the political strength of labor unions in most European countries, and the sobering experience of the Great Depression, most governments regard the maintenance of high rates of employment as a key economic goal. And because the arms industry has historically been a major provider of jobs in many European countries—especially in France, Great Britain, and West Germany—their governments have often sought to increase exports in order to generate new jobs or, in times of economic difficulty, to preserve jobs that might otherwise be lost.

Rationalizing Domestic Arms Production. For reasons of security as well as of prestige, the larger European nations seek to maintain a diversified arms industry comparable to (if smaller than) those of the two superpowers. But while the United States and the Soviet Union can sustain a relatively large military-industrial complex through domestic orders, no European country provides an internal market large enough to sustain a domestic arms industry at anywhere near economic rates of production. Exports are thus critically needed to justify the preservation of a large arms establishment.[41]

Political Influence. Like the two superpowers, the major European powers view arms transfers as an important source of influence in the Third World. Of course, compared to the United States and the Soviet Union, their objectives are more limited: most European governments seek to maintain close relations with a score of nations they consider important because of geographic location, economic links, or historical ties and obligations. Thus, France has placed particular emphasis on promoting stability in North Africa and the Middle East, while Great Britain has sought to preserve its ties with former colonies in the Persian Gulf area and sub-Saharan Africa.

These represent the principal motives underlying Soviet and European arms sales to the Third World. While any one or two of these may prevail in a given case, it is the clustering of these motives—each reinforcing the other—that drives the Soviet and European export programs. So long as this clustering persists, we can expect relatively high levels of sales to Third World countries.

But while this constellation of motives for large-scale arms exports may remain intact, this does not necessarily mean that there will be a steadily expanding market for Soviet (or European) arms.

Indeed, as we have discovered in the course of our investigation, the rate of arms transfers is governed as much by the demand in the marketplace (the "pull" factor) as by the desire of the supplier to sell (the "push" factor). No matter how much Moscow may want to increase its level of sales to the Third World, it cannot be assured of success if its present clients refuse to increase their level of spending and/or if new customers cannot be found. And while the U.S.S.R. was highly successful in boosting its arms exports in the late 1970s, there are some signs that this upward drive has leveled off as a result of slackened demand. Indeed, the CRS reported that Soviet sales dropped from $12.6 billion in 1982 to $4.2 billion in 1983, the lowest level in many years.[42]

The cause of the apparent decline in demand for Soviet arms is threefold: first, a number of Moscow's major clients (e.g., Algeria and Libya) made substantial purchases of high-tech Soviet gear in the late 1970s and are likely to postpone further orders until the new equipment is absorbed. Second, several other clients (e.g., India and Iraq) have recently indicated a strong desire to diversify their arms holdings in order to reduce their reliance on any one superpower. Finally, the Soviets have not succeeded in attracting many new customers since the invasion of Afghanistan, and the poor performance of their equipment in the 1982 Lebanon conflict is likely to discourage potential buyers.* These negative factors could be overridden, of course, by massive Iraqi purchases to replace equipment lost in the war with Iran, and continuing high-volume sales to Syria. But if present trends continue, we are likely to see a slackening of Soviet sales in the 1980s.

This assessment suggests that the Soviet export picture is not as rosy as some U.S. military analysts would have us believe. While Soviet sales could certainly shoot up again as a result of unforeseen developments, they could also remain at relatively low levels if the pull factor further evaporates. Nor is the drying up of demand the only problem Soviet policymakers might face: growing Soviet assis-

---

*As a result of Israeli/U.S. superiority in electronic warfare, *Business Week* reported on September 20, 1982, "the scorecard for Israel's June 9 raid on Soviet-built antiaircraft missiles in Lebanon was so lopsided that a former Israeli intelligence chief declares that 'shock tremors' must have ripped through Warsaw Pact countries, since the same missiles defend their air space." In response to such comments, the Soviet news agency Tass published a statement extolling the virtues of Soviet weaponry, and charging that Western "propaganda organs" had been "circulating deliberately false information on Soviet combat equipment."

tance to such dependencies as Afghanistan, Angola, Cuba, Ethiopia, and Vietnam have generated a significant drain on the Soviet economy and could prove intolerable if other costs (e.g., imports of food and technology) continue their upward climb. Furthermore, continued transfers to such countries as Libya and Syria could lead to Soviet involvement in an unwanted regional conflict. And since the potential for Soviet cooperation in future conventional arms control negotiations is likely to be determined by the perceived effectiveness of arms transfers in meeting their intended goals, it is important that we next examine the balance sheet for Moscow's military export program.

The Arms Export Balance Sheet: Soviet Gains and Losses

As we have seen, Soviet leaders are motivated by a wide range of political, military, and economic factors when approving arms transfers to the Third World, and, like their counterparts in the United States, they evidently believe in the efficacy of such transfers in achieving their intended objectives. This does not mean, however, that Soviet arms transfers have always delivered all of the benefits that have been ascribed to them; on many occasions, in fact, Moscow has discovered that arms transfers are an extremely unreliable instrument of policy, often producing results that are wholly inconsistent with fundamental national objectives. It is obvious, therefore, that the balance sheet on Soviet arms exports harbors significant losses as well as gains, and that both must be examined closely before calculating the bottom line on this program.[43]

In terms of gaining *presence*—establishing diplomatic relations and initiating political contact—there is no question that the Soviet arms export program has been highly successful. The U.S.S.R. now provides arms to some forty Third World nations, many of which cooperate with Moscow in other spheres. Arms transfers have also granted the U.S.S.R. other benefits: some Third World recipients (Libya, South Yemen, Vietnam) have allowed the Soviets to station reconnaissance and transport aircraft on their territory, and some have become active political partners as well, cooperating with Moscow on military initiatives in adjacent areas (as, for example, when Libya and South Yemen served as staging areas for Soviet/ Cuban operations in Angola and Ethiopia). Military sales have also, as we have seen, become a major source of hard currency.

These are respectable gains and no doubt explain the continuing Soviet involvement in arms exports. But however impressive, they cannot obscure one fundamental fact: Soviet arms transfers to the Third World have not resulted in lasting political *influence*—that is, an acknowledged capacity to alter or affect political-military decisionmaking by the leaders of recipient nations. Indeed, the record shows that the Soviets have often been frustrated in their attempts to use arms transfers to gain influence abroad, and that on occasions when they actually sought to apply pressure—as in Egypt in 1972 and Somalia in 1977—they were summarily and harshly rebuffed.[44]

In order to evaluate Moscow's performance in achieving its objectives via arms transfers, it is instructive to examine briefly the Soviet arms-supply relationship with a number of past and present recipients.

Egypt. President Gamal Abdel Nasser was the first Third World leader to request Soviet-bloc military assistance, and for twenty years Egypt was the leading Third World recipient of Soviet arms. Between 1955 and 1974, the U.S.S.R. provided Cairo with $3 billion in arms and military assistance, endowing Egypt with one of the most modern and well-equipped armies in the Third World. Furthermore, Moscow's original 1955 arms agreement with Cairo (which followed an earlier agreement with Czechoslovakia) became the model for Soviet military ties with dozens of other governments, thereby affording the U.S.S.R. access to many countries it had previously been excluded from, while allowing nationalistic Third World regimes to emphasize their independence from the traditional powers of the "First World" (Western Europe and North America). At the peak of Soviet influence in Egypt, during the resupply efforts that followed the 1967 Arab-Israeli war, Moscow had some 20,000 military advisors in the country and enjoyed almost unlimited access to naval facilities at Alexandria.

But however attractive to both parties, the Soviet-Egyptian relationship was not without its strains: Moscow repeatedly declined to supply Egypt with its most advanced offensive arms and counseled restraint on key Middle East disputes, while Cairo, for its part, persistently objected to the inadequate quality of Soviet deliveries and complained of the "arrogant" behavior of Russian military advisors. These strains grew more intense after Anwar Sadat succeeded Nasser, and in July 1972—only fourteen months after Cairo had signed a Treaty of Friendship and Cooperation with Moscow—Sadat canceled Soviet port privileges and expelled most of the Russian advisors. Fresh Soviet equipment was requested—and paid for in cash—during the October 1973 war with Israel, but Moscow never regained its privileged position in Egypt. Finally, in 1974, Sadat expelled the remaining Russian advisors and repudiated Egypt's $5 billion arms debt. For Moscow, the public loss of its oldest and most important client in the Middle East represented a humiliating foreign policy defeat. Other Arab nations—Iraq, Libya, Syria—have since become major Soviet clients, but none comes close to Egypt in terms of innate political or strategic significance.[45]

Somalia. The Soviet Union began providing arms to Somalia in 1963 and by 1969 had become that country's principal supplier. Over a fourteen-year period, Moscow supplied Somalia with about $1 billion in arms aid and deployed hundreds of military technicians to assist the Somalis in operation of all this new gear. As in Egypt, this arms-supply arrangement endowed Moscow with significant strategic benefits: President Siad Barre signed a Treaty of Friendship and Cooperation with the U.S.S.R. in 1974 and allowed the Russians to transform the port of Berbera into a major Soviet base on the Indian Ocean. But, again as in Egypt, the supply of arms did not provide Moscow with lasting political influence. In 1977, acting against Soviet advice, Barre sent Somali "volunteers" into the Ogaden region of Ethiopia in a barely disguised maneuver to seize the disputed area. When Moscow then provided emergency arms aid to the Ethiopians—ruled since 1974 by a self-styled Marxist regime—Barre ousted all Russian advisors, canceled Soviet basing privileges at Berbera, and repudiated the 1974 treaty. Although the break with Somalia was partly offset by expanded Soviet influence in Ethiopia, the loss of Berbera represented a significant strategic setback.[46]

Iraq. While Iraq remains a major recipient of Soviet arms, there are considerable strains in the Soviet-Iraqi relationship and evidence of a determined Iraqi effort to reduce its military dependency on the U.S.S.R. Between 1970 and 1979, Iraq acquired some $4.9 billion worth of arms from the U.S.S.R., more than any other Third World nation except Libya. This largesse has not, however, deterred President Saddam Hussein from seeking arms in the West (a $1.6 billion agreement for 60 Mirage F-1s was concluded with France in 1977), nor from opposing Moscow on other key issues (Iraq was notably forthright in its condemnation of the Russian invasion of Afghanistan). More significantly, Soviet arms aid has not provided the Soviets with any measure of political influence in Baghdad, as reflected in Hussein's 1980 decision to invade Iran in defiance of Soviet wishes. The Soviets have continued to supply Iraq with some arms and spare parts since the onset of the war, but it is possible that Hussein will shop elsewhere once the war is terminated.[47]

Libya. Often described in the West as an unblemished Soviet "success story" in Africa, Moscow's arms relationship with Libya is not without its problems and frictions. Since 1974 the U.S.S.R.'s number one arms customer in the Third World, Col. Muamar Qaddafi ordered an estimated $12 billion in modern arms by 1980, including top-rated MiG-23s, MiG-25s, Tu-22 bombers, and T-72 tanks. Qaddafi has also permitted the Soviets to stock combat equipment in Libya and to use Tripoli as a staging area for military supply operations elsewhere in Africa. Nevertheless, he has been outspoken in his opposition to Communism and has adamantly refused to provide Moscow with permanent naval facilities at Libyan ports. The Libyans have also engaged in overseas adventures that have jeopardized other Soviet interests (the 1983 Libyan incursion in Chad, for instance, alienated France along with several of the black African states being courted by Moscow) and have periodically threatened to ignite a regional war that could lead to an unwanted superpower confrontation. No doubt Moscow will continue to supply Libya—for the hard currency benefits, if nothing else—but it is doubtful that the Soviet-Libyan relationship will produce other significant benefits for the U.S.S.R.[48]

These four cases are fairly representative of the Soviet experience in using arms as instruments of influence and entree in the Third World. Admittedly, there are some brighter spots that could be mentioned—Cuba, South Yemen, and Vietnam remain close allies—but there are also other failures to recount—Indonesia and Sudan, among them—and an assortment of problem areas.[49] Algeria, for instance, appears determined to improve its ties with the West, and both Angola and Mozambique have resisted Soviet efforts to establish a formal military relationship involving bases and the like.[50] Syria, the number three Soviet recipient after Libya and Iraq, has repeatedly clashed with Moscow on fundamental issues (e.g., the 1976 Syrian occupation of Lebanon, which triggered a temporary suspension in Soviet arms deliveries) and appears determined to retain its distance from Moscow despite a continuing influx of sophisticated Soviet arms.[51]

This brief overview of Soviet arms programs suggests that the Soviet effort has produced mixed results at best, with some question as to whether the gains can be considered to outweigh the losses. "Although the Soviet Union can claim important successes to counterbalance [its] costly failures," Cynthia A. Roberts wrote in *Survival*, "the evidence suggests that arms transfers, by themselves, rarely, if ever, permit lasting gains." Nowhere is this more true than in the Middle East, she noted, where "the potential risks and costs of the still volatile Arab-Israeli conflict [and] the vacillating nature of Arab allegiances have clearly outpaced Moscow's ability to translate its weapons sales into meaningful political leverage."[52]

What accounts for this rather disappointing record? Although technical reasons are usually cited by Western analysts—the shoddy nature of Soviet arms, inadequate follow-up support, provocative behavior by Russian advisors, and so forth—the principal factor to be considered is that in almost every case the arms relationship is viewed by recipients as an alliance of convenience rather than of preference, and as one that can be severed whenever fundamental objectives necessitate an autonomous stance. Many former Soviet clients were visibly unhappy over their close association with the U.S.S.R. and wasted little time in ousting Russian advisors once the decision to break ties had been made.[53] As CDI noted in 1979, "Local conflicts and local problems matter more than great global issues for the course of an export program," and thus, "ten years of good relations can vanish with a regime change, or because the Soviets underestimate the determination of a customer to pursue policies the Soviets opposed."[54]

Ironically, the extent of Soviet (or, for that matter, American) leverage over its clients tends to diminish as the sophistication and quantity of arms transfers increases. The more powerful a recipient's arsenal becomes, the more likely it is to engage in aggressive or adventuristic behavior that conflicts with the interests of the supplier. "The arms suppliers themselves undermine their ability to dominate certain Third World conflicts," Barry Blechman, Janne Nolan, and Alan Platt observed in Foreign Policy, "by this very effort to secure political advantage by the transfer of increasingly sophisticated arms."[55] Thus, it was the big Soviet buildup in Egypt following the 1967 war that enabled Cairo to launch the 1973 war, and it was Soviet generosity in Somalia that helped induce Siad Barre to invade the Ogaden. High-tech deliveries to Iraq and Libya have likewise increased their capacity to engage in adventuristic behavior at the expense of long-term Soviet interests.

No doubt for this very reason, the Soviets have always tended to hedge their bets by supplying less-sophisticated equipment than that sought by their clients—thereby further jeopardizing their arms relationships. Although Moscow has progressively upgraded the equipment supplied to Third World clients, it has usually withheld its most capable systems and, on occasion, imposed other restraints to avoid provoking a regional conflict that could lead to a superpower clash. President Sadat of Egypt was visibly bitter over Moscow's failure to provide high-tech offensive arms prior to the October 1973 war with Israel, and the Syrians have repeatedly complained that the aircraft and missiles supplied to their country are no match for the U.S. arms sold to Israel.[56] These charges are borne out by examination of the arms supplied by the Soviets to their Middle Eastern clients, Cynthia A. Roberts observed in *Survival*. "In the first place, no Soviet aircraft in the region meet the high performance standards of the U.S.-supplied F-15 or F-16, much less their complement of air-to-air missiles. Second, and even more striking, is the complete absence in the area of any Soviet real-time early warning or electronic aircraft" comparable to the U.S. E-2CS and AWACS planes sold to Egypt, Israel, and Saudi Arabia.[57]

Such restraint has not, however, enabled the Soviets to escape the dilemmas posed by their massive arms transfer program. On one hand, they evidently feel compelled to maintain costly programs of dubious benefit rather than face the complete erosion of their overseas relationships; on the other, they fear that continued support for unpredictable and uncontrollable recipients could result in direct Soviet involvement in unwanted military conflicts abroad. As noted by Roger Pajak in *Survival*, recent conflicts in the Middle East have taught Moscow that "a special relationship with arms recipients can lead to risks of unwarranted military involvement and possible military confrontation with the United States."[58] This is particularly true in Syria, where Soviet efforts to placate Assad's desire for sophisticated weaponry have placed Soviet military personnel in close proximity to Israel and U.S. naval forces in the Mediterranean.[59]

These are sobering lessons and must give Soviet leaders considerable pause when confronted with major requests from unstable clients. So long as Moscow feels compelled to compete with Washington for influence and presence in the Third World, we can expect a continuing Soviet effort to boost its military exports to strategically placed clients. But given the problematical outcome of Soviet arms programs, we can also conclude that Soviet leaders would have real incentives to curb their exports in the context of a U.S.-Soviet agreement on multilateral restraint. Indeed, analyses of the Conventional Arms Transfer talks of 1977–78 suggest that the Russians were fully cognizant of these incentives and thus prepared to make significant concessions in return for U.S. restraint in areas such as the Middle East that had the greatest potential for a superpower confrontation. In discussing the CAT experience, chief U.S. negotiator Leslie Gelb surmised in 1979 that Moscow was motivated to adopt a conciliatory stance because "they have not always achieved what they hoped for politically through arms transfers and . . . their arms have been used in ways that were not intended."[60] And while the international climate did not permit a continuation of the CAT process beyond the preliminary stage, it did demonstrate that Moscow is sufficiently dissatisfied with the results of its arms program to consider a new family of arms control agreements with the United States.

Conclusion

As we have seen, the Soviet Union and the "big four" European powers are major suppliers of sophisticated arms to the Third World and are likely to remain so for the foreseeable future. As a result, Third World buyers now have access to more suppliers than ever before and, by playing upon the competitive impulse shared by all of these suppliers, can acquire increasingly sophisticated and capable military equipment. This process has exacerbated local controversies and increased the risk that such disputes will erupt in armed conflict. And because the superpowers are increasingly involved in the supply of technical military services to their principal clients, there is an increasing risk that such wars as do occur will provoke a U.S.-Soviet confrontation.

But while the risks posed by burgeoning arms transfers to the Third World are self-evident, there is no such certainty surrounding the purported benefits of such exports. In contrast to the widely held U.S. belief that arms transfers have provided Moscow with expanded power and leverage in the Third World, the record suggests that such exports have been unreliable instruments of influence and have exposed the U.S.S.R. to a significant risk of unwarranted involvement in local conflicts. While it is certainly true that Moscow has achieved some real gains in terms of overseas presence, it is questionable whether these gains really outweigh the losses.

From a purely economic point of view, the benefits for the Europeans from their arms exports appear more convincing: increased spending in imported oil has been partially offset by increased sales of military hardware, and export sales have helped sustain elaborate arms establishments. But these benefits have to be set against the potential costs of regional conflicts—Britain spent an estimated $1 billion in the Falklands to overcome the (mostly) European-supplied arms possessed by Argentina, and a future war in the Persian Gulf could choke off oil deliveries and thus produce a major economic crisis.

Clearly, these findings have considerable significance for our study of U.S. policy alternatives. To start with, this assessment of Soviet performance should reinforce our doubts about the utility of arms sales as an instrument of political and diplomatic leverage. As noted by Pierre, "the Soviet experience confirms that the provision of arms sales does not readily translate into lasting influence."[61] Given this reality, we can be much more skeptical about Pentagon claims of expanding Soviet presence—and thus the need for increased U.S. transfers to offset that presence. The fact that the Soviets have a conspicuous arms-supply relationship with a particular government now does not signify that this relationship will persist indefinitely, or that it is necessarily in America's interest to step up arms deliveries to that government's principal rivals.

More important than any of these conclusions, however, is the general finding that competition between the suppliers is making the world more dangerous for all countries, whatever their share of a particular market. As Barry Blechman, Janne Nolan, and Alan Platt noted in *Foreign Policy*, "the continuing escalation of arms transfers to increasingly autonomous Third World countries threatens both global stability and U.S. national interest."[62] In no way is this less true for the Soviets or the Europeans. While any given supplier may benefit politically or economically from a particular arms rivalry in the Third World, they all risk catastrophe in an uncontrolled conflagration.

For this reason, it is obvious that all major suppliers—as well as, in the end, all major recipients—have a strong vested interest in curbing the international traffic in conventional armaments. As we have seen, however, such restraints must by definition be multilateral to be effective: clearly, it does Washington (or Moscow, or Paris) no good to restrain its exports in the name of global stability if its clients turn elsewhere to make up for the shortfall in deliveries. Only mutual restraint on the part of all major suppliers will ensure a genuine reduction in global arms transfers.

Assuming, however, that all major suppliers can be convinced of the need for such cooperation, we still have the problem of overcoming the "primal motives" that underlie the arms traffic. As we have learned, leaders in both the West and East have come to expect a wide variety of benefits from arms sales and are thus understandably reluctant to consider any reduction in such exports. If we are to solicit their participation in a new round of arms control talks, therefore, we must offer concrete incentives to counterbalance the continuing influence of these primal motives. Such incentives cannot be merely negative in character—for example, the avoidance of war or diplomatic humiliation—but must also confer positive benefits—for example, new trade advantages or added political outlets.

It would be naive, at this point, to suggest that the major suppliers can be easily persuaded to negotiate collective restraints on their arms transfers. All that we have learned about the clustering of motives behind military exports indicates that it will prove extremely difficult to persuade supplier governments to impose real constraints on their foreign sales. But it should also be evident that the purported benefits of arms transfers are reaching a point of stable if not diminishing returns, while the potential risks of such sales are increasing at an exponential rate. As time goes on, therefore, the incentives to restrain will grow stronger—while the penalties for license will become increasingly catastrophic.

CHAPTER 11

Promoting Global Stability

An Alternative Policy Framework

At the outset of this book, I promised to explore the major foreign policy issues arising from the arms trade so that the reader will be able to play a more informed and effective role in future policy debates. At this point, we have nearly completed our task: we have examined the policies, procedures, and goals that have governed U.S. arms programs over the past twenty years and have watched how these programs actually performed in a number of key countries and regions. We have also investigated several special problem areas: the sale of arms-making technology, the export of police and paramilitary gear, and "gray-area" transfers to South Africa. In this process, we have made some preliminary observations about the relative effectiveness of arms transfers in achieving stated U.S. objectives—observations that, to a large degree, were confirmed by our analysis of Soviet and European arms sales. Now it is time to pull all of these observations together and to draw some final conclusions about the role of arms sales in U.S. foreign policy—and then, on that basis, to offer some recommendations for an alternative policy framework.

Such a framework need not incorporate a catalog of detailed legislative remedies; rather, it should provide a set of general principles that can be used in shaping new laws or regulations. These principles should clearly define the functions which arms exports may legitimately perform in the service of U.S. foreign policy and establish distinct constraints on the transfer of arms-making technology and internal security hardware. In addition, the framework should indicate what changes are needed in the existing decision-making process to ensure effective compliance with these principles and constraints. Composed in this manner, it could serve as a model for a new presidential initiative in this area, or for a new effort by U.S. lawmakers to revise the statutes governing arms transfers.

To begin this review, let us recall that in the "briefing" inserted into chapter 1 we identified three fundamental issues—national security, foreign policy, and relative economic benefit—that arise in all full-scale discussions of U.S. arms export policy. Now, having completed our study of the arms trade and its consequences, we can compose a second briefing—one that stresses the basic policy issues rather than the underlying trends. By definition, such a briefing must entail some political judgments as well as the statistical observations with which we have become familiar. These judgments will naturally reflect my perspective, but every effort will be made to rest them squarely on the findings accumulated in the course of this study.[1]

The Policy Environment

Arms transfers are an important instrument of U.S. foreign policy and have become increasingly more so during the past twenty years. Because of a decline in the more traditional expressions of military power—alliances, threats of intervention or "gunboat diplomacy," overseas bases and garrisons, and so forth—and the virtual disappearance of grant military assistance, arms sales have come to be seen as the principal U.S. mechanism for promoting U.S. security interests in the world at large. Even during the Carter administration, when some effort was made to reduce the outflow of arms, military sales played a key role in U.S. policy; under President Reagan, such exports came to be considered an essential instrument of U.S. policy—the equivalent, in the international sphere, of the massive military buildup in the United States. As suggested by Under Secretary of State James L. Buckley in 1981, "the Administration believes that arms transfers . . . complement and supplement our own efforts to improve our own defense capabilities and are an indispensable component of foreign policy."[2]

At the same time, arms transfers have decisively and irrevocably altered the world political-military environment in which U.S. policies are acted out. By selling their latest and most capable military systems, the United States and the other major arms suppliers have transformed many once-powerless Third World nations into major military contenders. Countries like Iraq, Israel, Libya, and Syria are now equipped with many of the same weapons possessed by the front-line states in NATO and the Warsaw Pact and are capable of sustaining warfare at unprecedented levels of violence and destructiveness. This transformation, combined with the industrial nations' dependence on imported raw materials and energy supplies, has converted many Third World areas into the world's leading crisis points; from now on, any hostilities arising in the Middle East or other volatile areas will have the potential to spark a major regional conflict and, conceivably, a superpower confrontation with thermonuclear potential. "The dramatic growth of conventional arms sales in both quantity and quality poses a grave danger to world stability," Andrew Pierre warned in 1983. "The United States and other countries risk being drawn into regional conflicts in the Third World which could escalate into a global conflagration."[3]

Given the growing importance of arms sales as an instrument of foreign policy, and the potential explosiveness of Third World battlefields, one would expect a corresponding increase in the degree of control exercised by U.S. policymakers and Congress over American military exports. Unfortunately, the opposite appears to be the case: except for the modest reforms introduced by President Carter, no recent U.S. administration has attempted to bring the arms trade under tighter national or international control. Indeed, one could conclude that the arms trade is rapidly slipping out of control, and that the momentum of this slippage is increasing with each passing year. As suggested by Rep. Tony P. Hall of Ohio, "we have opened a Pandora's Box which we may never be able to close again."[4]

America's growing loss of control over the arms trade can be delineated in a number of critical ways.

Volume. Net sales of U.S. arms and military equipment rose dramatically during the 1970s and are continuing to rise (though at a somewhat slower rate) in the 1980s. Total sales under the FMS program rose by an average annual rate of 153 percent between 1970 and 1982, from $1.1 billion to $21.3 billion, while FMS deliveries rose from $1.3 billion to $10.9 billion (in current dollars). Although U.S. law (specifically, the Arms Export Control Act) states unequivocally that reducing arms transfers is a fundamental American objective, no policy initiatives introduced to date have succeeded in reducing the long-term growth in exports. As a result, the United States is pouring more arms into the Third World than ever before, with an attendant increase in the war-making capabilities of recipient states—many of which harbor ambitions or resentments that could easily trigger a major conflict.

Sophistication. Sales of sophisticated weaponry have accounted for an ever-larger share of U.S. military exports over the past fifteen years and are expected to push U.S. sales levels to record heights in the years ahead. Carter's pledge to restrict sales of advanced arms to Third World buyers was repeatedly violated by the president himself, and Reagan has eliminated virtually all remaining constraints on sales of such equipment. The United States has been especially permissive in its sales to the Middle East, providing favored allies with such advanced gear as the AWACS radar surveillance plane, the F-15 and F-16 fighters, the M-60A3 tank, and the upgraded AIM-9L Sidewinder air-to-air missile. Because such transfers are also accompanied by comparable Soviet and Western European sales, U.S. exports are helping to sustain local arms races in the Middle East and other Third World areas that periodically threaten to explode into regional conflagrations. To make matters worse, some recipients of these arms have also acquired (or are attempting to acquire) the technology to produce nuclear weapons.

Proliferation of Clients. Whereas Washington once restricted arms transfers to close allies and the "forward defense countries" on the periphery of the Sino-Soviet bloc, now the tendency is to sell to any non-Communist government with sufficient cash or credit. In fiscal 1980, the United States sold arms to some 115 nations under the FMS and Commercial Sales programs, or about twice the figure for 1960.[5] In expanding the client pool for American munitions, U.S. authorities have invariably advanced the same "collective security" arguments used to justify the earlier choice of recipients; many of America's newer clients, however, have few historical or political ties to the United States and appear to seek arms more for parochial than for collaborative reasons. Indeed, many of the new entries to the client pool, such as North Yemen, Oman, Sudan, the United Arab Emirates, and Zaire, are engaged in regional rivalries or internal conflicts that are potentially destructive to long-term U.S. security interests. There is no reason to believe, moreover, that these countries are any more likely than the others to restrict the use of their American-supplied weapons to the defensive purposes specified by U.S. law; if anything, the proliferation of clients suggests a diminished rather than increased U.S. intent to control the uses to which its arms are ultimately put.

Exports of Technology and Military Skills. Accompanying the trend toward sales of increasingly sophisticated weapons has been a significant growth in sales of arms-making technology and military technical skills. As a result, more and more countries are acquiring the capacity to produce and export arms on their own, and more and more U.S. civilians are serving in sensitive military posts abroad. Although U.S. officials assert that such exports foster American security interests, it is obvious that they also pose significant risks: overseas arms producers can deliver U.S.-designed arms to other countries—some of which may become adversaries of the United States or its allies—while overseas concentrations of U.S. military technicians could become hostages of the host regime or targets for military attack by its rivals. Despite such risks, exports of this sort have been accorded even less attention in Washington than exports of finished military products.

Added together, these findings can be summarized as follows:

the United States is providing more and more countries with ever-larger quantities of increasingly sophisticated weapons, along with the skills to use them and the technology to reproduce them.[6]

To this must be added, of course, what we have learned about the international dimension of the arms trade: increased U.S. sales have been matched by the Soviet Union and the other major suppliers, thereby fueling regional arms races and augmenting the war-making capabilities of potential belligerents. When we consider the net military potential represented by the hundreds of billions of dollars worth of advanced arms supplied to Third World countries over the past fifteen years—as well as the hundreds of billions of dollars' worth of arms still in the pipeline—it is obvious that we are witnessing a global power shift of unprecedented dimensions. And we dare not underestimate the risks inherent in that shift: as Leslie Gelb of the State Department noted in 1978, "When these arms are delivered and when the recipients learn to use them, they will change the face of world politics; for the first time, many states throughout the world will have arms of much the same sophistication and quality as those of the few major powers."[7]

Something else must be said about these arms: there is a good chance that many of them will eventually be used. While the possessors of nuclear weapons have heretofore declined to use them for fear of mutual annihilation, no such inhibitions have yet prevented the use of conventional weapons. "Millions of words have been written in the past three decades about nuclear war and rightly so," the *New York Times* noted editorially in 1975. "But the arms that have killed more than ten million human beings since World War II have all been conventional weapons."[8] (Since this was written, another ten million people are believed to have lost their lives in conventional conflicts.) Whatever their professed commitment to peace and disarmament, most governments view conventional munitions as usable instruments of power that may be employed whenever national policy dictates the exercise of force. And while U.S. law explicitly restricts the use of U.S.-supplied arms to self-defense, U.N.-sponsored peacekeeping operations, and internal security, the recipients of these arms have not always let such limitations stand in the way of their using them for other purposes when they determined that their vital national interests were at stake. Thus the Israelis used their U.S.-supplied arms in the 1982 invasion of Lebanon, the Argentinians used their American weapons in the seizure of the Falklands, the Turks used theirs in the occupation of Cyprus, and so forth. Once a recipient breaks its ties with the United States, moreover, Washington loses all control over the use of American-supplied arms. Iran, for instance, continues to use its American hardware in the conflict with Iraq, while Libya has employed its U.S.-supplied aircraft in a number of foreign adventures. What all this means, of course, is that the United States is continuing to pour more and more arms into volatile Third World areas with no real assurance that they will not be used to undermine fundamental U.S. interests.

Most U.S. leaders acknowledge the risks posed by arms transfers, but argue that it is to our advantage to continue selling weapons so long as there are no established multilateral restraints on such exports. "We remain prepared to examine ways to pursue a regime of multilateral [arms transfer] restraint," then Under Secretary of State Buckley declared in 1981, but "we are not prepared . . . to sacrifice American interests and the interests of our friends abroad by seeking to go it alone."[9] Underlying this perspective is the belief that arms transfers deliver on the promises made for them—that on balance they do advance America's interests and those of its friends and allies. There is a growing body of evidence to suggest, however, that arms transfers are a relatively unreliable instrument of policy. Indeed, as we have seen, large-scale transfers of sophisticated arms can diminish rather than increase U.S. influence. Before we can draw any final conclusions on the validity of the prevailing U.S. approach, therefore, we must weigh the relative effectiveness of arms transfers in fulfilling their stated objectives.

Appraising the Risks and Benefits

Just how well, then, have arms sales performed? In responding, let us return to the three basic questions posed at the outset of this study, and then attempt to provide a final assessment.

Do Arms Sales Enhance U.S. National Security? If we mean by this, do arms transfers strengthen the self-defense capabilities of particular allies, then the answer is: sometimes. The record is clearest in the cases of countries located on the periphery of the Sino-Soviet bloc or otherwise threatened by hostile neighbors. Certainly postwar U.S. arms aid to Western Europe helped discourage Moscow from contemplating any further expansion of its European domain, and continued sales to the NATO powers have helped stabilize the existing European order. Arms transfers to other exposed countries, such as Israel, South Korea, and Taiwan, have also helped to discourage hostile action by potential aggressors.

We must not automatically assume, however, that in these cases arms transfers were the principal deterrent to aggression: equally important, in many cases, was the morale and fighting ability of the forces involved and the perceived determination of the population to resist conquest. When a nation is united in its will to combat aggression, arms aid can play an important role in strengthening its defense capability; in the absence of such determination, no amount of arms will guarantee a successful defense, as so many historical events have demonstrated. It also must be remembered that some of the armaments provided by the United States for defensive purposes have been used for offensive moves, usually at the expense of long-term U.S. security interests. Thus the 1974 Turkish intervention in Cyprus drove Greece out of NATO and jeopardized Western security in the Eastern Mediterranean, while the periodic Israeli incursions into Lebanon have embittered America's Arab allies (many of whom view Washington as the responsible party because of all the U.S. arms transfers to Israel) and thus undermined U.S. efforts to form a "strategic consensus" in the vital Persian Gulf area.

In the case of countries threatened by internal revolt, the record is less clear. When reasonably popular governments have been threatened by isolated guerrilla bands, as in Venezuela and Colombia, U.S. arms aid has contributed to the survival of the prevailing regime; when Washington has attempted to preserve an unpopular or undemocratic regime, as in Vietnam and Iran (under the Shah), the results have not been very encouraging. Massive U.S. military aid has, on occasion, helped sustain unstable regimes for considerable lengths of time—witness Batista's Cuba and Somoza's Nicaragua— but the net result has often been a legacy of anti-Americanism far more damaging than any short-term gains obtained from the survival of pro-U.S. potentates. In many cases, moreover, arms provided for defense against terrorists or revolutionary forces have been used instead to silence unarmed dissidents and protesters—thereby swelling the ranks of the insurgents and posing an increased security problem for the United States.

Examined in this fashion, U.S. national security can be said to have gained some benefit from conventional arms transfers on some occasions. But it is also necessary to view national security in another, broader perspective. This approach recognizes that in an increasingly interdependent world, the United States has a vested interest in the preservation of global stability. When even a minor local conflict can spread rapidly into a regional conflagration that might jeopardize U.S. access to essential raw materials or, worse, provoke a nuclear confrontation, it is obvious that our national security interests are best served if such conflicts are prevented altogether or are confined to the lowest level of violence possible. Seen from this perspective, the role of arms transfers in promoting national security is necessarily considerably far more limited: namely, to remove any incentive for a nation to go to war.

This function of arms transfers is fully acknowledged in U.S. policy. "Given the growing disorder that we confront today," Under Secretary Buckley suggested, arms transfers can "help to reestablish some sense of equilibrium."[10] Such equilibrium is achieved, in this view, by providing under-equipped U.S. allies with sufficient weaponry to deter aggression by stronger rivals. A frequently cited case-in-point is the Korean Peninsula, where U.S. aid to the South has heretofore succeeded in discouraging attack by the North. But this approach is necessarily one-dimensional: it assumes that some sort of power balance can be attained and preserved through the delivery of arms, whereas our analysis of the arms trade suggests that "equilibrium" is inherently unattainable in a world of multiple suppliers, and that every major delivery of sophisticated weaponry to one side in a rivalry will almost always provoke comparable (or larger) deliveries to the other side, leading to fresh arms requests by the original party, and so on. Once such a regional arms race has commenced, a fresh delivery of arms may, for a time, produce a temporary balance and therefore deter the outbreak of violence; inevitably, however, an imbalance will reappear, stimulating another—and more costly— round of arms transfers, or impelling the (currently) stronger side to launch a preemptive assault before the advantage shifts back to the other side. This has occurred every five to ten years in the Middle East and is likely to reoccur—at ever-increasing levels of violence— so long as the adversaries involved perceive an apparent advantage in preemptive attack.

Indeed, given the vast quantities of arms already transferred to the Third World, it appears that we have reached a point where each new round of arms transfers will embody a diminished capacity for the promotion of restraint. As nations acquire larger and larger stockpiles of sophisticated arms, they will become less likely to respect the interests of their principal suppliers, and more likely to pursue parochial interests that could expose their suppliers to considerable risk. "The current volume of transfers to the Third World is, of itself, a highly destabilizing force," Kevin G. Nealer of the Democratic Policy Committee noted in 1983. "The introduction of high technology weapons into a region can contribute substantially to localized arms races, raising the likelihood that political problems will be answered by military solutions."[11]

To make matters worse, modern arms have acquired a range and destructive capacity that make any conflict between two well-equipped adversaries an automatic threat to all neighboring countries—if for no other reason than that the fighting could spill over into adjacent countries' territory, or, as in the Iran-Iraq war, menace critical air and sea lanes. Under these circumstances, it is not hard to imagine a chain reaction of violence as one country after another joins the conflict in an effort to confine the fighting to the others' territory. Thus Jordan and Saudi Arabia have aided Iraq in its war with Iran in order to discourage further military action by the Iranians, and Israel has aided Iran in order to diminish the fighting power of Iraq. Given the deepening involvement of the superpowers in many Third World areas, moreover, it is not hard to see how such a chain reaction could precipitate a new world war. "The most apt historical analogy for the current period is the years preceding World War I," former Assistant Secretary of State Hodding Carter III suggested in 1982. "The Balkans of the 1980s could be the Middle East or Africa or Southeast Asia."[12]

If this analogy is even partially correct—and there is much evidence to suggest that it is—then any further arms deliveries to volatile Third World areas, from whatever sources, will further undermine global stability and thus represent a direct threat to the national security of the United States. This conclusion is not easily acknowledged by American policymakers—many of whom cling to a belief in the efficacy of arms transfers as an instrument of stability and influence—but follows nevertheless from our analysis of the world military environment. As suggested by Representative Hall, "The weapons we sell today could pull the United States and the world closer to the brink of war."[13] This outlook was confirmed, moreover, by the chairman of the Joint Chiefs of Staff, Gen. David C. Jones, in his annual "military posture statement" for fiscal 1982: "We enter the 1980s," he noted, "after a decade of pronounced growth in the inventories of advanced conventional weapons systems" of Third World countries. "The net effect has been that many developing nations have become armed to the point that they are capable of waging a war of great destructiveness, swiftness, and reach." And, as a consequence, "intra-regional conflicts in areas like Southwest Asia, Southeast Asia, Latin America, and Africa more than ever before threaten wide-spread death and devastation and portend harm to U.S. interests."[14]

On the basis of this prognosis, one is forced to conclude that, over the long run, increased arms exports are more likely to damage than to bolster U.S. national security. But what about the other purported benefits of military sales?

Do Arms Transfers Advance Other U.S. Foreign Policy Objec-

tives? Supporters of the U.S. arms export program have always argued that military sales benefit U.S. foreign policy by providing U.S. officials with enhanced political influence in recipient countries, by building close military-to-military ties, by providing access to bases, and so forth. But just how effective have such exports proven to be in providing these benefits? The answer, based on the studies conducted here, is: not very.

Let us take the issue of influence first. Arms transfers, according to the official doctrine, enhance American leverage by creating dependence on the United States for spare parts, training, follow-up support, and so forth. But while it is certainly possible to find cases where this may have occurred—the Philippines and South Korea, for example, have loyally supported U.S. policies in Asia over a thirty-odd-year period—the exceptions are far more conspicuous.

Let us look, for instance, at America's top three recipients over the past ten years: Iran, Saudi Arabia, and Israel. Despite steady increments in U.S. arms deliveries, U.S. officials were never able to persuade the Shah to adopt domestic reforms that might have saved his government; nor for that matter, have they persuaded the Saudis to endorse the Camp David peace plan or the Israelis to cease their military incursions into neighboring countries. In all these cases, the governments involved determined that particular national interests, as they perceived them, took precedence over any commitment or obligation to the United States. Many other examples could be cited—involving clients of the Soviet Union as well as of the United States—but all confirm the same conclusion: arms sales provide only a limited degree of influence over recipient governments, and whatever influence is acquired tends to vanish whenever fundamental issues are at stake. The premise that arms transfers provide significant leverage "doesn't withstand cursory examination," former Assistant Secretary Carter affirmed in 1982. "The Israelis do as they wish with American arms. So did the Turks on Cyprus. So do and have dozens of other nations." [15]

What, then, about military-to-military contacts, access to bases, and so forth? The same pattern is found here as with other forms of influence; when a recipient perceives a vested interest in close military and political ties with the United States, military sales can serve as a useful mechanism for strengthening these bonds; when, however, a recipient determines that its national interest requires an independent course, no amount of arms deliveries will assure compliance with U.S. priorities. Thus long-standing U.S. ties with Ethiopian military leaders did not prevent them from ousting Haile Selassie and imposing a socialist state; nor has the American alliance with Spain and Greece prevented them from placing tough new restrictions on American use of the U.S. bases in their country.

If arms transfers have been a relatively unreliable instrument when it comes to promoting certain U.S. interests, they have often succeeded in undercutting other U.S. objectives. Because transfers of high-tech arms usually entail follow-up deliveries of spare parts and services, such sales imply a long-term U.S. commitment to the recipient government. As we have seen, such a commitment can result in a close U.S. identification with regimes that are highly undemocratic and/or prone to engage in adventuristic military activities at the expense of America's own strategic interests. As noted by Senator Biden, "the placement of a weapon in the hands of an ally that is not particularly stable or of a regime that is not very beneficial to our area-wide interests ties us to a regime that we may very well not want to be tied to later."[16]

Arms transfers have also frustrated U.S. initiatives on behalf of economic development and human rights. Thus, massive arms purchases by debt-starved Third World nations have consumed funds needed for civilian projects, thereby undermining U.S. efforts to stimulate development. "Arms imports soak up foreign-exchange loans that could otherwise finance purchases of capital goods," Prof. Lance Taylor of MIT has noted. "Econometric studies suggest that each extra dollar spent on arms reduces domestic investment by 25 cents and agricultural output by 20 cents."[17] For countries like India and Pakistan that devote 20 percent or more of available government revenue to military expenditure, the potential for development—and thus for long-term stability—is significantly diminished. Similarly, transfers of internal security hardware have often been used to silence political dissidents—thereby frustrating U.S. initiatives in the area of human rights. While such transfers may contribute to the short-term security of pro-U.S. regimes, they are also likely to sow the seeds of anti-Americanism and thus cause long-term damage to U.S. interests.

It appears, therefore, that arms sales are an unreliable and sometimes counterproductive instrument of U.S. policy. As suggested by Representative Hall, "arms transfer policies seem destined, at best, to be weakly related to and, at worst, completely at odds with the actual arms transfer practices of an administration."[18]

Do Arms Transfers Benefit the U.S. Economy? Here we have some empirical evidence to go on: balance-of-payments data, R&D recoupments, employment figures, and so forth; if we look at these figures only, and view armaments as a mere trade commodity, then the answer is: yes, to a point. Military sales to the Middle East have undoubtedly helped reduce the U.S. trade imbalance with the oil-exporting countries and reduced the unit cost of some high-tech weapons acquired by America's own military forces. Particular sales have also contributed to the fiscal well-being of particular U.S. arms firms and the communities in which they are located.[19]

Some analysts suggest, however, that these benefits have been exaggerated and, when compared to U.S. economic activity as a whole, appear relatively insignificant. Although important in military terms, the $6.6 billion worth of arms exported by the United States in 1980 accounted for only about 3 percent of total U.S. exports, estimated by the ACDA to be over $220 billion.[20] Furthermore, the $800 million in R&D recoupments for 1976 amounted to less than 0.5 percent of the total Defense Department budget. And the 277,000 jobs attributed to foreign military sales by the U.S. Department of Labor in 1975 accounted for only 0.3 percent of a total work force of 80 million.[21] This is not to say that arms transfers do not play a significant economic role in some industries and in some communities. Nevertheless, as suggested by Andrew Pierre, arms transfers do not "occupy as important a role in the national economy as is often assumed by those who believe that economic imperatives must override any attempt to restrain arms sales."[22]

Those benefits that can be identified, moreover, must be balanced against any adverse economic effects of the arms trade. Such costs are, unfortunately, somewhat more difficult to measure. If we assume that the preservation of a large military-industrial capacity is generally beneficial to the U.S. economy, then a high level of arms exports will normally prove advantageous, since foreign sales absorb surplus productive capacity in times of reduced domestic arms spending. If, however, we conclude that an excessive military establishment can harm the U.S. economy—by absorbing capital, skills, and materials needed by the civilian economy—then export sales are especially harmful, since they ensure the survival of otherwise uneconomic enterprises. For most of the post–World War II era, economists generally viewed military spending as a boon to the economy; with the steady decline of many basic civilian industries, however, more and more economists have come to view defense spending as an obstacle to industrial revitalization and overall economic growth.[23] While it is not possible here to draw any final conclusions on this debate, it is enough to say that significant doubt remains about the relative economic benefit of arms transfers.

It appears that the case for arms transfers as a useful instrument of American policy is conspicuously weak. In some cases, and under some circumstances, military sales can help foster particular U.S. interests; on the whole, however, they appear to contribute relatively little toward the attainment of U.S. objectives and may, on occasion, contribute to their obstruction. Arms sales, in other words, have been oversold as an implement of policy.

But if the supposed benefits of arms transfers have been overestimated, the same cannot be said for the risks they pose to U.S. and world security. While American leaders have grudgingly concluded that the proliferation of nuclear technology—to friend and foe alike—represents a potential threat to long-term U.S. security, no such consensus has developed about the risk of conventional arms proliferation. Yet it is precisely such transfers that are contributing most of the potential for conflict in the "Balkans of the 1980s" and thus are lighting the fuse for a nuclear conflagration. As suggested by then Senator Walter F. Mondale in 1973, "the greatest danger to world peace may well lie not so much in the sudden outbreak of nuclear warfare between the superpowers, but in the step-by-step escalation of a local war fought with conventional weapons into an international war fought with nuclear weapons."[24]

If this is true—and common sense suggests that it could hardly be otherwise—then simple self-preservation demands that we strive to bring the arms trade under effective international control. Such a goal will not be easy to achieve—for, as we have seen, many powerful actors perceive a substantial vested interest in arms sales and can therefore be expected to resist the imposition of any new curbs on such exports. Nevertheless, the urgency of restraint is undeniable, and the penalties for inaction are steadily mounting. Hopefully, the growing international concern over global instability and nuclear war will lead more and more policymakers—and their constituents—to perceive a vested interest in conventional arms restraint.

Once U.S. leaders agree on the need for a new approach to arms transfers, they will have to commence the complex task of forging and implementing effective mechanisms of control. As we have learned, this will require both domestic reform and international cooperation. New procedures will have to be established, specific restrictions adopted, means of verification developed, and so forth. Many of these measures will have to emerge out of the negotiating process itself, and so cannot be delineated in advance. Nevertheless, much has been discovered in the course of this study that could prove applicable to the policy-formulation effort. It is appropriate, therefore, that we conclude with a draft overview of an alternative arms export control policy.

An Alternative Policy Framework

Since the foundation of this republic, the principal goal of U.S. foreign policy has been the creation of a just and peaceful world order wherein disputes are settled through negotiation rather than armed conflict. This goal is clearly stated in chapter 1 of the Arms Export Control Act: "an ultimate goal of the United States continues to be a world which is free from the scourge of war and the dangers and burdens of armaments; in which the use of force has been subordinated to the rule of law; and in which international adjustments to a changing world are achieved peacefully." In such a world, there would be no organized warfare, no permanent military establishments, and no traffic in the implements of war. While creation of such a world is presently beyond our grasp, we should never lose sight of this ultimate objective.

Looking at the world as it is, and wishing to avert a global catastrophe, our goal must be more expedient: the deterrence, containment, and control of military conflict. Clearly, arms transfers are capable of either fostering or impeding that goal. By strengthening the self-defense capabilities of exposed nations, they may promote deterrence; by provoking local arms races and exacerbating regional rivalries, they may provoke conflict. The task of the policymaker, therefore, is to establish guidelines for determining which outcome is most likely to result from particular sales. But because the stabilizing capacity of arms transfers has been consistently overestimated, and their provocative potential historically underestimated, the bias should always be against approval of a given sale unless it can be unambiguously shown that it will lower rather than raise the risk of violence. This basic principle is the cornerstone of a prudent arms export policy. "We must," Rep. Les Aspin affirmed, "be sure that if we give arms to other countries, they will use them in ways that further our national security interests. *This represents a relatively limited number of cases*" (emphasis added).[25]

The second fundamental premise of a sound military export policy is that arms transfers (and related deliveries of technology and services) should at all times be subordinated to the basic foreign policy goals of the United States. Each U.S. administration will, of course, interpret these goals in its own way. But such flexibility does not entail a license to subvert such fundamental national objectives as international stability, economic development, and human rights. Arms transfers must be conducted in accordance with these objectives, not independently of them.

In support of these principles, tough new restrictions should be imposed on the export of high-tech arms to volatile Third World areas. Such restrictions can be sufficiently flexible to allow exceptions on those rare occasions when a U.S. denial would clearly hinder deterrence, but tight enough to constrict the flow of sophisticated weaponry. These constraints should be particularly strict in the case of nuclear-capable delivery systems, disallowing the sale of such weapons to any nations known to be seeking a nuclear weapons capability. Similar restraints should be placed on the export of arms-making technology and on the sale of military technical services abroad.

To discourage excessive arms spending by economically troubled Third World countries, the United States should not provide arms credits or other sales incentives to nations with severe debt problems. Similar restrictions should also apply in cases where increased arms spending would consume resources needed for U.S.-supported development programs. At the same time, tougher constraints should be imposed on the sale of police and paramilitary gear to countries ruled by repressive and undemocratic regimes. In this context, all existing loopholes in the U.S. arms embargo on South Africa should be closed.

Implementation of an alternative policy of this sort will obviously require significant changes in the organization of the U.S. arms export establishment. As we have seen, the present decision-making system tends to favor the forces arrayed in favor of a proposed sale, rather than those that advocate caution. As a result, prior U.S. restrictions on the export of high-tech weaponry have been progressively eroded. Congress tried to remedy this situation in 1976 with passage of the Arms Export Control Act, but the particular approach adopted—entailing congressional review of proposed sales only after they have been fully negotiated by the executive branch— has proved deficient. Clearly, a whole new system of appraisal is needed to skew the bias in favor of restraint, and to ensure effective congressional oversight at an earlier point in the decisionmaking process. This may require shunting more of the export management function from the Department of Defense to the Department of State, or creation of new agencies independent of the existing arms sales bureaucracy. It could also involve the formation of a special congressional oversight committee modeled on the Select Committee on Intelligence, endowed with the authority to review pending transfers while they are still in the planning stage. Further, to prevent imprudent sales decisions, Congress and the public should be made aware of proposed sales long before they are sent over to Capitol Hill for formal ratification.

Improved management is also needed at the delivery end of the export system. A beefed-up enforcement capacity is required to ensure that equipment is delivered to the intended recipient, and that it is used exclusively for the purposes specified by U.S. law. Penalties must be established for governments and firms that violate U.S. regulations, and machinery established to adjudicate such violations. This may require expansion of the Customs Bureau's investigative staff, and appointment of a Special Prosecutor by the Justice Department to probe cases of possible government malfeasance.

As the world's number one supplier of arms and military services, there is much the United States can do by itself to control and curtail the international arms traffic. If U.S. restraint is not duplicated by the other major suppliers, however, the arms trade will continue to spin out of control. Accordingly, the promotion of international restraint must be a central goal of U.S. arms policy. To provide a forum for discussion of multilateral control measures, the Conventional Arms Transfer talks should be reconvened at the earliest possible date, with participation by European as well as Soviet and American delegations.[26]

It must be recognized, however, that multilateral cooperation will prove difficult to achieve unless Washington is prepared to help motivate restraint by providing incentives to the nations involved. In the case of the European suppliers, these can include a pledge by the Department of Defense to procure more of its military needs in Europe; in the case of the Soviets, they can include agreements to slacken arms competition in areas of strategic concern to Moscow. Prominent recipients of arms should also be invited to participate in this process and be offered incentives (security assurances, the deployment of U.N. peacekeeping forces, transfers of nonmilitary technology, etc.) for exercising restraint in their purchases. Needless to say, such incentives must be perceived as benefiting the United States as much as the other parties involved.

Clearly, the attainment of all these goals in the present political climate will prove extremely difficult unless there is a major shift in public consciousness on these issues. Without the backing of significant constituencies, even the most dedicated proponents of reform will be unable to alter existing U.S. policies—let alone those of other powers. Accordingly, any attempt to develop and implement an alternative arms export policy must be accompanied by a concerted educational effort designed to alert public opinion to the risks of uncontrolled exports and the benefits of restraint. Such an effort would have to counterbalance the various claims made on behalf of arms transfers by showing how such exports have been consistently oversold as an instrument of foreign policy. Furthermore, in those cases where restraint would cause economic hardship to domestic producers, federal assistance should be provided for the conversion of the facilities involved to alternative uses (with subsidized job training as needed).

This, then, is the framework for a just and prudent arms export policy for the United States. It would not eliminate arms transfers altogether, nor would it neglect essential features of national security. Rather, it would constrict the flow of weapons to volatile Third World areas, thereby promoting global stability and, by extension, U.S. national security. It would also restore effective government control over a program gone haywire and bring that policy into alignment with overall U.S. foreign policy objectives. Such an approach will not abolish the basic causes of instability and violence in the world—that will require a total transformation of the existing global order—but it will reduce the risk of war and help diminish the destructive violence of those wars that do occur. More importantly, it will help prevent the escalation of localized conflicts, and thus increase our chances of averting a nuclear holocaust.

Appendixes

Appendix 1. U.S. Military Exports by Program, Fiscal 1950–82
(million current dollars)

FMS = Foreign Military Sales Program

Recipient	FMS orders Arms & equipment	Construction	Total
E. Asia & Pacific, Total	19,001.0	—	19,001.0
Australia	6,160.6	—	6,160.6
Brunei	0.3	—	0.3
Burma	6.9	—	6.9
China	—	—	—
Hong Kong	—	—	—
Indochina (1950–54)	8.5	—	8.5
Indonesia	319.5	—	319.5
Japan	2,833.7	—	2,833.7
Kampuchea[b]	—	—	—
Korea, So.	3,877.4	c	3,877.4
Laos[b]	—	—	—
Malaysia	171.2	—	171.2
New Caledonia	—	—	—
New Zealand	210.3	—	210.3
Papua New Guinea	—	—	—
Philippines	224.8	—	224.8
Singapore	378.0	—	378.0
Taiwan	3,391.7	—	3,391.7
Thailand	1,415.2	—	1,415.2
Vietnam[b]	1.2	—	1.2
Other	1.5	—	1.5
Near East & So. Asia, Total	57,764.2	18,965.7	76,729.9
Afghanistan[b]	—	—	—
Algeria	—	—	—
Bahrain	12.6	—	12.6
Bangladesh	—	—	—
Egypt	5,369.5	20.0	5,389.5
India	80.5	—	80.5
Iran[d]	12,556.9	0.6	12,557.5
Iraq[b]	13.2	—	13.2
Israel	9,772.3	2.6	9,774.9
Jordan	1,772.7	0.8	1,773.5
Kuwait	950.1	1.0	951.1
Lebanon	166.0	—	166.0
Libya[b]	28.3	1.3	29.6

MAP = Military Assistance Program

FMS deliveries, total	Commercial Sales deliveries	MAP grants[a]
9,140.2	3,477.3	29,008.6
2,125.9	257.7	—
0.1	4.1	—
4.9	10.8	72.1
—	2.6	—
—	101.6	—
8.5	—	709.0
225.2	57.2	195.1
1,196.0	1,726.7	810.3
—	c	1,177.3
2,067.0	333.4	5,473.1
—	c	1,460.1
97.6	225.8	—
—	3.0	—
150.8	30.4	—
—	0.5	—
179.1	54.5	609.0
225.9	105.6	—
1,975.7	480.4	2,554.6
881.0	82.0	1,174.1
1.2	c	14,773.9
1.4	0.9	—
42,432.8	3,369.0	2,171.5
—	0.6	c
—	2.3	—
5.5	4.4	—
—	3.0	—
1,711.5	35.4	—
77.1	53.9	90.3
11,186.7	670.8	766.7
13.2	0.2	45.2
8,233.1	1,638.8	—
970.9	162.7	493.1
672.0	18.2	—
95.4	13.8	13.6
29.6	31.3	12.6

Appendix 1 (continued)

FMS = Foreign Military Sales Program

Recipient	FMS orders Arms & equipment	Construction	Total
Morocco	737.4	—	737.4
Nepal	0.1	—	0.1
Oman	98.7	1.8	100.5
Pakistan	2,070.8	—	2,070.8
Qatar	0.5	—	0.5
Saudi Arabia	23,297.2	18,937.5	42,234.7
Sri Lanka	c	—	c
Syria[b]	c	—	c
Tunisia	473.0	—	473.0
United Arab Emirates	24.0	—	24.0
Yemen, No.	340.5	c	340.5
Latin America, Total	2,273.8	4.6	2,278.4
Argentina	196.2	—	196.2
Bahamas	—	—	—
Belize	—	—	—
Bermuda	—	—	—
Bolivia	2.1	—	2.1
Brazil	303.7	—	303.7
Chile[b]	184.4	—	184.4
Colombia	70.2	—	70.2
Costa Rica	1.5	—	1.5
Cuba[b]	4.5	—	4.5
Dominican Republic	6.4	—	6.4
Ecuador	114.6	—	114.6
El Salvador	36.0	—	36.0
Guatemala	32.1	—	32.1
Guyana	—	—	—
Haiti	1.3	—	1.3
Honduras	28.4	—	28.4
Jamaica	0.2	—	0.2
Mexico	134.6	4.6	139.2
Neth. Antilles	—	—	—
Nicaragua	5.2	—	5.2
Panama	6.3	—	6.3
Paraguay	1.0	—	1.0
Peru	186.8	—	186.8
Trinidad-Tobago	0.1	—	0.1
Uruguay	22.5	—	22.5

	MAP = Military Assistance Program	
FMS deliveries, total	Commercial Sales deliveries	MAP grants[a]
544.0	73.5	29.6
0.1	0.1	1.7
59.4	7.2	—
548.8	46.7	650.3
0.4	8.2	—
17,896.3	566.2	23.9
c	0.1	3.2
c	1.4	—
98.7	10.2	40.3
7.7	19.8	—
282.6	0.2	1.0
1,402.3	479.6	766.8
188.2	100.0	34.0
—	0.4	—
—	0.5	—
—	1.2	—
2.0	5.0	32.7
273.9	103.2	207.2
177.8	8.8	80.5
57.4	27.1	83.2
1.5	1.4	2.9
4.5	—	8.6
5.8	3.7	22.6
63.8	24.3	32.0
23.0	2.5	87.7
30.9	5.8	16.3
—	0.9	—
1.3	2.1	2.4
12.8	6.1	16.6
0.2	1.5	2.1
95.9	18.8	c
—	1.2	—
5.2	4.3	7.7
5.4	40.4	4.5
1.0	2.9	9.3
163.8	34.0	75.0
0.1	1.4	—
19.4	2.5	40.8

Appendix 1 (continued)

FMS = Foreign Military Sales Program

	FMS orders		
Recipient	Arms & equipment	Construction	Total
Venezuela	935.7	—	935.7
Other	—	—	—
Africa, Total	753.9	—	753.9
Botswana	—	—	—
Cameroon	21.4	—	21.4
Ethiopia[b]	99.9	—	99.9
Gabon	2.2	—	2.2
Gambia	—	—	—
Ghana	0.7	—	0.7
Ivory Coast	—	—	—
Kenya	148.7	—	148.7
Liberia	17.8	—	17.8
Madagascar	c	—	c
Mali	0.2	—	0.2
Mauritania	—	—	—
Mauritius	—	—	—
Mozambique[b]	—	—	—
Niger	c	—	c
Nigeria	66.2	—	66.2
Rwanda	2.0	—	2.0
Senegal	c	—	c
Somalia	75.5	—	75.5
South Africa[b]	3.1	—	3.1
Sudan	230.5	—	230.5
Tanzania	—	—	—
Uganda[b]	—	—	—
Zaire	85.7	—	85.7
Zambia	—	—	—
Zimbabwe	—	—	—
Other	c	—	c
Europe & Canada, Total	34,820.4	8.6	34,829.0
Austria	201.3	—	201.3
Belgium	2,086.1	—	2,086.1
Canada	1,969.3	0.5	1,969.8
Denmark	1,187.1	—	1,187.1
Finland	0.2	—	0.2
France	511.3	—	511.3

MAP = Military Assistance Program

FMS deliveries, total	Commercial Sales deliveries	MAP grants[a]
268.3	78.3	[c]
—	1.0	0.9
526.5	109.5	253.3
—	0.4	—
5.3	14.1	0.2
86.4	1.5	183.3
2.2	3.4	—
—	0.3	—
0.5	0.6	—
—	0.6	0.1
112.8	7.1	10.0
4.4	2.3	11.3
[c]	0.6	—
0.2	[c]	1.9
—	0.2	—
—	0.1	—
—	0.4	—
[c]	0.2	0.1
46.8	47.3	—
0.6	[c]	—
[c]	0.3	2.6
14.5	[c]	15.0
3.1	18.6	—
176.7	0.1	1.7
—	3.0	—
—	0.5	—
72.8	5.8	26.3
—	1.1	—
—	0.4	—
[c]	0.5	0.1
22,320.0	6,727.7	18,876.4
163.6	31.7	96.3
1,199.3	267.0	1,203.8
1,596.5	1,405.1	—
796.2	95.3	587.3
[c]	17.2	—
405.2	281.9	4,045.1

Appendix 1 (continued)

FMS = Foreign Military Sales Program

Recipient	Arms & equipment	FMS orders Construction	Total
Germany, West	8,157.8	7.9	8,165.7
Greece	2,216.0	—	2,216.0
Iceland	0.5	—	0.5
Ireland	0.8	—	0.8
Italy	1,095.2	—	1,095.2
Luxembourg	4.6	—	4.6
Netherlands	3,463.8	—	3,463.8
Norway	1,836.4	—	1,836.4
Portugal	104.2	—	104.2
Romania	—	—	—
Spain	1,765.2	—	1,765.2
Sweden	147.0	—	147.0
Switzerland	1,159.8	—	1,159.8
Turkey	1,816.7	—	1,816.7
United Kingdom	7,008.6	0.3	7,008.9
Yugoslavia	88.6	—	88.6
Other	—	—	—
International Organizations[e]	1,648.1	—	1,648.1
Worldwide, Total	116,261.3	18,978.9	135,240.2

SOURCE: U.S. Department of Defense, *Foreign Military Sales, Foreign Military Construction Sales and Military Assistance Facts*, 1982 edition.

NOTE: Figures may not add up due to rounding.

[a]Includes Military Assistance Service–Funded (i.e., Vietnam War funding), but excludes training under International Military Education and Training program. Also excludes transfers of surplus U.S. military equipment under Excess Defense Articles program.

[b]No current U.S. arms export activity under FMS, MAP, or Commercial Sales programs.

[c]Less than $50,000.

[d]Figure for FMS orders reflects orders canceled by the late Shah's successors.

[e]Includes regional and general costs under MAP program.

MAP = Military Assistance Program

FMS deliveries, total	Commercial Sales deliveries	MAP grants[a]
7,196.1	1,280.0	884.8
1,598.8	295.8	1,674.9
0.5	0.7	—
0.8	3.0	—
806.3	904.8	2,243.7
3.8	12.4	7.8
1,519.9	381.7	1,178.1
1,093.1	153.7	862.2
29.1	21.9	499.5
—	3.7	—
975.2	335.5	693.4
99.5	277.9	—
694.4	109.8	—
983.5	58.9	3,197.3
3,142.6	771.9	1,012.9
15.3	17.6	689.6
—	1.4	—
833.1	242.2	3,548.1
76,654.8	14,405.2	54,624.8

Appendix 2. U.S. Arms Transfers to Third World Police Forces by Country, September 1976–May 1979

Region & country	Quantities delivered:		
	Gas grenades & projectiles	Gas guns	Canisters Mace
Latin America			
Antigua	116	—	—
Bahamas	421	—	—
Belize	310	—	—
Bermuda	212	12	—
Bolivia	—	—	—
Brazil	—	100	—
Cayman Is.	—	—	—
Colombia	48,020	30	—
Costa Rica	150	—	200
Ecuador	11,135	1,000	100
El Salvador	852	4	—
Guatemala	5,000	—	—
Guyana	4,000	—	—
Haiti	—	—	—
Honduras	1,700	—	—
Jamaica	2,550	32	100
Martinique	—	—	—
Mexico	2,640	6	1,000
Monserrat	200	—	—
Neth. Antilles	25	—	—
Nicaragua	500	—	—
Panama	1,000	—	—
Paraguay	48	—	—
Peru	5,785	—	—
St. Kitts	30	—	—
St. Lucia	50	—	—
St. Vincent	50	—	—
Surinam	—	—	—
Trinidad & Tobago	200	—	18
Turks & Caicos Is.	148	2	—
Uruguay	—	—	—
Venezuela	53,651	—	205
Virgin Is.	307	2	—
Total	139,100	1,188	1,623

| Quantities delivered: | | |
Rifles, carbines & submachine guns	Pistols & revolvers	Ammunition (1,000 rounds)
—	—	—
—	—	26
—	—	2
—	—	34
160	310	—
60	14	10
—	12	5
395	7,900	250
—	—	14
—	1,853	1,256
—	173	—
65	1,006	6,763
—	—	—
—	20	1
—	59	418
—	750	247
—	14	—
529	1,886	10
—	—	—
—	54	181
6,054	447	7,312
650	243	1,364
—	—	140
—	17,613	—
—	—	—
—	—	1
—	—	—
—	153	107
—	7	—
—	—	—
—	—	100
96	9,088	1,531
—	—	—
8,009	41,602	19,772

Appendix 2 (continued)

Region & country	Quantities delivered:		
	Gas grenades & projectiles	Gas guns	Canisters Mace
East Asia & Pacific			
Brunei	—	—	—
Fiji	16	—	—
Hong Kong	21,240	256	1,887
Indonesia	—	64	—
Korea, South	—	—	—
Macao	—	—	—
Malaysia	102,629	536	4,140
Papua New Guinea	20	—	3
Singapore	3,528	58	—
Tahiti	—	—	25
Taiwan	4,000	—	240
Thailand	4,315	—	—
Total	135,748	914	6,295
Africa			
Algeria	—	—	—
Botswana	500	—	—
Gambia	—	4	—
Ghana	5,000	—	—
Kenya	300	—	425
Lesotho	100	—	—
Liberia	—	10	175
Malta	—	—	—
Mauritius	300	33	—
Morocco	—	—	—
Nigeria.	88,042	210	—·
Senegal	—	—	—
Seychelles	—	—	—
Swaziland	—	—	—
Tanzania	—	—	—
Tunisia	12,550	120	50
Total	106,792	377	650
Near East & South Asia			
Abu Dhabi	3,100	3	—
Afghanistan	—	—	—
Bahrain	6,000	—	—
Bangladesh	2,300	43	—

	Quantities delivered:	
Rifles, carbines & submachine guns	Pistols & revolvers	Ammunition (1,000 rounds)
100	—	205
—	—	—
—	2,050	1,890
15,000	1,326	1,367
374	201	5
—	554	40
25,914	16,980	16,029
—	—	10
—	4,234	5,985
—	—	—
—	7,200	1,372
2,270	702	3,400
43,658	33,247	30,303
—	1,020	—
—	13	71
—	—	—
—	—	—
—	—	—
—	—	—
—	14,322	203
—	100	—
—	—	—
100	—	—
—	—	—
—	8	—
—	15	10
—	2	—
—	2	1
—	2,365	40
100	17,847	325
18	130	140
—	36	10
6	280	12
—	—	—

Appendix 2 (continued)

Region & country	Quantities delivered: Gas grenades & projectiles	Gas guns	Canisters Mace
Cyprus	900	20	—
Egypt	153,946	350	—
India	17,040	—	—
Iran	12,334	—	—
Iraq	—	—	—
Israel	16,557	75	300
Jordan	—	—	—
Kuwait	200	—	—
Lebanon	—	—	—
Nepal	225	14	—
Oman	13,000	160	—
Pakistan	8,370	—	2
Qatar	—	—	—
Saudi Arabia	—	—	—
Sri Lanka	—	16	—
Syria	—	—	—
Turkey	—	—	—
Total	233,972	681	302
World Total	615,612	3,160	8,870

SOURCE: Export licenses issued to U.S. arms firms by the Office of Munitions Control, U.S. Department of State.

Quantities delivered:		
Rifles, carbines & submachine guns	Pistols & revolvers	Ammunition (1,000 rounds)
—	200	120
—	2,419	328
—	—	—
—	3,060	10
—	420	—
—	166	3,959
—	3,003	150
15	—	101
—	5,198	70
—	—	—
100	—	30
—	970	49
—	646	100
—	14,326	330
—	—	25
—	72	—
—	3,000	—
139	33,926	5,434
51,906	126,622	55,834

Notes

Abbreviations

ACDA Arms Control and Disarmament Agency
AEI American Enterprise Institute for Public Policy Research
AWST *Aviation Week and Space Technology*
CBO Congressional Budget Office
CIA Central Intelligence Agency
CRS Congressional Research Service
DoD Department of Defense
DoS Department of State
DSAA Defense Security Assistance Agency
FOIA Freedom of Information Act
FY Fiscal Year
GAO General Accounting Office
GPO Government Printing Office
HCFA House Committee on Foreign Affairs
HCIR House Committee on International Relations
IISS International Institute for Strategic Studies (London)
SFRC Senate Foreign Relations Committee
SIPRI Stockholm International Peace Research Institute
USAID U.S. Agency for International Development

Basic References

The following citations are used throughout the notes to refer to basic references and statistical sources. In each case, the year(s) given refer to the edition being cited.

ACDA, *World Arms 1972–82* = Arms Control and Disarmament Agency, *World Military Expenditures and Arms Transfers, 1972–82*. (Earlier editions may have somewhat different title.)

DSAA, *FMS/MAP Facts 1983* = Defense Security Assistance Agency, *Foreign Military Sales, Foreign Military Construction Sales and Military Assistance Facts*, 1983 edition. (Earlier editions may have somewhat different title.)

IISS, *Military Balance 1983–84* = International Institute for Strategic Studies (London), *The Military Balance, 1983–1984*.

Jane's Aircraft 1980–81 = *Jane's All the World's Aircraft, 1980–1981*.

Jane's Ships 1980–81 = *Jane's Fighting Ships, 1980–1981*.

Jane's Weapons 1980–81 = *Jane's Weapons Systems, 1980–1981.*

SIPRI Yearbook 1983 = Stockholm International Peace Research Institute, *SIPRI Yearbook 1983: World Armaments and Disarmament.*

USAID, *U.S. Loans & Grants 45–79* = U.S. Agency for International Development, *U.S. Overseas Loans and Grants, July 1, 1945–September 30, 1979.*

1. The Global Arms Market

1. Jimmy Carter, Remarks at White House Reception, March 26, 1979 (White House Press Office transcript).
2. *Congressional Record* (March 27, 1979), p. S3424.
3. Quoted in *Wall Street Journal*, June 29, 1983.
4. DSAA, *FMS/MAP Facts 1983*, and earlier editions.
5. U.S. Comptroller General, *Foreign Military Sales—A Growing Concern*, p. 1.
6. Quoted in *New York Times*, October 19, 1975.
7. *Congressional Record* (May 14, 1979), p. S5726.
8. U.S. Congress, Senate, Committee on Foreign Relations, Subcommittee on Foreign Assistance, *U.S. Military Sales to Iran*, p. xiii.
9. For legislative history and description of these measures, see [Richard F. Grimmett], *Executive-Legislative Consultation on U.S. Arms Sales* (Report by the Congressional Research Service for the House Foreign Affairs Committee).
10. Quoted in *New York Times*, June 24, 1976.
11. For text of the Carter policy and description of its provisions, see U.S. Congress, House, Committee on Foreign Affairs, *Changing Perspectives on U.S. Arms Transfer Policy*, Report by the Congressional Research Service for the Subcommittee on International Security and Scientific Affairs, pp. 10–31, 122–23.
12. Quoted in *New York Times*, February 25, 1978. For discussion of the Carter policy in practice, see Grimmett, *Executive-Legislative Consultation*, pp. 13–20; and HCFA, *Changing Perspectives*, pp. 12–31. See also U.S. Congress, Senate, Committee on Foreign Relations, *Prospects for Multilateral Arms Export Restraint*, pp. 12–25.
13. For discussion, see Grimmett, *Executive-Legislative Consultation*, pp. 26–35.
14. Kevin G. Nealer, *An Unconventional Arms Policy: Selling Ourselves Short*, p. 2.
15. For elaboration of the pro-restraint argument, see Dick Clark, "Needed: A Policy of Restraint for United States Arms Transfers," *AEI Defense Review* 2 (1978): 2–15. See also Roger P. Labrie, John G. Hutchins, Edwin W. A. Peura, and Diana H. Richman, *U.S. Arms Sales Policy: Background and Issues*, pp. 35–60.
16. James L. Buckley, Address before the Aerospace Industries Association, Williamsburg, Va., May 21, 1981, as cited in HCFA, *Changing Perspectives*, pp. 124–26.

17. For elaboration of this position, see Bernard A. Schriever, "Jimmy Carter's Arms Transfer Policy: Why It Won't Work," AEI *Defense Review* 5 (1978): 16–28; and Labrie et al., *U.S. Arms Sales Policy*, pp. 61–80.

18. For summary of these arguments and counterarguments, see sources cited in notes 15 and 17, and Andrew J. Pierre, *The Global Politics of Arms Sales*, pp. 14–38.

19. For discussion of the methodological problems associated with arms trade data, see Frank Blackaby and Thomas Ohlson, "Military Expenditures and the Arms Trade: Problems of Data," *Bulletin of Peace Proposals* 13 (1982): 291–308; and Laurel A. Mayer, "U.S. Arms Transfers: Data Sources and Dilemmas," *International Studies Notes* 7 (Summer 1980): 1–7.

20. ACDA, *World Arms 1972–82*, p. 53, and earlier editions.

21. *SIPRI Yearbook 1982*, pp. 190–91.

22. Richard F. Grimmett, *Trends in Conventional Arms Transfers to the Third World by Major Supplier, 1976–1983*, p. 22, and earlier editions.

23. Ibid., pp. 16, 22.

24. Ibid., p. 16.

25. ACDA, *World Arms 1971–80*, p. 117; *SIPRI Yearbook 1982*, pp. 192–93.

26. DSAA, *FMS/MAP Facts 1983*, and earlier editions.

27. For further discussion of these channels, see Philip J. Farley, Stephen S. Kaplan, and William H. Lewis, *Arms across the Sea*, pp. 26–39, 43–53. See also William H. Cullin, *How to Conduct Foreign Military Sales*, part IV, pp. 9–11.

28. Detailed information on CS transactions can be found in U.S. Department of State, *Report Required by Section 657 of the Foreign Assistance Act*, published annually through fiscal 1981. On the use of CS channels to export police and paramilitary gear, see Michael T. Klare and Cynthia Arnson, *Supplying Repression*, pp. 56–73.

29. DSAA, *FMS/MAP Facts 1983*, and earlier editions.

30. Clark, "Needed: A Policy of Restraint," p. 3.

31. Grimmett, *Trends in Conventional Arms Transfers, 1976–82*, p. 28.

32. For detailed data on U.S. arms transfers to the Third World, see the annual "Arms Trade Register" in the *SIPRI Yearbook*. For description of these weapons and additional data on transfers, see Tom Gervasi, *Arsenal of Democracy II*.

33. The only complete listing of FMS transactions is the DSAA's computerized "FMS Case Listing," available upon request from the Department of Defense through the FOIA.

34. See the annual "Arms Trade Register" in the *SIPRI Yearbook*, and the country-by-country listings in successive editions of the IISS's *The Military Balance*. For discussion, see Caleb S. Rossiter, *U.S. Arms Transfers to the Third World: The Implications of Sophistication*.

35. See the register of licensing and coproduction agreements in the *SIPRI Yearbook 1982*, pp. 239–52.

36. U.S. Defense Security Assistance Agency, "Estimate of the Number of Officers and Employees of the USG and U.S. Civilian Contract Person-

nel in Foreign Countries for Assignments in Implementation of Sales and Commercial Exports under the Arms Export Control Act as of 30 Sept. 1983," unpublished document supplied through the FOIA. For background on the issue of technical military services, see Michael T. Klare, "America's White-Collar Mercenaries," *Inquiry* (October 16, 1978): 14–19; and U.S. Comptroller General, *Perspectives on Military Sales to Saudi Arabia.*

37. From copies of export licenses supplied to me by the Office of Munitions Control. For itemized breakdown of this data, see Klare and Arnson, *Supplying Repression,* pp. 122–65.

38. For a similar presentation of basic trends and patterns, see Farley et al., *Arms across the Sea,* pp. 1–18; and Pierre, *The Global Politics of Arms Sales,* pp. 3–14. See also Arms Control and Disarmament Agency, *The International Transfer of Conventional Arms.*

2. Primal Motives

1. U.S. Congress, Senate, Committee on Foreign Relations, *Foreign Military Sales,* Hearings, 90th Cong., 2d Sess., 1968, p. 42.

2. SFRC, *Prospects for Restraint,* p. 13.

3. U.S. Comptroller General, *Opportunities to Improve Decisionmaking and Oversight of Arms Sales,* p. 31.

4. I first addressed this issue in Michael T. Klare, "The Political Economy of Arms Sales," *Bulletin of the Atomic Scientists* 32 (November 1976): 11–18.

5. James L. Buckley, Testimony before the Subcommittee on International Security and Scientific Affairs, House Committee on Foreign Affairs, Washington, D.C., March 19, 1981 (U.S. Department of State transcript).

6. "Industry Observer," *AWST* (October 29, 1979): 11.

7. U.S. Congress, House, Committee on Foreign Affairs, *Mutual Development and Cooperation Act of 1973,* Hearings, 93rd Cong., 1st Sess., 1973, p. 116.

8. Francis J. West, Jr., "The U.S. Security Assistance Program: Giveaway or Bargain?" *Strategic Review* (Winter 1983): 52.

9. This inventory of export motives was developed on the basis of numerous interviews with senior officials of the departments of State and Defense, and through study of congressional hearings, GAO studies, trade publications, and other printed sources. For other perspectives on these motives and their relative importance, see ACDA, *The International Transfer of Conventional Arms,* pp. 43–82; Labrie et al., *U.S. Arms Sales Policy,* pp. 61–79; and Pierre, *The Global Politics of Arms Sales,* pp. 14–27.

10. This view is shared by other analysts of U.S. arms sales policy. See, for example, Pierre, *The Global Politics of Arms Sales,* pp. 45–72; and David J. Louscher, "The Rise of Military Sales as a U.S. Foreign Policy Instrument," *Orbis* 20 (Winter 1977): 933–64.

11. Buckley, Williamsburg Address, May 21, 1981.

12. Buckley, HCFA Testimony, March 19, 1981.

13. Labrie, et al., *U.S. Arms Sales Policy*, p. 62.

14. Buckley, HCFA Testimony, March 19, 1981.

15. Labrie, et al., *U.S. Arms Sales Policy*, p. 67.

16. Interview with William D. Perreault, Sr., Lockheed Corp., Burbank, Cal., August 27, 1974.

17. Labrie et al., *U.S. Arms Sales Policy*, pp. 67–68.

18. Quoted in *U.S. News and World Report* (March 4, 1982): 27.

19. See Pierre, *The Global Politics of Arms Sales*, pp. 136–88; and Labrie et al., *U.S. Arms Sales Policy*, pp. 67–69.

20. HCFA, *Mutual Development 1973*, pp. 116–17.

21. See Pierre, *The Global Politics of Arms Sales*, pp. 17–18.

22. West, "The U.S. Security Assistance Program," p. 52.

23. ACDA, *The International Transfer of Conventional Arms*, p. 49.

24. U.S. Congress, House, Committee on Foreign Affairs, *Fiscal Year 1975 Foreign Assistance Request*, Hearings, 93rd Cong., 2d Sess., 1974, p. 80.

25. U.S. Congress, House, Committee on Foreign Affairs, *Foreign Assistance Act of 1967*, Hearings, 90th Cong., 1st Sess., 1967, p. 118.

26. See *New York Times*, January 27, 1975; and "U.S. Military Aircraft Exports Pushed," *AWST* (May 28, 1973): 139–45.

27. Cited in *Washington Star*, November 25, 1978.

28. See Labrie et al., *U.S. Arms Sales Policy*, p. 70.

29. Ibid., p. 72. See also Jacques S. Gansler, *The Defense Industry* (Cambridge, Mass.: MIT Press, 1980), pp. 204–18.

30. U.S. Congress, Congressional Budget Office, *Budgetary Cost Savings to the Department of Defense Resulting from Foreign Military Sales*, p. ix.

31. Ibid., pp. 3–5. See also Labrie et al., *U.S. Arms Sales Policy*, pp. 72–73.

32. See Anthony Sampson, *The Arms Bazaar* pp. 249–55.

33. For discussion, see SFRC, *U.S. Sales to Iran*, pp. 4–12, 41–48.

34. For discussion, see HCFA, *Changing Perspectives*, pp. 32–55; and Pierre, *The Global Politics of Arms Sales*, pp. 62–68.

35. Quoted in *Arms Sales: A Useful Foreign Policy Tool?* (Washington, D.C.: American Enterprise Institute, 1982), p. 6.

36. *Congressional Record* (September 29, 1982), part III, p. H8018.

37. For further discussion of buyer motives, see ACDA, *The International Transfer of Conventional Arms*, pp. 43–82; and Pierre, *The Global Politics of Arms Sales*, pp. 129–271.

3. The Evolution of Doctrine

1. For discussion, see Louscher, "The Rise of Military Sales," pp. 933–64; Sampson, *The Arms Bazaar*, pp. 114–18.

2. DSAA, *FMS/MAP Facts 1979*, p. 1.

3. For discussion, see Stanley Karnow, "Weapons for Sale," *New Republic* (March 23, 1974): 21–23; "U.S. Military Aircraft Exports Pushed,"

pp. 139–45; and "U.S. Accelerates Aerospace Export Drive," AWST (June 2, 1975): 47–53.

4. For a sense of the debate at the time, see U.S. Congress, Senate, Committee on Foreign Relations, Subcommittee on Foreign Assistance, *Foreign Assistance Authorization: Arms Sales Issues.* See also U.S. Comptroller General, FMS—*A Growing Concern.*

5. For a discussion of the congressional initiative and the Arms Export Control Act, see Farley et al., *Arms across the Sea,* pp. 45–50.

6. Quoted in *New York Times,* June 24, 1976.

7. Quoted in *New York Times,* January 25, 1977.

8. For the text of the Carter statement, see HCFA, *Changing Perspectives,* pp. 122–23.

9. For an analysis of the Carter policy and contending evaluations, see: HCFA, *Changing Perspectives,* pp. 10–31; SFRC, *Prospects for Restraint,* pp. 12–18; Pierre, *The Global Politics of Arms Sales,* pp. 52–62; and Herbert Y. Schandler, *Implications of President Carter's Conventional Arms Trade Policy.* For a Carter administration perspective on the policy, see U.S. Department of State, *Arms Transfer Policy.*

10. Lucy Wilson Benson, "Turning the Supertanker: Arms Transfer Restraint," *International Security* 3 (Spring 1979): 8.

11. Quoted in *New York Times,* October 11, 1977.

12. *Munitions Control Newsletter* 50 (February 1978): 1.

13. U.S. Congress, House, Committee on International Relations, Subcommittee on Europe and the Middle East, *United States Arms Sales Policy and Recent Sales to Europe and the Middle East,* p. 52. The term "doublethink" was used by Sen. William Proxmire in a statement quoted in AWST (November 13, 1978): 13.

14. Quoted in *Washington Post,* March 29, 1980.

15. See SFRC, *Prospects for Restraint,* pp. 12–24.

16. Quoted in *Washington Post,* March 29, 1980.

17. For discussion, see Pierre, *The Global Politics of Arms Sales,* pp. 55–62; HCFA, *Changing Perspectives,* pp. 12–31; and Michael D. Salomon, David J. Louscher, and Paul Y. Hammond, "Lessons of the Carter Approach to Restraining Arms Transfers," *Survival* (September/October 1981): 200–208.

18. Cited in AWST (March 24, 1980): 8.

19. U.S. Congress, Senate, Committee on Foreign Relations, *U.S. Conventional Arms Transfer Policy,* p. 1.

20. HCIR, *United States Arms Sales Policy and Recent Sales to Europe and the Middle East,* pp. 40–41.

21. Cited in AWST (March 24, 1980): 8.

22. Nealer, *An Unconventional Arms Policy,* pp. 8–9.

23. For text of Buckley's Williamsburg Address, see HCFA, *Changing Perspectives,* pp. 124–26.

24. For text of the Reagan directive, see: HCFA, *Changing Perspectives,* pp. 127–28.

25. Quoted in *Newsweek* (December 15, 1980): 53.
26. For discussion of the Reagan policy, see HCFA, *Changing Perspectives*, pp. 32–55; Nealer, *An Unconventional Arms Policy*, pp. 10–19; Pierre, *The Global Politics of Arms Sales*, pp. 62–68; and Labrie et al., *U.S. Arms Sales Policy*, pp. 15–18.
27. For discussion of these initiatives, see "U.S. Weapons Exports Headed for Record Level," *Defense Monitor* 11 (1982): 3–6; and David R. Griffiths, "Reagan Administration Pushes Arms Transfers," AWST (June 8, 1981): 176–87.
28. Lt. Gen. Ernest Graves, Statement before the House Foreign Affairs Committee, Washington, D.C., March 19, 1981 (DoD transcript).
29. Christopher J. Dodd, "Arms Sales Non-Policy," *New York Times*, April 9, 1982.
30. Hodding Carter III, "Arms Sales and the Spread of Violence," *Wall Street Journal*, June 17, 1982.
31. James L. Buckley, Statement before the Senate Foreign Relations Committee, Washington, D.C., July 28, 1981, as cited in HCFA, *Changing Perspectives*, pp. 129–32.
32. For summary of the Defense Guidance, see *New York Times*, May 30, 1982.
33. William Clark, Remarks at Center for Strategic and International Studies, Georgetown University, Washington, D.C., May 21, 1982 (White House Press Office transcript).
34. For discussion, see HCFA, *Changing Perspectives*, pp. 67–85; "U.S. Will Sell Pakistanis F-16s," AWST (September 21, 1981): 23–24; and *Washington Post*, October 3, 1981.
35. For discussion, see HCFA, *Changing Perspectives*, pp. 56–66; *Washington Post*, October 3, 1981; and *New York Times*, April 9, 1982.
36. Quoted in *U.S. News and World Report* (March 8, 1982): 28.
37. Nealer, *An Unconventional Arms Policy*, pp. 14–19, 26–29.

4. The Implementation of Policy

1. Quoted in U.S. Comptroller General, *Opportunities to Improve Decisionmaking*, pp. 57–58.
2. Public Law 94–329, 90 Stat. 729, approved June 30, 1976. This statute superseded the Foreign Military Sales Act of 1968 (Public Law 90–629, 82 Stat. 1320). For full text of the AECA with statutory history and amendments, see U.S. Congress, Senate, Committee on Foreign Relations, and House, Committee on Foreign Affairs, *Legislation on Foreign Relations through 1981*, Joint Committee Print (Washington, D.C.: GPO, 1982), vol. 1, pp. 184–227.
3. Such rules and regulations are contained in the International Traffic in Arms Regulations, U.S. Code of Federal Regulations, title 22, chapter I, subchapter M, part 121.
4. For further clarification of the distinction between FMS and CS orders,

see Defense Security Assistance Agency, *Military Assistance and Sales Manual* part 3, as revised. See also Cullin, *How to Conduct Foreign Military Sales*, part 4, pp. 9–11.

5. For discussion, see "Weapons for the World Update," an annual report published by the Council on Economic Priorities (CEP) in New York City and published in the *CEP Newsletter*.

6. See Louscher, "The Rise of Military Sales," pp. 952–64.

7. For an overview of the Security Assistance Program, see Farley et al., *Arms across the Sea*, pp. 19–42. See also DSAA, *Military Assistance and Sales Manual*, part 1.

8. U.S. Department of Defense, Department of Defense Directive No. 5105.38, Defense Security Assistance Agency, August 10, 1978. For discussion of the DoD's role in arms exports, see Cullin, *How to Conduct Foreign Military Sales*, part 3, pp. 14–21.

9. For description, see Cullin, *How to Conduct Foreign Military Sales*, part 10, pp. 1–32.

10. Interview with Richard Violette, Deputy Director, DSAA, The Pentagon, Washington, D.C., October 11, 1979.

11. Interview with James Farber, Director, Office of Security Assistance and Sales, U.S. Department of State, Washington, D.C., October 16, 1979. For more on the State Department role in arms sales decisionmaking, see Cullin, *How to Conduct Foreign Military Sales*, part 3, pp. 10–11. See also the memorandum from Under Secretary of State Lucy Benson inserted in HCIR, *Recent Sales to Europe and the Middle East*, pp. 89–99.

12. Interview with Richard Violette, October 11, 1979. See also memorandum submitted by Lucy Benson in HCIR, *Recent Sales to Europe and the Middle East*, pp. 82–88; and Paul Y. Hammond, David J. Louscher, and Michael D. Salomon, "Controlling U.S. Arms Transfers: The Emerging System," *Orbis* 23 (Summer 1979): 317–52.

13. U.S. Comptroller General, *Opportunities to Improve Decisionmaking*, p. 31.

14. Ibid., p. 10. See also Cullin, *How to Conduct Foreign Military Sales*, part 3, pp. 1–21; and Hammond et al., "Controlling U.S. Arms Transfers," pp. 327–35.

15. For background on these procedures, see DSAA, *Military Assistance and Sales Manual*, part 3. See also Cullin, *How to Conduct Foreign Military Sales*, part 4, pp. 1–11; and Hammond, et al., "Controlling U.S. Arms Transfers," pp. 327–35.

16. Interview with James Farber, October 16, 1979.

17. Lt. Gen H. M. Fish, "Foreign Military Sales," *Commanders Digest* 17 (May 29, 1975): p. 6.

18. Leonard A. Alne, "The ABC of Military Exports," Remarks to the Aerospace Industries Association, San Francisco, Cal., May 1, 1974 (DSAA transcript).

19. U.S. Congress, Senate, Committee on Foreign Relations, Subcommittee on Multinational Corporations, *Multinational Corporations and*

U.S. Foreign Policy, Hearings, 94th Cong., 1st Sess., 1975, part 12, pp. 107–238 and 393–932. See also *New York Times*, June 5, 6, and 7, 1975; *Wall Street Journal*, July 18, 1975; and Sampson, *The Arms Bazaar*, pp. 143–53, 256, 272–74.

20. SFRC, *Multinational Corporations and U.S. Foreign Policy*, part 12, pp. 341–92 and 933–1171. See also *New York Times*, September 13, 1976, and May 27, 1977; and Sampson, *The Arms Bazaar*, pp. 128–40, 222–40, 274–78.

21. *New York Times*, June 22, 1975; *Wall Street Journal*, October 14, 1975. See also "Payoffs: The Growing Scandal," *Newsweek* (February 23, 1976): 26–33; and "Lifting the Lid on Some Mysterious Money," *Time* (June 23, 1975): 52–54.

22. For an extraordinary account of corruption in the arms trade written by a former DSAA official, see Donn R. Grand Pre, *Confessions of an Arms Peddler*. See also Sampson, *The Arms Bazaar*, pp. 180–221; William A. Schumann, "Foreign Payments Defended as Necessary," *AWST* (August 11, 1975): 21–22.

23. For Sampson's account of an "arms bazaar," see Sampson, *The Arms Bazaar*, pp. 11–14.

24. Dana Shor, "The Merchants of Death," *The Diamondback* (University of Maryland), October 18, 1978. For another account of this event, see Robert A. Miller, "The Arms Bazaar Was Bizarre," *Philadelphia Inquirer*, October 25, 1978.

25. For a glimpse at such activities, see "Paris Underscores Battle for Exports," *AWST* (June 6, 1977): 42–49.

26. U.S. Comptroller General, *Opportunities to Improve Decisionmaking*, pp. 31–32.

27. Interview with James Farber, October 16, 1979. See also memorandum submitted by Under Secretary of State Joseph J. Sisco in U.S. Congress, House, Committee on International Relations, Special Subcommittee on Investigations, *The Persian Gulf, 1975: The Continuing Debate on Arms Sales*, pp. 65–67.

28. Fish, "Foreign Military Sales," p. 6.

29. DSAA, *Military Assistance and Sales Manual*, part 3, pp. A1–A7, C3–C4. See also Cullin, *How to Conduct Foreign Military Sales*, part 3, pp. 1–4; and Hammond et al., "Controlling U.S. Arms Transfers," pp. 326–33.

30. Fish, "Foreign Military Sales," p. 6.

31. U.S. Comptroller General, *Opportunities to Improve Decisionmaking*, pp. 26–27. See also Hammond et al., "Controlling U.S. Arms Transfers," pp. 327–29.

32. U.S. Comptroller General, *Opportunities to Improve Decisionmaking*, p. 26. See also the memorandum submitted by Joseph Sisco in HCIR, *The Persian Gulf 1975*, pp. 65–67.

33. U.S. Comptroller General, *Opportunities to Improve Decisionmaking*, pp. 26–27.

34. Ibid., pp. 35–36.

35. Ibid., pp. 31–37. For an extraordinary account of bureaucratic infighting over arms transfers to the Shah of Iran in 1978–79, see the investigative report by Scott Armstrong in *Washington Post*, October 25, 1980.
36. U.S. Comptroller General, *Opportunities to Improve Decisionmaking*, pp. 29–31.
37. See Nealer, *An Unconventional Arms Policy*, pp. 14–18.
38. Grimmett, *Executive-Legislative Consultation*, pp. 10–35. A 1984 proposal to sell Stinger hand-held antiaircraft missiles to Jordan and Saudi Arabia was withdrawn by the Reagan administration when it became apparent that Congress would veto the sale (see *New York Times*, March 21, 1984).
39. For an introduction to this process, see U.S. Senate, Committee on Foreign Relations, *Arms Sales Package to Saudi Arabia*, Hearings, 97th Cong., 1st Sess., 1981.
40. Grimmett, *Executive-Legislative Consultation*, p. 4.
41. Ibid., p. 36.

5. The Limits of Policy

1. ACDA, *World Arms 1972–82*, pp. 13, 95–98.
2. ACDA, *World Arms 1971–80*, pp. 35, 77.
3. ACDA, *World Arms 1971–80*, p. 119.
4. Grimmett, *Trends in Conventional Arms Transfers, 1975–1982*, p. 19.
5. ACDA, *World Arms 1971–80*, p. 119.
6. Edward Lieuwen, "The Latin American Military," in U.S. Congress, Senate, Committee on Foreign Relations, Subcommittee on American Republics Affairs, *Survey of the Alliance for Progress*, Compilation of Studies and Hearings (Washington, D.C.: GPO, 1969), p. 113.
7. For text of the agreement with Ecuador (which served as a model for the others), see *Department of State Bulletin* (March 3, 1952): 336ff.
8. *New York Times*, April 28, 1953.
9. Luigi Einaudi, Hans Heymann, Jr., David Ronfeldt, and Caesar Sereseres, *Arms Transfers to Latin America: Toward a Policy of Mutual Respect*, pp. 1–2.
10. U.S. Congress, House, Committee on Appropriations, *Mutual Security Appropriations for 1960*, Hearings, 86th Cong., 1st Sess., 1959, p. 736.
11. For discussion of counterinsurgency doctrine and practice, see Douglas S. Blaufarb, *The Counterinsurgency Era* (New York: Free Press, 1977); Michael T. Klare, *War without End* (New York: Knopf, 1972); and William F. Barber and C. Neale Ronning, *Internal Security and Military Power*.
12. Quoted in Roger Hilsman, *To Move a Nation* (Garden City, N.Y.: Doubleday, 1967), p. 415.
13. See Theodore Sorenson, *Kennedy* (New York: Harper & Row, 1965), pp. 632–33; and Klare, *War without End*, pp. 31–55, 270–310.

14. Lieuwen, "The Latin American Military," p. 115.
15. Quoted in Barber and Ronning, *Internal Security*, p. 35.
16. HCFA, *Foreign Assistance Act of 1967*, p. 117.
17. Robert S. McNamara, *The Essence of Security* (New York: Harper & Row, 1968), p. 149.
18. Raymond J. Barrett, "Arms Dilemma for the Developing World," *Military Review* (April 1970): 33.
19. Einaudi et al., *Arms Transfers to Latin America*, p. 2.
20. Ibid., p. 3.
21. Ibid.
22. Nelson A. Rockefeller, "Quality of Life in the Americas," Report on a Presidential Mission for the Western Hemisphere, *Department of State Bulletin* (December 8, 1969): 516–18.
23. Charles A. Meyer, "U.S. Military Assistance Policy toward Latin America," *Department of State Bulletin* (August 14, 1969): 102.
24. HCFA, *Foreign Assistance Request*, FY75, p. 52.
25. Kenneth Rush, "Memorandum for the President," U.S. Department of State, Washington, D.C., April 3, 1973 (photocopy supplied through the FOIA).
26. DSAA, *FMS/MAPFacts 1979*, p. 3.
27. See U.S. Congress, Senate, Committee on Foreign Relations, *Guatemala and the Dominican Republic*, Staff Memorandum, 92nd Cong., 1st Sess., 1971; U.S. Congress, House, Committee on International Relations, *Torture and Repression in Brazil*, Hearings, 93rd Cong., 2d Sess., 1974. For discussion, see Jim Morrell, "Achievements of the 1970s: U.S. Human Rights Law and Policy," *International Policy Report* (November 1981): 1–8.
28. For legislative text of these measures, see SFRC and HCFA, *Legislation on Foreign Relations through 1981*, Part I, pp. 1–227. See also Morrell, "Achievements of the 1970s," pp. 1–8.
29. Quoted in *New York Times*, June 24, 1976.
30. For description and assessment of the Carter policy, see HCFA, *Changing Perspectives*, pp. 10–32, 122–23.
31. SFRC, *Prospects for Restraint*, p. 19.
32. *Washington Post*, October 26, 1978.
33. For discussion of Carter's backtracking on arms sales, see Michael Gordon, "Competition with the Soviet Union Drives Reagan's Arms Sales Policy," *National Journal* (May 16, 1981): 869–73. On El Salvador, see *Washington Post*, April 17, 1980; and John Eisendrath and Jim Morrell, "Arming El Salvador," *International Policy Report* (August 1982): 1–8.
34. Adm. Gordon J. Schuller, Statement before the Subcommittee on Inter-American Affairs, House Committee on Foreign Affairs, Washington, D.C., February 13, 1979 (DoD transcript).
35. Ibid.
36. See James Ott, "Industry Leaders Rap U.S. Export Policy," *AWST* (May 7, 1979): 19–20; and "U.S. Military Sales Policy Seen Aiding Other Nations," *AWST* (May 28, 1979): 105–106.

37. Jeane Kirkpatrick, "U.S. Security and Latin America," *Commentary* (January 1981): 29.
38. Jeane Kirkpatrick, "Dictatorships and Double Standards," *Commentary* (November 1979): 34–45.
39. See *Washington Post*, March 15, 1981; *New York Times*, March 18, 1981; and *San Francisco Chronicle*, June 19, 1981.
40. *New York Times*, June 3, 1981. See also HCFA, *Changing Perspectives*, pp. 56–66.
41. Buckley, Williamsburg Address, May 21, 1981.
42. For description and text of the Reagan policy, see HCFA, *Changing Perspectives*, pp. 32–55, 127–28.
43. DSAA, *FMS/MAP Facts 1982*, p. 4.
44. See *New York Times*, September 29, 1982.
45. Quoted in *Wall Street Journal*, March 19, 1981.
46. *SIPRI Yearbook 1980*, p. 88.
47. U.S. Department of Defense, *Security Assistance Program*, Congressional Presentation Document, FY 1984, pp. 18–34. Additional data from Policy Alternatives for the Caribbean and Central America, *Changing Course* (Washington, D.C.: Institute for Policy Studies, 1984), pp. 113–16.
48. See *New York Times*, February 4 and April 14, 1984.
49. Quoted in *New York Times*, March 11, 1983.
50. Quoted in *New York Times*, April 28, 1983. For more on the administration's position, see "Reagan Sounds the Alarm," *Newsweek* (March 14, 1983): 16–24; "A Big Stick Approach," *Time* (August 8, 1983): 16–24; and *New York Times*, July 26 and 28, 1983.
51. See *Washington Post*, March 18, May 5, and June 5, 1981. See also Cynthia Arnson, *El Salvador: A Revolution Confronts the United States* (Washington, D.C.: Institute for Policy Studies, 1982).
52. See *New York Times*, May 26 and 27 and July 23, 1983; *Washington Post*, July 1 and August 24, 1983.
53. See Lydia Chavez, "The Odds in El Salvador," *New York Times Magazine* (July 24, 1983): 14–19, 48; *New York Times*, May 26, 1983; *Washington Post*, June 15, 1983; and *Miami Herald*, July 1, 1983.
54. *New York Times*, August 3, 1983.
55. From text of Commission report as excerpted in *New York Times*, January 12, 1984.
56. Quoted in "More Money—and More Guns," *Newsweek* (January 23, 1984): 28. See also *New York Times*, January 12, 1984.
57. For discussion , see Pierre, *The Global Politics of Arms Sales*, pp. 232–49.
58. Ibid., pp. 237–39.
59. I first probed these "myths" in my testimony before the House Subcommittee on Inter-American Affairs. See U.S. Congress, House, Committee on International Relations, Subcommittee on Inter-American Affairs, *Arms Trade in the Western Hemisphere*, pp. 130–55.

60. Cecil Brownlow, "Second Chance in Latin America," *AWST* (November 25, 1974): 11.
61. David Ronfeldt and Caesar Sereseres, *U.S. Arms Transfers, Diplomacy, and Security in Latin America and Beyond*, p. 3.
62. Cecil Brownlow, "Report from Brazil," *AWST* (October 8, 1973): 7.
63. Quoted in "U.S. Military Sales Policy Seen Aiding Other Nations," p. 105.
64. Einaudi et al., *Arms Transfers to Latin America*, pp. 1–2.
65. U.S. Department of State, Bureau of Intelligence and Research, *Arms Sales in Latin America*, p. 10.
66. *Jane's Aircraft 1976–77*, p. 3.
67. Quoted in *Washington Post*, December 19, 1977.
68. See IISS, *Military Balance 1982–83*, pp. 98–109.

6. Arms and the Shah

1. Rep. Gerry E. Studds, "U.S. Entangled in Iranian Web," *Boston Evening Globe*, December 23, 1978.
2. DSAA, *FMS/MAP Facts 1978*, pp. 1, 4.
3. See Fred Halliday, *Iran: Dictatorship and Development* (Harmondsworth: Penguin, 1979), pp. 90–91; and Bruce R. Kuniholm, *The Origins of the Cold War in the Near East* (Princeton, N.J.: Princeton University Press, 1980), pp. 140–44.
4. See Kuniholm, *Origins of the Cold War*, pp. 148–208, 304–82; Alvin J. Cottrell, "Iran's Armed Forces under the Pahlavi Dynasty," in George Lenczowski (ed.), *Iran under the Pahlavis* (Stanford, Cal.: Stanford University Press, 1978), pp. 396–97; and Amin Saikal, *The Rise and Fall of the Shah* (Princeton, N.J.: Princeton University Press, 1980), pp. 29–35.
5. See Halliday, *Iran*, pp. 90–102; Leonard Binder, *Factors Influencing Iran's International Role* (Santa Monica, Cal.: RAND Corp., 1969), pp. 1–12.
6. See Binder, *Iran's International Role*, pp. 12–14; and Saikal, *Rise and Fall*, pp. 44–45. See also David Wise and Thomas C. Ross, *The Invisible Government* (New York: Bantam, 1965), pp. 116–20.
7. U.S. Congress, House, Committee on Foreign Affairs, *Mutual Security Act of 1954*, Hearings, 83rd Cong., 2d Sess., 1954, pp. 569–70.
8. See Halliday, *Iran*, pp. 75–83; Saikal, *Rise and Fall*, pp. 53–58; Binder, *Iran's International Role*, pp. 17–31; and Richard Cottam, *Nationalism in Iran* (Pittsburgh: University of Pittsburgh Press, 1964), pp. 286–311.
9. USAID, *U.S. Loans & Grants 45–77*, p. 17.
10. The NSC documents were identified in a letter to me from NCS Staff Secretary Jeanne W. Davis dated December 4, 1975, sent in response to a request under the FOIA. For discussion of the NSC study, see James H.

Noyes, *The Clouded Lens* (Stanford, Cal.: Hoover Institution Press, 1979), pp. 53–54.

11. Georgetown University, Center for Strategic and International Studies, *The Gulf: Implications of the British Withdrawal*, Special Report Series No. 8 (Washington, D.C.: Georgetown University, 1969), p. 9.

12. Ibid., p. 91.

13. U.S. Congress, House, Committee on Foreign Affairs, Subcommittee on the Near East and South Asia, *New Perspectives on the Persian Gulf*, p. 6. See also Noyes, *The Clouded Lens*, pp. 53–59.

14. HCFA, *New Perspectives on the Persian Gulf*, p. 39.

15. Interview, *Newsweek* (May 21, 1973): 44. For discussion of the Shah's imperial vision, see Saikal, *Rise and Fall*, pp. 136–47.

16. "The Rising Power of Iran," *U.S. News and World Report* (October 15, 1973): 104. See also Halliday, *Iran*, pp. 38–63.

17. Interview, *Newsweek* (May 21, 1973): 44.

18. SFRC, *U.S. Sales to Iran*, p. 4.

19. Ibid., pp. 14–32. For data on transfers of police equipment, see Klare and Arnson, *Supplying Repression*, p. 146.

20. SFRC, *U.S. Sales to Iran*, pp. xiii, 41.

21. HCFA, *New Perspectives on the Persian Gulf*, p. 39.

22. Ibid., pp. 33–37, 50–53. See also *New York Times*, July 14, 1975; and Noyes, *The Clouded Lens*, pp. 82–86.

23. Noyes, *The Clouded Lens*, p. 65.

24. SFRC, *U.S. Sales to Iran*, p. x.

25. HCFA, *Mutual Development 1973*, p. 110.

26. Quoted in *Kayhan*, International Edition, November 9, 1974.

27. SFRC, *U.S. Sales to Iran*, pp. 19–24.

28. Interview, *Newsweek* (May 21, 1973): 44.

29. Quoted in *California Business* (October 2, 1974): 32.

30. SFRC, *U.S. Sales to Iran*, p. 42.

31. See *New York Times*, February 23, 1976; *Wall Street Journal*, February 24, 1976; SFRC, *Multinational Corporations and U.S. Foreign Policy*, part 12, pp. 107–238, 393–932.

32. See *New York Times*, June 22, 1975; *Wall Street Journal*, October 14, 1975; and Sampson, *The Arms Bazaar*, pp. 241–59.

33. SFRC, *U.S. Sales to Iran*, p. 8.

34. Abdul Kasim Mansur (a pseudonym), "The Crisis in Iran," *Armed Forces Journal* (January 1979): 28.

35. Ibid, pp. 27–29.

36. "How Sudden Wealth Skewed a Nation's Economy," *U.S. News and World Report* (March 22, 1976): 56. See also *New York Times*, February 4, 1976.

37. Mansur, "Crisis in Iran," p. 29.

38. *New York Times*, June 15 and September 22, 1975; and *Times* (London), May 11, 1978.

39. For discussion, see George Ball, "What Brought Down the Shah," *Wash-*

ington Star, March 14, 1979; and Theodore H. Moran, "Iranian Defense Expenditures and the Social Crisis," *International Security* 3 (Winter 1978/79): 178–92.

40. *Washington Post*, September 25, 1975.
41. SFRC, *U.S. Sales to Iran*, p. 36; Noyes, *The Clouded Lens*, pp. 65, 82–86.
42. See Mansur, "Crisis in Iran," pp. 28–29; and Pierre, *The Global Politics of Arms Sales*, pp. 152–53.
43. Cited in *Washington Post*, October 25, 1980.
44. A moratorium on further sales to Iran was proposed by Sen. Edward Kennedy in 1975 and Sen. Robert Byrd in 1977. See *New York Times*, February 23, 1975; and "Byrd Calls for Moratorium on Iran Arms Sales," *Armed Forces Journal* (November 1977): 10. See also Michael T. Klare, "Hoist with Our Own Pahlavi," *Nation* (January 31, 1976): 110–14.
45. Pierre, *The Global Politics of Arms Sales*, p. 150.
46. *Washington Post*, October 25, 1980.
47. See "Iranian Priorities," *AWST* (August 14, 1978): 13.
48. *Washington Post*, November 9, 1978.
49. Quoted in *Wall Street Journal*, January 4, 1979.
50. Quoted in AEI, *A Useful Foreign Policy Tool?*, p. 6.

7. After the Shah

1. See "Iranian Priorities," p. 13; *Wall Street Journal*, February 6, 1979; and *Washington Post*, October 25, 1980. The "shock wave" reference appeared in *U.S. News and World Report* (February 19, 1979): 32.
2. Quoted in *Washington Post*, April 16, 1979.
3. See Pierre, *The Global Politics of Arms Sales*, pp. 142–88. See also the testimony of U.S. government officials in U.S. Congress, House, Committee on Foreign Affairs, Subcommittee on the Near East and South Asia, *The Persian Gulf 1974: Money, Politics, Arms and Power*; HCIR, *The Persian Gulf 1975*; and U.S. Congress, Senate, Committee on Foreign Relations, *Middle East Arms Sales Proposals*.
4. DSAA, *FMS/MAP Facts 1979*, p. 1.
5. See DSAA, *FMS/MAP Facts 1983*, pp. 3, 17.
6. Ibid., pp. 2–3, 16–17, and earlier editions.
7. ACDA, *World Arms 1971–80*, p. 117.
8. Grimmett, *Trends in Conventional Arms Transfers, 1975–82*, p. 18.
9. Estimate by Leslie Gelb in *New York Times*, January 24, 1982.
10. See IISS, *Military Balance 1983–84*, pp. 52–65.
11. Estimate by Leslie Gelb in *New York Times*, January 24, 1982.
12. DoD, *Security Assistance Program FY83*, p. 31.
13. I first addressed this issue in Michael T. Klare, "The Arms Overstock," *Harper's* (November 1979): 24–29.
14. *Washington Post*, February 4, 1979.

15. See *Wall Street Journal*, February 6, 1979; and *Washington Star*, April 17, 1979.
16. *Washington Post*, April 23, 1970.
17. See *Washington Star*, April 17, 1979; and *Washington Post*, April 23 and 26, 1979.
18. *Washington Post*, April 10, 1979.
19. Quoted in *New York Times*, February 11, 1979.
20. See *New York Times*, February 11, 1979. See also the long retrospective analysis by Scott Armstrong in *Washington Post*, November 1, 1981.
21. See Grimmett, *Executive-Legislative Consultation*, pp. 21–22.
22. *Washington Post*, February 12, 1979; and *New York Times*, February 12 and 17, 1979.
23. *AWST* (March 19, 1979): 26; and *Washington Post*, February 12, 1979.
24. See *Wall Street Journal*, February 12, 1979.
25. See *Christian Science Monitor*, February 14, 1979.
26. *Wall Street Journal*, February 16, 1979.
27. Ibid.
28. See James Cannon, "Pentagon's New Plan for Mideast Defense," *Business Week* (February 19, 1979): 44.
29. Quoted in *Los Angeles Times*, March 22, 1979.
30. See analysis by Christopher Wren in *New York Times*, March 8, 1979. See also Pierre, *The Global Politics of Arms Sales*, pp. 166–67.
31. Quoted in *New York Times*, March 8, 1979.
32. See *Christian Science Monitor*, February 20, 1979.
33. See *Washington Post*, April 16, 1979.
34. Quoted in *Chicago Tribune*, February 20, 1979. For assessment of Brown's trip, see "First SecDef to Visit Middle East," *Armed Forces Journal* (March 1979): 20–25.
35. Quoted in *Washington Star*, March 20, 1979.
36. *Washington Star*, April 3, 1979.
37. Quoted in *Washington Post*, April 11, 1979.
38. See the testimony by administration representatives in U.S. Congress, Senate, Committee on Foreign Relations, *Middle East Peace Package*.
39. Quoted in *Washington Star*, April 3, 1979.
40. *Congressional Record* (May 14, 1979), p. S5727.
41. *Congressional Record* (March 27, 1979), p. S3419.
42. *Wall Street Journal*, July 9, 1979.
43. *San Francisco Chronicle*, July 24, 1979.
44. See *New York Times*, September 12 and 14, 1979.
45. See *Washington Star*, January 21, 1980.
46. For text and analysis of the Carter address, see *New York Times*, January 24, 1980.
47. See *Wall Street Journal*, January 25, 1980; and *New York Times*, January 29, 1980.
48. Harold H. Saunders, Testimony before the Senate Foreign Relations Committee, Washington, D.C., March 20, 1980 (DoS transcript).

49. See *Washington Post,* January 4, February 28, and April 22, 1980; and *New York Times,* January 10 and 29 and April 22, 1980.

50. See analysis by John Goshko in *Washington Post,* February 10, 1980, and by Edward Cody in *Washington Post,* March 30, 1980.

51. Quoted in *Washington Post,* March 30, 1980. See also Pierre, *The Global Politics of Arms Sales,* pp. 168–69.

52. *Washington Post,* February 22 and 24, 1980.

53. *New York Times,* February 26, 1980.

54. Ibid.

55. Quoted in *Washington Post,* February 22, 1980.

56. Quoted in *AWST* (January 28, 1980): 22.

57. Quoted in *Washington Post,* March 30, 1980.

58. See *New York Times,* October 12, 1981.

59. See report on the visit of Egyptian Defense Minister Gen. Abou-Ghazala to Washington in the spring of 1981 in *AWST* (May 11, 1981): 74.

60. See analysis by William Beecher in *Boston Globe,* February 27, 1980. See also Amos Perlmutter, "Extricating the U.S. from a Mideast Aid Morass," *Wall Street Journal,* August 23, 1983.

61. See U.S. Comptroller General, *Perspectives on Military Sales to Saudi Arabia.* See also Pierre, *The Global Politics of Arms Sales,* pp. 175–84.

62. Charles Krauthammer, "Selling the Store to the Saudis," *New Republic* (May 9, 1981): 15.

63. Quoted in *Defense Monitor* 10 (1981): 3.

64. See Pierre, *The Global Politics of Arms Sales,* pp. 184–86; Grimmett, *Executive-Legislative Consultation,* pp. 21–35.

65. See SFRC, *Middle East Arms Sales;* and U.S. Congress, House, Committee on International Relations, *Proposed Aircraft Sales to Israel, Egypt, and Saudi Arabia.*

66. U.S. Library of Congress, Congressional Research Service, *Arms Sales to Saudi Arabia: AWACS and the F-15 Enhancements,* Issue Brief No. IB81078 (Washington: CRS, 1981), pp. 11–12.

67. Cited in Ibid., p. 11.

68. See Grimmett, *Executive-Legislative Consultation,* pp. 16–20.

69. *New York Times,* June 18, 1980.

70. Quoted in *New York Times,* June 18, 1980.

71. *Washington Post,* June 18, 1980.

72. *Washington Post,* June 21 and July 7, 1980.

73. See analysis by Scott Armstrong in *Washington Post,* November 1, 1981.

74. Ibid.

75. *Washington Star,* February 26, 1981.

76. Ibid.

77. *Washington Star,* March 3, 1981.

78. Quoted in *New York Times,* April 22, 1981. See also Grimmett, *Executive-Legislative Consultation,* pp. 22–23.

79. See *Washington Post,* September 29, 1981; *New York Times,* October

15, 1981. See also Grimmett, *Executive-Legislative Consultation,* p. 24.

80. See the exchanges in SFRC, *Arms Sales Package;* and U.S. Congress, House, Committee on Foreign Affairs, *Proposed Sale of Airborne Warning and Control Systems (AWACS) and F-15 Enhancements to Saudi Arabia.* Many of these arguments are also considered in U.S. Congress, Senate, Committee on Foreign Relations, *The Proposed AWACS/F-15 Enhancement Sale to Saudi Arabia,* Staff Report, 97th Cong., 1st Sess., 1981.

81. CRS, *AWACS and the F-15,* pp. 2–3.

82. Quoted in *New York Times,* April 22, 1981.

83. Interview, *U.S. News and World Report* (May 18, 1981): 67.

84. *New York Times,* October 7, 1981.

85. Interview, *U.S. News and World Report* (May 18, 1981): 67.

86. *New York Times,* October 2, 1981.

87. Krauthammer, "Selling the Store," p. 14.

88. *New York Times,* September 28, 1981.

89. *Washington Post,* October 6, 1981.

90. Quoted in *Newsweek* (October 19, 1981): 63.

91. *New York Times,* October 29, 1981.

92. Quoted in *New York Times,* October 29, 1981.

93. Quoted in *Wall Street Journal,* November 14, 1980.

94. Quoted in *New York Times,* February 13, 1982.

95. *New York Times,* February 13, 1982.

96. For discussion, see Abdul Kasim Mansur, "The American Threat to Saudi Arabia," *Armed Forces Journal* (September 1980): 47–60; and Krauthammer, "Selling the Store," p. 15. The limitations on U.S. leverage were again demonstrated in 1984, when Saudi Arabia adamantly refused to support the U.S.-backed Israeli-Lebanese peace agreement of May 1983 (*New York Times,* March 1, 1984).

97. DSAA, *FMS/MAP Facts 1980,* p. 1; and DoD, *Security Assistance Program FY83,* p. 31.

98. For discussion of the 1982 Lebanon war as a "testing ground" for U.S. arms, see *Washington Post,* June 11 and 17, 1982.

99. Quoted in *New York Times,* August 25, 1981.

100. Interview in *U.S. News and World Report* (May 18, 1981): 67.

101. Cited in *New York Times,* June 11, 1981.

102. *New York Times,* June 11, 1981.

103. See *New York Times,* April 2 and 4, 1983.

104. See *Washington Post,* April 6 and 10, 1978; *New York Times,* April 8, 1978; *San Francisco Examiner,* July 4, 1982; and *New York Times,* July 19, 1982.

105. Quoted in *Washington Post,* April 9, 1978.

106. Cited in *San Francisco Chronicle,* July 30, 1982.

107. See *International Herald-Tribune,* May 27, 1982.

108. Quoted in *New York Times,* March 19, 1981.

109. The 20,000 figure represents an estimate by international relief agencies and Lebanese officials of fatalities during the 1982 Lebanon war (*Los Angeles Times*, July 12, 1982).

110. This conclusion was evidently shared by Defense Department analysts cited in an extraordinary 1983 GAO report, *U.S. Assistance to the State of Israel*. An uncensored draft of the report, containing the DoD comments, was published by the American-Arab Anti-Discrimination Committee of Washington, D.C., as *U.S. Assistance to the State of Israel: The Uncensored Draft Report*.

8. Coproduction and Licensing

1. I previously explored these issues in Michael T. Klare, "America Exports Its Know-How," *Nation* (February 12, 1977): 173–78; and "The Unnoticed Arms Trade: Exports of Conventional Arms-Making Technology," *International Security* 8 (Fall 1983): 68–90.

2. For further discussion of these categories, see Congressional Research Service, *Issues Concerning the Transfer of United States Defense Manufacturing Technology* (Report prepared for the House Committee on International Relations), pp. 5–8.

3. Ibid., p. 1.

4. These figures were provided in a letter dated July 10, 1980, from Joseph P. Smaldone of the Office of Munitions Control to Dr. Stephanie Neuman of Columbia University.

5. See U.S. Department of Defense, Office of the Under Secretary for Research and Engineering, "Current Listing of Major Coproduction Programs," unpublished document obtained through the FOIA in 1982. For list of major licensing programs, see *SIPRI Yearbook 1982*, pp. 239–52.

6. Matthew Nimitz, Address before Aerospace Industries Association, San Diego, Cal., April 9, 1980 (DoS transcript).

7. CRS, *Issues Concerning the Transfer of Technology*, p. 7.

8. U.S. Comptroller General, *U.S. Military Coproduction Programs Assist Japan in Developing Its Civil Aircraft Industry*.

9. U.S. Defense Science Board, Task Force on Export of U.S. Technology, *An Analysis of Export Control of U.S. Technology—A DoD Perspective* (Washington, D.C.: DoD, 1976), p. vi.

10. See Bjorn Hagelin, "International Cooperation in Conventional Weapons Acquisition: A Threat to Armaments Control?" *Bulletin of Peace Proposals* 9 (1978): 144–55; Michael Moodie, "Vulcan's New Forge," *Arms Control Today* 10 (March 1980): 1–2, 6–8; Jan Oberg, "Third World Armament: Domestic Arms Production in Israel, South Africa, Brazil, Argentina, and India 1950–75," *Instant Research on Peace and Violence* 5 (1975): 222–39; and Thomas Ohlson, "Third World Arms Exporters—A New Facet of the Global Arms Race," *Bulletin of Peace Proposals* 13 (1982): 211–20.

11. For background on U.S. arms coproduction programs with these coun-

tries, see back editions of *Jane's Aircraft;* on current programs, see Caspar Weinberger, *U.S. Department of Defense, Annual Report to the Congress, Fiscal Year 1983* (Washington, D.C.: DoD, 1982), part 3, pp. 115–20.

12. For discussion, see Frederic M. Anderson, "Weapons Procurement Collaboration: A New Era for NATO?" *Orbis* 20 (1977): 965–90; and Michael R. Gordon, "Buy-America Weapons Drive—Another Thorn in Trans-Atlantic Relations," *National Journal* (August 14, 1982): 1416–18. See also U.S. Congress, Senate, Committee on Armed Services, *European Defense Cooperation,* Hearing, 94th Cong., 2d Sess., 1976.

13. See Congressional Research Service, NATO *Standardization: Political, Economic, and Military Issues for Congress,* Report Prepared for the House Committee on International Relations (Washington, D.C.: GPO, 1977); and U.S. Congress, House, Committee on Armed Services, Special Subcommittee on NATO Standardization, NATO *Standardization, Interoperability, and Readiness,* Report, 95th Cong., 2d Sess., 1978.

14. Quoted in *Wall Street Journal,* February 5, 1979.

15. William J. Perry, "The Role of Technology in Strengthening NATO," *NATO's Fifteen Nations* (February–March 1978): 55.

16. See Anderson, "Weapons Procurement Collaboration," pp. 977–85; Gordon, "Buy-America Weapons Drive," pp. 1416–18; Thomas R. Callaghan, "The Unbuilt Street: Defense Industrial Cooperation within the Alliance," *NATO's Fifteen Nations* (October–November 1982): 26–30; and Clarence A. Robinson, Jr., "NATO Weighs U.S. Action on Missiles," *AWST* (June 11, 1979): 86–100.

17. See text of Jefferson's talk before the American Defense Preparedness Association as excerpted in "Making Standardization Work," *AWST* (April 24, 1978): 11.

18. *Armed Forces Journal* (August 1982): 27. For more on Roland, see Bruce A. Smith, "Roland Missile Tests Prove Feasibility of European/U.S. Technology Transfer," *AWST* (September 11, 1978): 114–15; and Doug Richardson, "Roland: America's European Missile," *Flight International* (March 18, 1978): 765–68.

19. See Robert R. Ropelewski, "Five-Nation Coproduction Underway," *AWST* (May 2, 1977): 59–66; U.S. Comptroller General, *Sharing the Defense Burden: The Multinational F-16 Aircraft Program,* Report to the Congress (Washington, D.C.: GAO, 1977); and U.S. Comptroller General, *The Multinational F-16 Aircraft Program: Its Progress and Concerns.* See also *Los Angeles Times,* December 24, 1978; and *Wall Street Journal,* February 5, 1979.

20. See Robinson, "NATO Weighs U.S. Action," pp. 86–100; David R. Griffiths, "Weapons Family Concept Backed," *AWST* (April 9, 1979): 14–15; and Alton K. Marsh, "Arms Production Split Plans Advanced," *AWST* (June 5, 1978): 17–18.

21. Quoted in "F-16 Spurs European Industry Growth," *AWST* (September 1, 1980): 96.

22. For discussion, see Jack Baranson, "Technology Exports Can Hurt Us," *Foreign Policy* 25 (Winter 1976–77): 180–94; and "The Dangers of Sharing America's Technology," *Business Week* (March 14, 1983): 109–11.

23. Baranson, "Technology Exports Can Hurt Us," p. 186.

24. Quoted in *Wall Street Journal*, February 5, 1979.

25. Buckley, Williamsburg Address, May 21, 1981.

26. See Alton K. Marsh, "Pentagon Urges Coproduction Changes," AWST (June 7, 1982): 18–19; and William H. Gregory, "Offsets and Technology Transfer," AWST (July 26, 1982): 11.

27. The extent of these policy-oriented and managerial problems is revealed in the "Report of the DoD Task Group to Review International Coproduction/Industrial Participation Agreements," dated February 12, 1982. The Report, a copy of which was supplied to me by the Office of the Assistant Secretary of Defense for International Security Affairs, suggests that even within the Department of Defense there is much disagreement and lack of clarity on this issue.

28. From a list of coproduction agreements provided by the DoD and inserted in *The Congressional Record* (March 14, 1978), p. H2045.

29. *SIPRI Yearbook 1982*, pp. 239–52. On South Korea, see *New York Times*, April 1, 1982.

30. Quoted in *Washington Post*, December 19, 1977.

31. *Jane's Aircraft 1981–82*, pp. 1–3, 9–18; and *Jane's Weapons 1980–81*, pp. 26, 37, 846–48. See also *Wall Street Journal*, March 19, 1981; *Washington Post*, December 18, 1977, May 8, 1978, and March 15, 1981; SFRC, *Prospects for Restraint*, pp. 36–38; and Oberg, "Third World Armament," pp. 231–33. On Brazilian production, see Colin K. Winkelman and A. Brent Merrill, "United States and Brazilian Military Relations," *Military Review* (June 1983): 60–73.

32. See Ulrich Albrecht, Peter Lock, and Herbert Wulf, *Register of Arms Production in Developing Countries*. For discussion, see SFRC, *Prospects for Restraint*, pp. 34–41; Oberg, "Third World Armament," pp. 223–31, 233–35; Ohlson, "Third World Arms Exporters," pp. 211–20; and Richard R. Burt, *Developments in Arms Transfers: Implications for Supplier Control and Recipient Autonomy*, pp. 6–9. Dr. Stephanie Neuman of Columbia University has argued, however, that the general scarcity of technical resources in the Third World will severely limit the number of countries which will succeed in developing such a broad-based production capability. See Stephanie Neuman, "International Stratification and Third World Military Industries," *International Organization* 38 (Winter 1984): 167–97.

33. See Signe Landgren-Backstrom, "The Transfer of Military Technology to Third World Countries," in Helena Tuomi and Raimo Vayrynen (eds.), *Militarization and Arms Production*, pp. 193–204. See also Cecil Brownlow, "Brazil Presses to Build Aircraft Industry," AWST (January 2, 1975): 52–53; and Clarence A. Robinson, Jr., "Nation Seeks Larger Production Base," AWST (January 4, 1982): 41–44.

34. See Herbert J. Coleman, "Iran Seeks International Aircraft Role," *AWST* (May 21, 1973): 60–61; and *New York Times*, September 22, 1975.

35. On South Africa, see *New York Times*, October 27, 1977, and December 14, 1981; *Washington Post*, July 7, 1981; and Oberg, "Third World Armament," pp. 229–31. On Taiwan, see "Republic Seeks to Develop Its Own Weapons Systems," *AWST* (April 12, 1982): 46–53.

36. On Israel–South Africa links, see *New York Times*, May 21, 1977, February 10, 1978, and December 14, 1981; and *Christian Science Monitor*, December 16, 1980. On Israel-Taiwan ties, see *Wall Street Journal*, April 6, 1977. For discussion, see Raimo Vayrynen, "Semiperipheral Countries in the Global Economic and Military Order," in Tuomi and Vayrynen (eds.), *Militarization and Arms Production*, pp. 163–92.

37. *Washington Post*, December 18 and 19, 1977, and March 15, 1981.

38. See SFRC, *Prospects for Restraint*, pp. 35–38; and Ohlson, "Third World Arms Exporters," pp. 211–20. On Brazilian sales, see *Miami Herald*, April 17, 1977, and March 7, 1978; *Christian Science Monitor*, April 23, 1979; and "Brazil: A Major Contender in the Arms Business," *Business Week* (July 31, 1978): 45–46. On Israeli sales, see "IAI Latin American Sales Rise," *AWST* (December 9, 1974): 22; "Israel Expanding Exports to Aid Balance of Trade," *AWST* (June 2, 1975): 193–95; David A. Brown, "Arava Used as Aid to Israel Kfir Sales," *AWST* (February 2, 1976): 50–51; "Seeking New Markets for Military Aircraft," *Business Week* (August 28, 1978): 46–47; and "Peace with Egypt, But a Boom in Arms Sales," *Business Week* (April 2, 1979): 40.

39. See Albrecht et al., *Register of Arms Production*, pp. vi–xxxvi; Burt, *Developments in Arms Transfers*, p. 8; Landgren-Backstrom, "The Transfer of Military Technology," pp. 193–204; Oberg, "Third World Armament," pp. 222, 233–37; and Neuman, "International Stratification," pp. 174–81.

40. See *Jane's Aircraft 1981–82*, pp. 9–18; *Miami Herald*, May 24, 1978; and *Washington Post*, May 8, 1978.

41. On Brazil, see Brownlow, "Brazil Presses to Build Aircraft Industry," pp. 52–53. On Greece, see *New York Times*, March 3. 1982. On Turkey, see *New York Times*, January 1 and June 10, 1979. In May 1984, the United States agreed to the coproduction of F-16 fighters in Turkey (see "Turkey, U.S. Sign Agreement to Coproduce F-16 Fighters," *AWST*, May 14, 1984, p. 26).

42. Quoted in *Los Angeles Times*, December 21, 1970.

43. See *New York Times*, January 15, 1977; "Staunch Friends at Arms Length," *Time* (January 31, 1977): 30–31; and "U.S. Companies Oppose Lavi Aid," *AWST* (February 14, 1982): 16–19.

44. *New York Times*, April 1, 1982.

45. On Brazilian sales to Chile, see Cynthia Arnson and Michael Klare, "Law or No Law, the Arms Flow," *Nation* (April 29, 1978): 502–5. On Israeli sales to South Africa, see *New York Times*, January 15, 1976.

46. See Albrecht et al., *Register of Arms Production*, pp. vi–xxxvi.

47. For discussion, see Hagelin, "International Cooperation," pp. 144–55; Moodie, "Vulcan's New Forge," p. 8; Oberg, "Third World Armament," pp. 237–38; and Ohlson, "Third World Arms Exporters," pp. 211–20.
48. I have unsuccessfully attempted to obtain copies of these reports through the FOIA.
49. Nimitz, San Diego Address, April 9, 1980.

9. Arms Sales and Human Rights

1. Quoted in *New York Times*, April 15, 1977.
2. I first explored this link in Michael T. Klare, "Exporting the Tools of Repression," *Nation* (October 16, 1976): 365–70; and Michael T. Klare, *Supplying Repression*, 1st ed. (Washington, D.C.: Institute for Policy Studies, 1979).
3. See *New York Times*, February 3, 1981.
4. See "Arming America's Friends," *Newsweek* (March 23, 1981): 33–36; and Griffiths, "Reagan Administration Pushes Arms Transfers," pp. 176–87. On South Africa, see *Washington Post*, March 16, 1982.
5. For discussion, see Cynthia Arnson and Michael T. Klare, "Exporting Repression: U.S. Support for Authoritarianism in Latin America," in Richard Fagen (ed.), *Capitalism and the State in U.S.–Latin American Relations* (Stanford, Cal.: Stanford University Press, 1979), pp. 138–68.
6. For discussion, see Noam Chomsky and Edward S. Herman, *The Washington Connection and Third World Facism* (Boston: South End Press, 1979); and Edward S. Herman, *The Real Terror Network* (Boston: South End Press, 1982).
7. On El Salvador, see U.S. Congress, House, Committee on Foreign Affairs, Subcommittee on Inter-American Affairs, *U.S. Policy toward El Salvador*, Hearings, 97th Cong., 1st Sess., 1981; and U.S. Congress, House, Committee on Foreign Affairs, Subcommittee on Inter-American Affairs, *U.S. Policy Options in El Salvador*, Hearings, 97th Cong., 1st Sess., 1981. For background on the South Africa embargo, see U.S. Congress, House, Committee on Foreign Affairs, Subcommittee on Africa, *Implementation of the U.S. Arms Embargo*, Hearings, 93rd Cong., 1st Sess., 1973; and U.S. Congress, House, Committee on International Relations, Subcommittee on Africa, *United States-South Africa Relations: Arms Embargo Implementation*, Hearings, 95th Cong., 1st Sess., 1977.
8. Buckley, Williamsburg Address, May 21, 1981.
9. I first used this concept in Michael T. Klare, "The International Repression Trade," *Bulletin of the Atomic Scientists* 35 (November 1979): 22–27.
10. U.S. Comptroller General, *Stopping U.S. Assistance to Foreign Police and Prisons*, pp. 34–36.
11. Ibid., pp. 31–34. See also Klare and Arnson, *Supplying Repression*, pp. 44–55.

12. Klare and Arnson, *Supplying Repression*, pp. 56–73. A summary of the FOIA documents is provided in the appendix, pp. 122–65.
13. Ibid., pp. 74–83.
14. FMS and Commercial Sales transactions were tabulated annually in U.S. Department of State, *Report Required by Section 657 of the Foreign Assistance Act*, until discontinued in 1981.
15. I have a collection of FOIA requests that were denied by the two departments. See also Michael T. Klare, "Secretary Kreps Won't Talk," *Nation* (June 4, 1977): 678–79.
16. For a complete listing of individual FMS transactions by country, see DSAA, "FMS Case Listing."
17. DoD, *Security Assistance Program FY83*, pp. 89, 439.
18. For discussion, see Barber and Ronning, *Internal Security*; and Klare, *War without End*, pp. 270–310.
19. See Klare, *War without End*, pp. 311–64.
20. DSAA, "FMS Case Listing."
21. For descriptions of these weapons, see *Jane's Aircraft* and *Jane's Weapons Systems*.
22. DSAA, "FMS Case Listing." Additional information acquired from *SIPRI Yearbook 1981*, and earlier editions; and *Military Balance 1981–82*, and earlier editions.
23. For information on the activities of these agencies, see Amnesty International, *Amnesty International Report* (annual); Amnesty International, *Report on Torture* (New York: Farrar, Straus, Giroux, 1975); Amnesty International, *Torture in the Eighties* (London: Amnesty International, 1984); and periodic Amnesty International reports on particular countries. See also Thomas Plate and Andrea Darvis, *Secret Police* (New York: Doubleday, 1981).
24. U.S. Code of Federal Regulations, title 22, chapter I, subchapter M, *International Traffic in Arms*, part 121.1, The U.S. Munitions List.
25. Based on licenses issued by the U.S. Office of Munitions Control to major U.S. arms firms between September 1976 and May 1979. Copies of these licenses were provided to me following legal action under terms of the FOIA. For a complete listing of these licenses, see Klare and Arnson, *Supplying Repression*, pp. 122–65.
26. U.S. government findings on the human rights behavior of countries receiving U.S. assistance are reported annually in Department of State, *Country Reports on Human Rights Practices*, Report Required by Section 502B of the Foreign Assistance Act of 1961 as amended. (Title varies slightly from year to year.)
27. OMC, Export Licenses 1976–79.
28. OMC, Export Licenses 1976–79. See also Amnesty International sources cited in note 23.
29. For further discussion of these firms, see Klare and Arnson, *Supplying Repression*, pp. 67–73.
30. The term "police-industrial complex" was originally used in Steve Wright, "An Assessment of the New Technologies of Repression," in

Marjo Hoefnagels (ed.), *Repression and Repressive Violence* (Amsterdam: Swets and Zeitlinger, 1977), pp. 133–65. I first used the term "merchants of repression" in Michael T. Klare, "Merchants of Repression," *NACLA Report on the Americas* (July–August 1976): 31–38.

31. For additional information on these weapons, see *Jane's Infantry Weapons*; and Michael Dewar, *Internal Security Weapons and Equipment of the World* (New York: Charles Scribner's Sons, 1979).

32. *Times* (London), January 20, 1977.

33. *Southeast Asia Chronicle* no. 54 (January–February 1977): cover and 9, 21; no. 60 (January–February 1978): cover and 11; no. 69 (January–February 1980): 10–11, 31.

34. *Folha de São Paulo*, August 28, 1978.

35. U.S. Department of Commerce, Bureau of the Census, *FT410 Reports* (monthly).

36. U.S. Department of Commerce, Bureau of the Census, *Statistical Classification of Domestic and Foreign Commodities Exported from the United States*, Schedule B (Washington, D.C.: Department of Commerce, 1978); and Department of Commerce, *Export Administration Bulletin*, Supplement to Export Administration Regulations (December 29, 1977).

37. *FT410 Reports*.

38. Ibid.

39. *Los Angeles Times*, April 26, 1978.

40. From sales catalogues provided by the companies involved. On the Shok-Baton, see Amnesty International, *Evidence of Torture* (London: Amnesty International, 1977), pp. 27–31. On shock-baton sales to South Africa, see *New York Times*, September 21, 1982; and *Africa News* (October 18, 1982): 5.

41. For discussion of the "gray area" issue and U.S. compliance with the embargo, see the testimony by David Newsome in HCFA, *Implementation of the Embargo*, pp. 147ff. See also Michael T. Klare, "Evading the Embargo: Illicit U.S. Arms Transfers to South Africa," *Journal of International Affairs* 35 (Spring/Summer 1981): 15–28; and Maxwell J. Mehlman, Thomas H. Milch, and Michael V. Toumanoff, "United States Restrictions on Exports to South Africa," *American Journal of International Law* 73 (October 1979): 581–603.

42. Cited in Mohamed El Khawas and Barry Cohen (eds.), *The Kissinger Study of Southern Africa* (Westport, Conn.: Lawrence Hill, 1976), p. 104.

43. HCFA, *Implementation of the Embargo*, p. 58; HCIR, *U.S.–South Africa Relations*, p. 56.

44. IISS, *Military Balance 1981–82*, pp. 64–65.

45. For discussion, see International Aid and Defence Fund, *The Apartheid War Machine* (London: International Aid and Defence Fund, 1980), pp. 26–31; and Richard Leonard, *South Africa at War* (Westport, Conn.: Lawrence Hill, 1983), pp. 149–60.

46. See "Reagan and Southern Africa," *Africa News* (December 7, 1981):

6–8; *Washington Post*, March 16, 1982; and Thomas Conrad, "Legal Arms for South Africa," *Nation* (January 21, 1984): 41–45.

47. See *Washington Post*, August 8, 1982; and *Christian Science Monitor*, October 28, 1982.

48. See "South Africa Gets Another Large Computer," *Africa News* (September 27, 1982): 1–3. See also Thomas Conrad, *Automating Apartheid* (Philadelphia: American Friends Service Committee, 1982), pp. 40–60.

49. See *Christian Science Monitor*, October 28, 1982.

50. For discussion, see Laurie Nadel and Hesh Weiner, "Would You Sell a Computer to Hitler?" *Computer Decisions* (February 1977): 22–26.

51. For information on non-U.S. repression exports, see Wright, "New Technologies of Repression," pp. 161–65; and Klare and Arnson, *Supplying Repression*, pp. 100–108.

52. See Amnesty International, *Amnesty International Report, 1981* (London: Amnesty International, 1981), pp. 108–14; and Amnesty International, *Amnesty International Annual Report 1982* (London: Amnesty International, 1982), pp. 109–13.

53. Charles Maechling, Jr., "Counterinsurgency, Yes—But with Controls," *Washington Post*, February 12, 1981.

54. Quoted in *New York Times*, June 6, 1980.

10. A Look at the Competition

1. See *Washington Post*, December 1, 1979, and June 5, 1980; and *New York Times*, March 9, 10, 13, and 20, 1979. See also David R. Griffiths, "Congress Probes Yemeni Arms Policy," AWST (May 26, 1980): 82–84.

2. Quoted in *Washington Post*, June 5, 1980.

3. For an overview of the supply side of the arms trade, see Pierre, *The Global Politics of Arms Sales*, pp. 39–127. See also *SIPRI Yearbook 1982*, pp. 175–93.

4. Grimmett, *Trends in Conventional Arms Transfers 1975–82*, p. 10.

5. ACDA, *World Arms 1971–80*, pp. 117–20.

6. Anthony Cordesman, "U.S. and Soviet Competition in Arms Exports and Military Assistance," *Armed Forces Journal* (August 1981): 68. For a similar analysis, see F. Clifton Berry, Jr., "Military Aircraft Exports: Soviet Foreign Policy Tool," *Air Force* (March 1980): 72–75.

7. U.S. Department of Defense, *Soviet Military Power* (Washington, D.C.: DoD, 1981), p. 87.

8. See Bridget Gail, "'The Fine Old Game of Killing,' Comparing U.S. and Soviet Arms Sales," *Armed Forces Journal* (September 1978): 16–24.

9. *SIPRI Yearbook 1982*, pp. 175, 185–87.

10. U.S. Department of State, *Conventional Arms Transfers in the Third World, 1972–81*, p. 11.

11. Grimmett, *Trends in Conventional Arms Transfers 1975–82*, pp. 2–3.

12. Center for Defense Information, "Soviet Weapons Exports: Russian Roulette in the Third World," *Defense Monitor* 8 (January 1979): 2.
13. Grimmett, *Trends in Conventional Arms Transfers 1975–82*, p. 10.
14. ACDA, *World Arms 1971–80*, pp. 80–116.
15. ACDA, *World Arms 1970–79*, pp. 127–30.
16. Ibid.
17. See DoS, *Conventional Arms Transfers 1972–81*, pp. 9–10; and Pierre, *The Global Politics of Arms Sales*, pp. 73–82, 129–271.
18. See Pierre, *The Global Politics of Arms Sales*, pp. 83–122, 129–271.
19. See *SIPRI Yearbook 1982*, pp. 194–252, and the "Arms Trade Register" in earlier editions of this work. See also the sections on Soviet arms in *Jane's Aircraft* and *Jane's Weapons*.
20. Grimmett, *Trends in Conventional Arms Transfers 1975–82*, p. 16.
21. Ibid.
22. See the annual "Arms Trade Register" in the *SIPRI Yearbook*.
23. Ibid. For data on the arms inventories of Third World nations, see IISS, *Military Balance 1983–84*, and earlier editions.
24. U.S. Department of State, *Soviet and East European Aid to the Third World, 1981*, p. 2.
25. See Roger F. Pajak, "Soviet Arms Transfers as an Instrument of Influence," *Survival* 23 (July/August 1981): 168–69. On the Syrian deployments, see *New York Times*, March 2 and April 17, 1983.
26. This section draws on the following basic sources: Pierre, *The Global Politics of Arms Sales*, pp. 73–82; Pajak, "Soviet Arms Transfers," pp. 165–73; CDI, "Soviet Weapons Exports," pp. 1–8; and ACDA, *The International Transfer of Conventional Arms*, pp. 35–37, 44–52. Other sources include Joseph P. Smaldone, "Soviet and Chinese Military Aid and Arms Transfers to Africa," in Thomas H. Henriksen and Warren Weinstein (eds.), *Soviet and Chinese Aid to African Nations*, pp. 76–116; Rajan Menon, "The Soviet Union, the Arms Trade, and the Third World," *Soviet Studies* 24 (July 1982): 377–96; and Roger F. Pajak, "Soviet Military Aid to Iraq and Syria," *Strategic Review* (Winter 1976): 51–59.
27. Pajak, "Soviet Arms Transfers," p. 169.
28. Andrew J. Pierre, "Arms Sales: The New Diplomacy," *Foreign Affairs* (Winter 1981/82): 271.
29. Ibid., p. 272.
30. See Pajak, "Soviet Arms Transfers," p. 169; and Smaldone, "Soviet and Chinese Military Aid," pp. 76–116.
31. Pajak, "Soviet Arms Transfers," p. 169.
32. CDI, "Soviet Weapons Exports," p. 2.
33. See Menon, "The Soviet Union, the Arms Trade, and the Third World," p. 392.
34. See Cordesman, "U.S. and Soviet Competition in Arms Exports," pp. 66–67.
35. Pajak, "Soviet Arms Transfers," p. 171.

36. See Pajak, "Soviet Military Aid to Iraq and Syria," pp. 51–59.
37. U.S. Central Intelligence Agency, National Foreign Assessment Center, *Communist Aid Activities in Non-Communist Less Developed Countries, 1978*, p. 3.
38. U.S. Central Intelligence Agency, National Foreign Assessment Center, *Communist Aid to Less Developed Countries of the Free World, 1977* (Washington, D.C.: CIA, 1978), pp. 1–2.
39. This section draws on the following basic sources: Pierre, *The Global Politics of Arms Sales*, pp. 83–108; ACDA, *The International Transfer of Conventional Arms*, pp. 32–35, 67–77; and Sampson, *The Arms Bazaar*, pp. 154–88.
40. Pierre, *The Global Politics of Arms Sales*, pp. 83–99.
41. ACDA, *The International Transfer of Conventional Arms*, pp. 67–72.
42. Grimmett, *Trends in Conventional Arms Transfers 1976–83*, p. 16.
43. For other assessments of the "balance sheet," see Pierre, *The Global Politics of Arms Sales*, pp. 80–82; CDI, "Soviet Weapons Exports," pp. 4–5; Menon, "The Soviet Union, the Arms Trade, and the Third World," pp. 388–93; and Cordesman, "U.S. and Soviet Competition in Arms Exports," pp. 65–72.
44. See Menon, "The Soviet Union, the Arms Trade, and the Third World," pp. 388–93.
45. See Pierre, *The Global Politics of Arms Sales*, pp. 164–72; Menon, "The Soviet Union, the Arms Trade, and the Third World," p. 389; and CDI, "Soviet Weapons Exports," p. 4.
46. See Center for Defense Information, "Soviet Geopolitical Momentum: Myth or Menace?" *Defense Monitor* 9 (January 1980): 9–10. See also Menon, "The Soviet Union, the Arms Trade, and the Third World," p. 390.
47. See Pajak, "Soviet Military Aid to Iraq and Syria," pp. 52–54; Pierre, *The Global Politics of Arms Sales*, pp. 193–97; CDI, "Soviet Geopolitical Momentum," p. 17; and *New York Times*, November 17, 1982.
48. See Pierre, *The Global Politics of Arms Sales*, pp. 197–99; and CDI, "Soviet Geopolitical Momentum," p. 15.
49. See CDI, "Soviet Geopolitical Momentum," pp. 1–24.
50. Ibid., pp. 8–9.
51. See Pajak, "Soviet Military Aid to Iraq and Syria," pp. 54–57; Pierre, *The Global Politics of Arms Sales*, pp. 189–93; and Cynthia A. Roberts, "Soviet Arms-Transfer Policy and the Decision to Upgrade Syrian Air Defenses," *Survival* 25 (July/August 1983): 154–64.
52. Roberts, "Soviet Arms-Transfer Policy," p. 162.
53. See Pajak, "Soviet Arms Transfers," pp. 167–68; Berry, "Military Aircraft Exports," p. 74; and Smaldone, "Soviet and Chinese Military Aid," pp. 76–116.
54. CDI, "Soviet Weapons Exports," p. 4.
55. Barry M. Blechman, Janne E. Nolan, and Alan Platt, "Pushing Arms," *Foreign Policy* 46 (Spring 1982): 148.

56. See Berry, "Soviet Military Exports," p. 78; and Pajak, "Soviet Arms Transfers," pp. 167–68.
57. Roberts, "Soviet Arms-Transfer Policy," p. 160.
58. Pajak, "Soviet Arms Transfers," p. 167.
59. See *New York Times*, March 2 and April 17, 1983; *Boston Globe*, January 29, 1983; and *Washington Post*, December 3, 1982.
60. Quoted in CDI, "Soviet Weapons Exports," p. 8. See also Blechman et al., "Pushing Arms," pp. 141–48.
61. Pierre, "Arms Sales: The New Diplomacy," p. 273.
62. Blechman et al., "Pushing Arms," p. 148.

11. Promoting Global Stability

1. For a similar "briefing," prepared by the staff of Rep. Tony Hall of Ohio, see "Congressman Tony P. Hall Introduces Conventional Arms Transfer Limitation Legislation," *Congressional Record* (September 29, 1982), part 2, pp. H80818ff.
2. Buckley, SFRC Statement, July 28, 1981.
3. Quoted in "Strategy Proposed to Control World Sales of Conventional Arms," press release, Office of Rep. Tony Hall, Washington, D.C., February 7, 1983.
4. Quoted in Hall, "Strategy Proposed."
5. DSAA, *FMS/MAP Facts 1981*, and earlier editions.
6. For a similar assessment, see Hall, "Conventional Arms Transfer Limitation Legislation"; and Nealer, *An Unconventional Arms Policy*, pp. 7–8, 19–26.
7. U.S. Congress, House, Committee on Armed Services, *Indian Ocean Arms Limitations and Multilateral Cooperation on Restraining Conventional Arms Transfers*, Hearings, 95th Cong., 2d Sess., 1978, p. 16.
8. *New York Times*, January 27, 1975.
9. Buckley, SFRC Statement, July 28, 1981.
10. Buckley, Williamsburg Address, May 21, 1981.
11. Nealer, *An Unconventional Arms Policy*, p. 19.
12. Hodding Carter III, "Arms Sales and the Spread of Violence."
13. Quoted in Hall, "Strategy Proposed."
14. Gen. David C. Jones, *U.S. Military Posture for Fiscal Year 1982* (Washington, D.C.: DoD, 1981), p. 1.
15. Carter, "Arms Sales and the Spread of Violence."
16. Quoted in AEI, *Arms Sales: A Useful Foreign Policy Tool?*, p. 22.
17. Lance Taylor, "The Costly Arms Trade," *New York Times*, December 22, 1981.
18. Hall, "Conventional Arms Transfer Limitation Legislation."
19. See Labrie et al., *U.S. Arms Sales Policy*, pp. 70–76.
20. ACDA, *World Arms 1971–80*, p. 111.
21. Pierre, *The Global Politics of Arms Sales*, p. 26. See also CBO, *Budgetary Cost Savings*; and Labrie et al., *U.S. Arms Sales Policy*, pp. 46–51.

22. Pierre, *The Global Politics of Arms Sales*, p. 27.
23. See Wassily Leontief and Faye Duchin, *Military Spending;* Gordon Adams, *The Iron Triangle* (New York: Council on Economic Priorities, 1981); and Seymour Melman, *The Permanent War Economy* (New York: Simon & Schuster, 1974).
24. Quoted in *Aerospace Daily*, June 22, 1973.
25. Quoted in AEI, *Arms Sales: A Useful Foreign Policy Tool?*, p. 5.
26. The holding of bilateral (U.S.-Soviet) and multilateral conventional arms transfer limitation talks is also suggested by Hall in "Conventional Arms Transfer Limitation Legislation," and by Blechman et al. in "Pushing Arms," pp. 148–54.

Selected Bibliography

Books, Articles, and Monographs

Albrecht, Ulrich, Peter Lock, and Herbert Wulf. *Register of Arms Production in Developing Countries.* Hamburg: University of Hamburg, Working Group on Armaments and Underdevelopment, 1977.

Ball, Nicole, and Milton Leitenberg (eds.). *The Structure of the Defense Industry.* New York: St. Martin's Press, 1983.

Barber, William F., and C. Neale Ronning. *Internal Security and Military Power.* Columbus: Ohio State University Press, 1966.

Benson, Lucy Wilson. "Turning the Supertanker: Arms Transfer Restraint." *International Security* 3 (Spring 1979): 3–17.

Blechman, Barry M., Janne E. Nolan, and Alan Platt. "Pushing Arms." *Foreign Policy* 46 (Spring 1982): 138–54.

Burt, Richard R. *Developments in Arms Transfers: Implications for Supplier Control and Recipient Autonomy.* Santa Monica, Cal.: RAND Corporation, 1977.

Cahn, Anne Hessing, J. Kruzel, P. Dawkins, and J. Huntzinger. *Controlling Future Arms Trade.* New York: McGraw Hill, Council on Foreign Relations, 1977.

Center for Defense Information. "Soviet Weapons Exports: Russian Roulette in the Third World." *Defense Monitor* 8 (January 1979).

———. "U.S. Weapons Exports Headed for Record Level." *Defense Monitor* 11 (March 1982).

Clark, Dick. "Needed: A Policy of Restraint for United States Arms Transfers." *AEI Defense Review* 2 (1978): 2–15.

Cordesman, Anthony. "U.S. and Soviet Competition in Arms Exports and Military Assistance." *Armed Forces Journal* (August 1981): 65–72.

Cottrell, Alvin J. "The Foreign Policy of the Shah." *Strategic Review* (Fall 1975): 32–44.

Cullin, William H. *How to Conduct Foreign Military Sales.* Washington, D.C.: American Defense Preparedness Association, 1977.

Daly, John Charles (moderator). *Arms Sales: A Useful Foreign Policy Tool?* Washington, D.C.: American Enterprise Institute, 1982.

Einaudi, Luigi, Hans Heymann, Jr., David Ronfeldt, and Caesar Sereseres. *Arms Transfers to Latin America: Towards a Policy of Mutual Respect.* Santa Monica, Cal.: RAND Corporation, 1973.

Farley, Philip J., Stephen S. Kaplan, and William H. Lewis. *Arms across the Sea*. Washington, D.C.: Brookings Institution, 1978.

Frank, Lewis A. *The Arms Trade in International Relations*. New York: Praeger Publishers, 1979.

Gelb, Leslie. "Arms Sales." *Foreign Policy* 25 (Winter 1976–77): 3–23.

Gervasi, Tom. *Arsenal of Democracy II*. New York: Grove Press, 1981.

Gordon, Michael. "Competition with the Soviet Union Drives Reagan's Arms Sales Policy." *National Journal* 13 (May 16, 1981): 869–73.

Grand Pre, Donn R. *Confessions of an Arms Peddler*. Lincoln, Va.: Chosen Books, 1979.

Hammond, Paul Y., David J. Louscher, and Michael D. Salomon. "Controlling U.S. Arms Transfers: The Emerging System." *Orbis* 23 (Summer 1979): 317–52.

Hammond, Paul Y., David J. Louscher, Michael D. Salomon, and Norman A. Graham. *The Reluctant Supplier: U.S. Decisionmaking for Arms Sales*. Cambridge, Mass.: Oelgeschlager, Gunn and Hain, 1983.

Harkavy, Robert E. *The Arms Trade and International Systems*. Cambridge, Mass.: Ballinger, 1975.

Jones, Rodney, and Steven A. Hildreth. *Modern Weapons and Third World Powers*. Boulder, Colo.: Westview Press, 1984.

Kemp, Geoffrey. "Dilemmas of the Arms Traffic." *Foreign Affairs* 48 (January 1970): 274–84.

Klare, Michael T. "The International Repression Trade." *Bulletin of the Atomic Scientists* 35 (November 1979): 22–27.

———. "The Political Economy of Arms Sales." *Bulletin of the Atomic Scientists* 32 (November 1976): 11–18.

———. "The Unnoticed Arms Trade: Exports of Conventional Arms-Making Technology." *International Security* 8 (Fall 1983): 68–90.

Klare, Michael T., and Cynthia Arnson. *Supplying Repression*. 2d ed. Washington, D.C.: Institute for Policy Studies, 1981.

Labrie, Roger P., John G. Hutchins, Edwin W. A. Peura, and Diana H. Richman. *U.S. Arms Sales Policy: Background and Issues*. Washington, D.C.: American Enterprise Institute, 1982.

Leontief, Wassily, and Faye Duchin. *Military Spending*. New York and Oxford: Oxford University Press, 1983.

Louscher, David J. "The Rise of Military Sales as a U.S. Foreign Assistance Instrument." *Orbis* 20 (Winter 1977): 933–62.

Mallmann, Wolfgang. "Arms Transfers to the Third World: Trends and Changing Patterns in the 1970s." *Bulletin of Peace Proposals* 10 (1979): 301–307.

Menon, Rajan. "The Soviet Union, the Arms Trade, and the Third World." *Soviet Studies* 24 (July 1982): 377–96.

Moran, Theodore H. "Iranian Defense Expenditures and the Social Crisis." *International Security* 3 (Winter 1978/79): 178–92.

Nealer, Kevin G. *An Unconventional Arms Policy: Selling Ourselves Short*. Report of the Democratic Policy Committee, U.S. Senate. Washington, D.C.: Government Printing Office, 1983.

Neuman, Stephanie. "International Stratification and Third World Military Industries." *International Organization* 38 (Winter 1984): 167–97.

Neuman, Stephanie G., and Robert E. Harkavy (eds.). *Arms Transfers in the Modern World*. New York: Praeger Publishers, 1979.

Pajak, Roger F. "Soviet Arms Transfers as an Instrument of Influence." *Survival* 23 (July/August 1981): 165–73.

———. "Soviet Military Aid to Iraq and Syria." *Strategic Review* (Winter 1976): 51–59.

Pierre, Andrew J. "Arms Sales: The New Diplomacy." *Foreign Affairs* 60 (Winter 1981/82): 266–86.

———. *The Global Politics of Arms Sales*. Princeton, N.J.: Princeton University Press, 1982.

———(ed.). *Arms Transfers and American Foreign Policy*. New York: New York University Press, 1979.

Ra'anan, Uri, Robert L. Pfaltzgraff, Jr., and Geoffrey Kemp, (eds.). *Arms Transfers to the Third World*. Boulder, Colo.: Westview Press, 1978.

Ronfeldt, David, and Caesar Sereseres. *U.S. Arms Transfers, Diplomacy, and Security in Latin America and Beyond*. Santa Monica, Cal.: RAND Corporation, 1977.

Salomon, Michael D., David J. Louscher, and Paul Y. Hammond. "Lessons of the Carter Approach to Restraining Arms Transfers." *Survival* 23 (September/October 1981): 200–208.

Sampson, Anthony. *The Arms Bazaar*. New York: Viking Press, 1977.

Schriever, Bernard A. "Jimmy Carter's Arms Transfer Policy: Why It Won't Work." *AEI Defense Review* 2 (1978): 16–28.

Smaldone, Joseph P. "Soviet and Chinese Military Aid and Arms Transfers to Africa." In *Soviet and Chinese Aid to African Nations*, edited by Thomas H. Henriksen and Warren Weinstein. New York: Praeger Publishers, 1980.

Stanley, John, and Maurice Pearton. *The International Trade in Arms*. London: Chatto & Windus, 1972.

Stockholm International Peace Research Institute. *The Arms Trade with the Third World*. Stockholm: Almqvist & Wiksell, 1971.

———. *SIPRI Yearbook 1982: World Armaments and Disarmament*. Cambridge, Mass.: MIT Press, 1982.

Tahtinen, Dale R. *Arms in the Persian Gulf*. Washington, D.C.: American Enterprise Institute, 1974.

Thayer, George. *The War Business*. New York: Simon & Schuster, 1969.

Tuomi, Helena, and Raimo Vayrynen (eds.). *Militarization and Arms Production*. London: Croom Helm, 1982.

United Nations Association of the United States of America, National Policy Panel on Conventional Arms Control. *Controlling the Conventional Arms Race*. New York: U.N. Association of the U.S.A., 1976.

Whynes, David K. *The Economics of Third World Military Expenditure*. Austin: University of Texas Press, 1979.

Special Studies

ARMS CONTROL AND DISARMAMENT AGENCY

U.S. Arms Control and Disarmament Agency. *The International Transfer of Conventional Arms*. Report to the Congress, 93rd Cong., 2d Sess. Washington, D.C.: Government Printing Office, 1974.
———. *World Military Expenditures and Arms Transfers, 1972–1982*. Washington, D.C.: Government Printing Office, 1984.

CENTRAL INTELLIGENCE AGENCY

U.S. Central Intelligence Agency, National Foreign Assessment Center. *Communist Aid Activities in Non-Communist Less Developed Countries, 1978*. Washington, D.C.: CIA, 1979.
———. *Communist Aid Activities in Non-Communist Less Developed Countries, 1979 and 1954–79*. Washington, D.C.: CIA, 1980.

CONGRESSIONAL RESEARCH OFFICE OF THE LIBRARY OF CONGRESS

Grimmett, Richard F. *Trends in Conventional Arms Transfers to the Third World by Major Supplier, 1976–1983*. Washington, D.C.: CRS, 1984.
Rossiter, Caleb S. *U.S. Arms Transfers to the Third World: The Implications of Sophistication*. Washington, D.C.: CRS, 1982.
Schandler, Herbert Y. *Implications of President Carter's Conventional Arms Trade Policy*. Washington, D.C.: CRS, 1977.

GENERAL ACCOUNTING OFFICE

Comptroller General of the United States. *Foreign Military Sales—A Growing Concern*. Washington, D.C.: GAO, 1976.
———. *The Multinational F-16 Aircraft Program: Its Progress and Concerns*. Washington, D.C.: GAO, 1979.
———. *Opportunities to Improve Decisionmaking and Oversight of Arms Sales*. Washington, D.C.: GAO, 1979.
———. *Perspectives on Military Sales to Saudi Arabia*. Washington, D.C.: GAO, 1977.
———. *Stopping U.S. Assistance to Foreign Police and Prisons*. Washington, D.C.: GAO, 1976.
———. *U.S. Assistance to the State of Israel*. Washington, D.C.: GAO, 1983.
———. *U.S. Military Coproduction Programs Assist Japan in Developing Its Civil Aircraft Industry*. Washington, D.C.: GAO, 1982.
———. *U.S. Munitions Export Control Need Improvement*. Washington, D.C.: GAO, 1979.
———. *U.S. Security and Military Assistance: Programs and Related Activities*. Washington, D.C.: GAO, 1982.

U.S. DEPARTMENT OF DEFENSE

U.S. Defense Institute of Security Assistance Management. *The Management of Security Assistance*. 3rd ed. Wright-Patterson Air Force Base, Ohio, 1982.

U.S. Department of Defense. *Security Assistance Program.* Congressional Presentation Document, Fiscal Year 1984. Washington, D.C.: DoD, 1983.
U.S. Department of Defense, Defense Security Assistance Agency. *Military Assistance and Sales Manual.* Washington, D.C.: DoD, 1978.
———. *Foreign Military Sales, Foreign Military Construction Sales and Military Assistance Facts.* Washington, D.C.: DoD, 1983.

U.S. DEPARTMENT OF STATE

U.S. Department of State. *Arms Transfer Policy.* Report to the Congress. Washington, D.C.: Government Printing Office, 1977.
———. *Conventional Arms Transfers in the Third World, 1972–1981.* Washington, D.C.: Government Printing Office, 1982.
U.S. Department of State, Bureau of Intelligence and Research. *Arms Sales in Latin America.* Washington, D.C.: Government Printing Office, 1973.
———. *Soviet and East European Aid to the Third World, 1981.* Washington, D.C.: Government Printing Office, 1983.

Congressional Studies and Hearings

U.S. Congress, Congressional Budget Office. *Budgetary Cost Savings to the Department of Defense Resulting from Foreign Military Sales.* Washington, D.C.: Government Printing Office, 1976.
———. *The Effect of Foreign Military Sales on the U.S. Economy.* Washington, D.C.: Government Printing Office, 1976.
U.S. Congress, House, Committee on Foreign Affairs. *Executive-Legislative Consultation on U.S. Arms Sales.* Congress and Foreign Policy Series No. 7. Washington, D.C.: Government Printing Office, 1982.
———. *Proposed Sale of Airborne Warning and Control Systems (AWACS) and F-15 Enhancements to Saudi Arabia.* Hearings and Markup, 97th Cong., 1st Sess. Washington, D.C.: Government Printing Office, 1981.
U.S. Congress, House, Committee on Foreign Affairs, Subcommittee on International Security and Scientific Affairs. *Changing Perspectives on U.S. Arms Transfer Policy.* Report by the Congressional Research Service, Library of Congress, 97th Cong., 1st Sess. Washington, D.C.: Government Printing Office, 1981.
———. *U.S. Arms Transfer Policy in Latin America.* Hearing, 97th Cong., 1st Sess. Washington, D.C.: Government Printing Office, 1981.
U.S. Congress, House, Committee on Foreign Affairs, Subcommittee on the Near East and South Asia. *New Perspectives on the Persian Gulf.* Hearings, 93rd Cong., 1st Sess. Washington, D.C.: Government Printing Office, 1973.
———. *The Persian Gulf 1974: Money, Politics, Arms and Power.* Hearings, 93rd Cong., 2d Sess. Washington, D.C.: Government Printing Office, 1974.
U.S. Congress, House, Committee on International Relations. *Issues Concerning the Transfer of United States Defense Manufacturing Tech-*

nology. Report by the Foreign Affairs and National Defense Division, Congressional Research Service, 95th Cong., 1st Sess. Washington, D.C.: Government Printing Office, 1977.

————. *Proposed Aircraft Sales to Israel, Egypt, and Saudi Arabia*. Hearings, 95th Cong., 2d Sess. Washington, D.C.: Government Printing Office, 1978.

U.S. Congress, House, Committee on International Relations, Special Subcommittee on Investigations. *The Persian Gulf 1975: The Continuing Debate on Arms Sales*. Hearings, 94th Cong., 1st Sess. Washington, D.C.: Government Printing Office, 1975.

U.S. Congress, House, Committee on International Relations, Subcommittee on Europe and the Middle East. *United States Arms Sales Policy and Recent Sales to Europe and the Middle East*. Hearing, 95th Cong., 2d Sess. Washington, D.C.: Government Printing Office, 1978.

U.S. Congress, House, Committee on International Relations, Subcommittee on Inter-American Affairs. *Arms Trade in the Western Hemisphere*. Hearings, 95th Cong., 2d Sess. Washington, D.C.: Government Printing Office, 1978.

U.S. Congress, Senate, Committee on Foreign Relations. *Arms Sales and Foreign Policy*. Staff Study. 90th Cong., 1st Sess. Washington, D.C.: Government Printing Office, 1967.

————. *Arms Transfer Policy*. Report to Congress, 95th Cong., 1st Sess. Washington, D.C.: Government Printing Office, 1977.

————. *Middle East Arms Sales Proposals*. Hearings, 95th Cong., 2d Sess. Washington, D.C.: Government Printing Office, 1978.

————. *Middle East Peace Package*. Hearings, 96th Cong., 1st Sess. Washington, D.C.: Government Printing Office, 1979.

————. *The Proposed AWACS/F-15 Enhancement Sale to Saudi Arabia*. Staff Report, 97th Cong., 1st Sess. Washington, D.C.: Government Printing Office, 1981.

————. *Prospects for Multilateral Arms Export Restraint*. Staff Report, 96th Cong., 1st Sess. Washington, D.C.: Government Printing Office, 1979.

————. *U.S. Conventional Arms Transfer Policy*. Report to the Senate, 96th Cong., 2d Sess. Washington, D.C.: Government Printing Office, 1980.

————. *U.S. Military Sales to Iran*. Staff Report, 94th Cong., 2d Sess. Washington, D.C.: Government Printing Office, 1976.

U.S. Senate, Committee on Foreign Relations, Subcommittee on Foreign Assistance. *Foreign Assistance Authorization: Arms Sales Issues*. Hearings, 94th Cong., 1st Sess. Washington, D.C.: Government Printing Office, 1975.

Index